GREEK AND LATIN COMPOSITIONS

BY

RICHARD SHILLETO.

GREEK AND LATIN COMPOSITIONS

BY

RICHARD SHILLETO, M.A.

OF TRINITY COLLEGE,
LATE FELLOW OF PETERHOUSE, CAMBRIDGE.

CAMBRIDGE:

AT THE UNIVERSITY PRESS.

1901

CAMBRIDGE
UNIVERSITY PRESS

University Printing House, Cambridge CB2 8BS, United Kingdom

Cambridge University Press is part of the University of Cambridge.

It furthers the University's mission by disseminating knowledge in the pursuit of
education, learning and research at the highest international levels of excellence.

www.cambridge.org
Information on this title: www.cambridge.org/9781316626092

First published 1901
First paperback edition 2016

A catalogue record for this publication is available from the British Library

ISBN 978-1-316-62609-2 Paperback

PATRI AMANTISSIMO

HVNC LIBELLVM

D. D. D.

FILII SVPERSTITES

PREFACE.

AT the time of the death of the late Rev. Richard Shilleto, in 1876, it was known to us that there existed a large number of pieces of composition in Greek and Latin which were attributed to him, and which were in common use among old pupils and others engaged in tuition ; and, though it was not considered advisable to attempt a collection and publication of those in our own possession at that time, the idea of doing this in the future was always in our thoughts. Some few years ago, however, it was strongly represented to us that it was the opinion of a well-known public school master—an opinion which was entitled to serious consideration—that a really authentic collection of Mr Shilleto's compositions would be of distinct benefit to the cause of education ; whilst we ourselves had always felt that there was no guarantee for the genuineness of those pieces which were floating about in various schools and colleges, but which were yet credited with being his actual work. We therefore determined to take the matter in hand ourselves, and to make a collection of all those which were in our possession, of the authenticity of which there could be no reasonable doubt. Most of these, indeed almost all of them, were in Mr Shilleto's own handwriting ; and we satisfied ourselves, in regard to the few exceptions, that they also were really genuine. We had determined from the first that we would not apply to former pupils, who would no doubt have been pleased to assist us, but that we would content ourselves with such pieces of composition as we found amongst the papers which he left behind him. It is only right, however, for us to state that nothing was written with any idea of publication ; and that, therefore, as these pieces had been composed by him merely as models for the benefit of his pupils during a period extending over more than forty years, we felt that, in justice to his memory, we could publish nothing until it had been critically examined by some competent scholar. In preparing this volume for publication it should be added that no changes have been made beyond a few necessary verbal alterations; and the several pieces appear practically as Mr Shilleto left them.

It had been our intention, on the completion of our task, to approach the Syndics of the University Press at Cambridge—where almost the whole of Mr Shilleto's life was spent from 1828 to 1876—with a view to the publication of the work. But in this we were anticipated by the Syndics themselves, who intimated to us their willingness to publish a suitable selection from those compositions which we had in our possession—as the total amount of pieces would form a volume too bulky for publication. This offer was gladly accepted ; and the duty of examination and selection was most kindly undertaken by the Rev. C. E. Graves, Fellow and Tutor of St John's College, a former pupil of Mr Shilleto, and a friend of the family from his undergraduate days.

Mr Graves, with whom we have been in constant correspondence, is not only responsible for this selection, but he has also been good enough to see the work through the press ; and, whilst our thanks are first due to the Syndics of the University Press, we wish also to express our hearty and grateful acknowledgements to Mr Graves, as well as to all who may have associated themselves with him out of an affectionate regard for our father's memory and admiration for his scholarship.

E. R. SHILLETO.

W. F. R. SHILLETO.

September, 1901.

TRANSLATIONS

INTO GREEK VERSE

Alcides thus his race began,
O'er infancy he swiftly ran ;
The future god at first was more than man :
Dangers and toils, and Juno's hate,
Even o'er his cradle lay in wait,
And there he grappled first with Fate :
In his young hands the hissing snakes he press'd ;
So early was the deity confess'd :
Thus by degrees he rose to Jove's imperial seat ;
Thus difficulties prove a soul legitimately great.

DRYDEN.

Ἀπὸ βαλβίδων τοιόνδ' ἔλαχεν
δρόμον Ἀλκείδας, ἀταλᾶς ἄβας
ταχὺ τέρμ' ἀνύσας· ἦν δ' ἄρ' ὁ μέλλων
θεὸς ἐξ ἀρχῆς κρεῖσσόν τι βροτοῦ.
τί γάρ, ὅντινα πῆμ' ἐπιμαστίδιον
μόχθοι τ' ἐλόχων χὠ κότος Ἥρας;
καί νιν Μοίραις πρῶτ' ἀντίπαλον
σπάργαν' ἐδέρχθη
νεαρὸν νεαραῖς σύριγμ' ὄφεων
χερσὶ δαμάζονθ'· ὧδε νεογνὸς
φανθεὶς θεὸς ὤν, ὧδ' ὑψίβατον
Ζηνὸς προσέβα χρόνιος θάκημ'·
ὧδ' ὁ πόνος τοι
λῆμα κατ' αἶσαν μέγ' ἐλέγχει.

Mir.   Alas, now, pray you,
Work not so hard : I would the lightning had
Burnt up those logs that you are enjoin'd to pile !
Pray, set it down and rest you : when this burns,
'Twill weep for having wearied you. My father
Is hard at study ; pray now, rest yourself ;
He's safe for these three hours.

Fer.   O most dear mistress,
The sun will set before I shall discharge
What I must strive to do.

Mir.   If you'll sit down,
I'll bear your logs the while ; pray, give me that ;
I'll carry it to the pile.

Fer.   No, precious creature ;
I had rather crack my sinews, break my back,
Than you should such dishonour undergo,
While I sit lazy by.

Mir.   It would become me
As well as it does you : and I should do it
With much more ease ; for my good will is to it,
And yours it is against.

Pros.   Poor worm, thou art infected !
This visitation shows it.

Mir.   You look wearily.

Fer. No, noble mistress ; 'tis fresh morning with me
When you are by at night.   I do beseech you—
Chiefly, that I might set it in my prayers—
What is your name ?

Mir.   Miranda :—O my father,
I have broke your hest to say so !

Fer.   Admired Miranda !
Indeed the top of admiration ; worth
What's dearest to the world.

                                        SHAKESPEARE.

A. Μὴ πρός σε γούνων μὴ πονῶν ἄγαν πόνει.
εἰ γὰρ τάδ᾽ ἐξέπρησεν αἰθαλοῦσσα φλὸξ
τὰ πρέμν᾽ ἃ χῶσαι δεῦρ᾽ ἐπέσταλται τέλος.
ἄγ᾽ οὖν χαμαὶ θὲς τοῦτο καὶ κάμψον γόνυ·
καὶ γὰρ πυρωθὲν κλαύσεται τὸν σὸν κόπον.
ἀλλ᾽ ἐστὶ πρὸς Μούσαις γὰρ ὁ σπείρας πατήρ,
ἔξεστι δ᾽ ἀργεῖν κἀναπαύεσθαι δέμας,
δαρὸν γὰρ οὖν βέβαιος ἔνδον ἐμμένειν.
Φ. ἀλλ᾽, ὦ φίλη δέσποινα, μὴ δύνῃ σέλας
θεοῦ δέδοικα, πρὶν τόδ᾽ ἐξαντλεῖν χρέος.
A. κάθησ᾽· ἐγὼ δὲ βαστάσω τέως ξύλα.
δός μοι τόδ᾽, ὡς πρὸς ὄχθον ἐν μέρει φέρω.
Φ. μὴ δῆτα· πρίν γ᾽ ἄν, τιμιώτατον κάρα,
διαρραγείην νεῦρα, νωτιαῖα δὲ
λύοιμ᾽ ἂν ἄρθρ᾽, ἢ σοί γε τήνδ᾽ ἀτιμίαν
θείην ἄν, αὐτὸς μαλθακῶς παρήμενος.
A. ἀλλ᾽ οὐχὶ μᾶλλον σοί γ᾽ ἂν ἢ κἀμοὶ πρέποι·
ῥᾷον δ᾽ ἂν αὐτὴ τοῦθ᾽ ὑπουργοίην χρέος,
ἐγὼ γάρ εἰμ᾽ ἑκοῦσα σοὶ δ᾽ ἄκουσα φρήν.
Πρ. οἵα τάλαινα τῇδε πρόσκεισαι νόσῳ·
δηλοῖ γὰρ ἡ κέλευθος ἥνπερ ἐστάλης.
A. οἴμ᾽ ὡς καμόντος ὄμμα σοῦ κατηγορεῖ.
Φ. οὐ δῆτα, δέσποιν᾽· ἡμερήσιον σὺ γὰρ
ἐν εὐφρόνῃ παροῦσα σημαίνεις φάος.
πρὸς θεῶν ὅπως αἰτοῦντα μή μ᾽ ἀτιμάσεις,
ἄλλως τε κἂν εὐχαῖσι σοῦ μνείαν ἔχειν,
τί σ᾽ ἂν καλῶν τύχοιμ᾽ ἂν ἀψευδοῦς λόγου;
A. ἀλλ᾽ ἴσθ᾽ Ἀγαυὴν τοὔνομ᾽· ὦ πάτερ, σέθεν
λέγουσ᾽ ἐφετμῶν προδότις οὖσ᾽ ἐφηυρέθην.
Φ. ὡς εὐλόγως ἄρ᾽ ἦσθ᾽ ἐπώνυμος, κόρη,
ἣν οὐκ ἄγαιτ᾽ ἂν οὔτις εἰς ὑπερβολήν,
πάντων ὅσ᾽ ἔστι τιμιώτατον πολύ.

And when the dead by cruel tyrant's spite,
  Lie out to rav'nous birds and beasts expos'd,
His yearnful heart pitying that wretched sight,
  In seemly graves their weary flesh enclos'd,
    And strew'd with dainty flow'rs the lowly hearse;
    Then all alone the last words did rehearse,
Bidding them softly sleep in his sad sighing verse.

So once that royal maid fierce Thebes beguil'd,
  Though wilful Creon proudly did forbid her;
Her brother, from his home and tomb exil'd,
  (While willing night in darkness safely hid her)
    She lowly laid in Earth's all covering shade:
    Her dainty hands (not us'd to such a trade)
She with a mattock toils, and with a weary spade.

Yet feels she neither sweat, nor irksome pain,
  Till now his grave was fully finished;
Then on his wounds her cloudy eyes 'gin rain,
  To wash the guilt painted in bloody red:
    And falling down upon his gored side,
    With hundred varied 'plaints she often cry'd,
'Oh, had I died for thee, or with thee might have died!'
                        PHINEAS FLETCHER.

Κεἰ που τυράννων νηλεῶς ὕβρις νεκροὺς
ῥίψειεν ὠμοῖς θηρσί τ᾽ οἰωνοῖς θ᾽ ἕλωρ,
πολλῇ ξὺν αἰδοῖ πικρὸν ὄμμ᾽ ἐποικτίσας
τῶν πολλὰ τλάντων σώματ᾽ ὤγκωσεν τάφῳ
ἐξαιρέτοισι τύμβον ἄνθεσι στέφων·
κἀθ᾽ ὑστάτους ἀφῆκε κωκυτῶν γόους
αὐτὸς καθ᾽ αὑτὸν δυσθρόῳ θρηνῳδίᾳ
εὐναῖς ἐφυμνῶν ἡσύχως κοιμωμένων.
οὕτω δὲ Θήβας βασιλικὴ κλέπτει κόρη
ὠμοῦ βίᾳ Κρέοντος ἀντειρηκότος,
ἥτις πατρῴων τὸν κασίγνητον τάφων
καὶ πόλεος ἐκριφθέντα (νὺξ γὰρ ἀσφαλῆ
σκότῳ σφ᾽ ἑκοῦσ᾽ ἔκρυψεν) εὐσεβῶς χθονὸς
σκιᾷ περιστέλλει νιν ἐν περιπτυχεῖ,
ἁβρᾷ τε χειρὶ τῶνδ᾽ ἄιδρις ἐργμάτων
αὐτὴ δικέλλης καὶ γενῇδος ἅπτεται.
οὐ μὴν ἱδρῶτος οὐ πόνων ἐγεύσατο
πρὶν πᾶς ἐπλήσθη μόχθος· εἶτα δυσχίμῳ
βάψασα τραύματ᾽ ὀμμάτων πλημμυρίδι
ἔτεγγεν ὡς λύσουσα φοίνιον μύσος.
κἄπειτα πλευροῖς περιπεσοῦσ᾽ ᾑμαγμένοις
φίλως προσεῖπε μυρίοις οἰμώγμασιν·
ἢ ξυνθανεῖν χρῆν ἢ θανεῖν ὑπὲρ σέθεν.

Bel. A goodly day not to keep house, with such
Whose roof's as low as ours! Stoop, boys; this gate
Instructs you how to adore the heavens, and bows you
To a morning's holy office : the gates of monarchs
Are arch'd so high that giants may jet through
And keep their impious turbans on, without
Good morrow to the sun. Hail, thou fair heaven!
We house i' the rock, yet use thee not so hardly
As prouder livers do.

Gui.   Hail, heaven!

Arv.   Hail, heaven!

Bel. Now for our mountain sport : up to yond hill;
Your legs are young; I'll tread these flats. Consider,
When you above perceive me like a crow,
That it is place which lessens and sets off :
And you may then revolve what tales I have told you
Of courts, of princes, of the tricks in war :
This service is not service, so being done,
But being so allowed : to apprehend thus,
Draws us a profit from all things we see;
And often, to our comfort, shall we find
The sharded beetle in a safer hold
Than is the full-wing'd eagle. O, this life
Is nobler than attending for a check,
Richer than doing nothing for a babe,
Prouder than rustling in unpaid-for silk :
Such gain the cap of him that makes 'em fine,
Yet keeps his book uncross'd.

                                    SHAKESPEARE.

B. Κάλλιον ἤ τιν' ἔνδον οἰκουρεῖν φάος
οὕτω βραχεῖαν τὴν στέγην κεκτημένον.
κύπτοιτ' ἄν, ὦ τέκν'· ἥδε γὰρ φρενοῖ θύρα
ὀρθῶς σέβεσθαι προσκυνοῦντας οὐρανὸν
ἑωθινὰς κάμπτουσα πρὸς λιτὰς κάρα.
οὕτω δ' ἄρ' ὕψους αἱ τυραννικῶν στέγαι
μελάθρων ἀνήκουσ' ὥστε γηγενῆ σπορὰν
αὐταῖς μίτραισιν ἀνοσίοις διεκπερᾶν
μηδὲν προσεννέποντας ἡλίου κύκλον.
ὦ δῖος αἰθήρ, χαῖρ'· ἐνοικοῦντες πέτραις
ὥραν ὅμως ποιούμεθ' οὐχ ἥσσω σέθεν
τῶνδ' οἳ τρυφῶσιν εὐποτμωτέρᾳ χλιδῇ.
Γ. ὦ χαῖρε, καλλιφεγγὲς οὐρανοῦ σέλας.
A. χαίροις ἂν αὖθις ἐν τρίτοις προσφθέγμασιν.
B. εἶεν·
ὅπως δὲ θήρας ἀρξόμεσθ' ὀρεστέρας·
σφὼ μὲν πρὸς ὄχθον· νέα γὰρ ἡβᾶτε σκέλη·
ἐγὼ δ' ἔνερθεν αὖ καταστείψω πέδον.
ὅταν δ' ἄνωθεν οἷά τις κόραξ φανῶ
τότ' ἐννοεῖσθον ὡς ἐν ᾧπερ ἔσταμεν
οὕτως ἐλάσσων αὐτὸς ἢ μείζων πρέπει.
ὅπως δὲ μεμνήσεσθε τῶν εἰρημένων
μελάθρων ἀνάκτων καὶ φιλοψευδοῦς μάχης·
τὸ πραχθὲν οὗτοι πραχθὲν ὧδ' εἰργασμένον
ἀλλ' ἀξιωθέν· τῷ σκοπουμένῳ τάδε
οἷς ἂν βλέπῃ τις τοισίδ' ὠφέλημ' ἔνι.
παρηγορεῖται δ' ἔσθ' ὅτ' ἐννοίᾳ κέαρ,
ὅτανπερ εἰσορῶμεν ἀσφαλέστερον
τῷ λεπίσι μικραῖς κανθάρῳ πεφραγμένῳ
πορισθὲν ἕρκος ἀετοῦ τανυπτέρου.
χὠ βίος ὅδ' ἡμῶν μᾶλλον εὐγενέστερος
τοῦ τὰς τυράννων προσδοκᾶν ἐπιστολάς,
καὶ πλουσιώτερός γε τοῦ τὸν ὀρφανὸν
ἀποστερῆσαι, πλείονός τ' ἔχων τρυφῆς
τοῦ βυσσίνοις σοβοῦντας ἐγχλίειν στολαῖς·
οἵους ὁ λάμπρ' ὑφάσματ' ἐξειργασμένος
σέβει δεδορκώς, διαγράφει δ' οὐδὲν χρέος.

Const. A wicked day, and not a holy day!
What hath this day deserved? what hath it done,
That it in golden letters should be set
Among the high tides in the calendar?
Nay, rather turn this day out of the week,
This day of shame, oppression, perjury.
Or, if it must stand still, let wives with child
Pray that their burthens may not fall this day,
Lest that their hopes prodigiously be cross'd:
But on this day let seamen fear no wreck;
No bargains break that are not this day made:
This day, all things begun come to ill end,
Yea, faith itself to hollow falsehood change!

K. Phi. By heaven, lady, you shall have no cause
To curse the fair proceedings of this day:
Have I not pawn'd to you my majesty?

Const. You have beguiled me with a counterfeit
Resembling majesty, which, being touch'd and tried,
Proves valueless: you are forsworn, forsworn;
You came in arms to spill mine enemies' blood,
But now in arms you strengthen it with yours.

SHAKESPEARE.

K. Οὐχ ἱερὸν ἦμαρ εἶπας, ἀνίερον μὲν οὖν·
τί γὰρ δεδρακὸς τοῦ δ' ἐπάξιον φανὲν
χρυσηλάτοις τύποισιν ἀναγεγράψεται
ἐν ταῖς ἑορταῖς βουθύτοισιν ἤμασιν;
ἔδει γὰρ ἄλλων ἐκπεσεῖν νιν ἡμερῶν
ψεύδορκον αἰσχροποιὸν ἀνόσιον φάος.
εἰ δ' οὖν χρεὼν μένειν σφε, τῇδ' ἐν ἡμέρᾳ
θεοῖς ἀπεύχεσθ', ἥτις ἐγκύμων, φίλην
ὠδῖνα μήποτ' ἐκβαλεῖν, ὡς ἐλπίδων
σφαλεῖσ' ἂν ἀποτίκτουσα δύσμορφον τέρας.
πλὴν τῆσδε μηδεὶς ναυβάταις ναυαγίας
φόβος παρείη, καὶ τὰ μὴ τῆσδ' ἡμέρας
παγέντα συμβόλαια μὴ ψεύσειέ τις·
ὅσων δ' ἂν ἀρχαῖς κῦρος ᾖ φάος τόδε,
τέλους λάχοιεν δυσπότμου, καὐτὴ σαθρὰν
ὑγιὴς τρέποιτο πίστις εἰς ἀπιστίαν.
B. ἦ μήν, ἄνασσα, τῷδ' ἀρᾷ δίκης ἄτερ
τῷ καλλιφεγγεῖ κοὐδὲν αἰτίῳ φάει·
οὐ γὰρ κράτος πάντιμον οἶσθ' ὑπέγγυον;
K. κράτους μὲν οὖν κίβδηλον ἀλλάξας τύπον
παρηπάτησάς μ', ὃς δικαιωθεὶς τρίβῳ
καὶ προσβολαῖσι φαῦλος ὢν ἐλέγχεται.
ψεύδορκος εἶ, ψεύδορκος· ὅς γ' ἡμῶν μέτα
ὡς αἷμα δρέψων πολεμίων ἦλθες τότε,
νῦν δ' αὖτε τῷ σῷ τόδε βεβαιώσων πάρει.

Cyriack, this three years' day these eyes, though clear,
    To outward view, of blemish or of spot,
    Bereft of light, their seeing have forgot;
    Nor to their idle orbs doth sight appear
Of sun, or moon, or star, throughout the year,
    Of man, or woman. Yet I argue not
    Against Heaven's hand or will, nor bate a jot
    Of heart or hope, but still bear up and steer
Right onward. What supports me, dost thou ask?
    The conscience, friend, to have lost them overplied
    In Liberty's defence, my noble task,
Of which all Europe rings from side to side.
    This thought might lead me through the world's
        vain mask
    Content, though blind, had I no better guide.

MILTON.

Ὦ Κυρίακχε, λαμπρὰ κἂν ἰδεῖν φανῇ
τὰ τοῦδε τἀνδρὸς ὄμματ', οὐδ' ἐπάργεμα,
ὄψιν παλαιάν, τοῦ φάους τητώμενα,
ἔτος τόδ' ἤδη τρίτον ἐπεὶ διώλεσεν·
οὐδ' ἀσκόποις οὔθ' ἡλίου σέλας κύκλοις
οὔτ' ἀστέρων οὔτ' ὄμμα Λητῴας κόρης,
οὔτ' ἀνδρός, οὐ γυναικός, ἀνακυκλουμένων
μηνῶν πέφηνε πώποτ'—οὐδὲ μὴν ἐγὼ
χεῖράς τε καὶ τέχνημα μέμφομαι θεῷ,
οὐδ' ἐλπίδ' ἐντὸς καρδίας ἧσσον τρέφω·
ἀλλ' ἐμμένων ὀρθοῖσι σέλμασιν πλέω
εὐθεῖαν ἕρπων. ἀλλὰ γὰρ ζητεῖς μαθεῖν
ὅτῳ πεποιθὼς καρτερῶ· ξύνοιδ' ἐμοὶ—
ἀνθ' ὧν τά γ' ὄμματ' ὤλεσ'—ὧν ἐλευθέρας
πρόμος δίκης, καὶ πολλὰ κινδυνεύματα
ἤθλησα, φίλτατ', εὐγενοῦς ἔργου χάριν,
οὗπερ διῆλθε βάξις Εὐρώπην ὅλην.
βίου δ' ἂν ἥδ' ἔννοι' ἐν αἰόλου τύχαις
στέργοντ' ἄγοι μ' ἄν, καίπερ οὐ βλέπονθ' ὅμως,
μὴ τῇσδ' ὁδαγῷ χρώμενον βελτίονι.

                    Do you think
Such arrogance, or usurpation rather,
Of what is proper and peculiar
To every private husband, and much more
To him an emperor, can rank with the obedience
And duty of a wife ?   Are we appointed
In our creation—let me reason with you—
To rule or to obey ? or, 'cause he loves me
With a kind impotence, must I tyrannize
Over his weakness, or abuse the strength
With which he arms me, to his wrong ?   Shall I
His vassal, from obscurity raised by him
To this so eminent light, presume to appoint him
To do or not to do this or that ?

                                        MASSINGER.

Τοίαν γὰρ ἀξίωσιν, ἁρπαγὴν μὲν οὖν
τιμῆς πρεπούσης καὶ προσηκούσης πόσει
κἂν δημότης ᾖ παντί, δὶς τόσως δ' ἐμῷ
τύρανν' ἔχοντι σκῆπτρα, τήνδ' ἂν ἐννόμῳ
αὐχεῖς γυναικὸς ξυντρέχειν πειθαρχίᾳ;
φέρ' ἐννοώμεθ'· ἆρα θῆλυς ἄρσενος
κρατεῖ γένους θεσμοῖσιν, ἢ κρατούμεθα;
ἀκρατὴς ἔρωτός ἐσθ' ὅδ'· εἶτ' εὔνουν ἐμὲ
τήνδ' ἀσθένειαν δεῖ βιάζεσθαι, σθένει
ὅσῳ μ' ὁπλίζει χρωμένην ἐπὶ βλάβῃ;
πῶς ἐξ ἀμαυρῶν ἐς τόδ' ἐκπρεπὲς φάος
δούλη τις οὖσ' ἀρθεῖσα τλήσομαι πόθεν
τούτῳ τί χρὴ δρᾶν καὶ τί μὴ τάσσειν ἐγώ;

Casca. But wherefore did you so much tempt the heavens?
　　　It is the part of men to fear and tremble,
　　　When the most mighty gods by tokens send
　　　Such dreadful heralds to astonish us.
Cas.　You are dull, Casca, and those sparks of life
　　　That should be in a Roman you do want,
　　　Or else you use not. You look pale and gaze,
　　　And put on fear, and cast yourself in wonder,
　　　To see the strange impatience of the heavens:
　　　But if you would consider the true cause
　　　Why all these fires, why all these gliding ghosts,
　　　Why birds and beasts from quality and kind,
　　　Why old men, fools and children calculate,
　　　Why all these things change from their ordinance,
　　　Their natures and preformed faculties
　　　To monstrous quality,—why, you shall find
　　　That heaven hath infused them with these spirits,
　　　To make them instruments of fear and warning
　　　Unto some monstrous state.
　　　Now could I, Casca, name to thee a man
　　　Most like this dreadful night,
　　　That thunders, lightens, opens graves, and roars
　　　As doth the lion in the Capitol,
　　　A man no mightier than thyself or me
　　　In personal action, yet prodigious grown
　　　And fearful, as these strange eruptions are.

SHAKESPEARE.

A. Ὀργῆς δ' ἐπειρῶ τοῦ χάριν θείας ὅση;
   καίτοι βροτὸν χρὴ δειματούμενον τρέμειν
   σημεῖά γ' ἦν πέμποντες ὑψόθεν θεοὶ
   τοσῷδε καταπλήσσωσι κηρύκων κότῳ.

B. βραδύς τις ἴσθ' ὤν· χοῖα Ῥωμαίῳ πρέπει
   κέντροισι χρῆσθαι συμφύτοις ὀκνεῖς βίου,
   ἢ καὶ σπανίζεις· δεῖμα χλωρὸν ὀμμάτων
   ἔχει σ', ἀφῖξαί τ' εἴς τι θαῦμα φροντίδος
   τόνδ' εἰσορῶν ταραγμὸν οὐρανοῦ νέον.
   ἀλλ' αἰτίαν γὰρ εἰ λογίζεσθαι θέλεις,
   τί πῦρ τοσοῦτον πετόμεναί θ' αἵδε σκιαί,
   τί θήρ, τί δ' ὄρνις οὐ κατ' ἀξίαν γένους,
   τί θεσπιῳδεῖ παῖς γέρων τ' ἄφρων θ' ἅμα·
   τί ταῦθ' ἅπαντα κόσμον οὐ σῴζει, τέρας
   ἔκπαγλον εἴς τι τήν θ' ὑπάρχουσαν φύσιν
   καὶ τάξιν ἀλλάξαντα, τοισίδ' ἐννοεῖς
   θεόν τιν' ἐπιπνεῦσαι τάδ', ὥστε σὺν φόβοις
   ὑπερβίῳ τὸ μέλλον ἀγγέλλειν πόλει.
   λέγειν προσεικότ' ἄνδρα νυκτὶ τῇδ' ἔχω,
   στράπτοντα, βροντῶνθ', ὃς κενοῖ νεκρῶν τάφους,
   βρέμει τ' ἐν ὄχθοις οἷα Ταρπήοις λέων·
   ἄνδρ' ὄντα μείζον' οὔτ' ἐμοῦ τιν' οὔτε σοῦ
   πρὸς χειρὸς ἔργον, εἰς τέρας δ' ηὐξημένον
   φοβερόν, νεόρτων τῶνδε προσβολῶν δίκην.

Tim.   Commend me to them,
And tell them that, to ease them of their griefs,
Their fears of hostile strokes, their aches, losses,
Their pangs of love, with other incident throes
That nature's fragile vessel doth sustain
In life's uncertain voyage, I will some kindness do
    them:
I'll teach them to prevent wild Alcibiades' wrath.
First Sen. I like this well; he will return again.
Tim. I have a tree, which grows here in my close,
That mine own use invites me to cut down,
And shortly must I fell it: tell my friends,
Tell Athens, in the sequence of degree
From high to low throughout, that whoso please
To stop affliction, let him take his haste,
Come hither, ere my tree hath felt the axe,
And hang himself. I pray you, do my greeting
Flav. Trouble him no further; thus you still shall find him.
Tim. Come not to me again: but say to Athens,
Timon hath made his everlasting mansion
Upon the beached verge of the salt flood;
Who once a day with his embossed froth
The turbulent surge shall cover : thither come,
And let my grave-stone be your oracle.

                                 SHAKESPEARE.

T. Χαίρειν κελεύω· κἀνακούφισιν θέλων
λύπης ὀπάζειν, πολεμίας θ' ὁρμῆς φόβων,
κέντρων τ' ἔρωτος, μνησιπήμονός τ' ἄσης,
ἄλλων θ' ὁποῖα πήματ' οὐκ ἀκήρατον
σκάφος φέρειν εἴωθεν ἐν ῥόθῳ βίου,
χάριν νεμῶ τιν', ἀγρίου φρενῶν ὅπως
ὁ Κλεινίειος παῖς χόλου παυθήσεται.

A. προσίεταί με ταῦτά γ'· ἥξει γὰρ πάλιν.

T. ἐγγύς τι δένδρον τοισίδ' ἐμπέφυκέ μοι
ἀγροῖς, ὃ χρεία μ' ἡ παροῦσα προσκαλεῖ
ἄρδην τεμεῖν πρόρριζον, οὐδ' ἱδρυτέον
τὸ μὴ οὐ πέδῳ νιν ἐξισοῦν· στείχων δέ μοι
φίλοις τ' ἐμοῖσι φράζ', Ἐρεχθείδαις θ' ὁμοῦ
τοῖς τ' ἐν τέλει βεβῶσι τοῖς τ' ἀνωνύμοις,
διεξιὼν τὸν πάντα τάξεων κύκλον,
ὡς, ἤν τις αὐτῶν πημονὰς παῦσαι θέλῃ,
χρεὼν μολόντα δεῦρο σὺν σπουδῇ ποδός,
πρὶν ἀμφιπλῆγα δένδρον ἀξίνην τεμεῖν,
πλεκταῖς ἐν ἀρτάναισιν αὐτουργὸν θανεῖν.

Φ. οὐ σῖγ' ἀνέξει; μὴ σύ γ'· οὐ γὰρ εὐπιθής.

T. μή μοι πάλιν πρόσστειχ' ἔτ'· ἀλλ' ἰὼν φράσον
Τίμων' Ἐρεχθείδαισιν, ὡς τὸν εἰσαεὶ
μενοῦντ' ἐν ἀκτῆς κρασπέδοις ἁλιστόνου
ἐστήσατ' οἶκον· τοῦ δ' ἅπαξ καθ' ἡμέραν
μέλλει βαρύβρομον οἶδμα ῥυθιάδος ζάλης
καταψακάζειν λιβάσιν ἐκκρούστοις ἀφροῦ·
ὑμεῖς δ' ἐκεῖσ' ἐλθόντες, ὡς χρηστήριον,
οὕτω τάφον μου προσκυνεῖτ' αἰδούμενοι.

K. Phi.   Bind up your hairs.

Const. Yes, that I will; and wherefore will I do it?
I tore them from their bonds and cried aloud
'O that these hands could so redeem my son,
As they have given these hairs their liberty!'
But now I envy at their liberty,
And will again commit them to their bonds,
Because my poor child is a prisoner.
And, father cardinal, I have heard you say
That we shall see and know our friends in heaven:
If that be true, I shall see my boy again;
For since the birth of Cain, the first male child,
To him that did but yesterday suspire,
There was not such a gracious creature born.
But now will canker-sorrow eat my bud
And chase the native beauty from his cheek;
And he will look as hollow as a ghost,
As dim and meagre as an ague's fit,
And so he'll die; and, rising so again,
When I shall meet him in the court of heaven
I shall not know him: therefore never, never
Must I behold my pretty Arthur more.

Pand. You hold too heinous a respect of grief.

Const. He talks to me that never had a son.

K. Phi. You are as fond of grief as of your child.

SHAKESPEARE.

Φ. Κόσμησον αὖθις πλόκαμον ἀναδέτου κόμης.
Κ. δράσω τάδ' οὐκ ἄκουσα· τοῦ χάριν δ' ἐρῶ.
δεσμῶν δ' ἀποσπάσασα τοιάδ' ηὐχόμην·
εἰ γὰρ κόμην ὡς ἥδε χεὶρ ἐλευθεροῖ
οὕτω τέκνον λύσειε. νῦν δ' αὖθις πάλιν,
τοὐλευθέρου φθονοῦσα, δέσμιόν σφ' ἐγὼ
θήσω, τέκνου δεθέντος ἀθλιωτάτου.
ἱερεῦ, σέθεν δ' ἤκουσα πᾶς τις οὕνεκα
ἰδὼν ἐν Ἅιδου γνωριεῖ τὰ φίλτατα·
ὡς δ' ὧδ' ἐχόντων αὖθις ὄψομαι τέκνον.
ἐξ οὗ γὰρ ἄρσην πρῶτος ἐξέβλαστε παῖς
ἐς τόνδ' ὃς ἐχθὲς ἔσχεν ἀμπνοὰς βίου,
οὔπω πέφυκεν ἄλλος εὐειδέστερος.
νῦν δ' αὖ τὸ κάλλος τοὔμφυτον λύπη φθινὰς
ἐλᾷ παρειᾶς ἄνθος ὡραῖον τέκνου
βρύκουσα, κἀμενηνὸν εἴδωλον νεκροῦ
πεσόντος ἐν πληγαῖσι θανασίμοις νόσου
φαντάζεται παῖς οὑμὸς ἄψυχος σκιά·
χοὕτω θανεῖται· χὦταν ἐντύχω ποτὲ
ὧδ' ἀναφανέντι παιδὶ τῶν ἐκεῖ μέτα
οὐ γνωριῶ νιν· τοιγὰρ οὐκ ἐσόψομαι
τὸν καλλίπαιδ' Ἀρτοῦρον οὔποτ' αὖθις αὖ.
Π. ἄγαν τιν' ἄλγους φροντίδ', ὦ γύναι, τρέφεις.
Κ. παρήνεσας τάδ' αὐτὸς ὢν ἄπαις τέκνων.
Φ. λύπην ποθεῖν ἔοικας οὐχ ἧσσον τέκνου.

Give me my robe, put on my crown; I have
Immortal longings in me : now no more
The juice of Egypt's grape shall moist this lip :
Yare, yare, good Iras; quick. Methinks I hear
Antony call; I see him rouse himself
To praise my noble act; I hear him mock
The luck of Cæsar, which the gods give men
To excuse their after wrath; husband, I come :
Now to that name my courage prove my title!
I am fire and air; my other elements
I give to baser life. So; have you done?
Come then, and take the last warmth of my lips.
Farewell, kind Charmian; Iras, long farewell.
Have I the aspic in my lips? Dost fall?
If thou and nature can so gently part,
The stroke of death is as a lover's pinch,
Which hurts, and is desired. Dost thou lie still?
If thus thou vanishest, thou tell'st the world
It is not worth leave-taking.

SHAKESPEARE.

Δός μοι πέπλωμα κρατί τ' ἀμφίθες στέφος·
ἀθάνατος ἀρτίως με προσσαίνει πόθος.
ἀλλ' ἀμπέλου γὰρ οὔποτ' ἂν βρέχοιτ' ἔτι
γάνει τὰ χείλη τἀμὰ τῆς Αἰγυπτίας.
Ἴρα, σὺ δ' ἐγκόνησον· οὐχ ἕδρας ἀκμή.
κλύω γὰρ αὐδήν, ὡς ἔοικ', Ἀντωνίου,
ἰδοὺ δ' ἀνέστη τἄργα τἄμ' ἐπαινέσων·
ἢ οὐ κλύετ' ἐπεγγελῶντα Καίσαρος τύχῃ,
οἵαν θεοὶ φιλοῦσι δωρεῖσθαι βροτοῖς
πρόφασιν καλὴν δὴ τοῦ μεθύστερον κότου;
ἥκω πρὸς ἄνδρα τὸν ἐμόν· εἰ γὰρ εὐλόγως
ἐπώνυμοι καλοίμεθ' ἀνδρείας χάριν.
ἀλλ' αἰθέρος γὰρ κἀμπέχει πυρὸς φύσις
τὰ δ' ἄλλ' ἀφῆκα τῇ κακίονι ζόῃ.
ἀλλ' ἦ πέπρακται ταῦτα; δεῦρο χειλέων
θάλπος μολόντε λωτίσασθον ὕστατον.
χαίροις ἄν, Ἴρα, καὶ σύ, Χαρμία φίλη.
πίτνεις; τρέφω γὰρ κἀπὶ χειλέων ὄφιν;
εἰ δ' ἀσφαδάστως ὧδ' ἀπήλλαξαι φύσεως
ὡς δῆγμ' ἐραστοῦ καιρία πληγὴ μόρου,
λυπρὸν μὲν ἄλγος ἀλλ' ὅμως ποθούμενον.
μῶν ἡσυχάζεις; ὧδ' ἰοῦσ' ἀπαξιοῖς
γένος τὸ χαίρειν μὴ προσεννέπειν βροτῶν.

Great honours are great burdens; but on whom
They're cast with envy he doth bear two loads.
His cares must still be double to his joys
In any dignity; where, if he err,
He finds no pardon; and for doing well
At most small praise, and that wrung out by force.
I speak this, Romans, knowing what the weight
Of the high charge you have trusted to me is.
Not that thereby I would with art decline
The good or greatness of your benefit;
For I ascribe it to your singular grace,
And vow to owe it to no title else,
Except the gods, that Cicero's your Consul.
I have no urns, no dusty monuments,
No broken images of ancestors,
But for myself I have prepared this strength.

BEN JONSON.

Ἀρχῆς μὲν ἀεὶ δεινὸν ἄχθος ἂν λέγοις,
φθόνος δ᾽ ὅτῳ ξύνεστι τοῖσδ᾽ ἄχθος διπλοῦν·
ἐξουσία γὰρ ἀντὶ χαρμονῆς μιᾶς
διπλῆν νέμει μέριμναν· ὃς μὲν ἀμπλάκῃ
ξύγγνοιαν οὐδεὶς ἔσχε, τῷ δράσαντι δ᾽ εὖ
σπάνιός τ᾽ ἔπαινος καὶ παρ᾽ ἀκούσης φρενός.
τάδ᾽, ἄνδρες, ὑμῖν εἶπον οὐκ ἄιδρις ὢν
οἵωπερ ἀρχῆς ξυγκατέζευγμαι βάρει.
οὐχ ὡς ἀπώσων αἱμύλων λόγων μέτα
κάλλιστον ὂν τὸ δῶρον ὕψιστόν θ᾽ ἅμα·
καὶ γὰρ παρ᾽ ὑμῶν τῶν μάλ᾽ εὐμενῶν ἐμοὶ
καὶ θεῶν δεχόμενος οὐδενός τ᾽ ἄλλου χάριν
ὄμνυμι Ῥώμης ὕπατος ὡς πάρειμ᾽ ὅδε.
ἐπεὶ οὔτι κομπῶ τυμβόχωστ᾽ ὀγκώματα,
θηκῶν πατρῴων οὐδὲν ἀρχαῖον γάνος,
οὐ συντεθραυσμέν᾽ ἐν δόμοις ἀγάλματα,
αὐτὸς δ᾽ ἀφ᾽ αὑτοῦ τοῦτ᾽ ἐπικτῶμαι κράτος.

Go where thou mean'st. The ports are open ; forth.
The camp abroad wants thee, their chief, too long.
Lead with thee all thy troops out. Purge the city.
Draw dry that noisome and pernicious sink,
Which left behind thee would infect the world.
Thou wilt free me of all my fears at once,
To see a wall between us. Dost thou stop
To do that now commanded, which before
Of thine own choice thou art prone to ? Go. The Consul
Bids thee, an enemy, to depart the city.
Whither, thou'lt ask, to exile ? I not bid
Thee that. But ask my counsel, I persuade it.
What is there here in Rome that can delight thee ?
Where not a soul, without thine own foul knot,
But fears and hates thee. What domestic note
Of private filthiness, but is burnt in
Into thy life ? What close and secret shame
But is grown one with thine own infamy ?
What lust was ever absent from thine eyes ?
What lewd fact from thy hands ?

BEN JONSON.

Ἴθ᾽ ἔνθα χρῄζεις, ὡς ἀνεῳγμένων πυλῶν,
αὐτοῖς ὁπλίταις πᾶσι· τὸν ταγὸν στρατὸς
δαρὸν ποθεῖ θυραῖος· ἐξάντλει βαρὺν
ἄντλον, καθαίρων πατρίδ᾽, ὃς κακοσμίᾳ
μέλλει μιαίνειν σοῦ λελειμμένος χθόνα.
τῶν δειμάτων γάρ μ᾽ εἰσάπαξ ἐλευθεροῖς,
τοίχου μεταξύ γ᾽ ὄντος. ἆρ᾽ ὀκνεῖς τάδε
δρᾶν νῦν κελευσθείς, αὐτὸς ἃ σπεύδεις πάρος;
ἄπερρε· τήνδ᾽ ὡς ἐχθρὸν ἐκλιπεῖν πόλιν
ἄρχων κελεύω· ποῖ ποθ᾽ ὡς φευξούμενον;
τάχ᾽ ἄν μ᾽ ἔροιο· ταῦτ᾽ ἐπαγγέλλω μὲν οὔ·
πείθω γε μήν, σύμβουλον ἢν αἰτῇ μ᾽ ἔχειν.
τίς ἡδονὴ γὰρ ἐνθάδ᾽ ὄντος ἐν πόλει;
ἐν ᾗ φοβεῖταί σ᾽ ἢ στυγεῖ τίς ἔσθ᾽ ὃς οὐ
πλὴν σόν γε μιαρὸν πλῆθος; οἰκεία τίς οὐ
κηλὶς βίῳ ᾽ντέτηκεν αἰσχίστῳ σέθεν;
ποῖον δ᾽ ὄνειδος κρυπτὸν οὐδ᾽ ἄκρυπτον οὐ
εἰς ἓν κέκραται σῶν ἀναιδείᾳ τρόπων;
τίς σῶν ἄπεστιν ὀμμάτων ἔρως κακός;
ἔργου δὲ ποῖον χεῖρας οὐ χραίνει μύσος;

He's gone; and on his finger bears my signet,
Which is to him a sceptre. He is stern
As I am heedless; and the slave deserves
To feel a master. What may be the danger,
I know not: he hath found it, let him quell it.
Must I consume my life—this little life—
In guarding against all may make it less?
It is not worth so much. It were to die
Before my hour, to live in dread of death,
Tracing revolt ; suspecting all about me,
Because they are near; and all who are remote,
Because they are far.

BYRON.

Glorious and bright ! lo, here we bend
Before thy throne, trembling attend
Thy sacred pleasures : be pleased then
To shower thy comforts down, that men
May freely taste, in life's extremes,
The influence of thy powerful beams.

FORD.

Ἀλλ᾽ οἴχεται σφραγῖδά μου φορῶν, χερὸς
σκῆπτρόν τι κείνης, στερρὸς ὢν πρὸς ὄντ᾽ ἐμὲ
ἄβουλον ὀρθῶς· δεσπότην γὰρ ἄξιος
μαθεῖν ὁ δοῦλος. οἶδ᾽ ἐγὼ μὲν οὐ πόσον
τὸ δεινόν· εἰδὼς δ᾽ αὐτός, αὐτὸς εἰργέτω.
τί δεῖ μ᾽ ἀναλοῦν τόνδε τὸν βραχὺν βίον,
οὐκ ἄξιον τοσοῦδέ γ᾽, εἰ φυλάξομαι
ἅπαντα τὰ φθείροντα; προφθάσας γὰρ ἂν
οὕτω τελευτήν, θάνατον ἂν ζῴην τρέμων
στάσιν τ᾽ ἰχνεύων ποῦ 'στί, τοῖς μὲν οἴκοθεν
ὡς ἐγγὺς οὖσι πᾶσιν εἰς ὕποπτ᾽ ἰών,
τοῖς δ᾽ αὖ θυραίοις ὡς πρόσωθεν ἠμένοις.

Σέλας ὦ λαμπρόν, σεμνῶν πρὸ θρόνων
οἵδε πίτνοντες δεχόμεσθ᾽ ὁπόσ᾽ ἂν
σὺ θέλῃς τρομεροί· πρὸς ταῦτα θέλων
ἄφθον᾽ ἄνωθεν στάζοις χάριτος
μειλίγμαθ᾽, ὅπως δυσμαῖς τε βίου
     κἂν προτελείοις
πᾶς ἀπολαῦσαι σέθεν αὐγῆς.

Jes. I am never merry when I hear sweet music.
Lor. The reason is, your spirits are attentive :
      For do but note a wild and wanton herd,
      Or race of youthful and unhandled colts,
      Fetching mad bounds, bellowing and neighing loud,
      Which is the hot condition of their blood;
      If they but hear perchance a trumpet sound,
      Or any air of music touch their ears,
      You shall perceive them make a mutual stand,
      Their savage eyes turn'd to a modest gaze
      By the sweet power of music : therefore the poet
      Did feign that Orpheus drew trees, stones and floods;
      Since nought so stockish, hard and full of rage,
      But music for the time doth change his nature.
      The man that hath no music in himself,
      Nor is not moved with concord of sweet sounds,
      Is fit for treasons, stratagems and spoils;
      The motions of his spirit are dull as night
      And his affections dark as Erebus :
      Let no such man be trusted.

                                        SHAKESPEARE.

I. Κλύουσα μολπῆς οὐκ ἀνεπτόμην κέαρ.
Λ. ὁθούνεκ' εὖ μάλ' ἐντενεῖς τρέφεις φρένας.
    σκέψαι γὰρ ἀγέλην μάργον ἠγριωμένην,
    ἢ πωλικὴν ἀδμῆτα νεογενῆ φύσιν,
    σκιρτῶσαν αἰὲν ἐμμανῆ σκιρτήματα
    φρυάγμασίν τ' ὀρθοῖσιν ἐμβριμωμένην
    (οὕτως ἀνάσσων μυελὸς ἐνθερμαίνεται),
    εἴ πως κλύει σάλπιγγος εὐφθόγγου βοῆς
    ἤ τις δι' ὤτων ᾄσσεται μολπῆς χάρις,
    κοινὴν ἰδεῖν πάρεστιν ὡς ἔστη στάσιν
    μετέβαλέ τ' εἰς αἰδοῖον ὄμματ' ἄγρια,
    ὄψιν κρατηθεῖσ' αἰμύλου μολπῆς ὕπο.
    ἀνθ' ὧν ἀοιδὸς Ὀρφέα ποιεῖ δρυῶν
    εἴδη λίθους θ' ἕλκοντα καὶ σκληρὰς ῥοάς·
    δρυὸς γὰρ οὐ πέφυκεν οὐ πέτρας ἄπο
    οὐ μεστὸν ὀργῆς οὐδέν, ᾧ μολπὴ νέαν
    ἐν τῷ παραυτίκ' οὐ μεθήρμοσεν φύσιν.
    ὅσοις δὲ μηδεὶς ἐν φρεσὶν μολπῆς ἔρως
    φωνῶν ἀτέγκτοις νηδύμων ὁμαυλίας,
    στάσιν τε μηχάνημά τ' αἰόλον μάχης
    πλέκειν, ἄγειν τε καὶ φέρειν εὐμηχάνοις,
    οὗτος πόρον τῆς καρδίας νυκτὸς δίκην
    ἔθρεψ' ἀπαμβλυνθέντα, καὶ φίλους πόθους
    ὡς Ἐρεβόθεν δνόφοισιν ἐσκοτωμένους·
    τοιγὰρ τοιούτῳ μηδὲ πιστεύειν λέγω.

Fortuna loquitur.

I come not here, you gods, to plead the right
By which antiquity assign'd my deity,
Though no peculiar station 'mongst the stars,
Yet general power to rule their influence;
Or boast the title of omnipotent,
Ascrib'd me then, by which I rival'd Jove,
Since you have cancell'd all those old records:
But confident in my good cause and merit,
Claim a succession in the vacant orb.
For since Astraea fled to heaven, I sit
Her deputy on earth; I hold her scales,
And weigh men's fates out, who have made me blind
Because themselves want eyes to see my causes;
Call me inconstant, 'cause my works surpass
The shallow fathom of their human reason:
Yet here, like blinded Justice, I dispense
With my impartial hands their constant lots:
And if desertless impious men engross
My best rewards, the fault is yours, you gods,
That scant your graces to mortality.

THOMAS CAREW.

Οὐχ ὡς ἀπαιτήσουσα τὴν παγκληρίαν,
ἧς ἠξιώθην τῶν παλαιτέρων ὕπο
θεὸς γεγῶσα, καίπερ ἐν πανηγύρει
ἐξαίρετον μὲν οὐ λαχοῦσ᾽ ἄστρων ἕδραν
κοινὰς δ᾽ ἐποπτεύουσα συμπάντων ὁδούς·
οὐδ᾽ ὥς τι κομπάσουσα παγκρατὲς σέβας
οὗ πρὸς Δί᾽ αὐτὸν εἰς ἅμιλλαν ἱκόμην,
θεοί, πάρειμι δεῦρο· πῶς γάρ; οἵτινες
αὐτοὶ παλαιὰ γράμματ᾽ ἐξηλείψατε·
δίκῃ δὲ πίσυνος οὖσα κἀξιώματι
λαχεῖν ἔρημον ἀντιποιοῦμαι κύκλον·
ἐξ οὗ γὰρ ἐνθένδ᾽ ᾤχετ᾽ Ἀστραία φυγάς,
κείνης διάδοχος ἐν μέρει θακῶ θρόνους·
κείνης τάλαντ᾽ ἔχουσα τοῖς θνητοῖς ἐγὼ
ἐπισταθμῶμαι τὰς τύχας, οἵ μ᾽ ὀμμάτων
τυφλὴν ἔθηκαν οὐχ ὁρῶντες αἰτίας,
καλοῦσι δ᾽ ἀστάθμητον ὡς τά γ᾽ ἔργα μου
οὐ ξυμμετρεῖ λεπταῖσιν ἀνθρώπων φρεσί.
ἐνταῦθα δ᾽ ὥσπερ ὀμματοστερὴς Δίκη
κλήρους ἴσους ἴσαισι χερσὶ προσνέμω·
ἢν δ᾽ οὖν ἀνάξιός τις ἀνόσιος γέρα
λάχῃ τὰ τιμιώτατ᾽, αἰτία θεῶν
σπανίας νεμόντων χάριτας ἀνθρώπων γένει.

Lucio. Give't not o'er so: to him again, entreat him,
　　　Kneel down before him, hang upon his gown:
　　　You are too cold; if you should need a pin,
　　　You could not with more tame a tongue desire it:
　　　To him, I say!

Isab. Must he needs die?

Ang. 　　　　　　Maiden, no remedy.

Isab. Yes; I do think that you might pardon him,
　　　And neither heaven nor man grieve at the mercy.

Ang. I will not do't.

Isab. 　　　　But can you, if you would?

Ang. Look, what I will not, that I cannot do.

Isab. But might you do't, and do the world no wrong,
　　　If so your heart were touch'd with that remorse
　　　As mine is to him?

Ang. 　　　　　　He's sentenced; 'tis too late.

Lucio. You are too cold.

Isab. Too late? why, no; I, that do speak a word,
　　　May call it back again.　Well, believe this,
　　　No ceremony that to great ones 'longs,
　　　Not the king's crown, nor the deputed sword,
　　　The marshal's truncheon, nor the judge's robe,
　　　Become them with one half so good a grace
　　　As mercy does.
　　　If he had been as you and you as he,
　　　You would have slipt like him; but he, like you,
　　　Would not have been so stern.

　　　　　　　　　　　SHAKESPEARE.

Λ. Μή μοι πρόκαμνε, γονυπετὴς δ' αἰτουμένη
λίσσου μάλ' αὖθις κἀντέχου πεπλωμάτων.
ψυχρά τις ἦσθ' ἄρ'· εἰ γὰρ εὐτελοῦς τινὸς
χρεία σ' ἔχοι τις, οὐκ ἂν ἡσυχαιτέραν
γλῶσσαν νέμοις ἄν· εἶα λιπάρει μάλ' αὖ.

Ι. θανεῖν σφ' ἀνάγκη;

Α.   παρθέν', οὔ τι τῶνδ' ἄκος.

Ι. δοκεῖς γε μήν μοι τοῦτον ἂν κατοικτίσαι,
μήδ' ἄνδρ' ἐπ' οἴκτῳ, μή τιν' ἀσχαλᾶν θεῶν.

Α. οὐκ ἂν θέλοιμι.

Ι.   μῶν ἔχεις θέλων τὸ δρᾶν;

Α. ἂν μὴ θέλω 'γώ, μηδ' ἔχοντα δρᾶν λέγε.

Ι. ἆρ' οὖν δύναι' ἄν, ὥστε μηδὲν ἀμπλακεῖν,
εἰ σῆς θίγοι τοῦδ' οἶκτος ὡς κἀμῆς φρενός;

Α. ἀλλ' ὑστέρα προσῆλθες ἐπὶ δεδογμένοις.

Λ. ψυχράν τιν' ἐπὶ θερμοῖσι καρδίαν ἔχεις.

Ι. οὐχ ὑστέρα γε· πῶς γὰρ ὑστέραν λέγεις;
ἐπεὶ τὸ ῥίπτειν τ' ἀνακαλεῖν τ' αὖθις λόγον
ἐμοὶ πρόσεστιν· ἀλλά μοι πιθοῦ τάδε.
οὐ σεμνότιμον τοῦ προφερτάτου γέρας,
οὐ σκῆπτρ' ἄνακτος, οὐχὶ διάδοχον ξίφος,
ἱρά τε ῥάβδος, οὐ δικασπόλου στολή,
οὐδέν τι τούτων ἀξίωμ' αὐτῷ πρέπει,
τὸ μὴ οὐ τὸν οἶκτον δὶς τόσως ὑπερφέρειν.
εἰ γὰρ μετέπεσε σοί τε τοὐκείνου μέρος
τὸ σόν τ' ἐκείνῳ, καὐτὸς ὧδ' ἂν ἤμπλακες,
ἀλλ' οὐκ ἐκεῖνος στερρὸς ὧδ' ἂν ηὑρέθη.

Done to death by slanderous tongues
  Was the Hero that here lies:
Death, in guerdon of her wrongs,
  Gives her fame which never dies.
So the life that died with shame
Lives in death with glorious fame.
Hang thou there upon the tomb,
Praising her when I am dumb.

SONG.

Pardon, goddess of the night,
Those that slew thy virgin knight;
For the which, with songs of woe,
Round about her tomb they go.
  Midnight, assist our moan;
  Help us to sigh and groan,
    Heavily, heavily:
  Graves, yawn and yield your dead,
  Till death be uttered,
    Heavily, heavily.

SHAKESPEARE.

Ἄδε μὲν Ἡρὼ γαῖα καλύπτει,
ψιθυραῖς Ἡρὼ γλώσσαις φθιμένην·
θάνατος δ' ἀχέων ποινὰς μεγάλων
ἀντιδίδωσιν κλέος ἀθάνατον.
βιοτὰ δ' οὕτω θνήσκουσ' ἀκλεῶς
βίον εἴληχεν τὸν κλεινότατον.
δέλτος σὺ δέ μοι νῦν ἐπὶ τύμβῳ
      τῷδε κρεμαστὴ
σιγῶντος ἐμοῦ νιν ἐπαίνει.

σύγγνωθι θεά, πότνια νυκτός,
σὴν κτείνασιν παρθένον ἀδμῆτ'·
ἀνθ' ὧν τύμβους ἀμφιπολοῦμεν
λιγυροῖς θρήνοις ἐπιτυμβιδίοις.
σὺ δὲ νὺξ μεσάτη σύμμαχος ἡμῶν
μελέα μελέοις ἴσθι στοναχαῖς·
ἐπάνω τύμβοι τ' ἐκπροϊέντες
χάσκετε νεκρούς, ἔστ' ἂν θάνατος
      μέλεος μελέων
νεκύων πλήρωμα κενώσῃ.

Hastily rose our guide,
Leaving us at the board; awhile we lingered,
Then paced the beaten downward way that led
Right to a rough stream's edge, and there broke off;
The only track now visible was one
That from the torrent's further brink held forth
Conspicuous invitation to ascend
A lofty mountain.   After brief delay
Crossing the unbridged stream, that road we took,
And clomb with eagerness, till anxious fears
Intruded, for we failed to overtake
Our comrades gone before.   By fortunate chance,
While every moment added doubt to doubt,
A peasant met us, from whose mouth we learned
That to the spot which had perplexed us first,
We must descend, and there should find the road,
Which in the stony channel of the stream
Lay a few steps, and then along its banks;
And that our future course, all plain to sight,
Was downwards, with the current of that stream.

WORDSWORTH.

Ἡμᾶς δ᾽ ὁ πομπὸς σὺν τάχει θοινωμένους
λιπὼν ἀνέστη· κεἰς βραχὺν χρόνον μονῆς
στίβον τὸν εὐθὺς εἰς λάβρου χεῖλος ῥοῆς
κάτω φέροντα κἆτ᾽ ἄφαντον εἵρπομεν.
μόνον δὲ τἀπέκεινα χειμάρρου παρῆν
ὁρᾶν ἔτ᾽ ἴχνος οὐκ ἀσήμοισιν φραδαῖς
κελεῦον ὑψίκρημνον ἀμβαίνειν ὄρος.
χρόνον τιν᾽ ἐμμείναντες ἐξαμείβομεν
πόρον τὸν οὐ ζευχθέντα, κἀχόμεσθ᾽ ὁδοῦ,
ποδῶν ἄνω στείχοντες εἰς προθυμίαν,
ἔστ᾽ οὐ φθάσασι τοὺς προελθόντας φίλους
εἰσῆλθεν ἄπορον δεῖμα. σὺν τύχῃ δέ τῳ,
ἀμηχανοῦσι μᾶλλον ὡς προβαίνομεν,
ποιμήν τις ἀντέκυρσεν, ὃς φράζει λέγων
μολεῖν πρὸς αὐτὸν χῶρον ὃς πρὶν ἠπάτα,
ὡς ἐν πετρώδει κεῖσ᾽ ἀφιγμένους μυχῷ
ῥείθρου τιν᾽ εὑρήσοντας οὐ μακρὰν ὁδὸν
πάτον διελθόντ᾽, εἶτ᾽ ἰόντ᾽ ὄχθας πάρα·
κἀντεῦθεν ἄξοι, καὶ μάλ᾽ ἐμφανὴς ἰδεῖν,
κέλευθος ἡ μέλλουσα καὶ κατὰ ῥοήν.

Paulina.   I am sorry for't:
All faults I make, when I shall come to know them,
I do repent.   Alas! I have show'd too much
The rashness of a woman: he is touch'd
To the noble heart.   What's gone and what's past help
Should be past grief: do not receive affliction
At my petition; I beseech you, rather
Let me be punish'd, that have minded you
Of what you should forget.   Now, good my liege,
Sir, royal sir, forgive a foolish woman:
The love I bore your queen—lo, fool again!—
I'll speak of her no more, nor of your children;
I'll not remember you of my own lord,
Who is lost too: take your patience to you,
And I'll say nothing.
Leontes.   Thou didst speak but well
When most the truth; which I receive much better
Than to be pitied of thee.   Prithee, bring me
To the dead bodies of my queen and son:
One grave shall be for both: upon them shall
The causes of their death appear, unto
Our shame perpetual.   Once a day I'll visit
The chapel where they lie, and tears shed there
Shall be my recreation: so long as nature
Will bear up with this exercise, so long
I daily vow to use it.   Come and lead me
Unto these sorrows.

                                        SHAKESPEARE.

Π. Ἀλγῶ 'πὶ τούτοις· ἂν γὰρ ἀμπλάκω ποτὲ
εὐθὺς μετέγνωκ' ἀμπλακοῦσ' ὅταν μάθω.
φεῦ· ἄγαν ἔδειξα θῆλυς οὖσ' ἀβουλίαν·
ἀνδρὸς πρὸς ἧπαρ ἔθιγε γενναίου τάδε.
τὰ φροῦδα γάρ τοι μηκέτ' ὄντ' ἰάσιμα
οὔ φασι λυπεῖν θεμιτόν· ἀλλ' αἰτήμασιν
ἐμοῖσιν, ὦναξ, μὴ τοσόνδ' ἄλγος δέχου·
δίκης γὰρ αὐτὴ μᾶλλον ἀξία λαχεῖν
ἥτις σ' ἀνέμνησ' ὧν σ' ἐχρῆν ἀμνημονεῖν.
ἀλλ', ὦ φίλ' ὦναξ, ὦ τυραννικὸν κάρα,
φαύλῃ γυναικὶ τῇδε συγγνώμην ἔχε·
εὔνοι' ἀνάσσης προύτρεπεν τόσον φράσαι·
φεῦ τῆς ἀνοίας· δεύτερον τόδ' ἤμπλακον·
ἀλλ' οὔτ' ἂν αὐτῆς οὔτε τῶν παίδων πέρι
εἴποιμ' ἔτ' οὐδέν, οὐδ' ἀναμνήσω πόσιν
ἐμὸν τὸν αὐτῆς, ὃς βέβηκεν ἐκ τρίτων.
σὺ δ' ἀλλὰ τλήμων ἴσθι καὶ σιγήσομαι.
Λ. ἀλλ' εὖ γὰρ εἶπας κεῖνα τἀληθέστατα,
ἃ μᾶλλον οἴκτου τοῦδ' ἐδεξάμην σέθεν.
ἄγ' οὖν ὑφηγοῦ μοι πόδ' οὗ κεῖται τέκνον
ἄνασσά τ'· ἀμφοῖν σώμαθ' εἷς κρύψει τάφος
μόρου δ' ἐπ' αὐτοῖν αἰτία 'γγεγράψεται
ὄνειδος ἡμῖν εἰς τὸν αἰανῆ χρόνον.
ὅπου πρόκεινται δ' ἐμβατεύσομεν νεὼν
ἀεὶ κατ' ἦμαρ, καὶ δακρυρροῶν ἐκεῖ
τὸν αὐτὸς αὑτοῦ βουκολήσομαι πόνον.
μόχθοις δ' ἕως ἂν τοισίδ' ἀντέχῃ φύσις
χρῆσθαι τοσοῦτον εὔχομαι πανήμερος.
ἀλλ' εἶ' ὑφηγοῦ τἀμὰ πρὸς φρενῶν ἄχη.

      Have I so far lost
A father's power, that I must give account
Of my actions to my son ? or must I plead
As a fearful prisoner at the bar, while he
That owes his being to me sits a judge
To censure that which only by myself
Ought to be questioned ?   Mountains sooner fall
Beneath their vallies, and the lofty pine
Pay homage to the bramble, or what else is
Preposterous in nature, ere my tongue
In one short syllable yield satisfaction
To any doubt of thine—nay though it were
A certainty disdaining argument !
Since, though my deeds wore hell's black livery,
To thee they should appear triumphal robes,
Set off with glorious honour, thou being bound
To see with my eyes, and to hold that reason,
That takes or birth or fashion from my will.
           MASSINGER.

Ἀλλ' ἢ πατρῴας ἀμπλακόντ' ἐξουσίας
πατέρα τέκνῳ δεῖ πράξεων δοῦναι λόγον ;
ἢ καὶ χρεὼν τῷδ' ἀνδρὶ μὲν φεύγειν δίκην,
ὃς δ' ἐξ ἐμοῦ πέφυκεν αἵματος κριτὴν
ἔργων καθῆσθαι κἀπιτιμητὴν βαρύν,
ὁποῖ' ὑφ' ἡμῶν χρῆν ἐλέγχεσθαι μόνων ;
ναπῶν ἔνερθε πρὶν πέσοι ταπείν' ὄρη,
κύπτοι τ' ἀκάνθαις ἡ μάλ' ὑψαύχην πίτυς,
εἴτ' ἄλλο τῶνδ' ἔτ' ἐκνομώτερον φύσει,
πρὶν γλῶσσαν ἡμῶν κἂν ἔπους σμικροῦ χάριν
σοί τ' ἀπολογεῖσθαι τῇ θ' ὑποψίᾳ σέθεν,
κεἰ δῆλον εἴη τοὐπίκλημ' ἄνευ λόγου.
εἰ γὰρ τάδ' ἔργα Στύγιος ἠμπέσχε σκότος,
νικηφόρου χρῆν σοί γ' ὅμως δοκεῖν στολὴν
ἁβραῖσι ποικιλθεῖσαν εὐκλείας χλιδαῖς,
σοὶ γοῦν προσῆκον πάνθ' ὁρᾶν ὅπως ἐγώ,
ὅσ' ἂν δὲ πράγματ' ἐξ ἐμοῦ θελήματος
βλάστας ἔχει καὶ σχήμαθ', ἡγεῖσθαι λόγον.

Look, what I speak, my life shall prove it true ;
That Mowbray hath received eight thousand nobles
In name of lendings for your highness' soldiers,
The which he hath detain'd for lewd employments,
Like a false traitor and injurious villain.
Besides I say and will in battle prove,
Or here or elsewhere to the furthest verge
That ever was survey'd by English eye,
That all the treasons for these eighteen years
Complotted and contrived in this land
Fetch from false Mowbray their first head and spring.
Further I say, and further will maintain
Upon his bad life to make all this good,
That he did plot the Duke of Gloucester's death,
Suggest his soon-believing adversaries,
And consequently, like a traitor coward,
Sluiced out his innocent soul through streams of blood :
Which blood, like sacrificing Abel's, cries,
Even from the tongueless caverns of the earth,
To me for justice and rough chastisement ;
And, by the glorious worth of my descent,
This arm shall do it, or this life be spent.

SHAKESPEARE.

Ἦ μὴν ἐλέγξω κεἰ θάνοιμ' ὅσ' ἂν λέγω·
ὁ γὰρ Μοβραῖος μυρίας λαβὼν δραχμὰς
ὡς σοῖς δανείσων δῆθεν ὁπλίταις, ἄναξ,
οὗτος κατασχὼν εἰς τὰ μὴ πρέπουτ' ἔχει,
προδότης τις αἰσχρὸς κἀδικώτατος φανείς.
καὶ πρός γέ φημι κἀξελέγχοιμ' ἂν δορί,
εἴτ' ἐνθάδ' εἴτ' οὖν ἄλλοσ' εἰς ὅσον χθονὸς
οὐδείς τις Ἄγγλων πώποτ' ἔβλεψεν κύκλῳ,
ἅπαντα τὰν γῇ τῇδε τοῦ πολλοῦ χρόνου
ηὑρημέν' αἰσχρῶς καὶ μεμηχανημένα
ἀρχὴν Μοβραῖον τόνδε καὶ πηγὴν ἔχειν.
πρὸς τοῖς δέ φημι, πρὸς δὲ τοῦδ' ἀποφθίσας
ψυχὴν ἀπίστου πιστὰ προσφύσω τάδε,
Γλωστῆρος ὡς ἔρραψεν εἰς οὗτος μόρον,
τοὺς δυσμενεῖς τ' ἔπεισε πείθεσθαι ταχεῖς.
ἐκ τῶνδε τοίνυν μυρίων δι' αἱμάτων
προδότης παρωχέτευσεν ἄψυχος βίον.
τὰ δ' ἐξ ἀφώνων γῆς μυχῶν τιμωρίαν
θυτῆρος ἐν τρόποισιν Ἀβήλου βοᾷ,
κἀμοῦ κολαστοῦ προστυχεῖν καταξιοῖ.
καὶ τὴν ἐμὴν κατώμοσ' εὔκλειαν γένους
ἦ μὴν τάδ' ἔρξειν ἢ τελευτήσειν βίον.

So forth they rowed; and that Ferryman
With his stiffe oares did brush the sea so strong,
That the hoare waters from his frigot ran,
And the light bubles daunced all along,
Whiles the salt brine out of the billowes sprong.
At last far off they many Islandes spy
On every side floting the floodes emong:
Then said the knight; 'Lo! I the land descry;
Therefore, old Syre, thy course doe thereunto apply.'

'That may not bee,' said then the Ferryman,
'Least wee unweeting hap to be fordonne;
For those same Islands, seeming now and than,
Are not firme land, nor any certein wonne,
But stragling plots which to and fro doe ronne
In the wide waters: therefore are they hight
The Wandring Islands. Therefore doe them shonne;
For they have ofte drawne many a wandring wight
Into most deadly daunger and distressed plight.'

SPENSER.

Ἤρεσσον οὖν ἐνθένδε· χὠ πορθμεὺς ῥόθῳ
ἔψαιρεν ἅλμην καρτερῷ στερρᾶς πλάτης,
ὥστ᾽ ἐκ σκάφους μὲν πολιὸν ἐκθρώσκειν ὕδωρ,
κούφοισι δ᾽ ὀρχησμοῖσι καχλάζειν ἀφροῦ,
ἐκ κυμάτων γελῶντος ἁλμυροῦ σάλου.
χρόνῳ δὲ πολλὰς εἰσορῶσιν οὐ πέλας
νήσους ῥεούσας πανταχῇ διὰ ῥοῆς.
χὠ μὲν τάδ᾽ εἶπε· γῆν ὁρῶ· τοιγάρ, γέρον,
ἐκεῖσε πλοῦν θοῦ. μηδαμῶς, Χάρων ἔφη,
παθεῖν τι μή πως ἡμῖν ἄκουσιν τύχοι.
νῆσοι γάρ, ὡς ὁρᾶν μέν, αἵδ᾽ ἔχουσ᾽ ὅμως
οὐ χέρσον οὐδ᾽ οἴκησιν, ἀλλ᾽ ἀλώμεναι
πλάκες τρέχουσιν εὐρέων δι᾽ οἰδμάτων
ἐκεῖσε δεῦρό θ᾽· ὥστ᾽ ἐπωνομασμέναι
Πλαγκταὶ κέκληνται· τοιγὰρ εὐλαβοῦ σύ νιν·
ἐπέσπασαν γὰρ πολλὰ δὴ πλανωμένους
εἰς δεινὰ δυστυχήματ᾽ ὀλεθρίου δύης.

Since what I am to say must be but that
Which contradicts my accusation, and
The testimony on my part no other
But what comes from myself, it shall scarce boot me
To say 'not guilty': mine integrity
Being counted falsehood, shall, as I express it,
Be so received. But thus: if powers divine
Behold our human actions, as they do,
I doubt not then but innocence shall make
False accusation blush and tyranny
Tremble at patience. You, my lord, best know,
Who least will seem to do so, my past life
Hath been as continent, as chaste, as true,
As I am now unhappy; which is more
Than history can pattern, though devised
And play'd to take spectators. For behold me
A fellow of the royal bed, which owe
A moiety of the throne, a great king's daughter,
The mother to a hopeful prince, here standing
To prate and talk for life and honour 'fore
Who please to come and hear.

SHAKESPEARE.

Ἐπεὶ δὲ νῦν λέξαιμ' ἂν οὐδὲν ἄλλο πλὴν
ὡς ἀντεροῦσα τοῖς ἐμοῖς ἐγκλήμασιν,
αὐτή τ' ἐμαυτῆς μαρτυρῶ μί' οὖσ' ὕπερ,
τίς ὠφέλησις εἰ καταρνοίμην τὸ μή;
ψεῦδος γὰρ ἀξιοῦντι τοὐμὸν εὐσεβὲς
ἐμοῦ λεγούσης εἰκὸς ἂν ταύτῃ δοκεῖν.
εἰ δ' οὖν μέλει θεοῖσιν, ὥσπερ οὖν μέλει,
ἔργων βροτείων, κάρτ' ἐν ἐλπίσιν τρέφω
πεσεῖν ποτ' ἂν ψεύδορκον αἰσχύνῃ στόμα
ἐναντίον τῆς οὐδὲν αἰτίας, τὸ δὲ
τλῆμον παρασχεῖν κἀν ὑβρισταῖσιν φόβον.
ὦναξ, σὺ δ' οἶσθα, καίπερ οὐ δοκῶν ὅμως,
ὡς σῶφρον' ὡς πείθαρχον ὡς ἠσκημένον
βουλαῖσιν ἁγναῖς δεῦρ' ἀεὶ τείνω βίον,
ὡς τἀπὸ τοῦδε δυστυχῆ, ποίας λόγου
ὑπερβολῆς οὐ κρείσσον', ὃς θηρεύεται
σοφῶς θεατὰς κομψὰ ποικίλλων ἔπη;
ἴδεσθε γάρ με βασιλικῶν θ' ὁμευνέτιν
λέκτρων, λαχοῦσάν τ' ἐξ ἴσου μέρος θρόνων,
σεμνοῦ τ' ἄνακτος τέκνον, ἥ τ' ἐγεινάμην
παῖδ' ἐλπίδων ἔγκληρον, ὡς παραστατῶ
κλέους θ' ὕπερ ψυχῆς τε κωτίλλουσά τι
μῆκος πρόλεσχον τοὐπιόντος εἰσορᾶν.

Nay, said I not—
And if I said it not I say it now,
I'll follow thee through sunshine and through storm,
I will be with thee in thy weal and woe,
In thy afflictions, should they fall upon thee,
In thy temptations, when bad men beset thee,
In all the perils which must now press round thee,
And, should they crush thee, in the hour of death.
If thy ambition, late-aroused, was that
Which pushed thee on this perilous adventure,
Then I will be ambitious too—if not,
And it was thy ill-fortune drove thee to it,
Then I will be unfortunate no less.
I will resemble thee in that and all things
Wherein a woman may; grave will I be,
And thoughtful, for already is it gone,
The boon that Nature gave me at my birth,
My own original gaiety of heart.
All will I part with to partake thy cares,
Let but thy love my lesser joys outlast.

HENRY TAYLOR.

Οὐ γὰρ τάδ᾽ εἶπον; εἰ δὲ μή, τανῦν ἐρῶ.
καὶ γὰρ δι᾽ αἰθρίας τε χειμῶνός θ᾽ ὁμοῦ
εὖ καὶ κακῶς πράσσοντι σοὶ μεθέψομαι·
εἴτ᾽ ἐμπεσοῦσα δήξεται λύπη κέαρ,
εἴτ᾽ οὖν ποτ᾽ ἀνδρῶν ἐξ ὁμιλίας κακῶν
εἰς πεῖραν ἥξεις, κἀπὸ κινδύνων ὅσοι
τανῦν ἐφεστᾶσ᾽ εἴ τί σοι παθεῖν χρεών,
τότ᾽ οὐδὲ θνήσκων τοὐμὸν οὐ καμεῖ μέρος.
εἰ δ᾽ αὖτ᾽ ἐγερθεῖσ᾽ ἀρτίως ἀθλεῖν τάδε
φιλοτιμία σ᾽ ἐπῆρε κινδυνεύματα,
φιλότιμον ἦθος οὐδ᾽ ἔγωγ᾽ ἀναίνομαι·
εἰ δ᾽ οὖν ἀφορμὴ τῶνδέ σοι τὸ δυστυχές,
ξυνδυστυχεῖν ἕτοιμος, ἐν τούτοις θ᾽ ἅμα
κἂν οἷς τὸ θῆλυ καρτερεῖ μιμήσομαι,
σεμνὸν βλέπουσα δέργμα καὶ πεφροντικός·
πάλαι γὰρ ἥν ποθ᾽ ἡ φύσις γενέθλιον
δόσιν παρεῖχεν οἴχεται τὸ φαιδρόνουν.
τἄλλ᾽ ἂν προδοίην ὥστε σοὶ λυπημάτων
τῶν σῶν μετασχεῖν—ἡσσόνων μόνον γ᾽ ἔρως
ὁ σὸς ξυνείη χαρμονῶν ὑπερτελής.

                                    Mother,
What is done wisely is done well. Be bold
As thou art just. 'Tis like a truant child,
To fear that others know what thou hast done,
Even from thine own strong consciousness, and thus
Write on unsteady eyes and altered cheeks
All thou wouldst hide. Be faithful to thyself,
And fear no other witness but thy fear.
For if, as cannot be, some circumstance
Should rise in accusation, we can blind
Suspicion with such cheap astonishment,
Or overbear it with such guiltless pride,
As murderers cannot feign. The deed is done,
And what may follow now regards not me.
Consequence, to me,
Is as the wind which strikes the solid rock,
But shakes it not.

                                    SHELLEY.

Πρὸς τῷ δικαίῳ, μῆτερ, εὐθαρσὴς γενοῦ·
τὰ γὰρ σοφῶς εἰργασμέν' εἴργασται καλῶς.
πρὸς νηπίου γὰρ παιδός, ἥτις ὧδ', ἀφ' ὧν
σαυτῇ ξύνοισθ', οἷ' εἰργάσω φοβουμένη
μή τις ξυνειδῇ κάλλος, εἶτ' ἐν ὄμματι
γράφεις κατηφεῖ κάλλαγῇ παρηίδων
ὅσα στέγειν χρῆν· ἀλλ' ἔτ' ἐν σαυτῇ γενοῦ·
καὶ μηκέτ' ἄλλον μάρτυρ' ἢ τὸν σὸν φόβον
μηδένα φοβηθῇς· εἴ τι γὰρ γένοιτο νῷν
(καίτοι τόδ' οὐχ οἷόν τε) δεῖμ' ὑποψίας,
φαύλως βλεπόντων δέργμα θαύματος πλέον
ἐπάργεμος γένοιτ' ἂν ἥδ' ὑποψία,
ἢ κἂν καθιππασαίμεθ' ὡς ἀναιτίῳ
γοργὸν δεδορκόθ' οἷον οὐ πλάσειεν ἂν
μιαιφόνων τις. τοὔργον εἴργασται τόδε·
ἐμοὶ δὲ τοὐνθένδ' οὐκέθ' οἷ προβήσεται
μέλει· τί γὰρ τὸ μέλλον; οὐδὲν ἄλλο πλὴν
ῥιπὴ θυέλλης, ὡς ἐμοί γ', ἥτις πέτραν
βάλλει κραταιάν, ἡ δ' ἀκίνητος μένει.

O my love! my wife!
Death, that hath suck'd the honey of thy breath,
Hath had no power yet upon thy beauty:
Thou art not conquer'd; beauty's ensign yet
Is crimson in thy lips and in thy cheeks,
And death's pale flag is not advanced there.
Tybalt, liest thou there in thy bloody sheet?
O, what more favour can I do to thee,
Than with that hand that cut thy youth in twain
To sunder his that was thine enemy?
Forgive me, cousin! Ah, dear Juliet,
Why art thou yet so fair? shall I believe
That unsubstantial death is amorous,
And that the lean abhorred monster keeps
Thee here in dark to be his paramour?
For fear of that, I still will stay with thee;
And never from this palace of dim night
Depart again: here, here will I remain
With worms that are thy chamber-maids.

SHAKESPEARE.

Ὦ φιλτάτης δάμαρτος ὡραῖον δέμας,
Ἅιδης ὁ μελίπνουν ἐκπιὼν πνοῆς γάνος
ἀλλ' οὐδέπω τὸ κάλλος ἐκνικᾷ τὸ σόν,
οὐκ εὐμαρῆ χειρώματ'· ἔτι παρηίδων
φοινίσσεται τὸ σῆμα κἀπὶ χειλέων
ἥβης τὸ καλλίμορφον, οὐδ' Ἅιδης ἐκεῖ
ὠχρὸν φθορᾶς τρόπαιον ἀντέστησέ πω.
Τύβαλτε, σοὶ δὲ φοινίοις προκειμένῳ
πέπλοις τίν' ἔξω μεῖζον' ἀποδοῦναι χάριν
ἢ χερσὶν αἳ δίχ' ἄνθος ἔθρισαν τὸ σὸν
οὕτως ἐμαυτοῦ τοῦ μέγ' ἐχθίστου βροτῶν
ἥβην ἀποσπᾶν; ἀλλ', ἀνεψιοῦ κάρα,
ξύγγνοιαν ἴσχε· φιλτάτη δ' Ἰουλία,
τί καλλίπρωρος ὧδ' ἄρ' ἦσθ' ἰδεῖν ἔτι;
Ἅιδην ἄμορφον μῶν ἐρασθῆναί ποτε
ἐπεικάσας τύχοιμ' ἄν; εἶτ' ἀσώματον
ὠχρόν σ' ὑπὸ δνόφοισιν ἀμενηνὸν στύγος
ἔχειν παραγκάλισμα; ταῦτ' ἀποστέγων
ὅδ' ἐμμενῶ κάτοικος, οὐδ' ἄπειμ' ἔτι
μελάθρων σκοτεινῆς νυκτὸς εὐλαῖσιν γεγὼς
ταῖς σαῖσι προσπόλοισιν ὧδ' ὁμέστιος.

      Now give me leave,
My hate against thyself and love to him
Freely acknowledged, to give up the reasons
That made me so affected. In my wants
I ever found him faithful : had supplies
Of men and money from him, and my hopes,
Quite sunk, were by his grace buoyed up again :
He was indeed to me as my good angel
To guard me from all dangers. I dare speak,
Nay, must and will, his praise now, in as high
And loud a key, as when he was thy equal.
The benefits he sowed in me met not
Unthankful ground, but yielded him his own
With fair increase, and I still glory in it.
And tho' my fortunes, poor compared to his,
And Milan weighed with France appear as nothing,
Are in thy fury burnt, let it be mentioned
They served but as small tapers to attend
The solemn flame at this great funeral,
And with them I will gladly waste myself,
Rather than undergo the imputation
Of being base or unthankful.

            MASSINGER.

Ξύγγνωθι δή μοι, στόματος ἐξ ἐλευθέρου
ξυναινέσαντι σοὶ μὲν ἔχθος ὡς τρέφω
τούτῳ δὲ φιλίαν, ἣν ἀφηγῶμαι τορῶς
οἷόν νιν ὄντα κἀνθ' ὅσων στέρξας ἔχω.
εἴ του δεοίμην πιστὸς ὢν ὅπλων ἅλις
καὶ χρημάτων ἐπήρκεσ', ἐλπίδας τέ μοι
εὔφρων ἔσωζε, φελλὸς ὥς, τὰς ἐκ βυθοῦ,
ὡς ἵλεως δαίμων τις οὐδέν' ὄντιν' οὐ
ὑπεξελὼν κίνδυνον· οὐδ' ὀκνῶ λέγειν,
ἑκὼν μὲν οὖν λέξαιμ' ἄν, ὡς κἀμοὶ πρέπον,
τὸν τοῦδ' ἔπαινον νῦν τ' ἴσῃ παρρησίᾳ
καὶ πρόσθεν εὖτε σοὶ μετεῖχε τῶν ἴσων.
ἔδρασέ μ' εὖ βαθεῖαν οὐ λεπτήν τινα
σπείρας ἄρουραν, ἀλλ' ἀφ' ἧς καρπῶν φορὰν
τὴν πλείον' ἐξήμησε τῶν ἐσπαρμένων,
ἐφ' οἷς ἐπαυχῶ κἄτι νῦν· εἰ γὰρ τύχην
ἐμὴν πρὸς αὐτοῦ κρεῖσσον' εὐτελῆ νέμω,
ἄγων παρ' οὐδὲν τοὐμὸν ὡς πρὸς Κελτικὴν
πόλισμ', ὑπ' ὀργῆς νῦν σέθεν κεκαυμένην,
ἀλλ' οὖν τοσόνδ' ἔασον ἐξειπεῖν, ὅτι
ξυμβάλλεταί τι φέγγος ὧδ' ἀφαυρὸν ὂν
προπομπὸν ἀγλάϊσμα κηδείου πυρᾶς,
κἀγὼ σὺν αὐτῷ δέξομαι πρόφρων φθίνειν
ἢ δυσχάριστος ἤ τις ἀμνήμων κλύειν.

She dwelt among the untrodden ways
 Beside the springs of Dove,
A Maid whom there were none to praise
 And very few to love :

A violet by a mossy stone
 Half hidden from the eye !
Fair as a star, when only one
 Is shining in the sky.

She lived unknown, and few could know
 When Lucy ceased to be ;
But she is in her grave, and, oh,
 The difference to me !

WORDSWORTH.

Ἀβάτων οἴμων παρθένος ᾤκει
παρὰ ταῖς πηγαῖς ταῖσι Πελειάδος·
οὔτις ἐπήνει παρθένον ὕμνοις,
παῦροι δ' ἐφίλουν πάνυ παῦροι.
ὅσσοις ἴον ὡς ὅσον οὐκ ἀφανὲς
ψηφῖδος ὑπαὶ τῆς βρυοέσσης·
οἷος ἔλαμψεν πλάκας οὐρανίας
στεροπαῖς αἴθων μόνος ἀστήρ.
ἀγνὼς βίος ἦν, παύροις τε κόρης
γνωτὸς θάνατος τῆς ἡμετέρας·
ἡμῖν δὲ μόνοις (πολὺ γὰρ τὸ μέσον)
τύμβος νιν ἔχει πολύκλαυστον.

Look on the Vestals,
The holy pledges that the gods have given you,
Your chaste, fair daughters. Were 't not to upbraid
A service to a master not unthankful,
I should say these, in spite of your prevention,
Seduced by an imagined faith, not reason
(Which is the strength of nature), quite forsaking
The Gentile gods, had yielded up themselves
To this new-found religion. This I cross'd,
Discover'd their intents, taught you to use,
With gentle words and mild persuasions,
The power and the authority of a father,
Set off with cruel threats; and so reclaim'd them:
And, whereas they with torment should have died
(Hell's furies to me, had they undergone it!),
They are now votaries in great Jupiter's temple,
And, by his priest instructed, grown familiar
With all the mysteries, nay, the most abstruse ones,
Belonging to his deity.

MASSINGER.

Ἰδοῦ δὲ τήνδ᾽ ἀδμῆτα θυγατέροιν σποράν,
ἔρωτος ἁγνοῦ παρὰ θεῶν πιστώματα,
τὴν καλλίπαιδα παρθένων ξυνωρίδα·
ὀνειδίσαι μὲν τοὐμὸν οὐκ ἀμνήμονι
αἰδὼς λάτρευμα δεσπότῃ· ταύτας δ᾽ ὅμως
πίστει δοκούσῃ σοῦ παραινοῦντος βίᾳ
παρηγμένας λέγοιμ᾽ ἂν (οὐ γὰρ οὖν λόγῳ
ἐν ᾧπερ ἰσχὺς τῇ φύσει κεῖται μόνῳ),
ἱερῶν προδούσας νόμιμα τῶν ἐγχωρίων,
τελεταῖς ἐπακτοῦ ταισίδ᾽ ἐνδοῦναι θεοῦ.
ἁγὼ τορῶς φρονήματ᾽ ἐξιχνοσκοπῶν
ἠναντιώθην· κἀφρένωσ᾽ ὅτῳ τρόπῳ
λόγων ἐπῳδὰς μαλθακῶν παρηγόρους,
καὶ τὴν πατρῴαν συνδίκως ἐξουσίαν,
δειναῖς ἀπειλαῖς εὖ περιστέλλων κυροῖς.
οὕτω δ᾽ ἔπαυσα μὴ παραχθῆναι φρένας.
κᾆθ᾽, ἃς κακίσταις κατθανεῖν λώβαις ἐχρῆν
(φεῦ τῶν μ᾽ ἑλόντων, εἰ ᾽θανον, μιαστόρων),
νῦν προσπολοῦσι Ζηνὸς ὑψίστου δόμοις,
σκεθρῶς τε παιδεύσαντος ἱερέως, θεοῦ
τῶν σεμνοτίμων ἠθάδες μυστηρίων
κλύουσι, τῶν μάλιστ᾽ ἐν ἀρρήτοις λέγειν.

                    Sure, we thank you.
My learned lord, we pray you to proceed
And justly and religiously unfold
Why the law Salique that they have in France
Or should, or should not, bar us in our claim :
And God forbid, my dear and faithful lord,
That you should fashion, wrest, or bow your reading,
Or nicely charge your understanding soul
With opening titles miscreate, whose right
Suits not in native colours with the truth ;
For God doth know how many now in health
Shall drop their blood in approbation
Of what your reverence shall incite us to.
Therefore take heed how you impawn our person,
How you awake our sleeping sword of war :
We charge you, in the name of God, take heed ;
For never two such kingdoms did contend
Without much fall of blood ; whose guiltless drops
Are every one a woe, a sore complaint
'Gainst him whose wrong gives edge unto the swords
That make such waste in brief mortality.

                                        SHAKESPEARE.

Ἀλλ', ἴσθι, τῶνδε μυρίαν ἔχω χάριν.
λέγοις ἂν ἤδη, πανσοφώτατον κάρα,
ὁσίως δικαίως τ' εὖ σαφηνίσας τὸ πᾶν,
εἴτ' οὖν ἀπείργειν Σαλικὸς ὃς Κελτοῖς νόμος
κεῖται δικαίωμ' εἴτε μὴ τοὐμὸν σθένει.
ὅπως δὲ μὴ σύ, πιστὸς ὢν φίλος τ' ἀνήρ,
σκολιὰς παλαιῶν γραμμάτων κάμψεις στροφάς,
μηδ' ἐν πυκναῖσιν ἐξακριβώσας φρεσὶν
νόθην ἀνοίξεις συνθέτου σκῆψιν δίκης,
οἴας ἀναιδὲς σχῆμα τἀληθοῦς λόγου
μηδὲν ξυνᾴδει γνησίῳ μορφώματι.
ξυνίστορες γὰρ οἱ θεοὶ πόσοι φίλον
στάξουσιν αἷμα, νῦν μάλ' ἡβῶντες δέμας,
ὑπερμαχοῦντες ὧν ἂν αἴτιος γένῃ.
ἀνθ' ὧν ὅπως μὴ τἀμὰ θεὶς ὑπέγγυα
Ἄρεος τὸ νῦν καθεῦδον ἐπεγερεῖς ξίφος·
πρὸς θεῶν ἐπισκήπτω μάλ' ἐντροπήν σ' ἔχειν.
οὐ γὰρ τοιαῦται πώποτ' ἀλλήλαις μάχην
πόλεις ξυνῆψαν μὴ οὐ φόνοις ἡμαγμέναι·
σταγὼν δ' ἑκάστη τῶνδ' ἀναιτίων βλάβῃ
ἔσται πικρόν τ' ἔγκλημα τῷ πέρα δίκης
θήγοντι φάσγαν', οἳ ἀναλγήτῳ βίᾳ
βραχὺν βροτῶν αἰῶνα διαλυμαίνεται.

Duarte. You have bestowed on me a second life,
　　　　For which I live your creature, and have bettered
　　　　What nature framed imperfect : my first being
　　　　Insolent pride made monstrous ; but this later,
　　　　In learning me to know myself, hath taught me
　　　　Not to wrong others.

Doctor.　　　　　　　　Then we live indeed,
　　　　When we can go to rest, without alarum
　　　　Given every minute to a guilt-sick conscience
　　　　To keep us waking, and rise in the morning
　　　　Secure in being innocent : but when,
　　　　In the remembrance of our worser actions,
　　　　We ever bear about us whips and Furies,
　　　　To make the day a night of sorrow to us,
　　　　Even life's a burden.

Duarte.　　　　　　　　I have found and felt it ;
　　　　But will endeavour, having first made peace
　　　　With those intestine enemies, my rude passions,
　　　　To be so with mankind.

　　　　　　　　　　　　　　BEAUMONT.

A. Ἀνθ' ὧν ἔνειμας δευτέραν ἐμοὶ ζόην
καὶ τὴν πρὶν ἐξέπλησας ἐνδεᾶ φύσιν,
ζῶ σῆς τέχνασμα χειρός· ὃς πρὶν ἦ, κόρος
ὕβρις τ' ἀπηγρίωσέ μ'· ἡ δὲ νῦν φύσις
μαθόντ' ἐμαυτὸν εἰδέναι καὶ τοὺς πέλας
εὖ προυδίδαξε μὴ ἀδικεῖν.

B.   τούτοις βίος
ὁ βίος ἀληθὴς ἤν τις εἰς εὐνὴν πέσῃ
μηδὲν ξυνειδὼς δειμάτων ἐνθυμίων
οἵοις ξυνοικεῖ καρδία νοσοῦσ', ἄχους
ἄπαυστος, ὥστε βλέφαρα μὴ κοιμᾶν ὕπνῳ,
ἀνστῇ δ' ἑῷος εὐσεβεῖ χαίρων φρενί·
εἰ δ' αὖ τις αἰσχρῶν ἐργμάτων μεμνημένος
ταράσσεται μάστιγι τῶν Ἐρινύων
ἀνθ' ἡμέρας τε νυκτὸς αἰανῆς βάρος
ἤλλαξεν, αὐτὸς ὁ βίος οὐ βιώσιμος.

A. παθὼν τάδ' ἔμαθον· ὥστε τοῖσιν οἴκοθεν
ἐχθροῖσιν ὀργαῖς ἀγρίαις πειράσομαι
σπονδὰς ποιεῖσθαι πρῶτον, εἶτα τοῖς πέλας.

Cleo. The climate's delicate, the air most sweet,
Fertile the isle, the temple much surpassing
The common praise it bears.

Dion. I shall report,
For most it caught me, the celestial habits,
Methinks I so should term them, and the reverence
Of the grave wearers. O, the sacrifice!
How ceremonious, solemn and unearthly
It was i' the offering!

Cleo. But of all, the burst
And the ear-deafening voice o' the oracle,
Kin to Jove's thunder, so surprised my sense,
That I was nothing.

Dion. If the event o' the journey
Prove as successful to the queen,—O be 't so!—
As it hath been to us rare, pleasant, speedy,
The time is worth the use on 't.

Cleo. Great Apollo
Turn all to the best! These proclamations,
So forcing faults upon Hermione,
I little like.

Dion. The violent carriage of it
Will clear or end the business: when the oracle,
Thus by Apollo's great divine seal'd up,
Shall the contents discover, something rare
Even then will rush to knowledge. Go: fresh horses!

SHAKESPEARE.

K. Ἀβρὸς μὲν αἰθὴρ πνευμάτων δ' εὐήλιοι
στείχουσιν αὖραι καρπίμους νήσου γύας·
κρατεῖ δ' ὁ ναὸς τῶν ἐν ἀνθρώποις λόγων.

Δ. ἐγὼ δέ γ', οἷα πλεῖστα κατεπλάγην ἰδών,
τὰ θεῖα κεῖν' ἐσθήμαθ' (ὧδ' ἂν εὐλόγως
δοκεῖ καλεῖσθαι ταῦθ') ἑκὼν ἀπαγγελῶ
καὶ σεμνὸν αἰδοῦς σχῆμα τῶν ἠσκημένων.
φεῦ· οἷον τὸ θῦμ' ἔρεξαν ὡς μάλ' ἔννομον
καὶ σεμνότιμον κοὐ κατ' ἀνθρώπων φύσιν.

K. ὑπέρτατος δ' ὁ χρησμὸς οὐκ μυχοῦ συθεὶς
ὠτοστερὴς βρονταῖσι συγγενὴς Διὸς
οὕτω κατέσχε μ' ὥστε καὶ τὸ μηδὲν ἤ.

Δ. ἦν δ' ὡς ταχεῖά τ' ἀσμένοισί θ' ἥδ' ὁδὸς
αὐτοῖσιν ἡμῖν—εἴθε γὰρ ταύτῃ ῥέποι—
οὕτως ἀνάσσῃ νόστος ἢ σωτήριος,
χρονισθὲν ἦμαρ ἀξίαν ἔχει τριβήν.

K. ὦναξ Ἄπολλον, ταῦτ' ἀπαλλάξαι καλῶς.
ἃ δ' οὖν ἁμαρτεῖν Ἑρμιόνην βιάζεται
τοιαῦτα κηρυκεύματ' οὐ προσηκάμην.

Δ. ἀλλ' ἴσθι τῆσδε τῆς ἄγαν σπουδῆς ἄπο
ἤτοι λυθέντα ταῦτ' ἂν ἢ τελούμενα.
ὅταν δὲ τἀγγραφθέντ' ἀναπτύξῃ σαφῶς
ἐκ μάντεως ὁ χρησμὸς ἐσφραγισμένος,
δεινόν τι πρὸς φῶς ἵξεται σαφ' οἶδ' ὅτι.
ἀλλ' εἷα καινὸν ζεύξαθ' ἵππιον σθένος.

The land which warlike Britons now possesse,
And therein have their mighty empire raysd,
In antique times was salvage wildernesse,
Unpeopled, unmannurd, unprovd, unpraysd ;
Ne was it Island then, ne was it paysd
Amid the ocean waves, ne was it sought
Of merchants farre for profits therein praysd ;
But was all desolate, and of some thought
By sea to have bene from the Celticke maynland brought.

Ne did it then deserve a name to have,
Till that the venturous Mariner that way
Learning his ship from those white rocks to save,
Which all along the Southerne sea-coast lay
Threatning unheedy wrecke and rash decay,
For safëty that same his sea-marke made,
And namd it *Albion* : But later day,
Finding in it fit ports for fishers trade,
Gan more the same frequent, and further to invade.

SPENSER.

Ἦν νῦν Βρεταννοὶ γῆν ἔχουσ᾽ ἀρείφατοι,
ἀρχῆς τοσοῦτον ἔνθεν ὤρθωσαν κράτος,
χρονοῖς παλαιοῖς ἄβροτος ἦν ἐρημία,
ἀγνὼς ἄνανδρος ἀστιβὴς ἀνήροτος·
κοὐ ποντίαις πω νῆσος ἐξηρτημένη
ἐν ἀγκάλαισιν, οὐδ᾽ ἐκαρπώσαντ᾽ ἐκεῖ
ζηλωτὸν οἱ πρόσωθεν ἔμποροι βίον,
ἀλλ᾽ ἦν ἐρῆμος πᾶσα, χὥς φασίν τινες
πόρων δι᾽ ὑγρῶν Κελτικῆς ἐλθοῦσ᾽ ἄπο.
κοὐ κληδόνος πάροιθεν οἱ τότ᾽ ᾐξίουν,
πρὶν ναυβάτης τις ἐκτὸς εὔτολμος πετρῶν
λευκῶν σκάφος τῶν κεῖθεν ἐκσῶσαι μαθών,
πάσῃ παρ᾽ ἀκτῇ κειμένων τῇ πρὸς νότου,
σφαλερᾶς προφητῶν τοῖς ἀφροντίστοις φθορᾶς
ναυαγίων τε, σῆμα θείς νιν ἀσφαλὲς
ἐπωνόμαζε Λευκάδ᾽· ὕστερον δ᾽ ἔτι
λιμένων καλῶς ἔχουσαν ἰχθύων τ᾽ ἄγρας
πλείους κατῆσαν τάς τ᾽ ἄνω ᾽ζήτουν πλάκας.

Pul.   Still in his sullen mood ? no intermission
          Of his melancholy fit ?
Tim.   It rather, madam,
          Increases than grows less.
Pul.   Did he take
          No rest, as you could guess ?
Chry.   Not any, madam.
          Like a Numidian lion, by the cunning
          Of the desperate huntsman taken in a toil,
          And forced into a spacious cage, he walks
          About his chamber ; we might hear him gnash
          His teeth in rage, which open'd, hollow groans
          And murmurs issued from his lips, like winds
          Imprison'd in the caverns of the earth
          Striving for liberty ; and sometimes throwing
          His body on his bed, then on the ground,
          And with such violence, that we more than fear'd,
          And still do, if the tempest of his passions
          By your wisdom be not laid, he will commit
          Some outrage on himself.

                                        MASSINGER.

Π. Ἆρ' ὄμμ' ἔτι σκυθρωπός, οὐδὲ παῦλά πω
νόσου ματαίας;

Τ.   αὔξεται μὲν οὖν, γύναι,
νόσημα μᾶλλον ἢ καταφθίνει φρενός.

Π. οὐδ' ἔλαβέ γ' ὕπνος αὐτόν, ὥς γ' ἐπεικάσαι;

Χ. οὐ δῆτ'· ἐπεί τις ὡς Λιβυστικὸς λέων,
σοφῶς ἀγρευθεὶς δικτύων ἐν ἄρκυσιν
βίᾳ τ' ἐν ἔρκους περιβόλῳ κεκλημένος,
κοίτην διέρπει· κἀγκότως κλύειν παρῆν
ὀδόντας ὡς ἔθηγε, κἀξ ἀνεῳγμένων
κενοὺς ὑπεστέναζε χειλέων γόους,
στέναγμα δεινόν, οἷα πνεύματ' ἐν χθονὸς
μυχοῖσιν ἐγκρυφθέντα, κἀκ δεσμῶν πόρον
λύσεώς τιν' ἐκπονοῦντα· κᾆσθ' ὅτ' εἰς λέχος
ῥίπτει βιαίως, ἄλλοτ' εἰς πέδον δέμας,
φόβος δὲ νῦν τε καὶ τότ', ἢ πέρα φόβου,
ἢν μὴ θύελλαν κοιμίσῃς σοφῇ φρενί,
μή πού τι δεινὸν κεῖνος αὐτόχειρ πάθῃ.

You might have lived in servitude and exile,
Or safe at Rome, depending on the great ones ;
But that you thought these things unfit for men,
And in that thought you then were valiant.
For no man ever yet changed peace for war,
But he that meant to conquer. Hold that purpose.
There's more necessity you should be such
In fighting for yourselves, than they for others.
He's base that trusts his feet, whose hands are armed.
Methinks I see Death and the Furies waiting
What we will do, and all the Heaven at leisure
For the great spectacle. Draw then your swords ;
And if our destiny envy our virtue
The honour of the day, yet let us care
To sell ourselves at such a price, as may
Undo the world to buy us.

BEN JONSON.

Φεύγων ἂν ἔζης, ἦμαρ ἢ δοῦλον βλέπων,
ἢ τῶν σθενόντων ἐν κράτει Ῥώμην ἄνα
τὰ τοιάδ' ἀνδρὸς μὴ δοκῶν ἀνάξια·
ὡς δ' ὧδ' ἐχόντων ἦσθ' ἄρ' εὔψυχος τότε—
οὐδεὶς γὰρ οἶδ' ἠλλάξατ' εἰρήνης μάχην
ἄλλων κρατῆσαι μὴ θέλων· τούτων δ' ἔχου·
ὑμᾶς γὰρ ὧδε χρὴ διὰ στέρνων ἔχειν
ἄλλων ὑπερμαχοῦντας ἤ σφε τῶν πέλας.
κακοῦ γὰρ ὅπλ' ἔχοντα πιστεῦσαι ποσί.
Ἅιδην δοκῶ μὲν εἰσιδεῖν τ' Ἐρινύας
ἡμᾶς τανῦν βλέποντας οἷα πράξομεν,
σχολὴν δ' ἄγοντας τοὺς θεοὺς θεάματος
ἔκατι τοῦδε. νῦν ξίφη γυμνωτέα·
εἰ δ' ἡμῖν εὐψύχοισιν ἡ πεπρωμένη
κλέους φθονήσει τοῦδέ γ', ἄνδρες ἀλλ' ὅπως
τιμῆς τοσαύτης βίοτον ἀνταμείψομεν
ὥστ' ἐξολεῖται γαῖα πᾶσ' ὠνουμένη.

To be thus is nothing;
But to be safely thus.—Our fears in Banquo
Stick deep; and in his royalty of nature
Reigns that which would be fear'd: 'tis much he dares;
And, to that dauntless temper of his mind,
He hath a wisdom that doth guide his valour
To act in safety. There is none but he
Whose being I do fear: and, under him,
My Genius is rebuked; as, it is said,
Mark Antony's was by Caesar. He chid the sisters
When first they put the name of king upon me,
And bade them speak to him: then prophet-like
They hail'd him father to a line of kings:
Upon my head they placed a fruitless crown,
And put a barren sceptre in my gripe,
Thence to be wrench'd with an unlineal hand,
No son of mine succeeding. If 't be so,
For Banquo's issue have I filed my mind;
For them the gracious Duncan have I murder'd;
Put rancours in the vessel of my peace
Only for them; and mine eternal jewel
Given to the common enemy of man.

SHAKESPEARE.

Οὕτω μὲν οὐδὲν ἀσφαλῆ δ' οὕτως ἔχειν.
δεινὸς γὰρ ἐντέτηκε καρδίᾳ φόβος
Βάγκου· κρατεῖ δ' ἐν τῇ τυραννικῇ φύσει
τοιοῦτον οἷον κάρτα δειμαίνειν χρεών.
ἀνὴρ δὲ τολμᾷ πολλά, τῇ τ' εὐψυχίᾳ
προσιζάνει τὸ ξυνετόν, εὔσπλαγχνον κέαρ
οἷον κυβερνᾶν τἄργα δρᾶν ἐν ἀσφαλεῖ·
οὐδ' ἔστι πλὴν τοῦδ' ἄλλος οὗ φόβος μ' ἔχει
τοὐμὸν δ' ἐλέγχει λῆμ', ὁποῖ' Ἀντώνιον
πεπονθέναι λέγουσι πρὸς τὸν Καίσαρα.
οὗτος δ' ἐλοιδόρησε τὰς τρισσὰς κόρας
ὁθούνεχ' ἡμῖν κληδόνας τυραννικὰς
ἐπωνόμαζον, κἀκέλευσ' αὐτῷ λέγειν.
αἱ δ' ἀντεφώνουν μαντικοῖς προσφθέγμασι
πατέρα νιν ὡς ἔσοιτο βασιλικῆς σπορᾶς·
τοὐμὸν δ' ἀκάρπῳ κρᾶτ' ἐκόσμησαν στέφει,
αἰχμήν τ' ἄπαιδα χερσὶν εἰσεχείρισαν,
τῆς ἀλλοφύλου δεξιᾶς ποθ' ἁρπαγήν,
ἐμῶν γὰρ οὐδεὶς διαδόχους ἕξει θρόνους.
ὡς δ' ὧδ' ἐχόντων τῆσδ' ὑπὲρ Βάγκου σπορᾶς
ἐμὴν ἔχρανα καρδίαν μιάσματι,
ἔτλην τ' ἄνακτος εὐμενοῦς κλύειν φονεύς.
μόνων ἔκατι τῶνδε τὸν πρὶν ὄλβιον
κρατῆρ' ἀραίων ἐξέπλησα φαρμάκων,
καὶ τὴν ἐμὴν ἀθάνατον εὐκλείας χάριν
προύδωκα κοινῷ τῶν βροτῶν μιάστορι.

Timol.　We wrong ourselves, and we are justly punish'd,
　　　　To deal with bondmen, as if we encounter'd
　　　　An equal enemy.

Archid.　　　　　　　　They fight like devils;
　　　　And run upon our swords, as if their breasts
　　　　Were proof beyond their armour.

Timag.　　　　　　　　　Make a firm stand.
　　　　The slaves, not satisfied they have beat us off,
　　　　Prepare to sally forth.

Timol.　　　　　　　　They are wild beasts,
　　　　And to be tamed by policy.　Each man take
　　　　A tough whip in his hand, such as you used
　　　　To punish them with as masters : in your looks
　　　　Carry severity and awe ; 't will fright them
　　　　More than your weapons.　Savage lions fly from
　　　　The sight of fire ; and these, that have forgot
　　　　That duty you ne'er taught them with your
　　　　　　swords,
　　　　When, unexpected, they behold those terrors
　　　　Advanced aloft, that they were made to shake at,
　　　　'T will force them to remember what they are,
　　　　And stoop to due obedience.

　　　　　　　　　　　　　　　　MASSINGER.

A. Αὐτοὶ πρὸς αὐτοὺς πλημμελοῦντες ἐν δίκῃ
   ὀρθῶς κολαζόμεσθα, τοὺς δούλους γ᾽ ἔπι
   ἰόντες ὡς ἐπ᾽ ἐχθρὸν ἐξ ἴσης χερός.
B. καίτοι μάχονταί γ᾽ οἵδ᾽ ἀλαστόρων δίκην,
   ξίφεσιν ἐπεισπίπτοντες ὡς ὅπλων πλέον
   στέρνα στέγοντα.
Γ.   καρτεροῦντες ἔστατε·
   τροπῇ γὰρ οὐ στέργοντες οἱ δοῦλοι μιᾷ
   ὁρμώμενοι σπεύδουσιν ὡς ἐπ᾽ ἐξόδῳ.
A. σοφίᾳ τὸ δοῦλον θὴρ ὅπως δαμάζεται.
   ἀλλ᾽ εἰ ἕκαστος δεξιᾷ λαβὼν διπλῆν
   μάστιγ᾽, ὁποίᾳ δεσπότης ἐχρήσατο,
   ἐν ὄμμασιν φορῶμεν εὔσεπτον δέος.
   ἤτοι φοβήσει ταῦτά νιν μᾶλλον ξίφους.
   φεύγει λέων πῦρ χὠ μεγασθενὴς ἰδών·
   οὕτω δὲ χοἵδε τοῦ χρεὼν λελησμένοι,
   οὐ γάρ ποτ᾽ αὐτοὶ προυδιδάξατ᾽ ἔγχεσιν,
   ἀπροσδόκητον ἢν ἴδωσ᾽ ἐπηρμένον
   τὸ δεῖμ᾽, ὁποῖον ξυγγενὴς τρέμει φύσις,
   βίᾳ τάχ᾽ ἂν φρονοῖεν οἷα χρὴ φρονεῖν,
   εἴκοντες ὀρθῶς ἐννόμῳ πειθαρχίᾳ.

Thou seest this with a lovelorn maiden's eyes.
Cast thine eye round, bethink thee who thou art.
Into no house of joyance hast thou stepped,
For no espousals dost thou find the walls
Decked out, no guests the nuptial garland wearing,
Here is no splendour but of arms. Or think'st thou
That all these thousands are here congregated
To lead up the long dances at thy wedding?
Thou seest thy father's forehead full of thought,
Thy mother's eyes in tears : upon the balance
Lies the great destiny of all our house.
Leave now the puny wish, the girlish feeling,
O thrust it far behind thee.
Not to herself the woman must belong
Annexed and bound to alien destinies.
But she performs the best part, she the wisest,
Who can transmute the alien into self,
Meet and disarm necessity by choice,
And what must be, take freely to her heart,
And bear and foster it with mother's love.

COLERIDGE.

Σὺ γὰρ βλέπεις τάδ' οἷ' ἐρῶσα παρθένος.
κύκλῳ στρέφουσ' ὀφθαλμὸν ἥτις εἶ νόει.
οὐ γὰρ πατεῖς μέλαθρον ἡδονῆς γέμον,
οὐ νυμφικοῖς σοι τοῖχος ἔστεπται κλάδοις·
γαμβρὸς φορεῖ τίς στέφανον ὡς γαμουμένης;
πρέπει γὰρ οὐδὲν ἀγλάϊσμα πλὴν ὅπλων.
ἦ που χορεύειν σῶν χάριν νυμφευμάτων
οἱ μυρίοι δοκοῦσιν οἵδ' ἠλισμένοι;
ὅρα μὲν ὄμμα μητρὸς ὡς δακρυρροεῖ,
ὅρα δὲ πατέρα σὸν ξυνωφρυωμένον·
κεῖται γὰρ ὄλβος ἐν ῥοπῇ δόμων μέγας.
ἀνθ' ὧν μέθες μοι ταῦθ' ἃ νῦν μάτην φρονεῖς
πάλιν δικοῦσα παρθένειον ἵμερον.
ἐπεὶ οὐκέθ' αὑτῆς κυρία γυνὴ πέδαις
ἢ μηκέτ' οἰκείοισιν ἔζευκται πότμου·
ἡ δ' αὖ κρατίστη, τήνδ' ἐγὼ σοφὴν καλῶ,
τἀλλότριον ἥτις οἶδεν οἰκεῖον κτίσαι,
αὐτή τ' ἀνάγκην ἀντιοστατοῦσ' ὅπλων
γυμνοῦν, τὸ μέλλον τλᾶσ' ἑκουσία μένειν,
στέργειν τε βαστάζουσα μητρῴῳ πόθῳ.

The world had never taken so full note
Of what thou art, had'st thou not been undone ;
And only thy affliction hath begot
More fame, than thy best fortunes could have done :
For ever by adversity are wrought
The greatest works of admiration ;
And all the fair examples of renown
Out of distress and misery are grown.

How could we know that thou could'st have endur'd,
With a reposed cheer, wrong and disgrace ;
And with a heart and countenance assur'd
Have looked stern Death and horrour in the face ?
How should we know thy soul had been secur'd
In honest counsels, and in way unbase ;
Had'st thou not stood to show us what thou wer't,
By thy affliction that descry'd thy heart ?

It is not but the tempest that doth show
The seaman's cunning ; but the field that tries
The captain's courage : and we come to know
Best what men are, in their worst jeopardies.

DANIEL.

Εἰ μή ποτ' ἦσθα δυστυχὴς οὐκ ἂν σαφῶς
βροτοῖσιν ἐξέδειξας ὧν οἷός περ εἶ·
ἡ σὴ δ' ἄνολβος μοῖρα τίκτεται κλέος
τὸ μεῖζον ἢ κατ' εὐποτμωτάτην τύχην.
τοῖς γὰρ μεγίστοις θαύματός τ' ἐπαξίοις
μήτηρ πέφυκ' ἔργοισιν ἡ δυσπραξία·
τὰ πάντα τ' εὖ δεδραμέν', ὧν πύστις πάρα,
ἐκ πημονῶν ἔβλαστε κἀξ ἀμηχάνων.
τίς γάρ, τίς ἄν ποτ' ᾤετ' εὐσπλάγχνῳ φρενὶ
τλῆναί σ' ὄνειδος καὶ φέρειν ἀτιμίαν;
κρυερὸν τίς "Αιδην καρδίᾳ τ' εὐτλήμονι
ὀρθοῖς τ' ἐν ὀφθαλμοῖσιν ἀντίον βλέπειν;
τίς δ' ἂν ξυνῄδει σὴν καλοῖς βουλεύμασι
ψυχὴν ὁδοῖς θ' ἁγναῖσιν ἐστηριγμένην,
εἰ μὴ κατώφθης οἷος ἦσθ' ἐγκαρτερῶν
τοροῖσιν ἑρμηνεῦσι καρδίας δύαις;
ἤ τοι θύελλα ναυτίλων ἐμπειρίαν
σαφέστατ' ἐξέφηνε· κἂν μάχῃ δορὸς
ἀνδρεῖος ὢν ταγοῦχος ἐξετάζεται·
βροτῶν τ' ἀρίστη βάσανος ἡ δυσπραξία.

Agam. They have both deserved
         For their great service in this expedition,
         We should with calm and most impartial soul
         Hear and determine : therefore, if you please,
         Because the hours are precious, I shall
         Desire them lose no time.

Diom.   We all submit,
         And shall obey your prudence.

Agam.   You honour much
         Your Agamemnon. Princes, then to you.
         I hope you have brought hither with your persons
         Nothing but what your honours may consent to :
         Speak yourselves freely then ; these are your
              judges,
         Who are not only great in birth and titles,
         And therefore bring no thoughts to stain their
              honour,
         But bound by obligation of one country,
         Will love and do your name and valours justice.
         There lies your great reward, Achilles' arms,
         Forged by the subtle art of him, that framed
         Jove's thunderbolts, pride of Cyclopian labours :
         He that is meant by his kind stars to have
         The happy wearing of them next, may write
         Himself a champion for the gods and heaven,
         Against a race of giants that would scale it.
                                        SHIRLEY.

A. Ἀμφοῖν ὁμοίως ἀξίοιν ἐπ' ἀξίοις
εἰς τὴν στρατείαν ἔργμασιν φρενῶν ἴσῃ
πρέπει κλύοντας ἡσύχων κρῖναι ῥοπῇ.
ὥστ', εἰ τάδ' ὑμῖν ἀσμένοις, τώδ' ἀξιῶ
εὐθὺς λέγειν· σχολὴ γὰρ οὐ κέρδος φέρει.

Δ. σοφῇ προνοίᾳ πάντες οἵδ' ὑπείκομεν.

A. τιμῇ τὸν ἄνδρα πολλὰ τόνδ' ὀφέλλετε.
σφὼ δ' αὖ, ξυνωρὶς κοιράνων, προσεννέπω.
ὑμῖν πρὸς αὐτοῖς ἐλπὶς οὐδὲν ἄλλο πλὴν
δόξῃ ξυνῳδὸν δεῦρ' ἀφιγμένω φέρειν·
τοιγὰρ κελεύω πάντ' ἐλευθεροστομεῖν.
οὐ γὰρ μόνον κομποῦσιν εὔκλειαν γένους
οἵδ' οἱ κρινοῦντες, ὥστε λυμαντήριον
αἰδοῦς κομίζειν μηδέν, ἀλλὰ καὶ μιᾶς
ὅρκοις πάτρας δεθέντες ἐνδίκως κλέος
σφῷν εὐφιλεῖ τιμῶσι κἀνδρείαν φρενί.
κεῖται γέρας σφῷν κεδνόν, ὅπλ' Ἀχιλλέως,
γνώμης σοφῆς τεχνάσμαθ', ὃς τεύχει Διὸς
βροντάς, πόνων αὔχημα τῶν Κυκλωπίων.
ὁ δ' αὐτὰ μέλλων δεύτερος μάκαρ φορεῖν,
θεοῦ τυχών του πρευμενοῦς, οὗτος θεῶν
ὑπερμαχοῦντ' ἂν οὐρανοῦ θ' αὐτὸν γράφοι
Ὄλυμπον ἀμβαίνοντι γηγενεῖ στρατῷ.

What a true mirror
Were this sad spectacle for secure greatness !
Here they that never see themselves but in
The glass of servile flattery might behold
The weak foundation upon which they build
Their trust in human frailty.   Happy are those,
That knowing in their births they are subject to
Uncertain change, are still prepared and armed
For either fortune : a rare principle
And with much labour learned in wisdom's school.
For as these bondmen by their actions shew
That their prosperity, like too large a sail
For their small bark of judgement, sinks them with
A foreright gale of liberty, ere they reach
The port they long to touch at; so these wretches,
Swoll'n with a false opinion of their worth,
And proud of blessings left them, not acquired,
That did believe they could with giant arms
Fathom the earth, and were above their fates,
Those borrowed helps that did support them vanished,
Fall of themselves, and by unmanly suffering
Betray their proper weakness, and make known
Their boasted greatness was lent, not their own.

MASSINGER.

Οἷον κάτοπτρον τοῖς γ' ἐν ἀσφαλεῖ χλιδῇ
βεβηκέναι δοκοῦσιν ἥδ' ὄψις πικρά.
τῷ γοῦν ἑαυτὸν προσβλέποντι μηδαμῶς
πλὴν εἰς ἔνοπτρον δουλίου θωπεύματος
ἐνταῦθ' ἰδεῖν πάρεστ' ἐν ἀσφαλεῖ βάθρῳ
πυργοῦντι πίστιν αἰόλης θνητῶν τύχης.
ὅσοι δ' ὁρῶντες ἐκ νέων κοινούμενοι
τῶν ἀσταθμήτων ἀλλαγῶν μοῖραν διπλῆν
ὡπλισμένοι στέργουσιν, ὀλβίους λέγω·
ἐμπειρίᾳ γὰρ ἐκδιδάσκονται σοφοί,
σπαρνὸν δὲ τοῦθ' εὕρημα κοὐκ ἄτερ πόνου.
δοῦλοι μὲν ἔργοις οἵδε μηνύουσ' ὅτι
ἐν τῷ κατορθοῦν μὴ σοφῶς τοὐλεύθερον
ἔδυ περισσὸν λαῖφος ὡς σμικροῦ σκάφους
τέγγει πόδ', ἢν πρύμνηθεν ἵστηται πνοή,
πρὶν ἐξικέσθαι λιμένα τὸν ποθούμενον·
τλήμων δ' ὅδ' ὄχλος τἀξιώματος κεναῖς
ὠγκωμένος δόξαισι κἀπ' ὄλβῳ χλιδῶν,
ὃν παραλαβών τις αὐτὸς οὐκ ἐκτήσατο,
οἳ γῆν κραταιαῖς ἀμπέχειν ἐν ὠλέναις
Μοίρας θ' ὑπείκειν σφῶν ἐπαυχοῦσι σθένει,
φρούδου βεβῶτος τοῦδ' ἐρείσματος νόθου,
αὐτοὶ πίτνουσιν ἀσθενεῖς πεφασμένοι
γόοις γυναικείοισι, κᾆθ' ὁ κόμπος ὢν
ἀλλότριος οὐκ οἰκεῖος ἐξελέγχεται.

What, my young master? O my gentle master!
O my sweet master! O you memory
Of old Sir Rowland! why, what make you here?
Why are you virtuous? why do people love you?
And wherefore are you gentle, strong and valiant?
Why would you be so fond to overcome
The bonny priser of the humorous duke?
Your praise is come too swiftly home before you.
Know you not, master, to some kind of men
Their graces serve them but as enemies?

SHAKESPEARE.

Dr. Yes; you have blown his swoln pride to that vastness,
As he believes the earth is in his fathom.
This makes him quite forget his humble being.
And can I hope that he, that, only fed
With the imagined food of future empire,
Disdains even those that gave him means and life
To nourish such desires, when he's possessed
Of his ambitious ends (which must fall on him,
Or your predictions are false), will ever
Descend to look on me?

De.   Were his intents
Perfidious as the seas or winds, his heart
Composed of falsehood, yet the benefit,
The greatness of the good he has from you,
Must make him firm and thankful.

BEAUMONT AND FLETCHER.

Ὦ φίλτατόν μοι δεσπότου νέου κάρα,
ἥδιστον οἵπερ ζῶσιν, εὐμενέστατον,
τοῦ σοῦ πρέπεις μιμήματ' ἀρχαίου πατρός.
τίνος δ' ἕκατι δεῦρ' ἀφιγμένος κυρεῖς;
τί δ' ἐσθλὸς ἦσθα; τοῦ χάριν πᾶς τις φιλεῖ,
ὡς πρᾶον εὐτραφῆ δὲ καί τιν' ἄλκιμον;
τί δ' ἦν τοσαύτης αἴτιον προθυμίας
ἢ δυσκόλου σ' ἄνακτος ἀθλητὴν κρατεῖν
μέγα σθένοντ' ἐπῆρεν ἐν παλαίσμασιν;
θᾶσσον δ' ἔπαινος προύφθασεν σέθεν μολών.
οὐ γὰρ κάτοισθα, δέσποτ', οἰκεῖόν τινα
αὑτῷ κλέος τρέφοντα δυσμενέστατον;

ΔΡ. Ναί· τοῦδέ γ' ἐκ σοῦ κάρθ' ὑπερπλησθεῖσ' ὕβρις
αὐχεῖ χθόν' αὐτὴν ἀμπέχειν ἐν ὠλέναις.
ἤδη λέλησται φαῦλος ἐκ φαύλων τε φύς.
πῶς δ' ἐλπίσαιμ' ἄν, τὴν δοκοῦσαν ὃς τροφὴν
μόνον τέθραπται τοῦ γε μέλλοντος κράτους,
καὶ τοὺς πορόντας ἀφθόνως ἀπαξιῶν
τοσούσδ' ἐπαρκοῦνθ' ἱμέρους βόσκειν βίον,
φιλοτιμίας σχόντ' ἆθλον (οὐ τυχεῖν χρέων,
ἢ ψευδόμαντις εἶ σύ γ') εἶτ' ἀποβλέπειν
τλῆναί ποτ' ἄν νιν ἀσθένειαν εἰς ἐμήν;
ΔΕ. εἰ λῆμ' ὅπως ἢ κῦμ' ἄπιστον ἢ πνοή,
καὶ καρδία πᾶν ψεῦδος, ἀλλ' ὅμως ὅδε,
ἀρετῆς παθὼν εὖ τηλικαῦτα σῆς ὕπο,
οὐκ ἔσθ' ὅπως βέβαιον οὐχ ἕξει χάριν.

You shall no more be lodg'd beneath the trees,
Nor chamber underneath the spreading oaks.
Behold! I have devised you forms for tools
To square out timber, and perform the art
Of architecture, yet unknown till now;
I'll draw you forms of cities, towns and towers,
For use and strength: behold the models here.

See, here, a second art of husbandry,
To till the earth, to plough, to sow, to plant,
Devised by Saturn. Here is gold, refined
From grosser metals; silver, brass, and tin
With other minerals extract from earth.
I likewise have found out to make your brooks,
Rivers, and seas, by practice navigable.
Behold a form to make your crares and barks
To pass huge streams in safety, dangerless.

The last, not least, this use of archery;
The stringed bow and nimble-feather'd shaft.
By this you may command the flying fowl
And reach her from on high: this serves for war,
To strike and wound thy foemen from afar.

HEYWOOD.

Νῦν δ' οὐκέτ' αὖθις φυλλάδων ὑπὸ σκιᾷ
οἰκήσετ', οὐδ' ἔνερθε δασκίου δρυός·
ἰδοὺ γὰρ ὅπλων τῆς ξυλουργίας ἐγὼ
τύπους σοφῶν δὲ τεκτόνων πονήματα
ὑμῖν ἔδειξα νηπίοις οὖσιν τὸ πρίν.
καὶ σχήματ' οἴκων ἀστέων πύργων ἐγὼ
ἔγραψ' ἐρυμνῶν, χρησίμων· τύπος δ' ὅδε.
ἰδοῦ δὲ τέχνην δευτέραν γεωργίας,
σπείρειν φυτεύειν γηπονεῖν ἀροῦν Κρόνος
ἐξηῦρεν ὑμῖν· χρυσὸς ἀκραιφνὴς ὅδε,
χαλκὸς σίδηρος ἄργυρος τά τ' ἄλλ' ὑπὸ
χθονὸς κεκρυμμέν' ὠφελήματα βροτοῖς.
κἀγὼ δὲ ῥεῖθρα ποταμίους δ' ὑμᾶς πόρους
πέλαγός τε πλεῦσαι ξὺν χρόνῳ διδάξομαι·
τύπος γάρ ἐσθ' ὅδ', ᾧ γε χρωμένους ῥοὰς
ἔσται μεγίστας ναυσὶν ἀσφαλῶς περᾶν.
καὶ μὴν μέγιστον καίπερ ὕστατον λέγω
τόξων τόδ' ἔργον καὶ βελῶν ὠκυπτέρων,
ἔχουσι γὰρ ταῦθ' ὑψόθεν κιχεῖν πάρα
ὑμῖν πετανὸν ὄρνιν, ἐν δὲ ταῖς μάχαις
βαλεῖν ἀτράκτῳ τηλόθεν τὸν δάϊον.

It is not so ; thou hast misspoke, misheard ;
Be well advised, tell o'er thy tale again :
It cannot be ; thou dost but say 'tis so :
I trust I may not trust thee ; for thy word
Is but the vain breath of a common man :
Believe me, I do not believe thee, man ;
I have a king's oath to the contrary.
Thou shalt be punish'd for thus frighting me,
For I am sick and capable of fears,
Oppress'd with wrongs and therefore full of fears,
A widow, husbandless, subject to fears,
A woman, naturally born to fears ;
And though thou now confess thou didst but jest,
With my vex'd spirits I cannot take a truce,
But they will quake and tremble all this day.
What dost thou mean by shaking of thy head ?
Why dost thou look so sadly on my son ?
What means that hand upon that breast of thine ?
Why holds thine eye that lamentable rheum,
Like a proud river peering o'er his bounds ?
Be these sad signs confirmers of thy words ?
Then speak again ; not all thy former tale,
But this one word, whether thy tale be true.

SHAKESPEARE.

Οὐκ ἔστιν· εἰπὼν ἢ κλύων παρεσκόπεις·
ἀλλ' εὖ φρονῶν ὅπως τὰ σ' αὖθις ἀγγελεῖς,
λόγῳ γάρ ἐστι ταῦτα, τοῖς δ' ἔργοισιν οὔ.
πέποιθα μή σοι δεῖν πεποιθέναι τάδε,
τοῦ γὰρ τυχόντος ἀνδρὸς οἱ λόγοι σέθεν
κενὴ πνοή τίς ἐστιν· ἀλλά μοι πιθοῦ,
ὤνθρωπε, σοῖς γ' οὐ πειθόμεσθ' ἀγγέλμασιν.
ὅρκος γ' ἄνακτος εἰς ἐναντίον φέρει.
ἀλλ' οὔ τι χαίρων τῷδέ μ' ἐκπλήξεις φόβῳ·
νόσων γὰρ οὕνεκ' εἰμὶ πάγχυ τῶν φόβων,
κακοῖσι δ' αἰκισθεῖσα δειμάτων πλέα,
χήρα δ' ἀμερθεῖσ' ἀνδρὸς ἡσσῶμαι φόβων,
θῆλυς δὲ πρὸς πέφυκα κἀπὶ δείμασιν.
ἐὰν δὲ καὶ νῦν αἰνέσῃς παίζων λέγειν,
ἀλλ' οὐ δυναίμην οὐκέτ' ἂν τῇμῇ φρενὶ
σπονδὰς ποιεῖσθαι τῇ ταραχθείσῃ τὸ μὴ οὐ
τὴν ἡμέραν τρέμειν τε δειμαίνειν θ' ὅλην.
τί δὴ τινάσσεις τοῦ χάριν τὸ σὸν κάρα;
τί δ' ὧδε λυγρὸν ὄμμα προσδέρκει τέκνον;
τί δὴ θέλει στέρνοισιν ἐντεθεῖσα χείρ;
τίνος δ' ἔκατι ῥεῦμα δυσφιλὲς τόδε
τὸν σὸν κατέσχ' ὀφθαλμόν, οἶ' ὑπέρκοπος
ὄχθας ὑπερδραμόντος οἴδματος ῥοή;
μῶν τοῖσδε δηλοῖς ὡς τὰ πρὶν πιστὸς λέγων;
λέγοις ἂν αὖθις, μηδ' ἀναπτύξας τὸ πᾶν,
μόνον δὲ τοῦτ' εἰ μῦθος ἀψευδὴς ὁ πρίν.

All good people,
You that thus far have come to pity me,
Hear what I say, and then go home and lose me.
I have this day received a traitor's judgement,
And by that name must die: yet, heaven bear witness,
And if I have a conscience, let it sink me,
Even as the axe falls, if I be not faithful!
The law I bear no malice for my death;
'T has done, upon the premises, but justice:
But those that sought it I could wish more Christians:
Be what they will, I heartily forgive 'em:
Yet let 'em look they glory not in mischief,
Nor build their evils on the graves of great men;
For then my guiltless blood must cry against 'em.
For further life in this world I ne'er hope,
Nor will I sue, although the king have mercies
More than I dare make faults. You few that loved me,
And dare be bold to weep for Buckingham,
His noble friends and fellows, whom to leave
Is only bitter to him, only dying,
Go with me, like good angels, to my end;
And, as the long divorce of steel falls on me,
Make of your prayers one sweet sacrifice,
And lift my soul to heaven.

SHAKESPEARE.

Ὑμεῖς ὅσοι περ οἶδ' ἀφῖχθ' οἴκτῳ φρενὸς
τοσόνδε μου κλύοντες ἄψορροι πάλιν
ἐλθόντες οἴκαδ' εἶτα μὴ σώζεσθ' ἔτι.
ἔχω δὲ προδότου τῇδε θἠμέρᾳ δίκην,
καὶ τοὔνομ' ἡμῖν τοῦτο συντεθάψεται.
ἴστωρ γε μήν μοι Ζεὺς τό τε ξυνειδέναι,
εἰ γάρ τί μοι ξύνοιδα μὴ πιστὸς γεγώς,
ξίφους ῥέποντος εἰς κάρα καταρρέποι.
ἀλλ' οὐ νόμους γὰρ αἰτίους κρίνω μόρου,
οἳ μὲν πρὸς ἡμᾶς, ὅσα γε τἀγκεκλημένα,
δίκαι' ἔδρασαν· τοὺς δ' ἐρευνῶντας τρέφειν
ἐβουλόμην ἂν εὐσεβεστέρας φρένας.
οἷοι δ' ἂν ὦσι κάρτα συγγνώμην ἔχω·
ὅπως δὲ μηκέθ' οἶδ' ἐπεύξονται κακὰ
σπεύδοντες ἢ 'ν κλειναῖσι πυργοῦντες ταφαῖς·
βοᾷ δ' Ἐρινὺς τοῦ θανόντος ἐκδίκως.
κοὔτις πόθος μοι τοῦ γε πλείονος βίου,
οὐδ' εἴ γε πλείω τῶνδ' ὅσ' ἀμπλακεῖν ὀκνῶ
ἄναξ τρέφοι τὸν οἶκτον, οὐ σαίνω μόρον.
ὑμεῖς δ' ὅσοι στέργοντες, οὐ πολὺς λεώς,
τολμᾶτε ταγῷ δάκρυα Φηγούσσης νέμειν,
φίλων τε κεδνή θ' ἡλίκων παρουσία,
ὧν δὴ στέρεσθαι μόνον ἄχος κρεῖσσον μόρου,
εὔνων ὀπαδοὶ πρὸς τέλος θεῶν δίκην,
εὐχῶν κατάρχεσθ', εὖτ' ἀπαλλαγὴ μακρὰ
χάλυβος πεσεῖται, θυστάδ' εὔφημον βοήν,
ψυχήν τ' ἐς αἰπὺν οὐρανὸν προπέμπετε.

                                    Thy grave reproof,
If what thou dost desire were possible
To be effected, might well argue it
As wise as loving; but if you consider,
With what strong guards this tyrant is defended,
Ruffians and malcontents drawn from all quarters,
That only know to serve his impious will;
The citadels built by him in the neck
Of this poor city; the invincible strength
Nature, by art assisted, gave this castle;
And above all his fear—admitting no man
To see him, but unarmed, it being death
For any to approach him with a weapon;
You must confess, unless our heads were cannons
To batter down these walls, our weak breath mines,
To blow his forts up, or our curses lightning
To force a passage to him, and then blast him,
Our power is like to yours, and we like you
Weep our misfortunes.

                          BEAUMONT AND FLETCHER.

Εἰ μὲν γένοιτο τοῦθ' ὅπερ σπεύδεις τὸ δρᾶν,
ἢ τὰν φανείη κέρτομος ψόγος σέθεν
σοφῆς θ' ὁμοίως κὰκ φίλης λεχθεὶς φρενός·
εἰ δ' ἐννοήσεις τόνδ' ὀπαόνων ὅσον
πλῆθος στέγει τύραννον, ἐκ πάσης ὄχλος
προδοτῶν ἀλητῶν ξυμμεμιγμένος χθονός,
κλύειν θ' ἕτοιμος οἷα δυσθέως φρονεῖ,
ὅσοι δὲ πόλεως ἐγκαθίδρυνται λόφῳ
πύργοι ταλαίνης, ὡς δ' ἀνικήτῳ σθένει
φύσις τέχνη τε περιβαλεῖν ξυνόμνυτον
τεῖχος τόδ', εἶτα τῶνδ' ὑπερτελῆ φόβον
τοῦδ' ἀνδρός, ὅστις οὐδ' ἐᾷ προσεννέπειν
τῶν γ' ὅπλ' ἐχόντων οὐδέν, ὡς θανουμένων
πάντων, ὃς ἂν μὴ γυμνὸς ὢν ἆσσον μόλῃ.
ταῦτ' ἐννοοῦσα καὶ σὺ συμφήσεις ἐμοί,
εἰ μή τι χεῖρές θ' αἵδε μηχανῶν δίκην
τείχη κατασκάψουσι, καὶ τόδ' εὐτελὲς
πύργους κρυφαίως πνεῦμ' ἀϊστώσει πόλεως,
ἢ καὶ κεραυνὸς ὡς καταιβάτης ἀρὰ
σκήψασα τοῦτον αὐτὸν ἐμπρήσει φλογί,
ἴσον τόδ' ἀνδρῶν λῆμα θηλείᾳ φύσει,
ἄμφω θ' ὁμοίας ξυμφορὰς δακρύομεν.

Exton.   Great king, within this coffin I present
           Thy buried fear : herein all breathless lies
           The mightiest of thy greatest enemies,
           Richard of Bordeaux, by me hither brought.
Boling.   Exton, I thank thee not ; for thou hast wrought
           A deed of slander with thy fatal hand
           Upon my head and all this famous land.
Exton.   From your own mouth, my lord, did I this deed.
Boling.   They love not poison that do poison need,
           Nor do I thee : though I did wish him dead,
           I hate the murderer, love him murdered.
           The guilt of conscience take thou for thy labour,
           But neither my good word nor princely favour :
           With Cain go wander thorough shades of night,
           And never show thy head by day nor light.
           Lords, I protest, my soul is full of woe,
           That blood should sprinkle me to make me
             grow :
           Come, mourn with me for that I do lament,
           And put on sullen black incontinent :
           I'll make a voyage to the Holy Land,
           To wash this blood off from my guilty hand :
           March sadly after ; grace my mournings here ;
           In weeping after this untimely bier.

                                SHAKESPEARE.

E. Ὦναξ φέριστε, ξυντεθαμμένον δέος
τὸ σὸν στέγει τόδ᾽ ἄγγος· ἄψυχος δ᾽ ὅδε
ὁ πρὶν μέγιστος πολεμίων κεῖται σέθεν
Εὐκάρδιος, βάσταγμα τῆς ἐμῆς χερός.

B. οὗτοι σ᾽ ἐπήνεσ᾽, ὅς γ᾽ ἀνηκέστῳ χερὶ
ὄνειδος αἰσχρὸν ἐγκατέσκηψας τόδε
ἐς κρᾶτα τοὐμὸν ἔς τε πάνδημον πόλιν.

E. καὶ μὴν ἔτλην τόδ᾽ ἔργον ἐκ γλώσσης σέθεν.

B. ἀλλ᾽ οὔθ᾽ ὅτῳ δεῖ φαρμάκων αὐτὸς φιλεῖ
τὰ φάρμακ᾽, οὔτ᾽ ἐγὼ σέ· κεἰ θανεῖν σφ᾽ ἔδει,
φιλῶ θανόντα τὸν κτανόντ᾽ ἀποπτύσας.
σοὶ δ᾽ οὖν ἔπαινος οὔτε κείσεται χάρις
ἀνθ᾽ ὧν ἔδρασας, ἀλλὰ τὸ ξυνειδέναι
μύσος τὸ σαυτοῦ, χἄμα τῷ πρωτοκτόνῳ
πλάνητ᾽ ἀλᾶσθαι νυκτὸς ὀρφναίας σκότῳ,
καὶ μηκέτ᾽ αὐγαῖς ἡμέρας αἴρειν κάρα.
ἀλγεῖ γὰρ ἀλγεῖ φρήν, θεοὶ ξυνίστορες,
εἴ μοι χυθεὶς βλαστημὸν ἀλδαίνει φόνος.
ἴτ᾽ οὖν, ἄνακτες, ὡς τάχος φαιὰν στολὴν
πενθοῦντι συμπενθοῦντες ἀμφιβάλλετε.
κἀγὼ πρὸς ἱρὰν χειρὸς ἐκ μιαιφόνου
τόδ᾽ αἷμα νίψων ναυστολήσομαι χθόνα.
ὑμεῖς βάδην ἔπεσθε, κήδειον χάριν,
δάκρυσιν ἄωρον τήνδε θρηνοῦντες ταφήν.

Romont. You much weaken
The strength of your good cause, should you but think
A man for doing well could entertain
A pardon, were it offered : you have given
To blind and slow-paced Justice wings and eyes,
To see and overtake impieties,
Which from a cold proceeding had received
Indulgence or protection.
Charalois. Think you so ?
Romont. Upon my soul! nor should the blood you challenged,
And took to cure your honour, breed more scruple
In your soft conscience, than if your sword
Had been sheathed in a tiger or she-bear,
That in their bowels would have made your tomb.
To injure innocence is worse than murder :
But when inhuman lusts transform us, then
As beasts we are to suffer, not like men
To be lamented. Nor did Charalois ever
Perform an act so worthy the applause
Of a full theatre of perfect men
As he hath done in this.

MASSINGER.

P. Καλὴν σάφ᾽ ἴσθι σὴν ἀμαυρώσας δίκην
ὅστις νομίζεις τούς γε δρῶντας εὖ ποτ᾽ ἂν
ξύγγνοιαν εἰ νέμοι τις ἀσμένους λαβεῖν·
ἢ οὐκ οἶσθα βραδύπουν ὀμματοστερῆ θέμιν
πτεροῖσιν ὄμμασίν τε κοσμήσας, ὅπως
ὁρῶσα τὰσεβήματ᾽ ἐξιχνοσκοπῇ,
ὁποῖα τῶν πρὶν ψυχρότης τιμαόρων
ξυναινέσασα πρὸς τὸ μεῖζον ἤγαγεν.

X. μῶν ὡς δοκοῦντά σοι τάδ᾽ ἢ οὐ δοκοῦντ᾽ ἐρεῖς;

P. ψυχὴν ἐμὴν κατώμοσ᾽ ὡς δοκοῦντ᾽ ἐρῶ·
οὐ γὰρ φόνου τοῦδ᾽ οὕνεχ᾽, ὃν σὺ προὐκαλοῦ,
παιώνιόν τι τῶν ὑβρισθέντων γάμων,
ἐνθύμιον χρῆν μαλθακῇ θεῖναι φρενὶ
ἢ κεἰ λεαίνης ἢ 'ν σφαγαῖς ἄρκτου ξίφος
ἔβαψας, οἵων ἐν μυχοῖσι νηδύος
λαχεῖν ἔμελλες δυσπότμου τύμβου μέρος.
τό τοι μιαίνειν μεῖζον ἢ κτεῖναι λέγω·
ὅστις δ᾽ ἂν ὀργῶν μὴ κατ᾽ ἀνθρώπους ὕπο
ἐκθηριωθῇ, τόνδε καὶ θηρὸς δίκην
κτανεῖν προσῆκεν οὐ κατ᾽ ἄνδρ᾽ ἐποικτίσαι·
οὔπω γὰρ ἔργ᾽ ἔδρασας ἀξιώτερα
τυχεῖν ἐπαίνου κεἴ τις εὐσεβεστάτων
ἀνδρῶν ἀγείροι πρὸς κρίσιν πανήγυριν.

Luc.   Better forbear till Proteus make return.

Jul.   O, know'st thou not his looks are my soul's food?
         Pity the dearth that I have pined in,
         By longing for that food so long a time.
         Didst thou but know the inly touch of love,
         Thou wouldst as soon go kindle fire with snow
         As seek to quench the fire of love with words.

Luc.   I do not seek to quench your love's hot fire,
         But qualify the fire's extreme rage,
         Lest it should burn above the bounds of reason.

Jul.   The more thou damm'st it up, the more it burns.
         The current that with gentle murmur glides,
         Thou know'st, being stopp'd, impatiently doth rage ;
         But when his fair course is not hindered,
         He makes sweet music with the enamell'd stones,
         Giving a gentle kiss to every sedge
         He overtaketh in his pilgrimage.

                                    SHAKESPEARE.

Λ. Λῷόν γ᾽ ἐπισχεῖν ἔστ᾽ ἂν ἄψορρος μόλῃ.

I. οὐ γὰρ κάτοισθά μ᾽ ὡς ἅπασα βόσκομαι
τοῦδ᾽ ἀνδρὸς ὀφθαλμοῖσιν; ἀλλ᾽ ἐποίκτισον
οἴᾳ ξυνοικῶ δυστάλαιν᾽ ἀσιτίᾳ
δαρὸν τροφὴν ποθοῦσα τὴν ἐμὴν χρόνον.
εἰ γὰρ κατῄδης οἷ᾽ Ἔρως ἔσω δάκνει,
ἢ τἂν συ χιόνι ῥᾷον ἧπτες ἂν τὸ πῦρ
ἢ τοῖς λόγοις ἔρωτος ἐσβέννυς φλόγα.

Λ. ἀλλ᾽ οὐκ ἔρωτα ζάπυρον ἀξιῶ σβέσαι,
μᾶλλον δὲ λάβρον εἰργαθεῖν φλογὸς μένος
τὸ μὴ οὐχ ὑπέρφευ καὶ πέρα λόγου φλέγειν.

I. ὅσῳ δ᾽ ἂν εἴργῃς δὶς τόσον φλέγει τὸ πῦρ.
ἢ οὐκ οἶσθα τὴν ἕρπουσαν εὐμενεῖ ψόφῳ
ὡς δυσφόρως εἰρχθεῖσα θυμαίνει ῥοή;
ἢν ἐμποδὼν δὲ μηδὲν ᾖ, καλῷ δρόμῳ
στικταῖς ἐπὶ ψήφοισιν εὖ μινύρεται
χραίνουσ᾽ ἕκαστον δόναχ᾽ ἀβροῖς φιλήμασιν
ὅσοις ὁδοιποροῦσα συμπέπτωκέ ποι.

How yet resolves the governor of the town ?
This is the latest parle we will admit :
Therefore to our best mercy give yourselves ;
Or like to men proud of destruction
Defy us to our worst : for, as I am a soldier,
A name that in my thoughts becomes me best,
If I begin the battery once again,
I will not leave the half-achieved Harfleur
Till in her ashes she lie buried.
The gates of mercy shall be all shut up,
And the flesh'd soldier, rough and hard of heart,
In liberty of bloody hand shall range
With conscience wide as hell, mowing like grass
Your fresh-fair virgins and your flowering infants.
What is it then to me, if impious war,
Array'd in flames like to the prince of fiends,
Do, with his smirch'd complexion, all fell feats
Enlink'd to waste and desolation ?
What rein can hold licentious wickedness
When down the hill he holds his fierce career ?
We may as bootless spend our vain command
Upon the enraged soldiers in their spoil
As send precepts to the leviathan
To come ashore. Therefore, you men of Harfleur,
Take pity of your town and of your people,
Whiles yet my soldiers are in my command ;
Whiles yet the cool and temperate wind of grace
O'erblows the filthy and contagious clouds
Of heady murder, spoil and villany.
If not, why, in a moment look to see
The blind and bloody soldier with foul hand
Defile the locks of your shrill-shrieking daughters ;
Your fathers taken by the silver beards,

Τί δὴ δέδοκται τῆσδ᾽ ὃς ἡγεῖται πόλεως;
λόγων γὰρ ἥδε λοισθία κεῖται κρίσις.
ὡς τοίνυν οἰκτιοῦντος ἐνδοῦναι χρεών,
ἢ φοινίας μνηστῆρες ἐγκρατεῖς μάχης
προκαλεῖσθε τἄσχατ᾽ ἀντιτείνοντες κακῶν.
οὕτω γὰρ εἴην ταγός—ὡς δ᾽ ἐμοὶ κριτῇ
πρέπουσα κληδὼν εὐλόγως τ᾽ ἐπώνυμος—
ὡς πύργος οὗτος δουρίληπτος οὐ μόλις,
ἣν προσβάλω πάλιν γε μηχανάς, σποδῷ
ἐν αὐτὸς αὑτοῦ συμπεσὼν τεθάψεται.
οἴκτου δ᾽ ἅπασαι συγκεκλήσονται πύλαι,
κἂν τῷδ᾽ ὁπλίτης σκληρὸν ἀμβλυνθεὶς κέαρ,
φόνου κορεσθεὶς πάντα τ᾽ ἐν χειρῶν νόμῳ
μιαιφόνων θείς, σκήψεται δόμοις ὅπως
Ἅιδης ἄπληστος ὥστε γηγενῆ στάχυν
βρεφῶν τ᾽ ἄωτον εὐχλόους τ᾽ ἀμῶν κόρας.
τί γὰρ μέλει μοι τῶνδ᾽ ἔτ᾽, ἢν ἐνδὺς φλόγα
καπνῷ τε χρανθείς, οἷ᾽ ἄναξ ἀλαστόρων,
Ἄρης δύσαγνος πάντα τολμήσῃ κακὰ
διαφθορᾶς τε διαδρομῶν θ᾽ ὁμαίμονα;
τίς δ᾽ ἂν χαλινὸς ὕβριν ἂν κατασχέθοι
κάτω φερομένην ἐμμανῆ σκιρτήματα;
μάτην γὰρ εὐχή, χὤστις ἐκ βυθοῦ καλεῖ
λιταῖς τὸ κῆτος, χὠ μεμηνότ᾽ εἰς ἄγραν
αὐχῶν ἀπείργειν ἐντολαῖς στρατὸν κεναῖς.
τοιγὰρ τόδ᾽ ἄστυ τὸν λεών τ᾽ οἰκτείρατε,
ἕως ἔτ᾽ αἰδὼς τῷ στρατῷ πειθαρχίας,
ἕως ἔτ᾽ οἶκτος μετρίαις αὔραις πνέων
ἀτμὸν μυδῶντα καὶ νέφη διασκεδᾷ
λείας γέμοντα χάρπαγῆς φονορρύτου.
εἰ δ᾽ οὖν, ἐπόψεσθ᾽, οὐ μακροῦ χρόνου τριβή,
κόμην ὁπλίτην φόνιον αἰσχρουργῷ χερὶ
εἰκῇ μιαίνοντ᾽ ὀξυκωκύτων κορῶν,
πατρός τε πολιᾶς λαβόμενον γενειάδος

And their most reverend heads dash'd to the walls,
Your naked infants spitted upon pikes,
Whiles the mad mothers with their howls confused
Do break the clouds, as did the wives of Jewry
At Herod's bloody-hunting slaughtermen.
What say you ? will you yield, and this avoid,
Or, guilty in defence, be thus destroy'd ?

SHAKESPEARE.

I must commend
Your choice. The godlike son of the sea-goddess,
The unshorn boy of Peleus, with his locks
As beautiful and clear as the amber waves
Of rich Pactolus (roll'd o'er sands of gold,
Soften'd by intervening crystal), and
Rippled like flowing waters by the wind,
All vow'd to Sperchius as they were—behold them !
And him—as he stood by Polixena,
With sanction'd and with soften'd love, before
The altar, gazing on his Trojan bride,
With some remorse within for Hector slain
And Priam weeping, mingled with deep passion
For the sweet downcast virgin, whose young hand
Trembled in his who slew her brother. So
He stood i' the temple ! Look upon him as
Greece looked her last upon her best, the instant
Ere Paris' arrow flew.

BYRON.

σεμνὸν προσουδίζοντα κρᾶτα τείχεσι,
βρέφος τε λόγχαις γυμνὸν ἀναπεπαρμένον·
ἐν δ' αἱ τεκοῦσαι φοιτάσιν δρόμοις ποδῶν
φύρδην διαρρήξουσι κωκυτοῖς νέφη,
οἵοις Ἑβραῖαι τἄργα τῶν μιαιφόνων
γυναῖκες ἐστύγησαν Ἡρώδου κυνῶν.
τί δῆτα μέλλεις; λέξον· ἆρ' ὑπεκφυγεῖν
εἴκων τάδ'; ἢ τοιῷδ' ἐνεζεῦχθαι μόρῳ
ὧδ' ἀντιτείνων καὐτὸς ὢν ἐπαίτιος;

Οὐκ ἔσθ' ὅπως οὐ τήνδ' ἐπῄνεσ' αἵρεσιν·
ἰδοῦ γὰρ αὐτὸν θεῖον ἐναλίας θεοῦ
τέκνον, γεγῶτα παῖδα Πηλέως πατρός,
ἀκηράτους τε κρατὸς εὐμόρφου κόμας,
ὡς χρυσοφεγγῆ ψάμαθον εἰλίσσει κάτω
ἁβρῶς ῥέων Πακτωλὸς ὑαλίνῳ ποτῷ,
οὕτω δι' αὔρας, νάματος καλλιρρόου
δίκην, ἐθείρας ξανθὸς ἄσσεται πλόκος,
θρεπτήριον δώρημα πατρώᾳ ῥοῇ.
ἰδοῦ δὲ καί νιν, οἷος ὢν Πολυξένης
πέλας παρεστὼς βώμιος, μάλ' ἐννόμου
ψυχὴν ἔρωτος ἱμέρῳ τεθελγμένος,
νύμφην προσεῖδε Τρωϊκήν, κεύθων δ' ἔσω
ἐνθύμιόν τι κατθανόντος Ἕκτορος
Πριάμου τε δακρύοντος, οὐδ' ἄτεγκτος ὢν
πόθῳ κατηφοῦς καλλιπαρθένου κόρης,
ἢ χειρὶ χειρὸς ἔθιγεν οὐ φρίκης ἄτερ
ὑφ' ἧς ἀδελφὸς ὤλεθ'· ὧδ' ἀνακτόροις
ναοῦ παρέστη· λεῦσσε δ' οἷον ὕστατον
Ἑλλὰς προσεῖδεν ὄμμα τὸν προφέρτατον
πρὶν οἰστὸν ἀπὸ θώμιγγος ἰέναι Πάριν.

　　　　I see a man's life is a tedious one :
I have tired myself, and for two nights together
Have made the ground my bed.　I should be sick,
But that my resolution helps me.　Milford,
When from the mountain-top Pisanio show'd thee,
Thou wast within a ken : O Jove!　I think
Foundations fly the wretched ; such, I mean,
Where they should be relieved.　Two beggars told me
I could not miss my way : will poor folks lie,
That have afflictions on them, knowing 'tis
A punishment or trial ?　Yes ; no wonder,
When rich ones scarce tell true.　To lapse in fulness
Is sorer than to lie for need, and falsehood
Is worse in kings than beggars.　My dear lord !
Thou art one o' the false ones.　Now I think on thee,
My hunger's gone ; but even before, I was
At point to sink for food.　But what is this ?
Here is a path to't : 'tis some savage hold :
I were best not call ; I dare not call : yet famine,
Ere clean it o'erthrow nature, makes it valiant.
Plenty and peace breeds cowards : hardness ever
Of hardiness is mother.　Ho ! who's here ?
If any thing that's civil, speak ; if savage,
Take or lend.　Ho ! No answer ?　Then I'll enter.
Best draw my sword ; and if mine enemy
But fear the sword like me, he'll scarcely look on't.
　　　　　　　　　　　　　　　SHAKESPEARE.

Μακρός τις (ἔγνων δ' ἀρτίως) ἄρσην βίος.
κόπῳ παρεῖμαι, καὶ χαμαικοίτης δυοῖν
εἴληχα νυκτῶν τῶν παρελθουσῶν λέχος·
τὸ μὴ νοσεῖν δὲ καρτεροῦσ' ἐπήρκεσα.
λιμήν, σὺ δ' ἐγγύς, ἐξ ἐποψίου πάγου
Πεισάνορος δεικνύντος, ἦσθ' ἀπ' ὀμμάτων.
φεῦ· δοκοῦσιν οἴκων τοὺς ταλαιπώρους φυγεῖν
κρηπῖδες, οὗ γε χρῆν ἀποστροφῆς τυχεῖν.
πτωχώ γε μὴν δύ' εἰπέτην ὡς τῆς ὁδοῦ
οὐκ ἔσθ' ἁμαρτεῖν· κᾆτ' ἂν ὁ πτωχός, λαχὼν
ἀλγήματα, ψεύδοιτ' ἄν, ἐξειδὼς ὅτι
ἢ προσβολὴ τάδ' ἐστὶν ἢ 'λεγχος τρόπων;
καίτοι τί θαῦμα; τούς γε πλουσίους ὁρῶ
παύρους ἀληθεῖς· τἀμπλακεῖν δ' ἐξ ἀφθόνου
βίου κάκιον τοῦ μετ' ἐνδείας δόλου,
ψύθη τ' ἄνακτος χείρον' ἢ πτωχοῦ πέλει.
ὦ φίλτατ' ἀνδρῶν, ἦ σύ γ' εἰς ψεύστας τελεῖς;
μεμνημένῃ σου λῃστίς ἐστ' ἀσιτίας,
τροφῆς δὲ πρόσθεν πᾶσ' ἐτηκόμην σπάνει.
τί τοῦτο; πρὸς τίν' ὁ στίβος φέρει στέγην;
μῶν βαρβάρων οἴκησιν; οὐ θαρσῶ βοᾶν.
οὐκοῦν σιωπᾶν λῷον; ἀλλ' ἀσιτία
φύσιν θρασύνει πρὶν πανώλεθρον πεσεῖν.
ἡ πλησμονὴ γὰρ δειλὸν εἰρήνη θ' ἅμα
τίκτουσι· θάρσους δ' ἡ σπάνις μήτηρ ἔφυ.
ὠή, τίς ἐν πύλαισιν; εἰ γὰρ εὔξενοι,
λέγοιτ' ἄν· εἰ δ' ἄρ' ἄξενον φωνῶ, τροφὴν
δὸς ὡς τελούσης αὖθις ἢ χρυσὸν λαβών.
εἴσειμ'· ἐπεί τοι κοὐδενὸς φωνῆς κλύω.
καίτοι τόδ' ἔγχος πρόσθεν ἐξέλκειν θέλω·
εἰ γὰρ δέδοικεν ἐχθρὸς ὡσαύτως ἐμοί,
οὐδεὶς φόβος μοι μὴ οὐκ ἰδὼν ἀποστραφῇ.

Mon. Many a morning hath he there been seen,
With tears augmenting the fresh morning's dew,
Adding to clouds more clouds with his deep sighs ;
But all so soon as the all-cheering sun
Should in the furthest east begin to draw
The shady curtains from Aurora's bed,
Away from light steals home my heavy son,
And private in his chamber pens himself,
Shuts up his windows, locks fair daylight out
And makes himself an artificial night :
Black and portentous must this humour prove,
Unless good counsel may the cause remove.

Ben. My noble uncle, do you know the cause ?

Mon. I neither know it nor can learn of him.

Ben. Have you importuned him by any means ?

Mon. Both by myself and many other friends :
But he, his own affections' counsellor,
Is to himself—I will not say how true—
But to himself so secret and so close,
So far from sounding and discovery,
As is the bud bit with an envious worm,
Ere he can spread his sweet leaves to the air,
Or dedicate his beauty to the sun.
Could we but learn from whence his sorrows grow,
We would as willingly give cure as know.

SHAKESPEARE.

M. Πολλῶν δι' ὄρθρων κεῖσε φαίνεται παρών,
    δρόσον θ' ἑῴαν αὐξάνων δακρύμασι,
    νέφη τε νέφεσι προστιθεὶς βαρυστόνως.
    εὖτ' ἂν δὲ πρῶτος ἐσχάταις πρὸς ἀντολαῖς
    δνοφερὰ καλύμματ' ἐξέλῃ λέχους Ἔω
    ὁ πάντα θάλπων Ἥλιος, τότ' οἴκαδε
    υἱὸς βαρυνθεὶς λανθάνει φεύγων τὸ φῶς,
    κρυφθεὶς δίχ' ἄλλων ἡλίκων κατὰ στέγας,
    θύρας τε πακτοῖ λαμπρὸν ἐκκλείων φάος,
    νέαν τιν' αὑτῷ νύκτα μηχανώμενος.
    ἢ δεῖ τάδ' εἴς τι κρυερὸν ἐκβαίνειν τέρας,
    εἰ μὴ 'ποτρέψεις αἰτίαν εὔβουλος ὤν.
B. οἶσθ' αἰτίαν τῶνδ', εὐγενὲς θείου κάρα;
M. οὔτ' ἴσμεν οὔτε μανθάνω κείνου πάρα.
B. οὐδ' ἐξερευνᾷς λιπαρῶν τρόπῳ τινί;
M. αὐτός τε κἄλλων μυρίων πλῆθος φίλων.
    ὁ δ' αὐτὸς αὑτῷ συμφορὰς κοινούμενος
    ὥς ἐστιν αὑτῷ πιστὸς οὐκ ἔχω λέγειν,
    στέγει δὲ πυκνὴν οἰόφρων αὐτοῦ φρένα,
    ὡς μὴ 'ξικνεῖσθαι φροντίδων βυθοῦ τινά.
    κάλυξ ὁποῖα δυσχίμου δηχθεῖσ' ὑπὸ
    ἱπός, πρὶν αὔραις φύλλ' ἀναπτύξαι καλά
    δοῦναί τε κόσμον εὐπρόσωπον ἡλίῳ.
    εἰ γὰρ μάθοιμεν ἐξ ὅτου 'βλαστεν νόσος,
    ἑκὼν τάδ' εἰδείην ἂν ἰῴμην θ' ἑκών.

Should we be silent and not speak, our raiment
And state of bodies would bewray what life
We have led since thy exile. Think with thyself
How more unfortunate than all living women
Are we come hither : since that thy sight, which should
Make our eyes flow with joy, hearts dance with comforts,
Constrains them weep and shake with fear and sorrow ;
Making the mother, wife and child to see
The son, the husband and the father tearing
His country's bowels out. And to poor we
Thine enmity's most capital : thou barr'st us
Our prayers to the gods, which is a comfort
That all but we enjoy ; for how can we,
Alas, how can we for our country pray,
Whereto we are bound, together with thy victory,
Whereto we are bound ? alack, or we must lose
The country, our dear nurse, or else thy person,
Our comfort in the country. We must find
An evident calamity, though we had
Our wish, which side should win : for either thou
Must, as a foreign recreant, be led
With manacles thorough our streets, or else
Triumphantly tread on thy country's ruin,
And bear the palm for having bravely shed
Thy wife and children's blood.

SHAKESPEARE.

Εἰ καὶ σιωπήσαιμεν ἄφθεγκτοι λόγων,
δηλοῖ τὸ σῶμά θ' ἥ τε δυσπινὴς στολὴ
ἐπεὶ σὺ φεύγεις οἷον ἀντλοῦμεν βίον.
ἄγ' ἐννοοῦ γὰρ οὕνεκ' ἀθλιώταται
πασῶν ὅσαιπερ ζῶσιν αἵδ' ἀφίγμεθα·
ἦ γὰρ προσῆκε τερπνὸν ἐκκαλεῖν δάκρυ
παλτοῖς τ' ἐν ὀρχησμοῖσιν εὐφρᾶναι κέαρ,
ἡ σὴ πρόσοψις ἐξαναγκάζει πάλιν
κλαίειν τε κἀμφόβοισι σεισθῆναι δύαις,
εἴπερ γε μήτηρ υἱόν, ἄνδρ' ὁμευνέτις,
τέκνον τε τὸν σπείραντα νηλεεῖ χερὶ
διαρταμοῦντα σπλάγχν' ἐπόψεται χθονός.
μάλιστα δ' ἡμῖν νεῖκος ὀλέθριον τὸ σόν·
λιταῖς γὰρ εἴργεις μηδ' ἐποίχεσθαι θεοὺς
ὃ τοῖσί γ' ἄλλοις συμφορῶν παραψυχή·
πῶς γάρ ποτ' εὐξόμεσθα δυστυχεῖς ὑπὲρ
φίλης τε πατρίδος τῆς τε σῆς νίκης ἅμα;
δισσαῖν ἀνάγκῃ γοῦν μιᾷ προσήκομεν.
φεῦ· ἢ γὰρ προέσθαι πατρίδα φιλτάτην τροφὸν
πάντως ἄραρεν ἢ στερίσκεσθαι σέθεν,
καίτοι σὺ μούνη τῶν ἐκεῖ γε χαρμονή.
δῆλαι γὰρ εἰ καὶ δεχομέναις ἡμῖν πέσοι
νίκη τελευτὰς ἐσμὲν ἕξουσαι πικράς·
ἢ γάρ σε προδότην ὥς τιν' ἐξενωμένον
στείχειν ἀγυιὰς δέσμιον δι' ἄστεως
πάντως ἀνάγκη 'στ', ἢ ποσὶν νικηφόροις
τῇ δουριλήπτῳ δεῖ σ' ἐπεμβῆναι χθονί,
καὶ σῆς ξυνεύνου φερόμενος καλὸν κλέος
φόνῳ τέκνων τ' ἄναγνον αἱμάξεις χέρα.

Leonatus. You are pleased to interpret well;
Yet give me leave to say, in my own justice,
I have but express'd the promptness of my soul
To save you all; but 'tis not empty wishes
Can satisfy our mighty charge, a weight
Would make an Atlas double. A king's name
Doth sound harmoniously to men at distance,
And those who cannot penetrate beyond
The bark and out-skin of a commonwealth,
Or state, have eyes but ravish'd with the ceremony
That must attend a prince, and understand not
What cares alloy the glories of a crown;
But good kings find and feel the contrary.—
You have tried, my lord, the burden, and can tell
It would require a pilot of more years
To steer this kingdom, now impos'd on me,
By justice of my birth.

Cassander. I wish not life,
But to partake those happy days, which must
Succeed these fair proceedings; we are blest.
But, sir, be sparing to yourself: we shall
Hazard our joys in you too soon. The burden
Of state affairs impose upon your counsel;
'Tis fitter that we waste our lives, than you
Call age too soon upon you with the trouble
And cares that threaten such an undertaking.

SHIRLEY.

Λ. Εὖ μὲν τάδ' ἐξηγεῖσθε· συγγνώμη δέ μοι,
εἰ τῷ δικαίῳ ξυμμαχῶν τοσόνδ' ἐρῶ·
ὃς οὐδὲν ἄλλ' ἐξεῖπον ἢ προθυμίαν
ψυχῆς ἅπασιν ὑμὶν ὥσθ' ὑπηρετεῖν.
οὐ μὴν τοσούτοις ἔργμασίν γ' ἐπαρκέσει,
ὧν οὐδ' Ἄτλας ἂν ἄχθος ὀρθοῖτ' ἂν φέρων,
ἄλλως κενὴ βούλησις· ἡδὺ κληδόνος
τοῖς μὲν πρόσωθεν φθέγμα τῆς τυραννικῆς·
ὅστις δ' ἐρευνᾶν μὴ σθένει περαιτέρω
εἰ μὴ τὰ περιβόλαια τἄξωθεν πόλεως,
οὗτος μὲν ὄμματ' ἐκπλαγεὶς κόσμοις ὅσοι
σέβας περιστέλλουσιν οὐ τυραννικὸν
δίοιδεν ὡς δύαισι κίβδηλον φάος·
ἄναξ δ' ὁ κεδνὸς ἕτερα μανθάνει παθών.
σὺ δ' ἄχθος οἶσθα πεῖραν εἰσελθών, ὅτι
γεραιτέρου του δεῖ κυβερνήτου πόλεως
οἴακα νωμᾶν ἐπιτετραμμένου τανῦν
γένους κατ' ἀγχιστεῖα τοῦδ' ἐμοὶ τέλους.

Κ. ἀλλ' οὐκ ἔμοιγε πλείονος βίου πόθος
εἰ μὴ μετασχεῖν ἡμερῶν τῶν ὀλβίων
ἃς χρή γ' ἕπεσθαι τοῖς καλῶς κατηργμένοις.
τύχης γὰρ ἡμᾶς μακαρίας ὀλβίζομεν.
φεῖσαι δὲ σαυτοῦ, κοίραν'· ὡς κίνδυνος εἰ
τῶν ἐκ σέθεν σφαλούμεθ' ἐλπίδων πάρος.
ἄχθος δὲ τοῦτο τῆς πόλεως ἐγχείρισον
πιστοῖσι συμβούλοισιν, οἳ τρίβειν βίον
αὐτοὶ δίκαιοι μᾶλλον, ἢ σὺ προφθάσαι
σαυτῷ πρὸ καιροῦ γῆρας εἰσάγων πικρόν,
ὑπηρετῶν μόχθοισι καὶ λυπούμενος
ὁποῖ' ἀπειλεῖ τοισίδ' ἐγχειρήμασιν.

I left no ring with her : what means this lady ?
Fortune forbid my outside have not charm'd her !
She made good view of me ; indeed, so much,
That sure methought her eyes had lost her tongue,
For she did speak in starts distractedly.
She loves me, sure ; the cunning of her passion
Invites me in this churlish messenger.
None of my lord's ring ! why, he sent her none.
I am the man : if it be so, as 'tis,
Poor lady, she were better love a dream.
Disguise, I see, thou art a wickedness,
Wherein the pregnant enemy does much.
How easy is it for the proper-false
In women's waxen hearts to set their forms !
Alas, our frailty is the cause, not we !
For such as we are made of, such we be.
How will this fadge ? my master loves her dearly ;
And I, poor monster, fond as much on him ;
And she, mistaken, seems to dote on me.
What will become of this ?　As I am man,
My state is desperate for my master's love ;
As I am woman,—now alas the day !—
What thriftless sighs shall poor Olivia breathe !
O time, thou must untangle this, not I ;
It is too hard a knot for me to untie.

SHAKESPEARE.

Τίν' ἡ κόρη σφαγῖδα λειφθῆναι λέγει;
μορφῆς, ὃ μὴ γένοιτο, μῶν ἐμῆς ἐρᾷ;
εὖ γοῦν προσεῖδέ μ' ὄμμασιν· τόσον μὲν οὖν
ὥστ' ὄμματ' ἤδη προφθάσαι γλῶσσαν δοκεῖν,
προσεῖπε γάρ μ' ἔμπληκτα κοὐκέτ' ἔμφρονα.
κοὐκ ἔσθ' ὅπως οὐ τῆσδ' ἐρᾷ· σοφὸς δ' ἔρως
ἐν τῷδ' ἀγροίκῳ μ' ἀγγέλῳ προσεννέπει.
ἀναίνεται σφραγῖδα· τὴν δ' ἄναξ μὲν οὐκ
ἔπεμψεν, ἦ δ' ἄρ' ὡς ἔοικ' ἄρσην ἐγώ.
ὡς δ' ὧδ' ἐχόντων τῶνδέ γ', ὥσπερ οὖν ἔχει,
τὴν δυστάλαιναν χρῆν ὀνειράτων ἐρᾶν.
ψεῦδος, σὺ δ' ἦσθ' ἄρ' ἐμφανὴς πανουργία,
καθ' ἣν ἀλάστωρ πόριμος ὢν ἔρδει πολύ.
φεῦ· ὡς εὔπορόν τοι ψεῦδος εὔμορφον φρεσὶν
ἐν κηροπλάστοις θήλεσιν θεῖναι τύπους.
οὔκουν τὸ θῆλύ γ' αἴτιον, τὸ δ' ἀσθενές·
τοῖαι γὰρ ἡμεῖς οἷ' ὅθεν ξυγκείμεθα.
πῶς ταῦτα φῶ σύγκολλα; τῆσδ' ἄναξ ἐρᾷ,
ἐγώ θ' ὁμοίως ἡ τάλαινα δεσπότου,
ἐρᾶν δ' ἔοικεν ἥδε μωραίνουσ' ἐμοῦ.
πῶς οὖν τελεῖ τάδ'; ἦ μέν εἰμ' ἄρσην ἐγώ,
τἄμ' ἐστὶ δυσκόμιστα δεσπότου πόθῳ.
ἦ δ' αὖτε θῆλυς—φεῦ τρισαθλίας κόρης—
ὡς πολλὰ θρηνεῖν δεῖ μάτην στενάγματα.
χρόνῳ μέλει τοι κοὐκ ἐμοὶ λύειν τάδε·
ἀμήχανον γὰρ ἅμμα δύσλυτόν τ' ἐμοί.

Look, nymphs and shepherds, look,
What sudden blaze of majesty
Is that which we from hence descry,
Too divine to be mistook ?
    This, this is she
To whom our vows and wishes bend :
Here our solemn search hath end.

Fame, that her high worth to raise
Seem'd erst so lavish and profuse,
We may justly now accuse
Of detraction from her praise :
    Less than half we find express'd ;
    Envy bid conceal the rest.

Mark, what radiant state she spreads,
In circle round her shining throne,
Shooting her beams like silver threads :
This, this is she alone,
    Sitting, like a goddess bright,
    In the centre of her light.

Might she the wise Latona be,
Or the towered Cybele,
Mother of a hundred gods ?
Juno dares not give her odds :
    Who had thought this clime had held
    A deity so unparallel'd ?

                        MILTON.

Λεύσσετε νύμφαι, λεύσσετε ποιμένες,
οἷον ἄρ' ἡμῖν τόδε προσσαίνει
τηλόθεν αὐγῆς σέλας ἀφνίδιον
πολὺ θειοτέρας ἤ τιν' ἁμαρτεῖν.
πρὸς τήνδε λιταί, πρὸς τήνδε πόθος
πᾶς ἀνάκειται· τῇσδε φανείσης
        ὁσίους ὅσιοι
    μηκέτι μόχθους μετίωμεν.
φήμαις δὲ βροτῶν ταῖς μεγαλαύχοις
ὀπὶ γηρῦσαι πολυκομποτέρᾳ
πρόσθε δοκούσαις νῦν μέμψιν ἔχω
τοῦ γε δικαίου σφ' ἧσσον ἐπαινεῖν·
τοῦ δ' ἡμίσεος μεῖον ἀνειπὼν
        ὁ φθόνος εὗρεν
    τἄλλα παρ' αἶσαν κατακρύψαι.
λεύσσετε δ' οἵαν στεροπὴν σκεδάσασ'
ἀργυροπήνον λαμπάδ' ἵησιν
θάκων κύκλῳ μαρμαροέντων·
ἥδε κάθηται θεὸς ἀθανάτη
        κατέχουσα μέσην
    ἀκτῖν' αὐτὴ θεὸς αἴγλης.
τίς ἄρ' ἦσθ'; ἢ που Λητώ γε σοφήν,
ἤ σε προσείπω πυργοστέφανον
Κυβέλην ἑκατὸν θεῶν γενέτειραν;
σοὶ γὰρ ἂν Ἥρα μὴ οὐχ ὁρμηθεῖσ'
ἀπ' ἴσης οὐτἂν ἀντιφερίζοι·
τοιάνδε πλακῶν τίς ποτ' ἂν ηὔχει
        τῶνδ' ἐντόπιον
    κρείσσω τίνος οὐ θεὸν ἄλλης;

Drusilla. You new-create me. To conceal from you
My virgin fondness were to hide my sickness
From my physician. O dear aunt, I languish
For want of Diocles' sight! he is the sun
That keeps my blood in a perpetual spring;
But, in his absence, cold benumbing winter
Seizes on all my faculties. Would you bind me
That am your slave already in more fetters,
And in the place of service to adore you?
O bear me then (but 'tis impossible,
I fear, to be effected) where I may
See how my Diocles breaks through his dangers,
And in what heaps his honours flow upon him,
That I may meet him in the height and pride
Of all his glories, and there (as your gift)
Challenge him as mine own.

Delphia.   Enjoy thy wishes.
This is an easy boon, which, at thy years,
I could have given to any; but, now grown
Perfect in all the hidden mysteries
Of that inimitable art, which makes us
Equal even to the gods and nature's wonders,
It shall be done, as fits my skill and glory.

                    BEAUMONT AND FLETCHER.

ΔΡ. Ταῦτ' ἴσθ' ἀνηβῶσάν με· παρθένου δ' ἐμὸν
κρύπτουσ' ἔρωτά σ' ὧδε κρύπτοιμ' ἂν νόσον
κάμνουσ' ἰατρόν. ὦ κασιγνήτη πατρός,
πάλαι πόθῳ τέτηκα, Διοκλέους πόθῳ.
κείνου παρόντος ἠρινῷ Φοῖβος γάνει
θάλπει τόδ' αἷμα· δυσχίμῳ δ' ἀπὼν ἐμὰς
ψύχει φρένας πήγνυσιν· εἰ δὲ πλείοσιν
ἤδη με δούλην οὖσαν ἐζεῦχθαι πέδαις
καὶ μὴ λατρεύειν προσκυνεῖν δ' ὅπως θεὸν
χρήζεις, ἄγ' ἔνθα τὸν ἐμὸν ἄνδρ' ἐσόψομαι
(καίτοι φόβος μὴ ταῦτ' ἀμήχαν' ᾖ τὸ δρᾶν)
οἵῳ καταρρήγνυσι κίνδυνον σθένει,
μορφαὶ δ' ἐπιρρέουσι κληδόνων ὅσαι,
ὅπως ἐν ἀκμῇ τῆς ὑπερκόμπου χλιδῆς
ὑπαντιάζω, κᾆτ' ἐκεῖ, δῶρον χερὸς
τῆς σῆς, προσεννέπω νιν οἰκεῖον πόσιν.

Δ. πάντων μεθέξεις ὧν ἐπαυρέσθαι θέλεις·
δῶρον γὰρ εὐτελὲς τόδ', εὖτε σοὶ μέτρα
ταῦτ' εἶχον ἥβης, τοῦ τυχόντος ἦν λαχεῖν.
νῦν δ' αὖ τελειωθεῖσα κἀρρήτων ἴδρις
τελετῶν κλύουσα τῆς ἀμηχάνου τέχνης,
οἵαν λαχόντες καὶ θεοῖς ἰσούμεθα
πᾶσίν θ' ὁποῖον ἡ φύσις τίκτει τέρας,
κεδνῶς κρανῶ τάδ' ὥς τ' ἐπιστήμῃ πρέπει.

My fault being nothing—as I have told you oft—
But that two villains, whose false oaths prevail'd
Before my perfect honour, swore to Cymbeline
I was confederate with the Romans : so
Follow'd my banishment, and this twenty years
This rock and these demesnes have been my world ;
Where I have lived at honest freedom, paid
More pious debts to heaven than in all
The fore-end of my time.   But up to the mountains !
This is not hunters' language : he that strikes
The venison first shall be the lord o' the feast ;
To him the other two shall minister ;
And we will fear no poison, which attends
In place of greater state.   I'll meet you in the valleys.
How hard it is to hide the sparks of nature !
These boys know little they are sons to the king ;
Nor Cymbeline dreams that they are alive.
They think they are mine ; and though train'd up thus
 meanly
I' the cave wherein they bow, their thoughts do hit
The roofs of palaces, and nature prompts them
In simple and low things to prince it much
Beyond the trick of others.

SHAKESPEARE.

Οὐδὲν γὰρ αὐτὸς ἀμπλακὼν—ὡς πολλάκις
ἠκούσατ᾽, εἰ μὴ τἀμὰ πίσθ᾽ ὁρκώματα
κρατοῦντ᾽ ἐνόρκοις ψεύδεσιν δισσὼ στύγη
κατειπέτην ἄνακτι τῆσδε γῆς ὅτι
λάθοιμι Ῥωμαίοισι συμπαραστατῶν—
πρὸς ταῦτα φεύγω· καὶ τόδ᾽ εἰκοστὸν θέρος
οἰκῶ πέτραν τήνδ᾽ ἀντὶ τῆς ἄλλης χθονὸς
σώζων ἀμέμπτως δεῦρ᾽ ἀεὶ τοὐλεύθερον,
τοῖς θ᾽ ὑψόθεν θεοῖσιν εὐσεβῆ χρέα
τελῶν λατρείας πλεῖστα τοῦ πάρος χρόνου.
ἀλλ᾽, οὐ γὰρ ἀνδρὸς ταῦτα θηρευτοῦ λέγειν,
ὄρη προβῶμεν· χὠ φθάσας τόξοις νεβρὸν
βαλὼν ὅδ᾽ ἡμῖν δεσπόσει θοινάματος,
καὶ τῷδε δόρπον ἄτεροι προθήσομεν.
καὶ δεῖμ᾽ ἀπέσται φαρμάκων, οἷον φιλεῖ
δόμοις συνοικεῖν τοῖσιν ἀφνεωτέροις.
σφῷν δ᾽ ἐν μέσαισι ταῖς νάπαις ἐντεύξομαι.
τὴν συγγενῆ τοι δυσχερὲς κρύπτειν φλόγα·
παῖδες γὰρ οἵδε φύντες ἐκ τυραννικῆς
σπορᾶς λελήθασ᾽, ὥς τ᾽ ὀλωλότας πατὴρ
λέγει νιν αὐτὸς δῆθεν ὄντας ἐξ ἐμοῦ.
ὅμως δὲ φαύλως ἐν πέτρᾳ τεθραμμένων,
ἐν ᾗ κάρανα κύπτεται, τυραννικῶν
στεγῶν φρονήμαθ᾽ ἅπτεται· χἠ συγγενὴς
πράξεις ἐπαίρει καὶ κατ᾽ εὐτελεῖς φύσις
λῆμ᾽ ἢ κατ᾽ ἄλλους βασιλικώτερον φορεῖν.

Well, though it torture me, 'tis but the same;
My pang shall find a voice. From my youth upwards
My spirit walked not with the souls of men,
Nor looked upon the earth with human eyes;
The thirst of their ambition was not mine,
The aim of their existence was not mine;
My joys, my griefs, my passions, and my powers,
Made me a stranger; though I wore the form,
I had not sympathy with breathing flesh.
Nor midst the creatures of clay that girded me
Was there but one who—but of her anon.
I said, with men, and with the thoughts of men,
I held but slight communion; but instead,
My joy was in the wilderness, to breathe
The difficult air of the iced mountain's top,
Where the birds dare not build, nor insect's wing
Flit o'er the herbless granite; or to plunge
Into the torrent, and to roll along
On the swift whirl of the new breaking wave
Of river, stream, or ocean, in their flow.
In these my early strength exulted; or
To follow through the night the moving moon,
The stars and their development; or catch
The dazzling lightnings till my eyes grew dim;
Or to look, listening, on the scattered leaves,
While Autumn winds were at their evening song.
                                        BYRON.

Εἰ καὶ δάκνει μ', ὁμοῖον· οὐκ ἄλλως ἐρῶ·
φωνὴν γὰρ εὑρήσουσιν αἵδ' ἐμαὶ δύαι.
ἐκ νηπίου γὰρ οὐ ξυνωμίλησέ πω
φρεσὶν βροτείαις φρὴν ἐμή· γαῖαν δ' ἐγὼ
οὐκ ὄμμασιν προσεῖδον οἷ' ἄλλοι βροτοί.
φιλοτιμίας θ' ὅσων τέ τις σπουδὴ βίου
οὔπω μετεῖχον· ἐξενωμένον δ' ἔτι
ὀργή, φύσις μ' ἔθηκεν, ἀλγηδών, χαρά.
εἰ καὶ βρότειον ἀμφεβαλλόμην δέμας,
ἀλλ' οὔ τιν' ἔμπνουν ἠξίουν κοινωνίας,
καὶ πηλοπλάστων σπερμάτων μόνη τις ἦν
ἥτις μ' ἔσαινεν—ἧς ἐς ὕστερον λόγος.
ὃ γὰρ πρὶν εἶπον, ἀντὶ τοῦ φρονήμασι
βροτῶν ξυνεῖναι, πλήν γε τοῦ χρεὼν χάριν,
ἐρημία μ' ἔθελγεν· εἴτ' ὁρῶν ἔπι
μόγις κατασθμαίνοντ' ἀφιέναι πνοήν,
κρυσταλλοπήκτων ἔνθα μὴ χραίνει πέτραν
κώνωψ ἄφυλλον πτέρυγι, μηδ' ὄρνις ἔτλη
θεῖναί τις εὐνάς· εἴτε χειμάρροις δέμας
κρύψαι τρικυμίας τ' ἐν οἴδματος στρόβῳ
ῥεῖθρόν τε πόντον τ' αὖ ῥέοντα νωτίσαι.
τούτοις ἐφ' ἥβης νεαρὸς ὢν ἠγαλλόμην·
ἦν δ' ἀσμένῳ μοι ταῖς Σεληναίας ὁδοῖς
νυκτός τ' ὀπαδεῖν ἀστέρων πλανήμασι,
βλεφάροις τ' ἀμαυροῖς ἀστραπῆς ῥιπὰς ὁρᾶν,
κλύειν τ' ἀθροῦντα φυλλάδ' εὖτ' ὀπωριναὶ
ὕμνους ἔμελπον τοὺς πρὸς ἑσπέραν πνοαί.

King. You all look strangely on me : and you most ;
  You are, I think, assured I love you not.
Ch. J. I am assured, if I be measured rightly,
  Your majesty hath no just cause to hate me.
King. No !
  How might a prince of my great hopes forget
  So great indignities you laid upon me ?
  What ! rate, rebuke, and roughly send to prison
  The immediate heir of England ! Was this easy ?
  May this be wash'd in Lethe, and forgotten ?
Ch. J. I then did use the person of your father :
  The image of his power lay then in me :
  And, in the administration of his law,
  Whiles I was busy for the commonwealth,
  Your highness pleased to forget my place,
  The majesty and power of law and justice,
  The image of the king whom I presented,
  And struck me in my very seat of judgement ;
  Whereon, as an offender to your father,
  I gave bold way to my authority
  And did commit you. If the deed were ill,
  Be you contented, wearing now the garland,
  To have a son set your decrees at nought,
  To pluck down justice from your awful bench,
  To trip the course of law and blunt the sword
  That guards the peace and safety of your person.
                                    SHAKESPEARE.

E. Καινὸν τὸ πάντων βλέμμα κοὐχ ἥκιστα σόν.
ἐπεὶ οὐ φίλον μ' ὄνθ', ὡς ἔοικας, οἶσθά σοι.
Δ. ἐχθρὸν μὲν οὖν μοι κανόνι χρώμενον σαφεῖ
οὐκ εἰκὸς εἶναί σ', οἶδα, πάντιμον κάρα.
E. πῶς δ' οὔ; τόσης μὲν ἐλπίδος δεδραγμένον
τόσας δὲ λώβας σοῦ γε λωβηθένθ' ὕπο;
οὐ δεινὰ δεννάζων σύ μ' εἶτα δέσμιον
ἦγες Βρεταννικῶν τὸν ἄγχιστον θρόνων;
τάδ' οἰστά; Λήθης τίς τάδ' ἂν κλύζοι ῥοή;
Δ. κἀγὼ γάρ, ὦναξ, ἢ τότ' ἀντὶ σοῦ πατρός,
εἰκὼν ἐκείνου κυρίας ἐξουσίας·
ὅμως δ' ἐκείνῳ μ' ὄντα διάδοχον νόμων,
καὶ τἀγαθὸν σπεύδοντα παγκοίνῳ πόλει,
οὐκ ἀξιῶν σὺ τοὐμὸν αἰδεῖσθαι γέρας,
κῦρος τὸ παντόσεμνον ἐννόμου δίκης,
αἰδοῦς φοροῦντ' εἴκασμα τῆς τυραννικῆς,
θρόνοις μ' ἔπαισας ἐν μέσοις καθήμενον·
ἀνθ' ὧν πατρῷον ὡς ὑβρίζοντος σέβας
θαρσῶν ἐφῆκα τῷ κράτει τὰς ἡνίας,
δεσμοῖς σ' ἀπείργων· κεἰ τάδ' ἥμαρτον, σὺ δ' αὖ
νῦν σκῆπτρα κραίνων στέργε καὐτὸς εἰ σέθεν
βλαστὼν παρ' οὐδὲν θεσμὰ παῖς ἄγων τὰ σὰ
τῶν σεμνοτίμων ἐξελᾷ θάκων Δίκην,
σφήλας τε κῶλα τῶν νόμων ἀπαμβλυνεῖ
ξίφος τὸ τηροῦν σ' ἡσύχως ἐν ἀσφαλεῖ.

When last the young Orlando parted from you
He left a promise to return again
Within an hour, and pacing through the forest,
Chewing the food of sweet and bitter fancy,
Lo, what befel! he threw his eye aside,
And mark what object did present itself:
Under an oak, whose boughs were moss'd with age
And high top bald with dry antiquity,
A wretched ragged man, o'ergrown with hair,
Lay sleeping on his back: about his neck
A green and gilded snake had wreathed itself,
Who with her head nimble in threats approach'd
The opening of his mouth; but suddenly,
Seeing Orlando, it unlink'd itself,
And with indented glides did slip away
Into a bush: under which bush's shade
A lioness, with udders all drawn dry,
Lay couching, head on ground, with catlike watch,
When that the sleeping man should stir; for 'tis
The royal disposition of that beast
To prey on nothing that doth seem as dead:
This seen, Orlando did approach the man
And found it was his brother, his elder brother.

                                        SHAKESPEARE.

Ὅτ' ἀρτίως ἀπῴχετ' Ὀρλάνδος νέος
πάλιν μολεῖν ὑπέσχετ' οὐ μάλ' ἐς μακράν·
φοιτῶντι δ' ὕλης τῆσδ' ἀνὰ πτυχὰς βάδην,
Ἔρωτα τὸν γλυκύπικρον ἀναμασωμένῳ,
ὁποῖα συμβέβηκεν ἄξιον σκοπεῖν.
ἐκεῖσε γὰρ καὶ δεῦρο παρακλίνων κόρας
ἅπερ κατεῖδ' ἀκούσατ'· ἀρχαίας δρυὸς
σκιᾶς ἔνερθεν, ᾗ κλάδοι γήρᾳ μακρῷ
κατηρεφεῖς λειχῆνι, χὠ ξυνὼν χρόνος
γυμνόν νιν ἐψίλωσεν ὕψαυχεν κάρα,
δασὺς δυσαίων δυσπινεῖς ἔχων στολὰς
ἔκειτ' ἀνήρ τις ὕπτιος κοιμώμενος.
χλωρὸς δὲ χρυσόνωτός οἱ πέριξ ὄφις
δειρὴν ἐπλέχθη, πρός τ' ἀνεῳγμένον στόμα
πυκναῖς ἀπειλαῖς ἦγε λαιψηρὸν κάρα·
μεθεῖτο δ' ὡς Ὀρλάνδον ἐξαίφνης ὁρᾷ,
σπείρας θ' ἑλίσσων εἰσέδυ λόχμην, ἵνα
κατάσκιός τις ξηρὸν ἐξημελγμένη
οὖθαρ λέαιν' ἔκειτο, καὶ χαμαιπετὲς
νεύουσα κρᾶτα τὸν δαμένθ' ὕπνῳ γαλῆς
δίκην ἐτήρει προσδοκῶσ' ἀνάστασιν·
ἔνεστι γάρ τοι θηρὶ βασιλικὴ φύσις,
καὶ τοῦ θανεῖν δοκοῦντος οὐκέτ' ἂν θίγοι.
ταῦτ' οὖν ἰδὼν Ὀρλάνδος ἐγγύθεν σκοπεῖ
σκοπῶν δ' ἀδελφὸν ηὗρε τὸν γεραίτερον.

My name is Caius Marcius, who hath done
To thee particularly and to all the Volsces
Great hurt and mischief; thereto witness may
My surname, Coriolanus : the painful service,
The extreme dangers and the drops of blood
Shed for my thankless country are requited
But with that surname; a good memory,
And witness of the malice and displeasure
Which thou shouldst bear me: only that name remains;
The cruelty and envy of the people,
Permitted by our dastard nobles, who
Have all forsook me, hath devour'd the rest ;
And suffer'd me by the voice of slaves to be
Whoop'd out of Rome. Now this extremity
Hath brought me to thy hearth ; not out of hope—
Mistake me not—to save my life, for if
I had fear'd death, of all the men i' the world
I would have 'voided thee, but in mere spite,
To be full quit of those my banishers,
Stand I before thee here. Then if thou hast
A heart of wreak in thee, that wilt revenge
Thine own particular wrongs and stop those maims
Of shame seen through thy country, speed thee straight,
And make my misery serve thy turn : so use it
That my revengeful services may prove
As benefits to thee, for I will fight
Against my canker'd country with the spleen
Of all the under fiends. But if so be

Ὅδ' εἰμὶ Γάϊος Μάρκιος καλούμενος,
ὁ δεινὰ δράσας παντὶ μὲν Βόλσκων γένει
μέγιστα σοὶ δ' οὐχ ἧσσον ἐμβαλὼν πάθη,
ἃ τῶν ἁλόντων Κοριόλων ἐπώνυμον
συμμαρτυρεῖ μοι τοὔνομ'· ἐσχάτων δ' ἐγὼ
τὰ πλεῖστα κινδυνεύματ' ἀθλήσας πόνων,
καὶ δυσχαρίστου τῆσδ' ἐμῆς πάτρας ὕπερ
φόνιον σταλάξας αἷμα, τήνδ' ἐπώνυμον
τοιῶνδ' ἀμοιβὰς κληδόν' ηὑρόμην μόνας,
καλόν γε μαρτύρημα καὶ τεκμήριον
ἧς δυσμενείας βαρυκότου τ' ἔχθρας ὅδε
σοί γ' ἄξιος πάρειμι· τοῦτό μοι μόνον
ἔτ' ὄνομα λοιπόν· τἄλλα πάντ' ἀφείλετο
τὸ φθονερὸν ὄχλου μῖσος· οἱ δ' ἀνάλκιδες
ἄνακτες οὐκ ἔτλησαν ἀντειπεῖν, ἐμὲ
πάντων ἔρημον δουλίοις γλωσσῶν ῥόθοις
ἐῶντες αἰσχρῶς ἐκκεκηρῦχθαι πόλεως.
νῦν οὖν ὕβρισμα σῶν δόμων ἐφέστιον
τόδ' ἔσχατόν μ' ἔθηκεν οὐχ ὑπ' ἐλπίδων
βίον γε σώζειν—μηδὲ προσδόκα τόδε—
εἰ γὰρ προσῆν μοι τοῦ γε κατθανεῖν φόβος
σὲ πλεῖστα πάντων ἐξέφευγον ἂν βροτῶν·
ἔχθρᾳ γε μέντοι τοὺς ἐμοὺς ἀνδρηλάτας
δίκην τελείαν ἀντιτιμωρούμενος
πρὸς ταῦτα ταῖς σαῖς ὅδε παραστατῶ θύραις.
εἰ δ' οὖν ἔνεστι καρδίᾳ πλήρης κότου,
πρόθυμος οὖσ' οἰκεῖα τίσασθαι κακά,
παῦσαί τε τραύματ' αἴσχρ' ἅπερ τὴν σὴν πόλιν
πάλαι βλέπεις πάσχουσαν, ἐγκόνει τάχος,
καὶ τοὐμὸν ἄλγος τἀγαθὸν σπεύδοι τὸ σόν.
ὅπως δὲ χρήσει τῆσδ' ὅπη χειρὸς τίσις
εὐεργέτημα κείσεται· τῇ γὰρ πάτρᾳ
τῇ δυσχαρίστῳ διὰ μάχης ἐλθὼν κότῳ
τῷ τῶν ἔνερθεν χρήσομαι μιαστόρων.
εἰ δ' αὖτ' ἄπεστι τόλμα τῶνδ' αὖθίς τ' ὀκνεῖς

s.   9

Thou darest not this and that to prove more fortunes
Thou'rt tired, then, in a word, I also am
Longer to live most weary, and present
My throat to thee and to thy ancient malice;
Which not to cut would show thee but a fool,
Since I have ever follow'd thee with hate,
Drawn tuns of blood out of thy country's breast,
And cannot live but to thy shame, unless
It be to do thee service.

SHAKESPEARE.

King. Most subject is the fattest soil to weeds;
    And he, the noble image of my youth,
    Is overspread with them : therefore my grief
    Stretches itself beyond the hour of death :
    The blood weeps from my heart when I do shape
    In forms imaginary the unguided days
    And rotten times that you shall look upon
    When I am sleeping with my ancestors.
    For when his headstrong riot hath no curb,
    When rage and hot blood are his counsellors,
    When means and lavish manners meet together,
    O, with what wings shall his affections fly
    Towards fronting peril and opposed decay!
War. My gracious lord, you look beyond him quite :
    The prince but studies his companions
    Like a strange tongue, wherein, to gain the language,
    'Tis needful that the most immodest word
    Be look'd upon and learn'd; which once attain'd,
    Your highness knows, comes to no further use
    But to be known and hated. So, like gross terms,
    The prince will in the perfectness of time
    Cast off his followers; and their memory
    Shall as a pattern or a measure live,
    By which his grace must mete the lives of others,
    Turning past evils to advantages.

SHAKESPEARE.

ἄμιλλαν ἐλθεῖν εἰς τύχης, ἁπλῷ λόγῳ
παροίχεται δὴ τοῦ βίου κἀμοὶ πόθος·
σοί θ' ὅδε πρόχειρος τῷ τε σῷ πάλαι χόλῳ
πάρεστι λαιμός, ὃν τὸ μὴ σφάξαι σέθεν
σάφ' ἴσθι μώραν ἂν καταγνοίη φρένα·
σοὶ γὰρ δι' ἔχθρας αἰὲν εἱπόμην ἐγώ,
στέρνων τε τῆς σῆς πόλεος αἷμα μυρίον
ἔδρεψα, κοὐκ ἂν πλήν γε λυμεὼν σέθεν
ζῴην ἔτ', εἰ μὴ τὸ σὸν ὑπουργήσων χρέος.

A. Κακοῖς βρύει φυτοῖσιν ἡ βαθεῖα γῆ·
ἃ τόνδ', ἐμὴν ἡβῶντος εἰκόν' εὐγενῆ,
κατασκιάζει· τοιγαροῦν τοὐμὸν πέρα
τείνει τελευτῆς τῆς πεπρωμένης ἄχος.
στάζει δὲ δάκρυ καρδία φονόρρυτον,
φαντάζεται γὰρ ἡμάτων ἀκοσμία
χρόνος τ' ἀσελγής, οἷον εἰσόψεσθ' ἔτι
ἐμοῦ πατρῴοις ἐγκαθεύδοντος τάφοις.
ἦν γὰρ δρόμον σκιρτῶντος ἀχάλινον κάτω
σύμβουλον ὀργῆς ᾖ τὸ θερμανθὲν μένος,
αἰσχροῖς τ' ἀπαντᾷ πλοῦτος ἄφθονος τρόποις,
οἵοις πτεροῖς κίνδυνον ἡ 'πιθυμία
προὔπτον πέτοιτ' ἂν καὶ πρὸς ἀντήρη φθοράν.
B. ὦναξ, σὺ δ' υἱοῦ κάρτ' ἄγαν παρασκοπεῖς·
σπεύδει γὰρ οὗτος τοὺς ὀπάονας μαθεῖν
ὡς γλῶσσαν ἀλλόφυλον· ἧς κἂν αἰσχρὸν ᾖ
τὸ ῥῆμ' ἕκαστον ἐκδιδαχθῆναι χρεών,
ταύτῃ γ' ἐάν τις ἐντριβὴς μέλλῃ κλύειν·
κᾆθ', ὥσπερ οἶσθα καὐτός, οὐδὲν ἄλλο πλὴν
ἐχθαίρεται κατοφθέν. ὡς δ' αὕτως ὅδε,
χρόνου προβάντος, ῥημάτων αἰσχρῶν δίκην,
αἰσχρῶν ἑταίρων τῶνδ' ἀπαλλαχθήσεται·
ὧν μνῆστις ἐκδίδαγμα καὶ κανὼν σαφὴς
γένοιτ' ἄν, οἵῳ χρὴ σταθμώμενον βίους
ἄλλων ὄνησιν τῶν πρὶν ἐκπονεῖν κακῶν.

King.

> I muse my Lord of Gloucester is not come :
> 'Tis not his wont to be the hindmost man,
> Whate'er occasion keeps him from us now.

Queen.

> Can you not see ? or will ye not observe
> The strangeness of his alter'd countenance ?
> With what a majesty he bears himself,
> How insolent of late he is become,
> How proud, how peremptory, and unlike himself ?
> We know the time since he was mild and affable,
> And if we did but glance a far-off look,
> Immediately he was upon his knee,
> That all the court admired him for submission :
> But meet him now, and, be it in the morn,
> When every one will give the time of day,
> He knits his brow and shows an angry eye
> And passeth by with stiff unbowed knee,
> Disdaining duty that to us belongs.
> Small curs are not regarded when they grin ;
> But great men tremble when the lion roars ;
> And Humphrey is no little man in England.
> First note that he is near you in descent,
> And should you fall, he as the next will mount.
> Me seemeth then it is no policy,
> Respecting what a rancorous mind he bears
> And his advantage following your decease,
> That he should come about your royal person
> Or be admitted to your highness' council.

SHAKESPEARE.

Βασ. Γλωστὴρ πάλαι δὴ μὴ παρὼν θαυμάζεται·
φιλεῖ γὰρ οὗτος μὴ ἀπολείπεσθαι πρὸ τοῦ,
χρείας ὁποίας οὕνεκ᾽ οὐ πάρεστι νῦν.

Ἀν. οὔπω σὺ γὰρ δέδορκας; ἢ οὐ δοκεῖς ὁρᾶν
καινὸν πρόσωπον ἀρτίως ἠλλαγμένον;
οἷος τυραννικοῖσιν ἐγχλίει τρόποις,
ὡς σεμνότητος ἐκ νέας ὑπερχλιδᾷ
βίαιος αὑτῷ τ᾽ αὐτὸς οὐκέτ᾽ ὢν ἴσος;
καίτοι νιν οἶδ᾽ ὅτ᾽ εὐπροσήγορός τις ἦν,
εἰ δ᾽ ὄμμα παρακλίναιμι, τηλωπὸν θέαν,
ὁ δ᾽ εὐθὺς ἕδραν γονυπετῆ προύπιπτεν ἄν,
πειθαρχίας δὲ μέλαθρα πάντ᾽ ἐπήνεσεν.
ἢν δ᾽ ἐντύχωμεν νῦν γε κἀξ ἑωθινοῦ,
χαίρειν ὅτ᾽ οὔτις ἔσθ᾽ ὃς οὐ προσεννέπει,
σκυθρωπὸς ὄμμα καὶ ξυνωφρυωμένος
ὀρθοστάδην παρῆλθέ μ᾽ οὐ γουνούμενος
τιμῆς ἄμοιρον τῆς προσηκούσης ἐμοί.
σεσηρότος τοι σκύλακος οὔτις ἐντροπή·
ἀλλ᾽ εἰ λέων βέβρυχε χὠ μέγας τρέμει.
κοὐ τῶν τυχόντων οὗτός ἐστ᾽ ἐν Ἀγγλίᾳ·
ὢν γὰρ κατ᾽ ἀγχιστεῖά σοι γένους σκόπει
ὡς σοῦ πεσόντος ἔσθ᾽ ὅδ᾽ ἀμβάτης θρόνων.
οὔκουν τέλη λύει τόδ᾽, ὥς γ᾽ ἐμοὶ κριτῇ,
βαρύν τε θυμὸν τἀνδρὸς ἐννοουμένῃ,
κέρδος θ᾽ ὁποῖον σοῦ θανόντος ἄρνυται,
οὔτ᾽ ἐμπελάζειν τόνδε σοι, κλεινὸν σέβας,
οὔτ᾽ οὖν μετασχεῖν βασιλικῶν βουλευμάτων.

Welcome, good Robin. See'st thou this sweet sight?
Her dotage now I do begin to pity :
For, meeting her of late behind the wood,
Seeking sweet favours for this hateful fool,
I did upbraid her and fall out with her ;
For she his hairy temples then had rounded
With coronet of fresh and fragrant flowers ;
And that same dew, which sometime on the buds
Was wont to swell like round and orient pearls,
Stood now within the pretty flowerets' eyes
Like tears that did their own disgrace bewail.
When I had at my pleasure taunted her
And she in mild terms begg'd my patience,
I then did ask of her her changeling child ;
Which straight she gave me, and her fairy sent
To bear him to my bower in fairy land.
And now I have the boy, I will undo
This hateful imperfection of her eyes :
And, gentle Puck, take this transformed scalp
From off the head of this Athenian swain ;
That, he awaking when the other do,
May all to Athens back again repair,
And think no more of this night's accidents
But as the fierce vexation of a dream.
But first I will release the fairy queen.
      Be as thou wast wont to be ;
      See as thou wast wont to see :
      Dian's bud o'er Cupid's flower
      Hath such force and blessed power.

SHAKESPEARE.

Χαίροις ἂν ὦ τᾶν· ἢ σὺ τήνδ᾽ ὁρᾷς θέαν;
ἤδη βλέποντα μωρίαν οἰκτός μ᾽ ἔχει·
ὕλης γὰρ ἔνδον ἐντυχὼν τροφῆς γλυκὺ
γάνος δρεπούσῃ τῷδε τῷ σκαιῷ στύγει
πικρῶς ἐλοιδόρουν σφε κἀδιχοστάτουν.
λάσιον γὰρ ἀνδρὶ κρόταφον ἀνθέων πέριξ
ἤμπεσχε πλεκτῶν νεοδρόπων εὐοσμίᾳ·
δρόσος δὲ πρόσθεν κάλυκος αὐξηθεῖσ᾽ ἔσω,
κύκλοις ἑῴων μαργάρων ἀλιγκία,
νῦν αὖτε καλλίσταισιν ἀνθέων κόραις
ὡς σφῶν ὄνειδος δάκρυα δυσθυμοῦντ᾽ ἐπῆν.
ἐπεὶ δ᾽ ἐλοιδόρησα πρὸς χάριν φρενός,
ἡ δ᾽ αὖ λόγοισιν ἠπίοις παρίετο,
κἄπειτ᾽ ἐγὼ τὸ θνητὸν ἠξίουν βρέφος
λαβεῖν τὸ πλαστόν, ἡ δ᾽ ἐπείθετ᾽ ἐν τάχει,
εὐθὺς δ᾽ ἑκοῦσ᾽ ἐφεῖτο προσπόλων τινὶ
φέρειν ἐς οἴκους οὓς ἔχω θεὸς γεγώς.
δεδεγμένῳ δὲ παῖδα τὴν ἀπ᾽ ὀμμάτων
πάλιν δοκεῖ μοι δυσφιλῆ λῦσαι νόσον.
τὸ σὸν δὲ κρᾶτ᾽ ἄμορφον ἐξαιρεῖν ὅπερ
κεφαλὴν σκιάζει τοῦδ᾽ Ἀθηναίου ξένου,
ὅπως ἐγερθεὶς αὐτὸς οἵ τ᾽ ἄλλοι πάλιν
πρὸς τὴν πόλιν πέμψωσι νόστιμον πόδα,
μηδὲν λέγοντες εὐφρόνης ξυναλλαγὰς
εἰ μὴ ταράσσονθ᾽ ὡς ὀνειράτων κλόνον.
πρῶτον δ᾽ ἄνασσαν προφθάσω λύσας ἐμήν.
  οἷα πρὶν ἔφυς νῦν αὖτε γενοῦ,
    βλέπε δ᾽ ὀφθαλμοῖς οἵοισι πάρος·
  τοιάνδε κάλυξ ἱερὰν ἰσχὺν
      ἥδ᾽ Ἀρτέμιδος
  νικᾷ κακὸν ἄνθος Ἔρωτος.

Cesario.   I must acknowledge,
  Vittori has deserved, for many services,
  The love and honour of his country ; fought
  Her battles and brought conquest home, made tame
  The seas that threatened us, secured the land ;
  And Rome allowed some consuls, for less victories,
  Triumphs and statues.
Fabio.   Most excellent prince !
  How just he is !
Cesario.   But when opinion
  Of their own merit swells them into pride,
  Which sets a price on that which modesty
  Should count an act of their obedience,
  They forfeit the reward of thanks and honour,
  And betray poor and most vainglorious souls.
  Scipio and Antony and other Romans
  Deserved well of the Senate and were honoured ;
  But when they ran to faction, and pursued
  Ambitious ends to undo their country's peace,
  They were no longer patriots, but declared
  Rome's poison, and like gangrenes to the state,
  To be cut off, lest they corrupt the body.
                             SHIRLEY.

K. Πολλῆς ἐπάξιος μέν, οὐκ ἀρνήσομαι,
ἀνθ' ὧν δέδρακε, πᾶσι Νικάνωρ φίλοις
ἀστοῖσι τιμῆς· ὅστις ἐκ μάχης δόμοις
λάφυρ' ἐπασσάλευε, τὰν χέρσῳ τιθεὶς
βέβαια, λάβραν θ' ἡμερωμένην ἅλα·
χαλκοῦς γὰρ ἐν Ῥώμῃ τις ὡς νικηφόρος
ἔστηκεν, ἧσσον τοῦδ' ἀριστεύσας δορί.
Φ. ἄναξ φρονεῖ δίκαια κἀξ ὀρθῆς φρενός.
K. ὅτῳ δ' ἐπαρθεὶς ὄγκος ἢ κατ' ἀξίαν
πλείων ἀπαιτεῖ μισθὸν ὧν ὀφείλεται,
εἴπερ φρονεῖ τις θνητά, τῇ πειθαρχίᾳ,
τούτοις χάρις τ' ὄλωλε καὶ τιμῆς γέρας,
ἐπεὶ διαπτυχθέντες ὤφθησαν κενοί.
εὖ δρῶν τις εὖ πέπονθεν, ὡς βουλῆς ὕπο
Ἀντώνιός τε Σκιπίων τ' ἄλλων μέτα·
στάσει δ' ἐπαρθεὶς ὅστις ἂν κόσμον πόλεως
φιλοτιμίας ἕκατι τλῇ καταφθίσαι,
χρηστὸν πολίτην οὐκέτ', ἀλλὰ φάρμακον
κἀγὼ τίθημ' ὕπουλον, ὡς Ῥώμῃ, νόσον
πόλεως τομῶσαν μὴ τὸ σῶμ' ὅλον φθαρῇ.

Hip. 'Tis strange, my Theseus, that these lovers speak of.
The. More strange than true : I never may believe
These antique fables, nor these fairy toys.
Lovers and madmen have such seething brains,
Such shaping fantasies, that apprehend
More than cool reason ever comprehends.
The lunatic, the lover and the poet
Are of imagination all compact :
One sees more devils than vast hell can hold;
That is, the madman : the lover, all as frantic,
Sees Helen's beauty in a brow of Egypt :
The poet's eye, in a fine frenzy rolling,
Doth glance from heaven to earth, from earth to heaven ;
And as imagination bodies forth
The forms of things unknown, the poet's pen
Turns them to shapes and gives to airy nothing
A local habitation and a name.
Such tricks hath strong imagination,
That, if it would but apprehend some joy,
It comprehends some bringer of that joy ;
Or in the night, imagining some fear,
How easy is a bush supposed a bear !

                                        SHAKESPEARE.

Ἱπ. Δεινός γ' ἐρασταῖς τοῖσδ' ἀπήγγελται λόγος.

Θη. δεινός γε δῆτα μᾶλλον ἢ 'ληθέστερος.
οὔκουν ἔγωγε τοισίδ' ἀρχαίοις ποτ' ἂν
μύθοις πιθοίμην δαιμόνων τ' ἀθύρμασιν.
οἱ γοῦν ἐρασταὶ χοἰ μεμηνότες φρεσὶ
θερμαῖς ζέοντες ὧδε τῶν φαντασμάτων
πλάσσουσι μορφὰς ὥστε πλείον' ἐννοεῖν
ἢ ξυννοεῖν πέφυχ' ὁ σωφρονῶν λόγος.
ἐκ γὰρ περισσῶν πᾶς ξυνέστηκεν φρενῶν
ἔκφρων ἐραστὴς καὶ τὸν ὑμνῳδὸν λέγω.
χὠ μὲν μεμηνὼς πλείονας μιάστορας
κατεῖδεν ἢ κατ' ἀσπέτους "Αιδου μυχούς,
ὁ δ' αὖτ' ἐραστὴς καὐτὸς ἐξ ἴσου μανεὶς
Νειλῶτιν ὀφρὺν ἤκασεν Λήδης κόρῃ.
καὶ μὴν ἀοιδὸς λυσσάδας διαστρέφων
κόρας ἐλίγδην ὀμμάτων ἀπ' οὐρανοῦ
γῆν, ἄλλοτ' ἐκ γῆς οὐρανὸν προσδέρκεται·
κἂν ᾧ ζέουσα φροντὶς ἐξεργάζεται
τύπων ἀμόρφων σχήμαθ', ὑμνῳδὸς γράφων
μορφήν τιν' ἀντήλλαξε καὶ τῷ μηδενὶ
χώραν τιν' ὄνομά τ' ἀπονέμει τεταγμένον.
τοιαῦτ' ἀθύρει φροντὶς ἡ περισσόφρων,
ὥσθ' ἡδονήν τιν' εἰ θέλοι ποτ' ἐννοεῖν,
εὐθὺς προπομπὸν ξυννοεῖ τῆς ἡδονῆς·
ἢ νυκτὸς ὑπονοοῦσα λαθραῖον φόβον
λόχμην τιν' ἄρκτῳ ῥᾳδίως ἀπήκασεν.

If it be true,
Dread sir, as 'tis affirm'd, that every soil,
Where he is well, is to a valiant man
His natural country, reason may assure me
I should fix here, where blessings beyond hope,
From you, the spring, like rivers flow unto me.
If wealth were my ambition, by the queen
I am made rich already, to the amazement
Of all that see, or shall hereafter read
The story of her bounty : if to spend
The remnant of my life in deeds of arms,
No region is more fertile of good knights,
From whom my knowledge that way may be better'd,
Than this your warlike Hungary ; if favour,
Or grace in court could take me, by your grant,
Far, far beyond my merit, I may make
In yours a free election ; but, alas ! sir,
I am not mine own, but by my destiny
(Which I cannot resist) forced to prefer
My country's smoke before the glorious fire
With which your bounties warm me. All I ask, sir,
Though I cannot be ignorant it must relish
Of foul ingratitude, is your gracious license
For my departure.

                                        MASSINGER.

Εἰ δ' ὡς ἀληθῶς ἀνδρός, ὡς κρατεῖ λόγος,
ὦναξ, ἀρίστου πᾶσ', ἵν' ἂν πράσσῃ τις εὖ,
γῆ πατρίς, οὕτω τῆσδ' ἂν εἰκότως ἐγὼ
μέτοικος εἴην, τἀγάθ' οὗ παρ' ἐλπίδας
πηγῆς ἐπιρρεῖ ποταμὸς ὡς σέθεν πάρα.
εἰ γὰρ πόθος μοι χρημάτων, πλῆθος τόσον
ἤδη δέδωκ' ἄνασσα, τοῖς ὁρῶσί τε
χῶσοι πυθέσθαι χειρὸς ἀφθόνου δόσιν
μέλλουσι θαῦμα· ζῆν δὲ τοὐντεῦθεν βίου
σπεύδων ὅπλων ἀγῶσιν ἐν νικηφόροις
μάχης μάθοιμ' ἂν δὶς τόσως ἴδρις κλύειν·
εἰ γάρ τι κεδνοῖς κἄλλ' ἔθνος ταγοῖς βρύει
καὶ Παννονὶς γῆ πλεῖστον ἤδ' Ἄρει φίλη.
εἰ δ' αὖ μ' ἐπαίρειν βασιλικῆς σθένοι χάρις
στέγης, σὺ τιμῶν κάρτα μ' οὐ κατ' ἀξίαν
ἐλευθέραν τῆς ἐνθάδ' αἵρεσιν νέμεις·
ἀλλ' αὐτὸς αὑτοῦ κῦρος οὐκ ἔχω τάλας,
ἀλλ' ᾗ μ' ὑπείκειν δεῖ τὸ τῆς εἱμαρμένης
βιάζεται γῆς καπνὸν οἰκείας πάρος
πυρὸς προτιμᾶν ᾧ με σὴ θάλπει χάρις.
αἰσχρὸν μὲν οἶδ' ὄνειδος, ἀμνήμων τις ὢν
φανείς, ὅμως δὲ δὸς τοσόνδ' αἰτουμένῳ,
ἑκὼν ἑκόντι νόστιμον μολεῖν ὁδόν.

The night grows on, and you are for your meeting;
I'll therefore end in few. Be resolute,
And put your enterprise in act. The more
Actions of depth and danger are consider'd,
The less assuredly they are perform'd.
And thence it happ'neth, that the bravest plots
(Not executed straight) have been discover'd.
Say, you are constant, or another, a third,
Or more; there may be yet some wretched spirit,
With whom the fear of punishment shall work
'Bove all the thoughts of honour and revenge.
You are not now to think what's best to do
As in beginnings; but what must be done,
Being thus enter'd: and slip no advantage
That may secure you. Let 'em call it mischief:
When it is past, and prosper'd, 'twill be virtue.
Th' are petty crimes are punish'd, great rewarded.
                                        BEN JONSON.

Φθίνει μὲν ἡ νὺξ σοὶ δὲ κἀγορᾶς μέλει·
τοιγὰρ τάδ᾽ ἐν παύροισι συντόμως ἐρῶ.
ἄρχοις ἂν ἔργου καρτερῶν· ὅσῳ γὰρ οὖν
τοῖς τῆς βαθείας φροντίδος τολμήμασι
πλείων λογισμός, ἧσσον ἐκβαίνονθ᾽ ὁρῶ.
καὶ συμβέβηκε τοὺς μάλ᾽ ἀνδρείους δόλους
μή γ᾽ εὐθὺς ἐκπραχθέντας ὀφθῆναι πάρος.
εἰ γὰρ σὺ κεἴ τις ἄλλος ἢ καὶ πλείονες
ἐγκαρτεροῦσιν, ἀλλ᾽ ὅμως δειλὸς τάχ᾽ ἂν
εἷς τις φανείη, ζημίας ὅστις δέος
αἰδοῦς ἄγει πάροιθεν ἢ τιμωρίας.
ὃ φέρτατον δρᾶν οὐκέτ᾽ οἴεσθαι χρεών,
ὄντ᾽ οὐ παρ᾽ αὐτοῖς ἀλλ᾽ ἐν αὑτοῖσιν πόνοις,
ἀλλ᾽ οἳ ἀνάγκη· δεῖ δὲ μὴ παριέναι
μηδὲν δι᾽ ὧν βέβαιον ἐκπράξεις τέλος.
καὶ δὴ κλύει τάδ᾽ ἐν βροτοῖς πονηρία
ὀρθῶς πεπράχθω κἀρετὴ κεκλήσεται.
μεγάλοισι μισθός, ζημία φαύλοις κακοῖς.

                                   What angel shall
Bless this unworthy husband ? he cannot thrive,
Unless her prayers, whom heaven delights to hear
And loves to grant, reprieve him from the wrath
Of greatest justice.   Write, write, Rinaldo,
To this unworthy husband of his wife ;
Let every word weigh heavy of her worth
That he does weigh too light : my greatest grief,
Though little he do feel it, set down sharply.
Dispatch the most convenient messenger :
When haply he shall hear that she is gone,
He will return ; and hope I may that she,
Hearing so much, will speed her foot again,
Led hither by pure love : which of them both
Is dearest to me, I have no skill in sense
To make distinction : provide this messenger :
My heart is heavy and mine age is weak ;
Grief would have tears, and sorrow bids me speak.
                                   SHAKESPEARE.

Τίς ἂν ποτ᾽ ἄνδρα τόνδ᾽ ἀνάξιον θεὸς
δέχοιτ᾽ ἂν εὔφρων; οὐ γὰρ οὖν πράξει καλῶς
εἰ μή τις εὐχαῖς ἧς κλύων χαίρει θεὸς
φιλεῖ τε δοῦναι τὰς λιτὰς τελεσφόρους
δίκης μεγίστης πῆμ᾽ ἀποστρέψει κότου.
ὦ πρέσβυ, σοὶ δὲ χρὴ μέλειν γράψαι τάχος
τῷ τῆς δάμαρτος τῷδ᾽ ἀναξίῳ πόσει.
ὅπως δ᾽ ἕκαστον ἀξίας ἰσόρροπον
ἔσται τὸ γραφθέν, ἣν ἀναξίαν ἄγει.
ἐμὴν δὲ λύπην καρδίας ὑπερτάτην,
εἰ καὶ μόλις κατήσθετ᾽, ἔγγραψον πικρῶς.
ὅπως δὲ πέμψεις ὅστις εὔζωνος πάρα.
τάχ᾽ ἂν δ᾽ ἀκούσας ὡς ἀποίχεται γυνὴ
ἄψορρος ἥξει· δεῦρό τ᾽ ἐλπίς, ἢν μάθῃ
τοσόνδε, καὐτὴν νόστιμον βῆναι πόδα
ἔρωτος ἁγνοῦ πανδίκως ἡγουμένου.
πόθος μὲν ἀμφοῖν· ἀλλ᾽ ὅτου πλέων πόθος
οὐκ ἴδρις εἰμὶ τοῦ διαιρεῖσθαι τόδε.
τὸ σὸν μελέσθω δ᾽ ἄγγελον ζητεῖν ὅπου.
βαρεῖα μὲν φρὴν καὶ τὸ γῆρας ἀσθενές,
λύπη δ᾽ ἀπαιτεῖ δάκρυον, ἀλγηδὼν λόγους.

I know you all, and will awhile uphold
The unyoked humour of your idleness :
Yet herein will I imitate the sun,
Who doth permit the base contagious clouds
To smother up his beauty from the world,
That, when he please again to be himself,
Being wanted, he may be more wonder'd at,
By breaking through the foul and ugly mists
Of vapours that did seem to strangle him.
If all the year were playing holidays,
To sport would be as tedious as to work ;
But when they seldom come, they wish'd for come,
And nothing pleaseth but rare accidents.
So, when this loose behaviour I throw off
And pay the debt I never promised,
By how much better than my word I am,
By so much shall I falsify men's hopes ;
And like bright metal on a sullen ground,
My reformation, glittering o'er my fault,
Shall show more goodly and attract more eyes
Than that which hath no foil to set it off.
I'll so offend, to make offence a skill ;
Redeeming time when men think least I will.

SHAKESPEARE.

Κάτοιδα πάντας κἀς βραχὺν χρόνον μονῆς
ὀργὰς ἀκόσμους ἀργίας ξυνοίσομεν.
ἐν τῷδε γὰρ τὸν ἥλιον μιμήσομαι·
ὅστις πρὸς ἀνδρῶν ὄμμαθ' ὑδρηλοῦ νέφους
νοσῶδες αἶσχος καλλονὴν κρύπτειν ἐᾷ,
ὅπως, ὅταν τὸν πρόσθεν ἀλλάξῃ κύκλον,
ποθούμενος λάχῃ τι θαύματος πλέον,
ἀτμοῦ μυδῶντος εἰ διαρρήξει πνοάς,
οἵαις πνιγῆναι 'μελλεν ἐγκρυφθὲν σέλας.
εἰ δ' οὐνιαυτὸς πᾶς ἑορτάζειν θέλοι
ἴσος σχολῆς τ' ἂν καὶ πόνου γένοιτ' ὄχλος·
σπαρνὴ δ' ἑορτῶν ἀσμένοις παρουσία,
τὰ γὰρ μόλις ξυμβάντα πᾶς ἀσπάζεται.
οὕτω δ' ἀποστὰς τῶν ἀνειμένων τρόπων
τίσας θ' ὁποῖον οὐχ ὑπεσχόμην χρέος,
ὅσῳ γ' ἀμείνων ἢ καθ' ἀπηγγειλάμην
φανήσομαί τις ἐλπίδας ψεύσω βροτῶν·
κᾆθ', οἳ ἀφεγγεῖ χρυσὸς ἐν πέδῳ πρέπει,
ἀρετὴ πλέον στίλβουσα κἀξ ἁμαρτιῶν
κεδνόν τι δείξει καὶ περίβλεπτον βροτοῖς,
οἷον μόνον καθ' αὑτὸ κάλλος οὐκ ἔχει.
οὕτω δ' ἁμαρτὼν τἄμ' ἁμαρτάνω σοφῶς
ἀπροσδόκητος ἀντίποιν' εὑρὼν χρόνου.

Age.   Welcome to the morn!
The eastern gates unfold, the priest approaches;
And lo! the sun is struggling with the gloom,
Whose masses fill the eastern sky, and tints
Its edges with dull red:—but he will triumph;
Bless'd be the omen!

Med.   God of light and joy
Once more refresh us with thy healing beams!
If I may trace thy language in the clouds
That wait upon thy rising, help is nigh—
But help achieved in blood.

Ion.   Say'st thou in blood?

Med.   Yes, Ion!—why, he sickens at the word,
Spite of his new-born strength;—the sights of woe
That he will seek have shed their paleness on him.
Has this night's walk shown more than common
          sorrow?

Ion.   I passed the palace where the frantic king
Yet holds his crimson revel, whence the roar
Of desperate mirth comes mingling with the sigh
Of death-subdued robustness, and the gleam
Of festal lamps 'mid spectral columns hung
Flaunting o'er shapes of anguish made them
          ghastlier.
How can I cease to tremble for the sad ones
He mocks—and him the wretchedest of all?
                                    TALFOURD.

A. Ὦ χαῖρ' ἑῷον φέγγος· οἴγονται πύλαι
τοῦ μάντεως παρόντος αἱ πρὸς ἀντολάς.
ἰδοὺ δνόφοισιν ἥλιος λυγίζεται
ὅσοι πόλον πιμπλᾶσιν, ἐμβάπτων φλογὶ
ἄκρους ἀφαυρὸν βάμμα· νικήσει δ' ὅμως.
ἐδεξάμην τὸν ὄρνιν.

M.   ὦ χαρᾶς δοτὴρ
φέγγους τε δαῖμον, λαμπάσιν παιωνίοις
θάλποις ἂν αὖθις· εἰ δ' ἃ σημαίνεις λέγων
προπομπὰ τῶν σῶν ἀντολῶν δηλοῖ νέφη,
ἐπάρκεσις πάρεστι σὺν φόνῳ γε μήν.

I.   ἦ σὺν φόνῳ πάρεστιν;
M.   οὐκ ἄλλως ἐρῶ.
φρίσσει κλύων τάδ' ὁ σθένων ἥβῃ νέᾳ,
ποιεῖ γὰρ ὠχρὸν καὐτὸν ὧν μέλλει τυχεῖν
φαντάσματ' ὠχρά· μῶν ἄχους φαντάζεται
μεῖζόν τι κοινοῦ τῆσδε νυκτὸς ἐν τρίβῳ;

I.   μέλαθρα παρῆλθον οἷς ὁ βακχεύων ἄναξ
οἰνῶπ' ἔτ' ἴσχει κῶμον, ἔνθ' ὑλάγματα
χαρᾶς ἀτερποῦς μίγνυται στενάγμασι
τοῖς τῶν σθενόντων θανασίμων ὀλουμένων·
δνοφεραῖσι δ' ἐν στήλαισιν αἰωρουμένων
ἐπισκιάζει λαμπάδων γαῦρον σέλας
μορφὰς ἀμόρφους δέργμα φρικῶδες βλέπειν.
πῶς οὐ τρέσαιμ' ἂν τῶνδ' ὑπὲρ τῶν ἀθλίων
εἰς οὓς ὑβρίζει καὐτὸς ὢν τρισάθλιος;

When I have said, make answer to us both.
Lo, in this right hand, whose protection
Is most divinely vow'd upon the right
Of him it holds, stands young Plantagenet,
Son to the elder brother of this man,
And king o'er him and all that he enjoys :
For this down-trodden equity, we tread
In warlike march these greens before your town,
Being no further enemy to you
Than the constraint of hospitable zeal
In the relief of this oppressed child
Religiously provokes.   Be pleased then
To pay that duty which you truly owe
To him that owes it, namely this young prince :
And then our arms, like to a muzzled bear,
Save in aspect, hath all offence seal'd up ;
Our cannons' malice vainly shall be spent
Against the invulnerable clouds of heaven ;
And with a blessed and unvex'd retire,
With unhack'd swords and helmets all unbruised,
We will bear home that lusty blood again
Which here we came to spout against your town,
And leave your children, wives and you in peace.

SHAKESPEARE.

Κἀμοῦ κλύοντας νῷν ἀμείβεσθαι λέγω.
ἡ δεξιὰ γὰρ ἥδ', ἐνώμοτος θεῶν
ὅρκοις βοηθεῖν τοῦ παρεστῶτος δίκῃ,
τὸν παῖδ' ἔχει τόνδ', ἔρνος ἐκ Σπαρτῶν γένους
ὃν ἔτεκε τἀνδρὸς τοῦδ' ὁ πρεσβεύων κάσις
αὐτοῦ τ' ἄνακτα τῆς θ' ὅλης παμπησίας.
τῆς λακπατήτου τῆσδ' ὑπὲρ δίκης πατῶ
χλοερὰ πρὸ πύργων πεδία δυσμενῆ στίβον,
ὧν ἐχθρὸς ὑμῖν οὐδὲν ἄλλο πλὴν ὅσον
ὑπερμαχοῦντα τοῦδ' ὑβρισθέντος βρέφους
ὁσία μ' ἀπαιτεῖ· ξένιον αἰδεσθεὶς θεὸν
ἔχω προθύμως· τοιγαροῦν αἰδοῦς σέβας
ὑμῖν δεδόχθω τῆς προσηκούσης τίνειν
ᾧπερ προσήκει, παιδὶ τῷ νέῳ λέγω.
οὕτω μέν, ἄρκτος οἷα φιμωθείς, ὅπλα
εἰ μὴ κατ' ὄμμα πάντ' Ἄρης ἐσφράγισεν·
οὕτω δ' ἀναλοῖ τοξότης ὀργὴν κενὴν
ἄτρωτα βέλεσιν οὐρανοῦ βάλλων νέφη·
χἠμεῖς καλὴν φοροῦντες εὐοργησίαν
ἔγχη τ' ἄθραυστα καὶ κυνᾶς ἀκηράτους
σπαργῶν τόδ' αἷμ' ἄψορρον οἴκαδ' οἴσομεν,
ὃ πρὸς πόλιν στάξοντες οἵδ' ἀφίγμεθα,
ἐῶντες ὑμᾶς σὺν γυναιξὶ σὺν τέκνοις.

Weep no more, nor sigh, nor groan ;
Sorrow calls no time that's gone :
Violets plucked the sweetest rain
Makes not fresh nor grow again :
Trim thy locks, look cheerfully ;
Fate's hid ends eyes cannot see :
Joys as winged dreams fly fast ;
Why should sadness longer last ?
Grief is but a wound to woe :
Gentlest fair, mourn, mourn no moe.

FLETCHER.

Παῦσαι δακρύων παῦσαι δὲ γόων.
χρόνον οἰχόμενον τί καλεῖ λύπη;
ῥόδα γὰρ δρεφθέντ᾽ οὐκ ἔτι θάλλειν
ὄμβροι παρέχουσ᾽ οὐδ᾽ ἥδιστοι.
βλέπε φαιδρωπὸν κοσμοῦσα κόμην·
κρύφιον Μοίρας ὄμματα λήθει
τέλος· ὡς πτηνῶν θᾶσσον ὀνείρων
χάρματα φεύγει· τί δὲ χρὴ μίμνειν
μόχθοις νέον ὂν τραῦμ᾽ οἰμωγήν;
    σὺ δέ μοι τὸ λίαν,
παρθένε, πένθος κατακοίμα.

TRANSLATIONS

INTO GREEK PROSE

And therefore it was great injustice in Plato, though springing out of a just hatred of the rhetoricians of his time, to esteem of rhetoric but as a voluptuary art, resembling it to cookery, that did mar wholesome meats, and help unwholesome by variety of sauces to the pleasure of the taste. For we see that speech is much more conversant in adorning that which is good than in colouring that which is evil ; for there is no man but speaketh more honestly than he can do or think ; and it was excellently noted by Thucydides in Cleon, that because he used to hold on the bad side in causes of estate, therefore he was ever inveighing against eloquence and good speech, knowing that no man can speak fair of courses sordid and base. And therefore, as Plato said elegantly, ' That virtue, if she could be seen, would move great love and affection ': so, seeing that she cannot be showed to the sense by corporal shape, the next degree is to show her to the imagination in lively representation : for to show her to reason only in subtilty of argument was a thing ever derided in Chrysippus, and many of the Stoics, who thought to thrust virtue upon men by sharp disputations and conclusions, which have no sympathy with the will of man.

BACON.

Διὸ καὶ μεγάλην τινὰ ἀδικίαν ἠδίκησε Πλάτων,
καίπερ ἀπὸ δικαίας πάνυ ἔχθρας τῶν τότε ῥητόρων
ὁρμωμένην, τὸ ἀποκαλεῖν ὥσπερ ἀπολαυστικὴν παρα-
σκευὴν τὴν ῥητορικήν, ἀπεικάζων τῇ ὀψοποιϊκῇ, ἥπερ ἄρα
σιτία τὰ μὲν ὑγιεινὰ λυμαίνοιτο τοῖς δὲ μὴ βοηθοίη διὰ
ποικιλίας ὄψων ὡς δὴ τῇ γεύσει χαριουμένη. σύν-
ισμεν γὰρ τῷ λόγῳ πολὺ μᾶλλον κοσμητικῷ ὄντι τοῦ
ἀγαθοῦ ἢ τοῦ κακοῦ κομμωτικῷ, ἐπεὶ οὐδεὶς ὅστις οὐ
κάλλιον λέγει ἢ καθ' ἃ ποιεῖ ἢ καὶ οἴεται· ὥστε
μετρίως εἴρηται περὶ Κλέωνος τῷ Θουκυδίδῃ, ὅτι ἐν τῷ
πολιτεύεσθαι ἀεὶ εἴχετο τοῦ χείρονος, διὰ ταῦτα ἀεὶ
λοιδοροῦντος τὴν δεινότητα καὶ ῥητορικήν, εἰδότος ἄρα
ὅτι οὐδεὶς εὖ ἂν λέγοι περὶ τῶν φαυλοτέρων καὶ
αἰσχιόνων. ὅθεν καὶ συμβαίνει, καθάπερ ὁ Πλάτων
κομψῶς εἶπε περὶ τῆς ἀρετῆς, ὅτι δεινοὺς ἂν παρεῖχεν
ἔρωτας αὑτῆς, εἰ εἰς ὄψιν ᾔει, οὕτως, ἅτε οὐ καταληπτὴν
οὖσαν οὐδεμιᾷ τῶν διὰ τοῦ σώματος αἰσθήσεων, τὸ ἐπὶ
τούτοις ἐμφαίνεσθαι δεῖν τῇ φαντασίᾳ στίλβουσαν ὡς
ἐναργέστατα. ἐπεὶ τὸ τῇ γε διανοίᾳ ἐμφανίζειν αὐτὴν
διὰ λόγου ποικιλίας οὐδεὶς ὅστις οὐ καταγελᾷ τῶν
τε ἄλλων πολλῶν Στωϊκῶν καὶ δὴ καὶ Χρυσίππου,
οἰομένου δεῖν διὰ τῶν ἀκριβῶν μεθόδων καὶ συλλογισμῶν
ἄκουσιν ἐπεμβάλλειν τὴν ἀρετήν, ὧν οὐδὲν μετέχουσιν
αἵ γε ἀνθρώπιναι ὀρέξεις.

I need not recall the events of that and of the precedent years of the war. Not only the arms of France had been defeated on every side, but the inward state of that kingdom was already more exhausted than it had ever been. She went on indeed, but she staggered and reeled under the burden of the war. Our condition, I speak of Great Britain, was not quite so bad : but the charge of the war increased annually upon us. It was evident that this charge must continue to increase, and it was no less evident that our nation was unable to bear it without falling soon into such distress, and contracting such debts, as we have seen and felt, and still feel. The Dutch neither restrained their trade, nor overloaded it with taxes. They soon altered the proportion of their quotas, and were deficient even after this alteration in them. But, however, it must be allowed that they exerted their whole strength ; and they and we paid the whole charge of the war. Since therefore by such efforts as could not be continued any longer, without oppressing and impoverishing these nations to a degree that no interest except that of their very being, nor any engagement of assisting an alliance *totis viribus* could require, France was reduced, and all the ends of the war were become attainable ; it will be worth your lordship's while to consider why the true use was not made of the success of the confederates against France and Spain, and why a peace was not concluded in the fifth year of the war.

BOLINGBROKE.

Τὰ δὲ πεπολεμημένα καὶ τότε καὶ ἐν τοῖς ἔτι
πρότερον ἔτεσιν οὐδὲν δεῖ ὑπομνῆσαι εἰδότας. ἡ μὲν
γὰρ Γαλατία οὐχ ὅτι τὰ ὅπλα πανταχόθεν ἤδη ἡσσῆτο,
ἀλλὰ καὶ τὰ οἴκοθεν τότε δὴ ὥσπερ οὐδεπώποτε κατ-
αναλωμένα ἦν. οὐ μὴν ἀλλὰ ἔτι ὀρθουμένη διετέλει,
σφαλλομένη μέντοι καὶ ὅσον οὐ πταίουσα διὰ τὸ ἄχθος
τὸ τοῦ πολέμου· τὰ δὲ ἡμέτερα πράγματα, τὰ τῆς
Βρεταννίας λέγω, οὐ μὰ Δί᾽ οὐχί πω κακῶς οὕτω
διέκειτο, τὰ δὲ ἀναλώματα τὰ κατ᾽ ἐνιαυτὸν ἐπὶ τὸ
μεῖζον ηὐξάνετο. οὐδέ γε ἄδηλα ἦν οὔτε ταῦτα ἂν ἔτι
μᾶλλον ἐπιδιδόντα, οὔτε ἡ πόλις αὐτὴ ἀδύνατος ἐσομένη
ὑπενεγκεῖν μὴ οὐκ εἰς τοσαύτην μὲν τὴν ἀπορίαν
καταστᾶσα, τοσαῦτα δὲ ὀφειλήματα ὀφείλουσα, ὅσα
μέχρι τοῦ δεῦρο ὁρῶμέν τε καὶ αἰσθανόμεθα. οἱ δὲ
Βαταυοὶ τὴν ἐμπορίαν οὔτε κατεῖχον, οὔτε εἰσφορὰς
πραξάμενοι ἐπίεζον· ἀλλ᾽ ὕστερον τὸ ἐπιβάλλον μέρος
μεταβαλόντες καὶ ὡς ἐνδεέστεροι ἐγένοντο. οὐ μὴν
ἀλλ᾽ ἐκεῖνό γε ὁμολογητέον, ὅτι οὐδὲν ἐκλιπὲς ἦν ὅσα
γε τὸ κατ᾽ αὐτούς· ἐκεῖνοι δὲ σὺν ἡμῖν πάντα τὰ τοῦ
πολέμου ἀναλώματα ὑπήνεγκαν. ἐπειδὴ τοίνυν τὰ
τοιαῦτα ταλαιπωροῦντες οἷα διακαρτερῶν τις ἐπὶ τοσοῦτον ἔμελλε τὰς πόλεις ταύτας κατατρίψειν καὶ κατανα-
λώσειν, ὅσον οὔτε δι᾽ οὐδὲν τῶν συμφερόντων εἰ μὴ
αὐτοῦ τοῦ περιεῖναι ἕνεκα ἐνεχώρει, οὔτε συνθήκη
οὐδεμία βοηθείας τοῖς συμμάχοις παντὶ σθένει κατὰ τὸ
δυνατὸν ἂν ἀναγκάζοι, παρεστησάμεθα τὴν Γαλατίαν
καὶ ὅσα βουλόμενοι ἠρξάμεθα τοῦ πολέμου ἤδη κατα-
ληπτὰ ἐγένετο, ἄξιον ἂν εἴη ἐξετάσαι τί ἦν τὰ κωλύοντα
τοὺς συμμάχους μὴ ἱκανῶς χρήσασθαι τοῖς κατωρθω-
μένοις πρὸς Γαλάτας καὶ Ἴβηρας, μηδὲ ποιήσασθαι
εἰρήνην ἐν τῷ πέμπτῳ ἔτει τοῦ πολέμου.

The immediate occasion which led to Draco's legislation
is not recorded, and even the motives which induced him
to impress it with that character of severity to which it
owes its chief celebrity, are not clearly ascertained. We
know, however, that he was the author of the first written
laws of Athens : and as this measure tended to limit the
authority of the nobles, to which a customary law, of which
they were the sole expounders, opposed a much feebler
check, we may reasonably conclude that the innovation did
not proceed from their wish, but was extorted from them by
the growing discontent of the people. On the other hand,
Draco undoubtedly framed his code as much as possible in
conformity to the spirit and the interests of the ruling
class, to which he himself belonged ; and hence we may
fairly infer that the extreme rigour of its penal enactments
was designed to overawe and repress the popular movement
which had produced it. Aristotle observes that Draco
made no change in the constitution ; and that there was
nothing remarkable in his laws, except the severity of the
penalties by which they were sanctioned. It must however
be remembered that the substitution of law for custom, of
a written code for a fluctuating and flexible tradition, was
itself a step of great importance ; and we also learn that he
introduced some changes in the administration of criminal
justice, by transferring causes of murder, or of accidental
homicide, from the cognizance of the archons to the magistrates called *ephetes* ; though it is not clear whether he
instituted, or only modified or enlarged, their jurisdiction.

THIRLWALL.

Τὰ δὲ πρὸς τὸ νομοθετεῖν τὸν Δράκοντα εὐθὺς
προοδοποιοῦντα οὔτε λέγεται, ἅ τε διανοούμενος τοσαύτην τῇ νομοθεσίᾳ ἐνεσημήνατο τὴν ὠμότητα ὥστε δι᾽
αὐτὴν ταύτην ὀνομαστοτάτην εἶναι, οὐδὲ ταῦτα διηκρί-
βωται ἱκανῶς. φαίνεται δ᾽ οὖν πρῶτος γράψας νόμους
Ἀθηναίοις· ἐπειδὴ δὲ τοῦτο παραιρεῖσθαι ἔμελλέ τι
τῆς τῶν εὐπατρίδων ἐξουσίας, ᾗ νόμος τις ἄγραφος
πρότερον ὑπάρχων αὐτῶν γε ἐξηγουμένων πολὺ ἀσθε-
νέστερον ἦν ἐμπόδιον, οὐκ ἂν ἀλόγῳ τις τεκμηρίῳ λέγοι
χρώμενος ὅτι οὐ μᾶλλον βουλομένοις τούτοις ἐνεωτερίσθη
ἢ βιαζομένοις διὰ τὸν τῶν δημοτῶν ἀεὶ ἐπιδιδόντα
θόρυβον. τοὐναντίον δὲ φαίνεται Δράκων τοὺς νόμους
θεὶς κατὰ νοῦν τε καὶ πρὸς τὸ συμφέρον ὅτι μάλιστα
τοῖς δυνατοῖς, ὧν καὶ αὐτὸς ἦν· ὃ καὶ σημεῖον ὅτι κατα-
πλῆξαί τε καὶ κατέχειν βουλόμενος τὴν τῶν πολλῶν
κίνησιν, ἢ καὶ αἰτία ἦν τοῦ νομοθετεῖν, οὕτω δὴ τὴν
ἐσχάτην τῶν ἐπιτιμιῶν ἀκρίβειαν εἰκότως εἰσήνεγκε.
τῆς γοῦν πολιτείας οὔ φησιν Ἀριστοτέλης οὐδὲν μετα-
βαλεῖν αὐτόν, οὐδ᾽ ἐνεῖναι ἄλλο οὐδὲν ὅ τι καὶ λόγου
ἄξιον τοῖς νόμοις ἀλλ᾽ ἢ ὅτι χαλεπαῖς ταῖς ζημίαις
κατειλημμένοι εἶεν. οὐ μὴν οὐδὲ ἐκεῖνο δεῖ λεληθέναι
ὅτι τὸ νόμον ἀντὶ ἔθους ἀντικαταστῆσαι, ἀνταλλάξαντα
τῆς ἀβεβαίου καὶ εὐμεταβόλου παραδοχῆς τὰ γεγραμ-
μένα, τοῦτο αὐτὸ προὔργου τι ἐγένετο· λέγεται δὲ καὶ
ἔστιν ἃ νεωτερίσαι περὶ τοῦ τοὺς ἀδικοῦντας δικάζειν,
τὰ περὶ φόνου τοῦ τε ἑκουσίου καὶ τοῦ ἀκουσίου μετε-
νεγκὼν ἀπὸ τῶν ἀρχόντων εἰς τοὺς ἐφέτας καλουμένους,
καίπερ ἄδηλον ὂν εἴτε καταστήσας τὸ ἀρχεῖον τοῦτο
εἴτε ἐπανορθούμενος ἢ καὶ μείζω τὰ γέρα ἐγχειρίσας.

First, for the king our sovereign himself, who is the principal person you are to eye in this business; his grace doth profess, that he truly and constantly desireth to reign in peace. But his grace saith, he will neither buy peace with dishonour nor take it up at interest of danger to ensue; but shall think it a good change, if it please God to change the inward troubles and seditions, wherewith he hath been hitherto exercised, into an honourable foreign war. And for the other two persons in this action, the French king and the duke of Britain, his grace doth declare unto you, that they be the men unto whom he is of all other friends and allies most bounden: the one having held over him his hand of protection from the tyrant; the other having reached forth unto him his hand of help for the recovery of his kingdom. So that his affection toward them in his natural person is upon equal terms. And whereas you may have heard that his grace was enforced to fly out of Britain into France, for doubts of being betrayed; his grace would not in any sort have that reflect upon the duke of Britain, in defacement of his former benefits; for that he is throughly informed that it was but the practice of some corrupt persons about him, during the time of his sickness, altogether without his consent or privity.

BACON.

Πρῶτον μὲν ὁ βασιλεὺς ὁ ἡμέτερος—τοῦτον γὰρ δὴ πρῶτον ἐνταῦθα ἐπισκεπτέον κατὰ τὸ προσῆκον τοῦ ἀξιώματος—δηλοῖ ὅτι ὡς ἀληθῶς οὐδὲν ἄλλο βούλεται ἢ ὅπως εἰρηνεύων διατελεῖ. τὴν μέντοι εἰρήνην αὐτὴν οὔτ' ἄν φησι τῆς δυσκλείας ὠνεῖσθαι, οὔτ' ἐπὶ πολλῷ τῷ γενησομένῳ κινδύνῳ δανείζεσθαι· ἡγεῖται δὲ ἐπὶ τὸ βέλτιον περιστῆναι ἂν τὰ πράγματα, σὺν τοῖς θεοῖς εἰπεῖν, εἰ τῶν οἰκείων ταραχῶν καὶ στάσεων μέχρι τοῦ δεῦρο πεπειραμένος πόλεμον ἐν τῇ ἀλλοτρίᾳ οὐκ ἄδοξον ἀνταλλάξαιτο. ἔπειτα πρὸς ἐκείνους πρὸς οὓς ἐν τῷ παρόντι ἐστὶν ἡ σκέψις, λέγω δὲ τὸν Γαλάτην καὶ τὸν Ἀρμορικόν, τοσοῦτον ὁ βασιλεὺς ἀποφαίνεται ὅτι τούτοις οὐχ ἥκιστα τῶν ἄλλων φίλων καὶ ἐνσπόνδων κεῖται παρ' αὐτῷ εὐεργεσία, ὧν ὁ μὲν ὑπερέσχε τὴν χεῖρα ἵνα μή τι πάθοι ὑπὸ τοῦ τυράννου, ὁ δὲ ὤρεξεν αὐτῷ βοηθοῦσαν σπεύδοντι τὴν κάθοδον· ὥστε ὅσα γε πρὸς τὴν φύσιν αὐτοῦ μηδὲ πρὸς ἕτερον μᾶλλον σπουδάζειν. εἰ δ' ἄρα καὶ ἀκηκόατε περὶ τοῦ βασιλέως, ὡς φοβούμενός ποτε μή τις προδῷ αὐτὸν ἐξ Ἀρμορικῆς καταφύγοι εἰς Γαλατίαν, οὐδὲ τοῦτο ἀξιοῖ οὐδαμῶς τῷ Ἀρμορικῷ καταμέμφεσθαι ὥστε μηκέτι μεμνῆσθαι τῶν προτέρων εὐεργεσιῶν, τοσοῦτον εὖ κατειδὼς ὅτι τὰ τοιαῦτα ἐβουλεύσαντο τῶν παρ' αὐτῷ τινὲς σύμβουλοι καὶ μισθωταὶ λανθάνοντες αὐτὸν ἅτε χαλεπῶς ἐν τῷ τότε νοσοῦντα, καὶ οὐ συγκαταινέσαντα ἀλλ' οὐδὲ συνειδότα.

No Grecian lawgiver ever thought of entirely abolishing ancient usage, and becoming according to the modern phrase the framer of a new constitution. In legislating they only reformed. Lycurgus, Solon, and the others, so far from abolishing what usage had established, endeavoured to preserve everything which could be preserved, adding only several new institutions and improving those already in existence. If therefore we possessed the whole of the laws of Solon, we should by no means find them to contain a perfect constitution. But to compensate for that, they embraced, not only the rights of individuals, but also morals, in a much higher degree than the latter can be embraced in the view of any modern lawgiver. The regulation of private life, and hence the education of youth, on which the prevalence and continuance of good morals depend, formed one of their leading objects. They were convinced that the state would otherwise be incapable of governing itself. To this it must be added, that in these small commonwealths, in these towns with their territories, many regulations could be made and executed which could not be put into operation in a powerful and widely extended nation. Whether these regulations were always good, and always well adapted to their purpose, is quite another question. It is our duty at present to show from what point of view those lawgivers were accustomed to regard the art of regulating the state, and the means of preserving and directing it.

HEEREN.

Τὰ δὲ παλαιὰ νόμιμα παντάπασιν ἀνελεῖν καὶ
ὥσπερ νῦν λέγουσι καινῆς τινὸς δημιουργὸς γενέσθαι
πολιτείας οὐδ' εἷς ᾤετο δεῖν τῶν Ἕλλησι νομοθετούντων,
οὔτε Λυκοῦργος οὔτε Σόλων οὔτ' ἄλλος ὁστισοῦν,
νόμους τιθεὶς οὐδὲν ἄλλο ἢ ἐπανορθούμενος. οὐ γὰρ
ὅπως τὰ νόμῳ καθεστῶτα διέλυον ἀλλὰ καὶ πάντα
διασώζεσθαι τὰ ἐνδεχόμενα ἐπεχείρουν, τὰ μὲν ἔστιν
ὅτε προστιθέντες, τὰ δὲ ἤδη ὑπάρχοντα ὅπως ἐπιδώσει
σπουδὴν ποιούμενοι. εἰ τοίνυν ὅσα ἐνομοθέτει ὁ Σόλων
πάντα ἐσῴζετο, οὐκ ἂν πάνυ εἰκὸς τέλειόν τι ἐνεῖναι
αὐτοῖς εἶδος πολιτείας. ἀντὶ μέντοι τούτων οὐ τῶν
καθ' ἕκαστον δικαίων μόνον ἐπεμελοῦντο ἀλλὰ καὶ τῶν
ἠθικῶν, καὶ ταῦτα πολὺ μᾶλλον ἢ κατὰ τὴν τῶν νῦν
νομοθετῶν ὁτουοῦν ἐπιμέλειαν. τῶν γὰρ πρὸς τὸν
ἴδιον ἑκάστῳ βίον καὶ δι' αὐτὸ τῆς τῶν νέων παιδείας
καθ' ἣν κατέχει τε καὶ συμμένει ἡ ἠθικὴ ἀρετή, εἴπερ
καί του ἄλλου καὶ τούτων μάλιστα ἐπωρέγοντο, πεπεισ-
μένοι ὡς ἄρα τούτων μὴ ὑπαρχόντων αὐτὴ ἑαυτῆς
ἄρχειν ἀδύνατος ἂν εἴη ἡ πόλις. δεῖ δὲ μηδ' ἐκεῖνο
λεληθέναι, ὅτι ἐν ταύταις ταῖς σμικραῖς πόλεσιν αὐταῖς
τε καὶ τοῖς περικειμένοις χωρίοις πολλὰ ἐνεδέχετο
ἐγγενέσθαι καὶ τελειωθῆναι ἀμήχανα ἐν μείζονί τινι
καὶ δυνατωτέρῳ ἔθνει. εἰ δὲ τὰ νόμιμα ταῦτα ἀεὶ
ἀγαθά τε ἦν καὶ πρὸς τὸ τέλος τὸ προκείμενον ἀρκούν-
τως εἶχεν, ἄλλης ἂν εἴη ἀπορίας· τοσοῦτον δ' οὖν ἐν
τῷ παρόντι δεῖ ἀποδεῖξαι πρὸς τί ἐκεῖνοι ἀποβλέποντες
τῆς τε τοῦ διοικεῖν τὴν πολιτείαν τέχνης εἴχοντο, καὶ
διὰ ποίων εὖ οἰκήσει καὶ ταχθήσεται ἐσκοποῦντο.

Solon. Let me put to you a few questions, near to the point : you will answer them, I am confident, easily and affably. Pisistratus, have you not felt yourself the happier, when, in the fulness of your heart, you have made a large offering to the gods ?

Pisistratus. Solon, I am not impious : I have made many such offerings to them, and have always been the happier.

Sol. Did they need your sacrifice ?

Pis. They need nothing from us mortals ; but I was happy in the performance of what I have been taught is my duty.

Sol. Piously, virtuously, and reasonably said, my friend. The gods did not indeed want your sacrifice : they, who give every thing, can want nothing. The Athenians do want a sacrifice from you : they have an urgent necessity of something ; the necessity of that very thing which you have taken from them, and which it can cost you nothing to replace. You have always been happier, you confess, in giving to the gods what you could have yourself used in your own house : believe me, you will not be less so in giving back to your fellow citizens what you have taken out of theirs, and what you very well know they will seize when they can, together with your property and life.

LANDOR.

Σόλ. Φέρε δή, ὀλίγα ἄττα σε ἔρωμαι οὐκ ἄπο
τρόπου· σὺ γὰρ ῥᾳδίως ἂν οἶμαι ἀποκρίναιο καὶ οὐδὲν
δυσχεραίνων. μέμνησαί που, ὦ Πεισίστρατε, εὐδαι-
μονέστερον διακείμενος, ὁπότε ὡς χάριν ἀποδώσων
ἱκανήν τινα τοῖς θεοῖς ἐδωρήσω θυσίαν.

Πεισ. οὐ γὰρ ἀσεβής τίς εἰμι, ὦ Σόλων· πολλὰ
τὰ τοιαῦτα δωρησάμενος αὐτοῖς μέμνημαι καὶ πολλάκις
ἀεὶ δὲ ἥδιον διακείμενος.

Σόλ. μῶν ὡς δεομένοις τι τῆς σῆς θυσίας;

Πεισ. οὐδὲ γὰρ ἑνὸς παρ' ἡμῶν θνητῶν γε ὄντων
δέονται· ἡδόμην μέντοι ἃ ὡς προσήκοντά μοι ἔμαθον
ταῦτα διαπραττόμενος.

Σόλ. εὐσεβῶς γὰρ σὺ καὶ δικαίως καὶ νουνεχόντως λέγεις· ἐπεὶ οἱ μὲν θεοὶ οὐ πάνυ ἐδέοντο τῆς
σῆς θυσίας. τίνος γὰρ ἂν ἐνδεεῖς εἶεν οἵ γε αὐτοὶ
πάντα δωρούμενοι; οἱ δέ γε Ἀθηναῖοι ἀπαρχῆς τινὸς
δέονται παρὰ σοῦ. ἔστι γὰρ οὗ χρεία τις αὐτοὺς κατε-
πείγει, τούτου αὐτοῦ ὃ ἀφῄρησαι αὐτοὺς καὶ ἔχοις ἂν
προῖκα ἀποδοῦναι· καὶ ὅτι μὲν ἀεὶ ἥδιον διάκεισαι τοῖς
θεοῖς ταῦτα ἀπονέμων οἷς ἔνδον παρὰ σαυτῷ χρῆσθαι
ἐνεδέχετο, καὶ αὐτὸς ὁμολογεῖς· εὖ δ' ἴσθ' ὅτι οὐδὲν
ἧττον ταὐτὸν ἂν πάσχοις ἐὰν καὶ τοῖς πολίταις ἀποδῷς
ὃ ἀφελόμενος αὐτοὺς ἀδαπάνως ἂν ἀποδοίης. εὐδαι-
μονέστερος γοῦν ὢν, ὡς καὶ αὐτὸς φής, τοῖς θεοῖς ἐκεῖνα
ἀπένειμας ὅσοις οἴκοι παρὰ σεαυτῷ ἐξῆν χρῆσθαι·
ταῦτα δὲ ἃ ἀφῄρησαι τοὺς πολίτας οἴκοθεν παρ' αὐτῶν
ἀποδιδοὺς οὐδὲν ἧττον ἴσθι ἐσόμενος, ὅταν δυνηθῶσιν
ἁρπασομένους εὖ εἰδὼς αὐτά τε καὶ τὰ χρήματά σου
καὶ δὴ καὶ τὴν ψυχήν.

There were in the town five and twenty hundred foot, and a regiment of horse and dragoons; the line about the town was finished; yet in some places the graff was wider and deeper than in others. The castle within the town was very well prepared, and supplied with great store of provisions to endure a siege. The opinions were several: the officers of the Cornish were of opinion that it was best to proceed by way of approach; because, the ground being very good, it would in a very short time be done; and since there was no army of the enemy in a possibility to relieve it, the securest way would be the best: whereas the works were so good, that they must expect to lose very many men; and if they were beaten off all their summer hopes would be destroyed; it not being easy again to make up the spirit of the army for a new action. Besides, they alleged, the well-affected party in the city, which was believed to be very great, would, after they had been closely besieged three or four days, have a greater influence upon the soldiers, and be able to do more towards the surrender, than they could upon a storm, when they would be equally sensible of the disorder of the soldiers, and their own damage by plunder, as the other; and the too late example of the executed citizens would keep men from offering at any insurrection in the city.

CLARENDON.

Ἦσαν δὲ ἔνδον πεζοὶ μὲν πεντακόσιοι καὶ δισχίλιοι, τῶν δὲ ἱππέων καὶ ἱπποτοξοτῶν τέλος ἕν· ἐπετετέλεστο δὲ ἤδη ὁ μὲν περίβολος τῶν τειχῶν, ἡ δὲ τάφρος ἔστιν ᾗ βάθους καὶ εὔρους ἱκανῶς εἶχεν, ἔστι δ' ᾗ ἐνέλιπεν. ἡ δὲ ἀκρόπολις τά τε ἄλλα πάνυ εὖ παρεσκευασμένη ἦν καὶ τοῖς σιτίοις ὡς ἐπὶ πολιορκίαν. καὶ ἄλλοι μὲν ἄλλας γνώμας ἀπεφαίνοντο· τοῖς δὲ ἐν τέλει οὖσι τῶν Δαμνονίων ἐδόκει χῶμα ποιήσαντας μᾶλλον ἢ διὰ προσβολῆς πυιητέα εἶναι τὴν ἐπιχείρησιν· ἐπιτηδείας γὰρ οὔσης τῆς γῆς οὐ διὰ πολλοῦ κατορθώσεσθαι τὴν πεῖραν· καὶ ἅμα τῶν πολεμίων οὐδενὸς ἐν δυνάμει ὄντος ὥστε βοηθῆσαι τὸ ἀσφαλέστατον καὶ βέλτιστον. εἰ δὲ μή, ἰσχυρῶν ὄντων τῶν τειχισμάτων, εἰκὸς εἶναι πολλούς τινας ἂν ἀπολέσαι, ἡσσηθεῖσι δὲ ἐν ἀνελπίστῳ ἤδη εἶναι τὰ ἔς γε τὸ παρὸν θέρος· οὐδὲ γὰρ ῥάδιον παραθαρσύνειν τοὺς στρατιώτας ὥστε ἀναμάχεσθαι. πολλοὺς δὲ καὶ ὄντας ὡς εἰκὸς τοὺς ἐν τῇ πόλει τὰ ἑαυτῶν φρονοῦντας, ἐπειδὰν τρίτη ἢ τετάρτη ἡμέρα γένηται πολιορκουμένοις, μᾶλλον πείσειν τοὺς ἔνδοθεν, καὶ πολὺ μᾶλλον ξυνοίσειν ἐς τὴν ὁμολογίαν ἢ κατὰ προσβολήν, εἰ γένοιτο, ἅτε ὑπὸ τῶν στρατιωτῶν ἀτακτούντων καὶ λείαν ποιουμένων καὶ αὐτοὺς οὐδὲν ἧσσον διαφθαρησομένους· τοὺς δὲ ἄρτι ζημιωθέντας θανάτῳ τῶν ἀστῶν μεγίστην ἂν εἶναι ἀποτροπὴν τοῦ μηδένα ἔτι στασιάζειν ἐν τῇ πόλει.

Ambition is like choler, which is an humour that maketh men active, earnest, full of alacrity and stirring, if it be not stopped; but if it be stopped and cannot have its way it becometh adust, and thereby malign and venomous : so ambitious men, if they find the way open for their rising, and if they still get forward, they are rather busy than dangerous; but if they be checked in their desires they become secretly discontent, and look upon men and matters with an evil eye, and are best pleased when things go backward; which is the worst property in a servant of a prince or state. Therefore it is good for princes, if they use ambitious men, to handle it so that they be still progressive, and not retrograde; which, because it cannot be without inconvenience, it is good not to use such natures at all; for if they rise not with their service, they will take order to make their service fall with them. But since we have said it were good not to use men of ambitious natures, except it be upon necessity, it is fit we speak in what cases they are of necessity. Good commanders in the wars must be taken, be they never so ambitious; for the use of their service dispenseth with the rest; and to take a soldier without ambition is to pull off his spurs. There is also great use of ambitious men in being screens to princes in matters of danger and envy; for no man will take that part except he be like a seeled dove, that mounts and mounts because he cannot see about him. There is use also of ambitious men in pulling down the greatness of any subject that overtops; as Tiberius used Macro in the pulling down of Sejanus.

BACON.

Η δὲ φιλοτιμία ὡμοίωταί τι τῇ χολῇ, ἢ σπου-
δαστικούς τε καὶ δραστηρίους παρέχει τοὺς ἀνθρώπους,
καὶ προθυμίας ἅμα μεστοὺς καὶ ἰτητικούς, ἐὰν ἄρα
μηδὲν κωλύῃ· εἰ δὲ μή, ἀπορίας οὔσης τοῦ μὴ πόρρω
ἰέναι, οὕτω δὴ φλεγματώδης γίγνεται ὥστε εἰς τὸ βλαβερὸν καὶ νοσῶδες ἀποκριθῆναι. ὡς δ᾽ αὕτως καὶ οἱ
φιλότιμοι, ὅσοι μὲν ἂν πόρου τυχόντες τοῦ προϊέναι
διατελῶσιν ἀεὶ ἐπιδιδόντες πολυπραγμονέστεροι ἂν
εἶεν ἢ ἐπικινδυνότεροι· οἳ δ᾽ ἂν κολουθῶσι ταῖς ἐπιθυ-
μίαις λάθρᾳ δυσκολαίνουσι, βασκαίνοντες ἅμα τοῖς
ἀνθρώποις τε καὶ τοῖς πράγμασι, καὶ εἰς τὸ ὀπίσω
ἀναχωρούντων ἐφηδόμενοι. ὃ καὶ κάκιστον κέκτηται ὁ
τῷ βασιλεῖ ἢ τῇ πόλει ὑπηρετῶν. διὸ καὶ προσήκει
τοῖς βασιλεῦσιν, εἴπερ χρῶνται τοῖς φιλοτίμοις, οὕτω
μεταχειρίζεσθαι ὅπως τις ἀεὶ προχωρήσεται ἀλλὰ
μὴ ἀναχωρήσεται· τοῦτο δ᾽ ἐπειδὴ ἀδύνατον ἄνευ τοῦ
ἀσυμφόρου, οὐ πάνυ δεῖ ταῖς τοιαύταις χρῆσθαι
φύσεσιν· ἐὰν γὰρ μὴ ἅμα τῇ χρήσει καὶ αὐτοὶ αὐξά-
νωνται, οὕτω πράξουσιν ὅπως ἅμα σφίσιν αὐτοῖς καὶ
ἡ χρῆσις σφαλήσεται. ἐπεὶ δὲ ἀσύμφορον ἦν τοῖς
τοιούτοις χρῆσθαι ὅτι μὴ ἐξ ἀνάγκης, λοιπὸν διελθεῖν
ἐν οἷς καιροῖς ἀναγκαῖοί εἰσιν. πρῶτον μὲν ἐπὶ τῶν
πολέμων ἀγαθοῖς χρηστέον τοῖς στρατηγοῖς, κἂν ὦσιν
ὅτι μάλιστα φιλότιμοι· ἥ τε γὰρ ὠφέλεια αὐτῶν τἆλλα
πάντα ἀφανίζει, ὅ τε στρατηγὸς ἀφιλότιμός τις ὢν
ταὐτὸν δύναται καὶ εἴ τις τὰ ὅπλα ἀφέλοιτο. ἔπειτα
μεγάλην ἔχουσι τὴν ῥοπὴν οἱ φιλότιμοι προβεβλημένοι
τοῖς βασιλεῦσιν, ἐπικινδύνων ὄντων τῶν καιρῶν καὶ
φθονερῶν· οὐδὲ γὰρ ἂν εἰς ταῦτα ὑπομένοι μὴ οὐ
προσόμοιος ὢν περιστερᾷ κεκαλυμμένῃ τοὺς ὀφθαλμούς,
ἢ ἀναπετομένη διατελεῖ, ἅτε ἀδυνατοῦσα τὰ κύκλῳ
ὁρᾶν. ἔτι δὲ ὠφέλιμοι οἱ τοιοῦτοι εἰς τὸ τὸν ὑπερέ-
χοντα ἀεὶ τῶν πολιτῶν καταβάλλειν, καθάπερ διὰ
Μάκρωνος καθεῖλε τὸν Σηϊανὸν ὁ Τιβέριος.

When our ministers had once departed from the
straight line of British policy, the difficulty of returning to it became every year greater, and the inclination
every year less. We continued busy and bustling in every
court of Europe. We negotiated against the Emperor in
concert with France, and gave her thereby the means of
regaining more of that credit and influence in the Empire,
which she had formerly had, than she could have acquired
without our assistance. We contrived to make peace
abroad almost as chargeable to us as war. Abuses of every
kind were suffered at home. Trade was neither eased nor
encouraged ; and the gradual payment of our debt was
utterly neglected by a minister rather desirous to keep his
country under this oppression than ignorant of the means
to deliver her from it. Whilst we acted in this manner,
France grew frugal, she made the debts she could not pay
sit more lightly upon her, she raised her credit, and she
extended her commerce. In short, her strength increased,
and ours diminished. We were reduced to a state of weakness we had never felt before ; and this very weakness was
urged as a reason for bearing tamely the losses our merchants sustained, and all the affronts our government
received, lest we should be drawn into a war by using
reprisals, the common right of nations.

BOLINGBROKE.

Οἱ δὲ προεστῶτες ἐπειδὴ ἅπαξ ἀπενενεύκεσαν τοῦ ἀπὸ τῆς εὐθείας κατὰ τὰ πάτρια πολιτεύεσθαι, καθ' ἕκαστον ἔτος τοῦ ἐπανιέναι ἥ τε ἀπορία καὶ ὁ ὄκνος ἤδη ἐπεδίδου. ἐχρώμεθα γὰρ ἑκασταχοῦ τῆς Εὐρώπης πολυπραγμοσύνῃ καὶ πολυπειρίᾳ. πρῶτον μὲν τοῖς Γαλάταις ἐπὶ τῷ Καίσαρι συνεπράττομεν, ὥστε δι' ἡμῶν αὐτοὺς πλέον τοῦ πρότερον παρὰ τοῖς ἐκείνου πολίταις ὑπάρχοντος ἀξιώματος καὶ δυνάμεως ἀναλαβεῖν ἢ ὅσον ἐνεδέχετο μὴ καὶ ἡμῶν συμβοηθησάντων. ἔπειτα τὰ μὲν ἔξωθεν ἐπράττομεν ὅπως μηδὲν ἧττον εἰρηνευόντων δαπανήσεται ἢ καὶ πολεμούντων, τὰ δὲ οἴκοθεν πάντα καὶ παντοῖα διαφθειρόμενα περιεωρῶμεν. τοῖς δὲ χρηματιζομένοις τίς παρ' ἡμῶν βοήθεια; τίνι μὲν οὖν οὐ βάρος; ἐπεὶ τό γε ταξαμένους ἀποδοῦναι τὰ κοινῇ ὠφειλημένα οὐδ' ἐπῄει τῷ πολιτευομένῳ μᾶλλον ὅπως συμμενεῖ τοῖς πολίταις ἡ τοσαύτη ταλαιπωρία ἢ ἀγνοοῦντι δι' ὧν ἐνδέχεται ἀπολῦσαι. καὶ ἡμεῖς μὲν τὰ τοιαῦτα ἐπολιτευόμεθα· οἱ δὲ Γαλάται φειδόμενοί τε καὶ τὰ χρέα ἐξαλείφοντες μὲν οὐ ῥᾷον δὲ ὑποφέροντες ἀξιόχρεῳ ἐγένοντο καὶ δι' αὐτὸ καὶ τὴν ἐμπορίαν ἐπηύξησαν. συνελόντι δὲ εἰπεῖν, ἡμεῖς μὲν ἠλαττούμεθα, ἐκεῖνοι δὲ μείζους ηὐξάνοντο. εἰς τοσοῦτον τοίνυν ἡμεῖς ἀσθενείας καθεστήκειμεν ὅσον οὐδεπώποτε πρότερον· καὶ ταύτην αὐτὴν ἀπελογούμεθα ὁπότε ῥᾳθυμοῦντες περιΐδοιμεν ὅσα αὐτοὶ μὲν ὑβριζοίμεθα τοῖς δὲ ἐμπόροις ζημία γίγνοιτο, μὴ δή, εἰ σύλαις χρησαίμεθα, ὅπερ κοινῇ ὑπάρχει τοῖς ἅπασι νόμιμον, περιπέσοιμεν πολέμῳ.

The English ambassadors, having repaired to Maximilian, did find his power and promise at a very great distance ; he being utterly unprovided of men, money, and arms, for any such enterprise. For Maximilian, having neither wing to fly on, for that his patrimony of Austria was not in his hands, his father being then living, and on the other side, his matrimonial territories of Flanders being partly in dowry to his mother-in-law, and partly not serviceable, in respect of the late rebellions ; was thereby destitute of means to enter into war. The ambassadors saw this well, but wisely thought fit to advertise the king thereof, rather than to return themselves, till the king's farther pleasure were known ; the rather, for that Maximilian himself spake as great as ever he did before, and entertained them with dilatory answers : so as the formal part of their ambassage might well warrant and require their farther stay. The king hereupon, who doubted as much before, and saw through his business from the beginning, wrote back to the ambassadors, commending their discretion in not returning, and willing them to keep the state wherein they found Maximilian as a secret, till they heard farther from him.

BACON.

Οἱ δὲ παρ' Ἄγγλων πρέσβεις ἀφικόμενοι ὡς Μαξιμιλιανὸν τήν τε δύναμιν καὶ ἃ ὑπέσχετο ὡς διὰ πλείστου ἀπέχοντα κατέλαβον, ἅτε πάνυ ἀπαράσκευον ὄντα στρατιᾶς τε καὶ χρημάτων καὶ ὅπλων ὡς ἐπὶ τήν γε τοιαύτην πεῖραν. ὁ γὰρ Μαξιμιλιανὸς ἀπορηθεὶς καὶ κατ' ἀμφότερα—οὔτε γάρ πω τὰ παρὰ τοῦ πατρὸς ἔτι ζῶντος τὰ πρὸς ἕω χωρία παρειλήφει, ἅ τε ἡ γυνὴ προῖκα ἐπηνέγκατο τῆς Βελγικῆς τὰ μὲν κατοκώχιμα ἔτι εἶχεν ἡ πενθερὰ τὰ δὲ διὰ τὰς νεωστὶ στάσεις ἀνωφέλητα ἦν—κατὰ ταῦτα οὖν πάντων ἐνδεὴς ἦν ἐς τὸν πόλεμον. οἱ δὲ πρέσβεις, ταῦτα καὶ αὐτοὶ εὖ εἰδότες, ὅμως ἅτε φρόνιμοι ὄντες γνώμην ἐποιοῦντο μᾶλλον ἀπαγγέλλειν τῷ βασιλεῖ ἢ αὐτοὶ ἐπαναχωρεῖν πρὶν πυθέσθαι ὅ τι δοκοίη αὐτῷ, ἄλλως τε καὶ ὅτι ὁ Μαξιμιλιανὸς αὐτὸς τὰ αὐτὰ ἃ καὶ πρότερον ἐκόμπει, φιλανθρωπευόμενος ἀεὶ καὶ ἀποκρινόμενος ἐς ἀναβολάς· ὥστε κατὰ τὸν λόγον τῆς πρεσβείας ἀναγκαῖον εἶναι διατρίβειν ἐς τὸν πλείονα χρόνον. ὁ δὲ βασιλεύς, ὑποπτεύσας τοσοῦτον καὶ πρότερον ἅτε αὐτὸς πάντα τὰ ἐξ ἀρχῆς διϊδών, ἐπιστολὴν τοῖς πρέσβεσιν ἀντέπεμψεν, ἅμα μὲν τὴν ξύνεσιν ἐπαινῶν οὐκ ἀναχωρούντων, ἐν τῷ αὐτῷ δὲ στέγεσθαι ἀξιῶν τὰ περὶ τοῦ Μαξιμιλιανοῦ ἕως ἂν ἐπὶ τὸ πλέον παρ' ἑαυτοῦ πύθωνται.

The speech which he addressed to the Assembly may be taken as one instance out of numbers of these solemn and volunteered declarations. He considered, he said, as great criminals, those who by personal ambition compromised the small amount of stability secured by the Constitution; that if the Constitution contained defects and dangers, the Assembly was competent to expose them to the eyes of the country; but that he alone, bound by his oath, restrained himself within the strict limits traced by that act. He declared that the first duty of authorities was to inspire the people with respect for the law by never deviating from it themselves; and that his anxiety was not, he assured the Assembly, to know who would govern France in 1852, but to employ the time at his disposal, so that the transition, whatever it might be, should be effected without agitation or disturbance; for, said he, the noblest object and the most worthy of an exalted mind is not to seek when in power how to perpetuate it, but to labour incessantly to fortify, for the benefit of all, those principles of authority and morality, which defy the passions of mankind and the instability of laws.

KINGLAKE.

Ὧν δὲ μετὰ σπουδῆς οὗτος καὶ αὐτεπάγγελτος προεῖπεν ἐξειλέχθω ἓν ἀπὸ πολλῶν ἡ δημηγορία ἡ πρὸς τὴν ἐκκλησίαν. πανουργοτάτους γὰρ ἔφη λογίσασθαι ὅσοι διὰ τὰς ἰδίας φιλοτιμίας τὸ βέβαιον, καὶ ὡς σμικρὸν ὄν, ὃ παρέχοι ἡ τῆς πολιτείας κατάστασις εἰς κίνδυνον προάγοιεν. εἰ δὲ ταύτῃ ἐνυπάρχοι ἐνδεές τι ἢ βλαβερόν, τὴν ἐκκλησίαν μὲν ἐνδέχεσθαι φανερὸν ποιεῖν πρὸ τῶν ὀμμάτων τοῖς πολίταις, αὐτὸς δὲ τῷ ὅρκῳ πιστωθεὶς μόνος τῶν ἄλλων κατέχειν ἑαυτὸν μέχρι τῶν ἀκριβῶν ὅρων ὧν ὁ νόμος ὡρίσατο. δεῖν γὰρ πρῶτον τοὺς ἄρχοντας τοῖς ἀρχομένοις δέος τὸ προσῆκον τῷ νόμῳ ἐμποιεῖν, αὐτοὺς μηδοτιοῦν παραβαίνοντας. διεμαρτύρατο δὲ ἦ μήν, ὅστις, ἐπειδὰν αὐτῷ ἡ ἀρχὴ πέρας σχῇ, ἄρξει τῆς Γαλατίας, τοῦτο μὴ προθυμεῖσθαι προϊδεῖν, ἀλλὰ τῷ χρόνῳ τῷ περιόντι οὕτω χρῆσθαι ὥστε τὴν μεταβολήν, οἱαδήποτε ἔσοιτο, ἄνευ ταραχῆς καὶ θορύβου γενέσθαι· τῷ γὰρ μεγαλοψύχῳ ἐκεῖνο δοκεῖν γενναιότατον εἶναι καὶ ἑαυτοῦ ἀξιώτατον, μὴ ὅταν αὐτὸς ἄρχῃ ὅπως ἀΐδιος ἔσται ἡ ἀρχὴ ἐπιζητεῖν, ἀλλὰ καὶ συνεχῶς ἀεὶ διαπονεῖσθαι ὑπὲρ τῆς τοῦ κοινοῦ σωτηρίας ὅτῳ τρόπῳ ἰσχυρότατα γενήσεται τὰ ἐπιτηδεύματα οἷς ἐξουσία καὶ δικαιοσύνη χρώμεναι καρτεροῦσιν ὁμοίως πρὸς τὰς ἀνθρωπίνας ἐπιθυμίας καὶ τὸ τῶν νόμων ἀβέβαιον.

Euphranor. Tell me, Alciphron, is your genuine philosopher a wise man or a fool?

Alciphron. Without question the wisest of men.

Euph. Which is to be thought the wise man, he who acts with design, or he who acts at random?

Alc. He who acts with design.

Euph. Whoever acts with design, acts for some end: doth he not?

Alc. He doth.

Euph. And a wise man for a good end?

Alc. True.

Euph. And he showeth his wisdom in making choice of fit means to obtain his end?

Alc. I acknowledge it.

Euph. By how much therefore the end proposed is more excellent, and by how much fitter the means employed are to obtain it, so much the wiser is the agent to be esteemed.

Alc. This seems to be true.

Euph. Can a rational agent propose a more excellent end than happiness?

Alc. He cannot.

Euph. Of good things the greatest good is the most excellent.

Alc. Doubtless.

Euph. Is not the general happiness of mankind a greater good than the private happiness of one man, or of some certain man?

Alc. It is.

Euph. Is it not therefore the most excellent end?

Alc. It seems so.

Euph. Are not those men who pursue this end by the properest methods to be thought the wisest men?

Alc. I grant they are.

Euph. Which is a wise man governed by, wise or foolish notions?

Alc. By wise doubtless.

Euph. It seems then to follow, that he who promotes the general wellbeing of mankind by the proper necessary means is truly wise and acts upon wise grounds.

BERKELEY.

Εὐφ. Εἰπέ μοι, ὦ Ἀλκίφρον, πότερον σοφός τίς ἐστιν ἢ ἠλίθιος ὅ γε ὡς ἀληθῶς φιλόσοφος;

Ἀλκ. σοφώτατος μὲν οὖν.

Εὐφ. πότερος δὲ σοφὸς νομιστέος ὁ μετὰ λόγου πράττων ἢ ὁ εἰκῇ;

Ἀλκ. ὁ μετὰ λόγου.

Εὐφ. ὃς δ᾽ ἂν μετὰ λόγου πράττῃ, πράττει που πρὸς τέλος τι ἀποβλέπων· ἢ οὔ;

Ἀλκ. ἀνάγκη.

Εὐφ. ὁ δέ γε σοφὸς πρὸς ἀγαθόν τι τέλος;

Ἀλκ. φαίνεται.

Εὐφ. καὶ ἐνταῦθά γε δηλοῖ τὴν σοφίαν, τῷ ἐκλέγεσθαι ὅσα ἂν ἐπιτήδεια ᾖ πρὸς τὸ τέλος;

Ἀλκ. σύμφημι.

Εὐφ. οὐκοῦν ὅσῳ μὲν ἄμεινον τὸ τέλος τὸ προκείμενον, ὅσῳ δὲ ἐπιτηδειότερα τὰ πρὸς τὸ τέλος, τοσούτῳ σοφώτερος ὁ πράττων νομιστέος;

Ἀλκ. εἰκός τοῦτό γε.

Εὐφ. τί δέ; ἆρά τι τέλος κάλλιον τῆς εὐδαιμονίας προθείη ἂν ὅ γε λόγῳ πράττων;

Ἀλκ. οὐδέν.

Εὐφ. τῶν δὲ ἀγαθῶν δήπου τὸ ὑπερβάλλον τῷ ἀγαθῷ καὶ κάλλιον ἂν εἴη;

Ἀλκ. κάλλιον μέντοι.

Εὐφ. οὐκοῦν μεῖζον ἀγαθὸν ἡ κοινὴ συμπάντων εὐδαιμονία τῆς ἑνός γέ του ἢ καὶ τοῦδε;

Ἀλκ. μεῖζον γάρ.

Εὐφ. συμβαίνει ἄρα κάλλιστον εἶναι τέλος τοῦτο;

Ἀλκ. ἔοικεν.

Εὐφ. οὐκοῦν καλεῖς σοφωτάτους εἶναι τοὺς διὰ τῶν ἐπιτηδειοτάτων ὁδῶν τούτου ἐπορεγομένους;

Ἀλκ. ἔγωγε.

Εὐφ. ὁ δὲ σοφὸς ἄγεται πότερον σοφίᾳ ἢ ἀφροσύνῃ;

Ἀλκ. σοφίᾳ δήπου.

Εὐφ. κινδυνεύει ἄρα συμβαίνειν, ὅστις τοῖς πρὸς τὸ τέλος ἀναγκαίοις οὖσιν ὀρθότατα χρώμενος σπεύδει τὸ κοινὸν συμπάντων ἀγαθόν, τοῦτον ὡς ἀληθῶς σοφὸν εἶναι καὶ πράττειν σοφίᾳ.

Ἀλκ. οἶμαι κινδυνεύειν καὶ τοῦτο.

s.   12

There he cast anchor, and, to prove the affections of the people, sent some of his men to land, making great boasts of the power that was to follow. The Kentish men, perceiving that Perkin was not followed by any English of name or account, and that his forces consisted but of strangers born, and most of them base people and freebooters, fitter to spoil a coast than to recover a kingdom; resorting unto the principal gentlemen of the country, professed their loyalty to the king, and desired to be directed and commanded for the best of the king's service. The gentlemen entering into consultation, directed some forces in good number to show themselves upon the coast ; and some of them to make signs to entice Perkin's soldiers to land, as if they would join with them ; and some others to appear from some other places, and to make semblance as if they fled from them, the better to encourage them to land. But Perkin, who, by playing the prince, or else taught by secretary Frion, had learned thus much, that people under command do use to consult, and after to march in order, and rebels contrariwise run upon an head together in confusion ; considering the delay of time, and observing their orderly and not tumultuary arming, doubted the worst.

BACON.

Ἐνταῦθα δὲ καθορμισάμενος, καὶ βουλόμενος ἀπο-
πειρᾶσθαι τῶν αὐτόθεν ὡς ἔχοιεν εὐνοίας, ἄνδρας τῶν
σφετέρων ἀπεβίβασε τὴν μέλλουσαν ἔτι κατάγεσθαι
δύναμιν μεγαλύνοντας. τοὺς δὲ Καντίους, οὔτε γὰρ
ἔλαθεν αὐτοὺς ὅτι οὐδεὶς ὅστις καὶ λόγου ἄξιος τῶν
ἐπιχωρίων μετὰ Περκίνου εἴη, ὁρῶντές τε τὴν στρατιὰν
ἀλλόφυλον οὖσαν, ἀνθρώπους μοχθηροὺς καὶ λῃστὰς
οἴους τῆς παραθαλασσίας μᾶλλον τέμνειν ἢ τὴν βασι-
λείαν ἀναλαβεῖν, ὡς τοὺς ἐκεῖ αὐτοῦ δυνατωτάτους
ἐτράποντο, ἅμα μὲν ἐπαγγελλόμενοι τὴν εὔνοιαν, ἐν
τῷ αὐτῷ δὲ ἐδέοντο ὅπως τις ἄρξει καὶ ἐξηγήσεται ὡς
ἂν μάλιστα ξυμφέρῃ τῷ βασιλεῖ. οἱ δὲ διαβουλευσά-
μενοι ἐκέλευον μέρος τι οὐκ ὀλίγον φανεροὺς εἶναι ἐν
τῷ αἰγιαλῷ, καὶ τοὺς μὲν σημεῖα ἄραντας ἐπισπάσασθαι
τοὺς μετὰ Περκίνου ἐς ἀπόβασιν ὡς προσχωρησομένους
δή, τοὺς δὲ ἔδει ἄλλους ἄλλοθεν ἀναφανῆναι φυγὴν
προσποιουμένους, ἐάν πως θαρσαλεώτερον ἀποβῆναι
προθυμῶνται. ὁ δὲ Πέρκινος, ἤτοι αὐτὸς ὑποκρινόμενος
βασιλεὺς εἶναι ἢ Φρίωνος διδάσκοντος τοῦ γραμματέως,
τοσοῦτον δ' οὖν εὖ ᾔδει τοὺς μὲν πειθαρχοῦντας ὅτι
βουλευσάμενοι οὕτως ὡς ἄν τις προστάσσῃ πορεύεσθαι
φιλοῦσι, οἱ δὲ ἐπαναστάντες τοὐναντίον ἀξυντάκτως
αὐτοὶ ἑαυτοῖς ἐμπαλάσσονται· ἀναλογισάμενος δὲ τὴν
διατριβὴν καὶ τὴν ὅπλισιν αἰσθόμενος ἐν κόσμῳ οὖσαν
καὶ ἐν οὐδενὶ θορύβῳ ἤδη ὑπώπτευε μὴ πάθῃ τὰ
ἔσχατα.

As to the abuses of anger, which it is to be observed may be in all different degrees, the first which occurs is what is commonly called passion ; to which some men are liable, in the same way as others are to the epilepsy, or any sudden particular disorder. This distemper of the mind seizes them upon the least occasion in the world, and perpetually without any real occasion at all : and by means of it they are plainly, every day, every waking hour of their lives, liable and in danger of running into the most extravagant outrages. Of a less boisterous, but not of a less innocent kind, is peevishness ; which I mention with pity, with real pity to the unhappy creatures, who, from their inferior station, or other circumstances and relations, are obliged to be in the way of, and to serve for a supply to it. Both these, for aught that I can see, are one and the same principle : but as it takes root in minds of different makes, it appears differently, and so is come to be distinguished by different names. That which in a more feeble temper is peevishness, and languidly discharges itself upon everything which comes in its way ; the same principle in a temper of greater force and stronger passions, becomes rage and fury. In one, the humour discharges itself at once ; in the other, it is continually discharging. This is the account of passion and peevishness, as distinct from each other, and appearing in different persons. It is no objection against the truth of it, that they are both to be seen sometimes in one and the same person.

BUTLER.

Ὅσα δὲ ἁμαρτάνουσι περὶ ὀργάς, ἃ ἐνδέχεται κατὰ
πάντα γίγνεσθαι διαφέροντα τῷ μᾶλλον καὶ ἧττον,
πρῶτον ἐπέρχεται τὴν ὀργιλότητα καλουμένην ἐπι-
σκέψασθαι, ᾗ εἰσὶν οἱ πεφύκασιν ἔνοχοι, καθάπερ καὶ
ἄλλοι ἐπιληπτικοὶ ἢ καὶ πρὸς ἄλλην τινὰ ἀποκεκρι-
μένην νόσον τῶν ἐξ αἰφνιδίου. ἡ δὲ καταβολὴ αὕτη
τῆς ψυχῆς ἐφ' ὁποιᾳοῦν προφάσει καταλαμβάνει τοὺς
τοιούτους, ἢ καὶ πολλάκις ἐπ' οὐδεμιᾷ, ὥστε διὰ ταύτην
δῆλον ὅτι ὁσημέραι καὶ δὴ καὶ πλειστάκις τῆς ἡμέρας
μὴ καθεύδοντες κινδυνεύουσιν εἰς τὰ ἀτοπώτατα προ-
χωρεῖν. τὴν δὲ σφοδροτέραν μὲν οὐ συγγνωμονικὴν
μέντοι οὐδὲν ἧττον λέγω δυσκολίαν. ἧς καὶ μεμνημένος
ἐποικτείρω τοὺς ἀθλιωτάτους τούτους, ὅστις ἤτοι ὑπο-
δεέστερος ὢν ἢ καὶ ἄλλως πως ἢ κατά τι ἢ πρός τι
διακείμενος μήτε ἐκποδὼν στῆναι δύναται τρέφειν τε
τὸ πάθος ἀναγκάζεται. ἀμφοῖν δή, ὅσα γε ἐμοὶ δοκεῖ,
μία καὶ ἡ αὐτὴ ἀρχὴ ἂν εἴη· ἄλλης μέντοι ἐν ἄλλῳ
ἐμφυομένης, ἀλλοία καὶ τὰ εἴδη, ὥστε διορισθῆναι ἰδίῳ
ἑκάτερον ὀνόματι. ἡ γὰρ ἀσθενεστέρας τινὸς φύσεως
ἐπιτυχοῦσα, καὶ πρὸς ὅ τι ἂν ᾖ ἐμποδὼν πρὸς τοῦτο
ἀνειμένως ἀποδιδοῦσα, ἔστω δυσκολία· ἡ δὲ αὐτὴ ἐπὶ
σφοδροτέρας τε καὶ βιαιοτέρας ψυχῆς εἰς μανίαν τε καὶ
ἀγριότητα ἀπεκρίθη. καὶ ἐνταῦθα μὲν εἰσάπαξ ἀπο-
δέδωκεν, ἐκεῖ δὲ οὐδέποτε παύεται. περὶ δὲ τῆς ὀργιλό-
τητος καὶ δυσκολίας ὡς ἑκατέρας ἀλλοίας οὔσης καὶ ἐν
ἑτέρῳ ἑτέρας ἀναφαινομένης ἐπὶ τοσοῦτον εἰρήσθω·
οὐδὲν δέ τι ἐλέγχει τὰ λεγόμενα ὅτι ἐν τῷ αὐτῷ ἔστιν
ὅτε συνδυάζεσθον.

What were her triumphs afterwards ? What was her success after she proceeded on the new plan ? I shall say something on that head immediately. Here let me only say, that the glory of taking towns and winning battles is to be measured by the utility that results from those victories. Victories, that bring honour to the arms, may bring shame to the councils, of a nation. To win a battle, to take a town, is the glory of a general, and of an army. Of this glory we had a very large share in the course of the war. But the glory of a nation is to proportion the end she proposes to her interest and her strength : the means she employs to the ends she proposes, and the vigour she exerts to both. Of this glory, I apprehend, we have had very little to boast of at any time, and particularly in the great conjuncture of which I am speaking. The reasons of ambition, avarice, and private interest, which engaged the princes and states of the confederacy to depart from the principles of the grand alliance, were no reasons for Great Britain. She neither expected nor desired anything more than what she might have obtained by adhering to those principles. What hurried our nation then with so much spirit and ardour into those of the new plan ?

BOLINGBROKE.

Ποία δὲ τὰ μετὰ ταῦτα ἡ πόλις τρόπαια ἔστησεν;
τί δὲ προὐχώρησεν αὐτῇ τὸ καινὸν τοῦτο ἐπιτήδευμα
ἐνστησαμένη; ἀλλὰ τούτων πέρι ἐρῶ τι αὐτίκα δὴ
μάλα, τοῦτο αὐτὸ ἐν τῷ παρόντι ὑπειπών, ὅτι τοῖς τὰς
πόλεις ἐκπολιορκοῦσι καὶ νικῶσι τὰς μάχας ὅσον τὸ
τῶν ἐνθένδε ἀποβησομένων συμφέρον τοσαύτη συμβέβηκεν εἶναι καὶ ἡ εὐδοξία. ἐνδέχεται γὰρ ταῖς πόλεσι
τὴν αὐτὴν νίκην καλὴν μὲν τοῖς στρατευομένοις, αἰσχίστην δὲ τοῖς πολιτευομένοις δόξαν περιάπτειν. εὐδοκιμεῖ
γὰρ ὁ μὲν στρατηγὸς αὐτός τε καὶ τοῖς περὶ αὐτὸν
χρώμενος νικῶν τὰς μάχας καὶ τὰς πόλεις ἐκπολιορκῶν,
ἡ δέ γε πόλις μέχρι τοῦ τε συμφέροντος καὶ τῆς
δυνάμεως ὁριζομένη τὸ τέλος τὸ προκείμενον, καὶ ὅσοις
μὲν χρῆται ἀναφέρουσα εἰς τοῦτο, τὸ δὲ πρόθυμον εἰς
ἀμφότερα. καὶ ἐκείνης μὲν τῆς εὐκλείας πλεῖστον
μετῆν ἡμῖν ἐν τῷ πολέμῳ, ταύτης δέ γ’, οἶμαι, μεταποιεῖσθαι οὐδέποτε εἴχομεν, ἐν δὲ τῷ τότε χρόνῳ
οὐδ’ ὁτιοῦν. ὅ τι γὰρ διανοούμενοι οἱ ἄλλοι, ἤτοι βασιλεύς τις ἢ πόλις, εἴτε διὰ πλεονεξίαν, εἴτε φιλοτιμίαν,
εἴτε καὶ τὸ ἰδίᾳ ἕκαστοι συμφέρον θεραπεύοντες, ἀπέ-
στησαν τῆς ὅτε ἡ ἐπὶ μεγάλοις συμμαχία συγκατέστη
προαιρέσεως, τούτων οὐδὲν Βρεταννοὶ ὄντες διενοήθημεν,
ἅτε οὐδὲν ἄλλο οὔτε ἀξιοῦντες οὔτε ἐφιέμενοι τῶν
γενομένων ἂν ἐχομένοις ἐκείνης τῆς προαιρέσεως—
τίνι οὖν ἐπαιρόμενοι προθυμότερον καὶ προπετέστερον
ἐπὶ τὴν καινὴν ταύτην ὡρμήσαμεν;

Another error, that hath also some affinity with the former, is a conceit that of former opinions or sects, after variety and examination, the best hath still prevailed and suppressed the rest : so as, if a man should begin the labour of a new search, he were but like to light upon somewhat formerly rejected, and by rejection brought into oblivion ; as if the multitude, or the wisest for the multitude's sake, were not ready to give passage rather to that which is popular and superficial than to that which is substantial and profound ; for the truth is, that time seemeth to be of the nature of a river or stream, which carrieth down to us that which is light and blown up, and sinketh and drowneth that which is weighty and solid.

Another error, of a diverse nature from all the former, is the over early and peremptory reduction of knowledge into arts and methods, from which time commonly sciences receive small or no augmentation. But as young men, when they knit and shape perfectly, do seldom grow to a farther stature, so knowledge, while it is in aphorisms and observations, it is in growth ; but when once it is comprehended in exact methods, it may perchance be farther polished and illustrated, and accommodated for use and practice, but it increaseth no more in bulk and substance.

BACON.

Ἄλλο τοίνυν ἁμαρτάνεται παραπλήσιόν τι τῷ προειρημένῳ, ὅστις οἴεται τῶν προτέρων δοξῶν τε καὶ προαιρέσεων πολλῶν τε οὐσῶν καὶ μετὰ ποικιλίας ἐξεταζομένων τὴν ἀρίστην ἀεὶ ἐκνενικηκέναι ἀφανίσασαν τὰς ἄλλας, ὥστε εἴ τις ἄρα πάλιν ἐξ ἀρχῆς τὸ αὐτὸ προσταλαιπωροίη διερευνώμενος κινδυνεύοι ἂν ἐπιτυχεῖν τῷ πάλαι ἀποδοκιμασθέντι καὶ δι᾽ αὐτὸ καὶ ἀμνηστουμένῳ· ὡς δὴ οὐκ ἂν τὸ πλῆθος καὶ δὴ καὶ αὐτοὶ οἱ χαρίεντες τοῦ πλήθους ἕνεκα ῥᾷον συγχωροῖεν τῷ πιθανῷ τε καὶ ἐπιπολῆς κειμένῳ ἢ τῷ ὄγκου τε καὶ μεγέθους εὖ ἔχοντι. τὸ δὲ ὁ χρόνος ῥείθρῳ τινὶ ἢ ποταμῷ πέφυκε παρόμοιος εἶναι, ὃς τὸ μὲν κοῦφον καὶ πεφυσημένον καταφέρει πρὸς ἡμᾶς, τὸ δὲ στερεὸν καὶ βαρύσταθμον κατέκλυσέ τε καὶ κατεπόντισεν. ἔτι δὲ καὶ ἄλλως ἁμαρτάνει ἀλλότριόν τι τῶν προειρημένων ὁ τὴν ἐπιστήμην εἰς τέχνας τινὰς καὶ μεθόδους πρωιαίτερον βιαζόμενος, ὅθεν ὡς ἐπὶ τὸ πολὺ ἤ τι ἢ οὐδὲν ἐπιδιδόασιν αἱ μαθήσεις. ἀλλὰ καθάπερ τὰ μειράκια διηρθρωμένα τε ἤδη καὶ εἰς τέλος ἀφιγμένα τῆς εὐμορφίας, οὐδέποτε ὡς ἔπος εἰπεῖν ἐπὶ τὸ μεῖζον αὐξάνεται, ὡς δ᾽ αὔτως καὶ ἡ ἐπιστήμη ἐν ἀφορισμοῖς μὲν οὖσα καὶ ζητήσεσιν ἐν ἐπιδόσει ἂν εἴη, ἐπειδὰν δὲ τάχιστα ἐν ἀκριβέσι μεθόδοις τις συμπεριλάβῃ, ἐνδέχεται μὲν εἰ τύχοι ἔτι μᾶλλον διασαφεῖν τε καὶ ἐκκαθαίρειν ὥστε ἱκανωτέραν εἶναι πρὸς τό τε πράττειν καὶ χρῆσθαι, τῷ μέντοι ὄγκῳ ἢ ἀριθμῷ οὐδὲν ἔτι διατελεῖ ἐπιδιδοῦσα.

The king, without any alteration in his countenance by all that insolent provocation, told them, that he was their king, they his subjects, who owed him duty and obedience ; that no parliament had any authority to call him before them ; but that they were not the parliament, nor had any authority from the parliament to sit in that manner ; that of all the persons who sat there, and took upon them to judge him, except those persons who being officers of the army he could not but know whilst he was forced to be amongst them, there were only two faces which he had ever seen before, or whose names were known to him. And after urging their duty that was due to him, and his superiority over them, by such lively reasons and arguments as were not capable of any answer, he concluded, that he would not so much betray himself and his royal dignity, as to answer any thing they objected against him, which were to acknowledge their authority ; though he believed that every one of themselves, as well as the spectators, did in their consciences absolve him from all the material things which were objected against him.

CLARENDON.

Ὁ δὲ βασιλεὺς μεταλλάξας τὴν ὄψιν πρὸς τὴν ὕβριν καὶ ἐπήρειαν οὐδοτιοῦν ἔφη αὐτὸς μὲν ἄρχειν ἐκείνους δὲ ἀρχομένους ἑαυτῷ κατὰ τὸ προσῆκον δεῖν πειθαρχεῖν, ἅμα λέγων ὅτι αὐτὸς μὲν ἀνεύθυνος εἴη τῇ βουλῇ, ἐκείνοις δὲ οὔτε μετεῖναι τῆς βουλῆς, οὔτε ἐπιτετράφθαι ὑπὸ τῆς βουλῆς τό γε τοιοῦτον δικάζειν. ἔτι δὲ τοὺς καθημένους καὶ δικάζειν οἰομένους δεῖν, τοὺς μὲν εἰδέναι ὅτι στρατηγοὶ εἶεν τῶν ἐναντίων ὡς βίᾳ συγγενόμενος αὐτοῖς, τῶν δὲ εἰ μὴ δυοῖν μόνοιν οὔτε ἑωρακέναι πω τὰ πρόσωπα οὔτε τὰ ὀνόματα ἀκηκοέναι. ἰσχυρισάμενος δὲ σφόδρα φανεροῖς καὶ ἀνεξελέγκτοις λόγοις καὶ ἀποδείξεσιν ἅ τε προσήκοι αὐτῷ παρ' ἐκείνων καὶ ὅσον ὑπερβαλλόντως ἔχοι, τελευτῶν ἐπεῖπεν ὅτι οὐ καταισχύνειν ἐθέλει αὐτόν τε καὶ τὸ ἀξίωμα τὸ βασιλικὸν ἀπολογούμενος πρὸς τῶν ἐγκεκλημένων ὁτιοῦν, ἵνα μὴ συμφῇ ἐπ' ἐκείνοις τὸ κῦρος εἶναι, καίπερ οὐκ ἀγνοῶν ἐκείνους αὐτούς τε καὶ τοὺς ἄλλους τοὺς παρόντας ὅτι τῶν ἐγκλημάτων ὅσα καὶ λόγου ἄξια πάντων οὐδεὶς ὅστις οὐκ ἀφίησιν, εἰ προνοεῖται ὅπως μὴ ἐπιορκήσει.

It may be said again, that a king of France has power enough by the constitution of that government to support a minister who checks corruption, reforms abuses, and maintains a frugal management of the public revenue. But it may be asked, how a minister, who should undertake this, could be supported in a government like ours, where he would be sure to have for his enemies all those who have shared so long the public spoils or who hope to share them, and where these enemies would have the means and opportunities of supplanting him, notwithstanding the protection of his master? I answer, by the parliament. How many ministers have there been, to whom much national mischief was imputed justly, and no one national good could be ascribed, and who were long supported by the favour of the crown, and by the concurrence of the two houses, which this favour and their own management procured them? Shall these supports be sufficient for a wicked or weak minister; and shall innocence and ability, with the same favour and better management, be reckoned for nothing? I cannot think so ill even of the present age, as degenerate as it is. It is degenerate, no doubt : but I have heard men complain of this degeneracy, who promoted it first, and sought their excuse in it afterwards.

BOLINGBROKE.

Ἀλλὰ νὴ Δί' ὁ μὲν Γαλάτης ἱκανῶς ἔχει ἐκ τῶν ἐκεῖ καθεστώτων τῷ συμβούλῳ βοηθεῖν ὅστις παύσει μὲν τοὺς διαφθεροῦντας, ἐπανορθώσει δὲ τὰ ἐσφαλμένα, ἔτι δὲ σωφρονιεῖ εἰς εὐτέλειαν τὰ δημοσίᾳ ἀναλισκόμενα· τὸν δὲ ἐν τῇ οἵᾳ παρ' ἡμῖν πολιτείᾳ τῷ τοιούτῳ ἐπιχειροῦντα τίς ἂν ἀσφαλῆ παρέχοι, μέλλοντά γε ἀπεχθέσθαι πρὸς ἅπαντας τοὺς ἐπὶ τοσοῦτον χρόνον ἤδη τῶν ἐκ δημοσίου κεκλεμμένων ἤτοι μετέχοντας ἢ ἐλπίζοντας, ἄνδρας εὐπορίᾳ τε καὶ εὐκαιρίᾳ χρωμένους τοῦ ὑποσκελίζειν αὐτόν, καὶ ταῦτα βοηθοῦντος αὐτοῦ τοῦ βασιλέως; τάχ' ἂν γὰρ καὶ τοῦτό τις ἂν ἀμφισβητήσειεν. ἀλλὰ διὰ τῆς συγκλήτου. πόσοις γὰρ ἤδη τῶν πολιτευομένων, ὧν κακὰ μὲν εἰς τὴν πόλιν παμπλήθη δικαίως κατηγορήθη ἀγαθὸν δὲ οὐδοτιοῦν, ἅμα μὲν ἐβοήθησεν ἡ τοῦ βασιλέως εὔνοια, ἅμα δὲ ἑκούσης ἔτυχον τῆς τε βουλῆς καὶ τῆς ἐκκλησίας διὰ τὴν τοιαύτην εὔνοιαν καὶ αὐτοὶ τῇ ἑαυτῶν δεξιότητι χρώμενοι; εἶτα τῷ μὲν πονηρῷ ἢ ἀσυνέτῳ συμβούλῳ ἱκανὴ ἔσται αὕτη ἡ βοήθεια, τῷ δέ γε δικαίῳ καὶ φρονίμῳ τῆς τε αὐτῆς εὐνοίας ἀξιωθέντι καὶ αὐτῷ δεξιωτέρῳ ὄντι παρ' οὐδὲν νομισθήσεται; ἀλλ' οὐδὲ τῆς νῦν γενεᾶς ἔγωγ' ἂν τοσαύτην ἀδικίαν καταγνοίην, πονηρᾶς μὲν οὔσης ὡς πάντες ἂν σύμφαιεν· ἀκούω δέ τινας καταμεμφομένους τὴν πονηρίαν, οἳ πρῶτον μὲν προήγαγον εἶτα αὐτὴν ταύτην ἀπελογήσαντο ὑπὲρ τῆς σφετέρας.

The honourable gentlemen are so ingenuous as to confess that our affairs, both abroad and at home, are at present in the utmost distress : but, say they, you ought to free yourselves from this distress, before you inquire how, or by what means, you were brought into it. Sir, according to this way of arguing, a minister that has plundered and betrayed his country, and fears being called to account in parliament, has nothing to do but to involve his country in a dangerous war, or some other great distress, in order to prevent an inquiry into his conduct, because he may be dead before that war is at an end or that distress got over. Thus, like the most villainous of all thieves, after he has plundered the house, he has nothing to do but to set it in a flame, that he may escape in the confusion. It is really astonishing to hear such an argument seriously urged in this house ; but, say these gentlemen, if you found yourself upon a precipice, would you stand to inquire how you were led there, before you considered how to get off ? No, Sir : but if a guide had led me there, I should very probably be provoked to throw him over, before I thought of anything else ; at least, I am sure I should not trust to the same guide for bringing me off, and this, Sir, is the strongest argument that can be used for an inquiry.

Οὗτοι τοίνυν τὰ μὲν παρόντα πράγματα, τά τε ἐνθάδε καὶ τὰ ἔξωθεν, ἐν πάσῃ ἀπορίᾳ εἶναι ὡς ἁπλοῖ δή τινες ὄντες ὁμολογοῦσι· δεῖν μέντοι ἀπαλλαγέντας τῆς ἀπορίας οὕτως ἤδη ὅπως καὶ ὁπόθεν καθέστατε εἰς αὐτὴν ἐξετάζειν. καίτοι κατά γε τὸν λογισμὸν τουτονὶ τὸν ῥήτορα τὸν κλέψαντα τὰ τῆς πόλεως καὶ προδόντα αὐτήν, φοβούμενον μὴ εὐθύνας δῷ ἐν ὑμῖν, οὐδὲν ἄλλο δεῖ ἢ τὴν πόλιν ἀνηκέστῳ πολέμῳ ἢ ἄλλῃ τινὶ τῶν μεγίστων ἀπορίᾳ περιβαλόντα ὅπως μὴ ἐξετάσει τις τὰ πεπολιτευμένα προκαταλαβεῖν. ἐνδέχεται γὰρ δὴ πρὶν πέρας ἔχειν τὸν πόλεμον ἢ ἐκ τῆς ἀπορίας περιγενέσθαι αὐτὸν τελευτῆσαι. ὡσπερανεὶ ὁ κακουργότατος τῶν λῃστῶν, λείαν ποιησάμενος τὴν οἰκίαν, μηδὲν ἄλλο ἢ ἐμπρήσειεν αὐτήν, ἵνα δὴ τῶν ἄλλων θορυβουμένων αὐτὸς ἀποδρᾷ. ταῦτα γὰρ παρ᾽ ὑμῖν τινες σπουδῇ πάνυ ἰσχυρίζονται, ὃ καὶ ἐγὼ ὡς ἀληθῶς θαυμάζω. ἀλλά φασιν οὗτοι· σὺ γὰρ ἄν, εἰ ἐπὶ κρημνοῦ τύχοις γενόμενος, καθήμενος, οἶμαι, πρότερον ἐξετάζοις τίνι τρόπῳ ἐκεῖσε ἀνέβης, ἀλλ᾽ οὐ τί ἂν ποιῶν καταβαίης βουλεύσαιο; οὐκ ἂν οἶμαι τοῦτό γε. εἰ δὲ ἡγεμόνι τινὶ χρώμενος ἀνέβην, εἰκότως ἂν ὀργιζόμενος πρῶτον μὲν κατεκρήμνισα αὐτόν, ἔπειτα τὰ ἐντεῦθεν ἂν ἐσκοπούμην. τοσοῦτο δ᾽ οὖν οἶδα, οὐκ ἂν ἔτι τῷ αὐτῷ πειθοίμην μέλλων γε εἰς τὸ ἀσφαλὲς καταβῆναι· ᾧ καὶ οὐχ ἥκιστα ἰσχυριζόμενος παραδείγματι λέγω ὅτι ποιητέον ἐστὶ τὴν ἐξέτασιν.

The proverbial truth tells us 'extremes meet,' as in this case also is verified; whereas the mean which our Church holds will never meet with either extreme; they parted off from it; and, however slight the original divergence, become more and more widely separated from it, and never again join. To a careless or superficial thinker, the mean seems likely to join the extreme, because it has in it some quality which is wanting to the other extreme; but it is not so; it agrees with the extreme, not in essentials, but in something incidental; the rash man appears to have one quality in common with the brave one, in that he exposes himself to danger; the brave man's caution may readily appear like cowardice; and so the rash thinks the brave cowardly, and the coward holds him to be rash; whereas the exposing himself to danger or no, is but an accident; the principle on which he does it, or refrains from it, is that which constitutes his character; he then will neither be rash nor cowardly; but the coward will be rash, and the rash will be cowardly, if emergencies so determine. Prodigality and avarice seem to be contraries; yet are they continually united, as in Catiline, '*alieni appetens, sui profusus*'; he who is simply liberal will be neither, though by either extreme he will be confounded with the other. 'Extremes meet,' because they proceed on no settled principle, but on passion; they are guided by no internal rules, but are blown about, this way or that, by the force of outward circumstances; the mean goes on fixed principles, and therefore holds on an even course, undeviating and therefore never approximating to either extreme.

PUSEY.

Τὸ δὲ λεγόμενον ἔχεσθαι ἀλλήλων τὰ ἄκρα φαίνεται κἀνταῦθα συμβαίνειν. τὸ δὲ μέσον τὸ τῆς ἡμετέρας ἐκκλησίας οὐδ' εἰς ἕτερον τούτοιν μηδέποτε συνδράμῃ. ἀπεστήτην γὰρ αὐτοῦ, καὶ δι' ὁποσουανοῦν τὸ ἐξ ἀρχῆς ἀποκλίναντε ἐπὶ τὸ πλέον ἔτι ἀεὶ διίστασθον, ὥστε μηδέποτε αὖθις εἰς ἓν συντείνειν. τῷ μὲν δὴ οὑτωσὶ εἰκῇ σκοπουμένῳ κινδυνεύοι ἂν τὸ μέσον τῷ ἑτέρῳ τοῖν ἄκροιν συναρμόττειν, ἅτε ἐνυπάρχον τι τούτῳ ὃ τῷ ἑτέρῳ ἐλλείπει· τὸ δὲ συνᾴδετον ἀλλήλοιν οὐ κατὰ τὴν οὐσίαν ἀλλὰ κατὰ συμβεβηκός. οἷον δοκεῖ κοινόν τι εἶναι τῷ ἀνδρείῳ πρὸς τὸν θρασὺν ἢ ἄμφω φιλοκίνδυνοι· ἡ δὲ εὐλάβεια τοῦ ἀνδρείου ῥᾳδίως ἂν δειλία νομίζοιτο· ὅθεν καὶ ἀποκαλοῦσιν αὐτὸν ὁ μὲν θρασὺς δειλὸν ὁ δὲ δειλὸς θρασύν· τὸ δὲ συμβέβηκεν αὐτῷ κινδυνεύειν ἢ μή· ἡ δὲ προαίρεσις καθ' ἣν πράττει ἢ οὔ, τοῦτο αὐτὸ κρίνει τὸ ἦθος. οὔκουν οὗτός γε οὔτε θρασὺς οὔτε δειλὸς ἂν εἴη· ὁ δὲ δειλὸς θρασὺς καὶ ὁ θρασὺς δειλὸς ὡς ἂν ἡγῆται τὰ ἀποβαίνοντα. φαίνεται δὲ καὶ ἀσωτία καὶ ἀνελευθερία ἐναντία· πολλάκις μέντοι συνδυάζονται, οἷον ἐπὶ Κατιλίνου λέγεται, ἐφίεσθαι μὲν τῶν ἀλλοτρίων τῶν δ' οἰκείων προΐεσθαι. ὁ δὲ ἁπλῶς ἐλεύθεριος οὐδέτερος ἂν εἴη, καίπερ τῶν ἄκρων ἑκατέρου πρὸς ἑκάτερον ἀπωθουμένων· ἔχεται δὲ ἀλλήλων τὰ ἄκρα, ἅτε ἀπὸ πάθους ὁρμώμενα ἀλλ' οὐ βεβαίως κατὰ προαίρεσιν. οὔτε γὰρ ὑπὸ τῶν ἔνδοθεν ἀρχῶν κινεῖται, ἄγεταί τε ἑκατέρωσε ὑπὸ τῶν ἐκτός· ἡ δὲ μεσότης βεβαίως πορεύεται καὶ ὡς ἂν ὁ λόγος· διὸ καὶ ὀρθῶς καὶ ἀμεταβόλως ὥστε μηδ' ἑτέρῳ τοῖν ἄκροιν σύνεγγυς εἶναι.

At that time came more confident advertisement, though false, not only to the lord admiral, but to the court, that the Spaniards could not possibly come forward that year ; whereupon our navy was upon the point of disbanding, and many of our men gone ashore : at which very time the Invincible Armada, for so it was called in a Spanish ostentation throughout Europe, was discovered upon the western coast. It was a kind of surprise ; for that, as was said, many of our men were gone to land, and our ships ready to depart. Nevertheless the admiral, with such ships only as could suddenly be put in readiness, made forth towards them ; insomuch as of one hundred ships there came scarce thirty to work. Howbeit, with them, and such as came daily in, we set upon them, and gave them the chase. But the Spaniards, for want of courage, which they called commission, declined the fight, casting themselves continually into roundels, their strongest ships walling in the rest, and in that manner they made a flying march towards Calais. Our men by the space of five or six days followed them close, fought with them continually, made great slaughter of their men, took two of their great ships, and gave divers others of their ships their death's wounds, whereof soon after they sank and perished ; and, in a word, distressed them almost in the nature of a defeat ; we ourselves in the mean time receiving little or no hurt.

BACON.

Ἐν δὲ τούτῳ ἦλθεν ἀγγελία οὐ μόνον τῷ ναυάρχῳ ἀλλὰ καὶ τοῖς ἐν τέλει ψευδὴς μὲν πολλῷ δὲ μᾶλλον ἰσχυριζομένων, ὡς ἄρα οὐχ οἷοί τ᾽ εἶεν ἐπιέναι τό γε ἔτος τοῦτο οἱ Ἴβηρες· οὗ δὴ ὅσον οὐ διελέλυτο τὸ ναυτικὸν ἡμῶν, καὶ πολλοὶ ἤδη καὶ ἀπεβεβήκεσαν ἐκλιπόντες τὰς ναῦς. κατὰ δὲ τὸν καιρὸν αὐτὸν τοῦτον ὁ ἀήσσητος δὴ καλούμενος στόλος, ἐλλόγιμος γὰρ ἤδη ἐγένετο ἐς τὴν ἤπειρον ὡς τῶν Ἰβήρων ἐπὶ πολὺ μεγαλυνόντων, φανερὸς ἦν καταπλέων τὰ πρὸς ἑσπέραν· καὶ ἔλαθέ πως καταπλέων· πολλοί τε γὰρ ἤδη ἀπελελοίπεσαν τὰς ναῦς, ὥσπερ εἴρηται, αὐταί τε ἤδη ἔμελλον ἀποπλεῖν. ὁ δὲ ναύαρχος ὅμως δι᾽ ὀλίγου αἰφνιδίως παρασκευασάμενος ὅσας δὴ ναῦς ἐποιεῖτο τὸν ἐπιπλοῦν, ἀπὸ γὰρ τῶν ἑκατὸν μόλις ἀνήγετο τριάκοντα. ταύτας δ᾽ οὖν ἔχοντες καὶ ὁπόσαι παραγένοιντο ὁσημέραι ἐπιθέμενοι αὐτοῖς ἐδιώκομεν. οἱ δὲ Ἴβηρες, εἴτε καὶ ἀνδρείᾳ ἐλλιπεῖς εἴτε καὶ ὡς ἔφασαν κατὰ τὰ ἐπεσταλμένα, διαναυμαχῆσαι μὲν οὐκ ἤθελον, κύκλους δὲ ἀεὶ ἑαυτῶν ταξάμενοι, τῶν πλωιμωτέρων ἐντὸς ἀποκλεισασῶν τὰς ἄλλας, οὕτω δὴ φυγὴν ἐποιοῦντο ἐπὶ τοῦ Ἰτίου λιμένος. ἡμεῖς δὲ ἐς πέντε μάλιστα ἢ ἓξ ἡμέρας κατὰ πόδας διώκοντες, καὶ πολλὰς μὲν προσβολὰς ποιούμενοι πολλοὺς δὲ ἀποκτείναντες, τὰς μὲν δύο ναῦς εἵλομεν, αἱ δὲ ἄλλαι οὐκ ὀλίγαι κατατετραυματισμέναι κατέδυσαν καὶ οὕτω δὴ ἀπώλοντο· ὥστε καὶ ὡς ξυνελόντι εἰπεῖν οἱ μὲν ἐταλαιπωροῦντο οὐδὲν ἧσσον ἢ κρατούμενοι, αὐτοὶ δὲ ἤ τι ἢ οὐδὲν ἐβλαπτόμεθα.

The sophists at first embraced in their course of instruction philosophy as well as rhetoric. But that which they called philosophy was, as with the scholastic philosophers, the art of confounding an opponent by syllogisms and sophisms; and the subjects about which they were most fond of speculating were some of those metaphysical questions, respecting which we ought to learn that we never can know anything. This kind of reasoning, when disputation and speaking were taught, was very closely connected with rhetoric. Afterwards the sophists and rhetoricians formed distinct classes; but the different classes which Isocrates distinguished in his old age could hardly have been so decidedly marked in his youth.

The precepts and the very name of the sophists became odious among the ancients: and it would be vain to attempt to free them entirely from the reproaches cast on them by philosophers and by the comic poets. But yet they cannot be deprived of the glory of having made the higher classes of their nation sensible of the necessity of a liberal education. They rose rapidly and extraordinarily, because they were closely connected with the wants of the times. In states where all subjects were discussed orally, and where everything was just beginning to improve, instructors in logic and rhetoric could not but be acceptable. But in two respects, by reducing eloquence to a mere art of disputing, and by degrading or ridiculing the popular religion, they soon became injurious and even dangerous to the state.

HEEREN.

Τὸ μὲν οὖν πρῶτον ῥητορικὴν ἅμα καὶ φιλοσοφίαν ἐπηγγέλλοντο οἷοί τ᾽ εἶναι διδάσκειν οἱ σοφισταί. ᾧ μέντοι ἐπωνόμαζον φιλοσοφίαν, καθάπερ καὶ παρὰ τοῖς ἀπὸ σχολῆς καλουμένοις, καὶ παρὰ τούτοις τέχνη τις ἐγένετο τοῦ τὸν προσδιατρίβοντα συλλογισμοῖς καὶ ἀπάτῃ λόγου χρωμένους εἰς ἀπορίαν ἐμβάλλειν. ὧν γοῦν ἀσμεναίτατα πέρι ἐσκοποῦντο νοητὰ ἄττα ἦν, περὶ ὧν τοσοῦτον δεῖ μανθάνειν ὅτι οὐδαμῶς οὐδέποτε ἐπιστητὰ ἂν εἴη. ὁ δὲ τοιοῦτος λογισμὸς διδασκόντων τῶν τότε τὸ ἀμφισβητεῖν καὶ ὅπως τις δεινὸς λέγειν ἔσται ὡς ἐγγυτάτω εἴχετο τῆς ῥητορικῆς. ὕστερον δὲ χρόνῳ οἱ σοφισταὶ καὶ ῥήτορες ἑτέραν ἑκάτεροι τάξιν εἶχον. καίτοι ἅς γε ἤδη γέρων ὢν διωρίσατο Ἰσοκράτης σχολῇ γ᾽ ἂν εἶεν οὕτω παγίως νεωτέρου ὄντος ἀποκεχωρισμέναι. τὰ δ᾽ οὖν δόγματα τὰ τῶν σοφιστῶν καὶ δὴ καὶ αὐτὸ τὸ ὄνομα ἐπίφθονον τοῖς πάλαι ἐγένετο, ὥστε ὁ παντάπασι μέλλων ἀπολύειν ὧν ἔψεγον οἵ τε φιλόσοφοι καὶ οἱ κωμῳδοδιδάσκαλοι ὥσπερ ἂν ὕδραν τέμνοι. οὐ μὴν οὐδὲ τοῦ πεῖσαι τοὺς τῶν ἐπιχωρίων βελτίονας ὡς ἀναγκαῖον εἴη ἡ ὀρθὴ παιδεία δίκαιοί εἰσι τὸν ἔπαινον τοῦτον ἀφαιρεθῆναι, θαυμασίως δ᾽ ὡς ἐν βραχεῖ χρόνῳ ἐλλόγιμοι ηὐξήθησαν ἅτε τὰς τότε χρείας ὡς μάλιστα ἀποπληροῦντες. ὅπου γὰρ οὐδὲν ὅ τι οὐκ ἀπεστοματίζετο καὶ πάντα ἤδη ἐπὶ τὸ βέλτιον ἐπεδίδου, οὐδεμία μηχανὴ ἔν γε τοσαύταις πόλεσι μὴ οὐκ εὐδοκιμεῖν τοὺς διαλεκτικὴν καὶ ῥητορικὴν διδάσκοντας. οὐ μὴν ἀλλὰ δυοῖν ἔνεκα, τὸ μὲν ὅτι ἐριστικήν τινα τέχνην τὴν τοῦ λέγειν δεινότητα ἐβιάζοντο εἶναι, τὸ δὲ τὴν περὶ τὰ θεῖα νόμισιν ἤτοι κατασμικρίζοντες ἢ εἰς γέλωτα τρέποντες δι᾽ ὀλίγου οὐχ ὅτι βλαβεροὶ ἀλλὰ καὶ ὀλέθριοι ἐγένοντο ταῖς πόλεσιν.

But, Sir, in wishing to put an end to pernicious experiments, I do not mean to preclude the fullest enquiry. Far from it. Far from deciding on a sudden or partial view, I would patiently go round and round the subject, and survey it minutely in every possible aspect. Sir, if I were capable of engaging you to an equal attention, I would state that, as far as I am capable of discerning, there are but three ways of proceeding relative to this stubborn spirit, which prevails in your colonies, and disturbs your government. These are, to change that spirit, as inconvenient, by removing the causes, to prosecute it as criminal, or to comply with it as necessary. I would not be guilty of an imperfect enumeration; I can think of but these three. Another has indeed been stated, that of giving up the colonies; but it met so slight a reception, that I do not think myself obliged to dwell a great while upon it. It is nothing but a little sally of anger; like the frowardness of peevish children; who, when they cannot get all they would have, are resolved to take nothing.

BURKE.

'Αλλ', ὦ ἄνδρες, βουλόμενος ἀποπαύειν τὰ μετὰ κινδύνου ἐγχειρήματα, οὔκουν ἐθέλω τὸν ἀκριβέστατον ἐξετασμὸν ἐμποδίζειν, οὐδὲ πολλοῦ δεῖ· οὐ γὰρ ὅπως ἐπιπολῆς οὑτωσὶ οὐδὲ κατὰ μέρος διακρίνω ταῦτα, ἀλλὰ καθ' ἡσυχίαν δοκεῖ μοι πανταχόθεν περισκοπεῖν, καθ' ἕκαστον πάντῃ πάντως διορῶντα ὡς ἂν μάλιστα δύνωμαι. εἰ δ' ἐπ' ἐμοὶ εἴη πείθειν καὶ ὑμᾶς εἰς τὸ καὶ αὐτοὺς προσέχειν ὁμοίως τὸν νοῦν, δηλώσαιμ' ἂν ὅτι καθ' ὅσον γε ἐπ' ἐμοί ἐστι τὸ προϊδεῖν, τρεῖς μόναι ὑπάρχουσιν ὁδοὶ τοῦ ἰέναι, εἴ τις μέλλει τῇ ἀσελγείᾳ ταύτῃ ἀντιστῆναι, οἵα κατέχει τὸ παραυτίκα ἐν ταῖς ἀποικίαις ἡμῶν καὶ συνταράττει τὴν πολιτείαν. ταύτην γὰρ ἤτοι μεταβάλλειν δεῖ ὡς ἀνεπιτήδειον οὖσαν, ἀφανίσαντας τὰς ἐμποιούσας αἰτίας, ἢ ὡς ἄδικον εἰς δίκην ὑπακτέον, ἢ καὶ ὡς ἀναγκαίαν ἐατέον. ἐγὼ μὲν γὰρ οὐδὲν ἄλλο ὁρῶ, καίπερ σπεύδων τὴν αἰτίαν ἀποφυγεῖν τοῦ ἐνδεέστερον ἀπαριθμῆσαι. οὐ μὴν ἀλλὰ εἰσὶν οἱ τέταρτον τοῦτο μαντεύονται, ὡς ἄρα δεῖ αὐτονόμους ἀφεῖναι. καίτοι ὀλίγοι δὴ ἦσαν οἱ τοῦτό γε ἀποδεχόμενοι, ὥστε μηδ' ἐμοὶ προσήκειν, ὥς γε ἐμαυτὸν πείθω, ἐν τούτῳ μᾶλλον ἔτι διατρίβειν. τί γὰρ ἄλλο φαίνεται ἢ ἀσθενής τις ὀργὴ ἀπορρέουσα, οἵα δυσκολία παιδίων τινῶν ἀγανακτούντων, καὶ εἰ μὴ πάντα ὅσα βούλονται κατέχειν ἔξεστιν οὐδ' ὁτιοῦν ἑτοίμως ἂν λαμβανόντων;

Philonous.   It seems then that by sensible things you mean those only which can be perceived immediately by sense.

Hylas.   Right.

Phil.   Doth it not follow from this, that though I see one part of the sky red, and another blue, and that my reason doth thence evidently conclude there must be some cause of that diversity of colours, yet that cause cannot be said to be a sensible thing, or perceived by the sense of seeing ?

Hyl.   It doth.

Phil.   In like manner, though I hear variety of sounds, yet I cannot be said to hear the causes of those sounds.

Hyl.   You cannot.

Phil.   And when by my touch I perceive a thing to be hot and heavy, I cannot say with any truth or propriety, that I feel the cause of its heat or weight.

Hyl.   To prevent any more questions of this kind, I tell you once for all, that by sensible things I mean those only which are perceived by sense, and that in truth the senses perceive nothing which they do not perceive immediately : for they make no inferences. The deducing therefore of causes or occasions from effects and appearances, which alone are perceived by sense, entirely relates to reason.

Φιλ. Τὰ δὲ αἰσθητά, ὡς ἔοικας, τοιαῦτά που ὑπολαμβάνεις εἶναι οἷα ἡ αἴσθησις ἀπὸ τοῦ εὐθέος καταλαμβάνει.

Ὑλ. ὑπολαμβάνω γάρ.

Φιλ. οὐκοῦν ἐκ τούτων γε συμβαίνει ὅτι τὰ τοῦ οὐρανοῦ ὁρῶν τὸ μὲν ἐρυθρὸν φαινόμενον τὸ δὲ κυανοῦν, καὶ ἐνθένδε συλλογιζομένης τῆς διανοίας ὡς ὑπάρχοντος αἰτίου τινὸς τῆς ἐναντιότητος ταύτης, ὅμως οὐ δίκαιος ἂν εἴην περὶ τοῦ αἰτίου λέγων ὡς αἰσθητοῦ ὄντος καὶ διὰ τῆς ὄψεως καταληπτοῦ;

Ὑλ. συμβαίνει μὲν οὖν.

Φιλ. ὡσαύτως δὲ ὅτι φωνὰς ἀκούων παντοδαπάς, οὐ μέντοι ἀκούω καὶ τὰς αἰτίας αὐτῶν;

Ὑλ. συμβαίνει καὶ τοῦτο.

Φιλ. καὶ δὴ καὶ ὅτι ἐφαπτόμενός του καταλαμβάνω μὲν διὰ τῆς ἐπαφῆς ὅτι θερμόν ἐστι καὶ βαρύ, τῆς δὲ αἰτίας ἑκατέροιν, λέγω δὲ τῆς θερμότητος καὶ βαρύτητος, οὐκ ἐφάπτομαι, εἴπερ μέλλει τις ἀληθῶς λέγειν καὶ μετρίως;

Ὑλ. ἵνα τοίνυν μὴ ἀδολεσχῇς πλείω τοιαῦτα ἐρόμενος, συλλήβδην ἐρῶ ὅτι τὰ αἰσθητὰ δοκεῖ μοι εἶναι τοιάδε οἷα τῇ αἰσθήσει καταληπτά ἐστι. τῷ δὲ ὄντι οὐδενὸς πάνυ αἱ αἰσθήσεις αἰσθάνονται οὗ μὴ ἀπὸ τοῦ εὐθέος αἰσθάνονται· οὐδὲν γὰρ ἄρα συλλογίζονται. ὥστε τὸ συλλογίζεσθαι τὰς αἰτίας καὶ τὰς προφάσεις ἀπὸ τῶν συμβαινόντων καὶ τῶν φαινομένων, ἅπερ καὶ μόνα δὴ καταληπτά ἐστι διὰ τῆς αἰσθήσεως, τοῦτο οὐδενὸς ἄλλου ἢ τοῦ λογιστικοῦ ἂν εἴη.

Phil. This point, then, is agreed between us, that sensible things are those only which are immediately perceived by sense. You will further inform me, whether we immediately perceive by sight anything beside light and colours and figures : or by hearing, anything but sounds : by the palate, anything beside tastes : by the smell, beside odours : or by the touch, more than tangible qualities.

Hyl. We do not.

Phil. It seems, therefore, that if you take away all sensible qualities, there remains nothing sensible.

Hyl. I grant it.

Phil. Sensible things, therefore, are nothing else but so many sensible qualities, or combinations of sensible qualities.

Hyl. Nothing else.

Phil. Heat then is a sensible thing.

Hyl. Certainly.

Phil. Doth the reality of sensible things consist in being perceived ? or is it something distinct from their being perceived, and that bears no relation to the mind ?

Hyl. To exist is one thing, and to be perceived is another.

Phil. I speak with regard to sensible things only : and of these I ask, whether by their real existence you mean a subsistence exterior to the mind, and distinct from their being perceived ?

Hyl. I mean a real absolute being, distinct from and without any relation to their being perceived.

BERKELEY.

Φιλ. ταῦτα τοίνυν ὡμολογήσθω παρ' ἐμοί τε καὶ σοὶ ὅτι τοιαῦτά ἐστι τὰ αἰσθητὰ οἷα ἡ αἴσθησις ἀπὸ τοῦ εὐθέος καταλαμβάνει· ἐκεῖνο δὲ ἔτι ἀναπλήρωσόν μοι, εἰ διὰ μὲν τῆς ὄψεως ἀπὸ τοῦ εὐθέος οὐδὲν ἄλλο αἰσθανόμεθα ἀλλ' ἢ φῶς καὶ σχήματα καὶ χρώματα, διὰ δὲ τῆς ἀκοῆς φωνάς, διὰ δὲ τῆς γεύσεως χυμούς, διὰ δὲ τῆς ὀσφρήσεως ὀσμάς, διὰ δὲ τῆς ἐπαφῆς τὰ ἁπτά;

Τλ. οὐδὲν ἄλλο.

Φιλ. κινδυνεύει ἄρα, ἢν πάντα ἀφέλῃς δι' ὧν τις ἄν τι αἰσθάνοιτο, οὐδὲν ἔτι αἰσθητὸν μένειν;

Τλ. ὁμολογῶ.

Φιλ. ἄλλο τι οὖν λέγεις τὸ αἰσθητὸν ἢ ὁσαδήποτε ποιεῖ τὴν αἴσθησιν ἢ ἄθροισίν γε τούτων;

Τλ. οὐδὲν ἄλλο.

Φιλ. οὐκοῦν θερμὸν αἰσθητόν τι;

Τλ. πῶς γὰρ οὔ;

Φιλ. τί οὖν; τὸ εἶναι τὰ αἰσθητὰ τὸ αὐτό ἐστι καὶ τὸ αἰσθάνεσθαι ἡμᾶς αὐτά, ἢ κεχωρισμένον τι τούτου καὶ οὐδὲν τῇ διανοίᾳ ἡμῶν προσῆκον;

Τλ. ἕτερον μὲν τὸ εἶναι, ἕτερον δὲ τὸ τοὺς αἰσθανομένους ἔχειν.

Φιλ. μέμνησο μέντοι ὅτι τὰ αἰσθητὰ μόνον λέγω· πυνθάνομαι δὲ περὶ τούτων εἰ σὺ εἶναι αὐτὰ λέγων ὡς ἀληθῶς οὐσίαν τινὰ λέγεις ἔξω τῆς διανοίας ὑπάρχουσαν πρὸς οὐδένα λόγον τοῦ αἰσθάνεσθαί τινα αὐτά;

Τλ. ἁπλῶς καὶ ἄντικρυς οὐσίαν λέγω καὶ ταῦτα εἴτε τις αἰσθάνεται εἴτε μή.

It was never doubted but a war upon pirates may
be lawfully made by any nation, though not infested or
violated by them.   Is it because they have not *certas sedes*
or *lares*?   In the piratical war, which was achieved by
Pompey the great, and was his truest and greatest glory ;
the pirates had some cities, sundry ports, and a great part
of the province of Cilicia ; and the pirates now being have
a receptacle and mansion in Algiers.   Beasts are not the
less savage because they have dens.   Is it because the
danger hovers as a cloud, that a man cannot tell where it
will fall; and so it is every man's case ?   The reason is
good, but it is not all, nor that which is most alleged.   For
the true received reason is, that pirates are *communes
humani generis hostes* ; whom all nations are to prosecute,
not so much on the right of their own fears, as upon the
band of human society.   For as there are formal and
written leagues, respective to certain enemies ; so is there
a natural and tacit confederation amongst all men, against
the common enemy of human society.   So as there needs
no intimation or denunciation of the war ; there needs no
request from the nation grieved ; but all these formalities
the law of nature supplies in the case of pirates.   The same
is the case of rovers by land ; such as yet are some cantons
in Arabia, and some petty kings of the mountains, adjacent
to straits and ways.

BACON.

Καὶ ὅτι οὐ θέμις πρὸς τοὺς λῃστὰς πόλει ἡτινιοῦν ποιεῖσθαι πόλεμον, καὶ ταῦτα μηδὲν ἀδικοῦντας μηδὲ βιαζομένους, οὐδείς πω ἠμφεσβήτησε. τί γάρ; ἢ ὅτι οὐδεμίαν οἴκησιν καὶ δίαιταν ἀφωρισμένην κέκτηνται; καίτοι ἔν τε τῷ λῃστικῷ καλουμένῳ πολέμῳ, ὃν πολεμήσας Πομπήιος ὁ μέγας ταύτην ὡς ἀληθῶς μεγίστην δόξαν ἠνέγκατο, οἱ τότε λῃσταὶ πόλεις τινὰς εἶχον καὶ λιμένας ἔστιν οὓς καὶ μέρος τι οὐκ ὀλίγον Κιλικίας, καὶ τοῖς νῦν ἀποστροφὴ ὑπάρχει καὶ οἴκησις ἡ Νομαδική. οὐδὲ γὰρ ἧττον ὠμὰ ὅσα τῶν θηρίων σπηλαίοις κατῴκηται. ἢ τοῦτο αἴτιον ὅτι ὥσπερ νεφέλη τις ἐπικρέμαται ὁ κίνδυνος, ἄδηλον ὂν ὅποι καὶ κατασκήψει, ὥστε οὐδενὶ ὅτῳ οὐ μέλει τοῦτό γε; εἰκότως ἔχει καὶ αὕτη ἡ αἰτία, ἐλλείπει μέντοι τι, καὶ ἄλλην τινὰ οἱ πλεῖστοι αἰτιῶνται. ἡ γὰρ ἀληθὴς καὶ νενομισμένη ἥδε· οἱ γὰρ τοιοῦτοι κοινοί εἰσι τοῦ ἀνθρωπίνου γένους πολέμιοι, οἷς πᾶσαν πόλιν ἐπεξελθεῖν δεῖ, οὐ μᾶλλον κατὰ τὸ δίκαιον τοῦ ἰδίου ἑκάστην δέους ἕνεκα, ἢ ὡς ἐπὶ συνδέσμῳ τῆς πρὸς ἀλλήλους κοινωνίας. οὐ γὰρ μόνον πρὸς τοὺς ἀφωρισμένους πολεμίους ἐπὶ ῥητοῖς συγγραφόμεθα συμμαχίας, ἀλλὰ καὶ φύσει τις ὑπάρχει ἄγραφος συνωμοσία ὡς ἐπὶ τῷ κοινῷ συμπάντων πολεμίῳ. διὸ καὶ οὐδὲν δεῖ οὔτε ἐπαγγέλλειν πόλεμον τοὺς μέλλοντας, οὔτε βοηθείας δεῖσθαι τοὺς ἀδικουμένους· τὰ τοιαῦτα γὰρ ἐκεῖ μὲν ἐπὶ ῥητοῖς κεῖται, ἐνταῦθα δὲ ὁ φυσικὸς νόμος εἴ τι ἐλλείπει ἀναπληροῖ. ἀρκεῖ δὲ καὶ τὸ αὐτὸ καὶ ἐπὶ τῶν κατὰ γῆν λῃστείας ποιουμένων· οἷον ἔτι νομίζουσιν ἔστιν ἃ Ἀραβίας πολίσματα καὶ οἱ τῶν ὀρεινῶν βασιλεῖς ὁδῶν ἢ στενοπόρων καλῶς κείμενοι.

The Areopagus had repaired to the general assembly
to give its opinion respecting the project of a citizen
named Timarchus, who was soon after proscribed for the
depravity of his manners. Autolycus addressed them in
the name of the whole court. This senator, educated in
the simplicity of the ancient times, and a stranger to the
shameful abuse to which the most ordinary terms of conversation are now perverted, suffered a word to drop from
him, which, misconstrued from its real sense, admitted of
an allusion to the licentious life of Timarchus. The whole
of the assembly applauded him in a transport, and Autolycus, astonished, assumed a severer countenance. After
a moment's pause, he attempted to proceed ; but the people,
putting an arch construction on the most innocent expressions, never ceased to interrupt him by a confused noise
and immoderate bursts of laughter. A distinguished citizen
now rising, exclaimed, ' Are not you ashamed, Athenians,
to be guilty of such indecency in presence of the Areopa-
gites ?' The people answered that they felt all the venera-
tion due to the majesty of that tribunal : but that there
were circumstances in which it was impossible to restrain
themselves within the bounds of decorum. What virtues
must not this body have possessed, to have established and
maintained so high an opinion of the respect due to it in
the minds of the people ; and what good might it not have
produced, had they known how to value it as it deserved ?

ANACHARSIS.

Τῆς δὲ βουλῆς τῆς ἐξ Ἀρείου πάγου πρόσοδόν ποτε
πρὸς τὴν ἐκκλησίαν ποιησαμένης, ἔδει γὰρ ἀποφαίνεσθαι
τὴν γνώμην περὶ τοῦ εἰσηγήματος τῶν πολιτῶν τινός,—
Τίμαρχος ἦν αὐτῷ ὄνομα, ὃς καὶ οὐ πολλῷ ὕστερον διὰ
τὴν ἀσέλγειαν ἠτιμώθη,—ὑπὲρ τῶν ἄλλων Αὐτόλυκός
τις ἐδημηγόρει. ὁ δὲ βουλευτὴς οὗτος πεπαιδευμένος
μὲν κατὰ τὴν ἀρχαιοπρεπῆ εὐήθειαν τῶν τρόπων, ξένος
δὲ ὢν τῆς αἰσχρουργίας ᾗ οἱ νῦν καταχρώμενοι τῶν
ῥημάτων καὶ τὰ συνηθέστατα παραστρέφουσιν, ἔλαθεν
ἑαυτόν τι εἰπὼν ὃ εἴ τις τὴν εἰωθυῖαν ἀξίωσιν ἀνταλλάτ-
τοι ἐδόκει τὴν Τιμάρχου ἀσέλγειαν αἰνίττεσθαι. ὁ μὲν
οὖν δῆμος ὑπερησθεὶς ἀνεκρότησεν· ὁ δὲ Αὐτόλυκος
ἐκπεπληγμένος ἔτι μᾶλλον ἐσκυθρώπαζεν, ὀλίγον δὲ
ἐπισχὼν ἤδη προῄει τοῦ λόγου. οἱ δὲ τὰ μηδὲν ἀσχή-
μονα τῶν ὀνομάτων πάνυ κακοήθως ἐπὶ τὸ γέλοιον
ἐκλαβόντες οὐδεπώποτε ἐπαύσαντο θορυβοῦντες. ἐνταῦθα δὲ ἀναστὰς ἀνὴρ τῶν πολιτῶν οὐκ ἀδόκιμος,
οὐκ αἰσχύνεσθε, ἔφη, ὦ ἄνδρες Ἀθηναῖοι, εἰ τοιαῦτα
ἀσχημονεῖτε, καὶ ταῦτα παρούσης τῆς βουλῆς τῆς ἐξ
Ἀρείου πάγου; οἱ δὲ ἀπεκρίναντο ὅτι τὴν μὲν βουλὴν
θαυμάζοιεν κατὰ τὸ ἀξίωμα ὃ καὶ προσήκοι αὐτῇ· εἶναι
μέντοι ὅτε ἀδύνατα εἴη μέχρι τοῦ πρέποντος ὁρίζεσθαι
τὸν γέλωτα. οἵας τὸ συνέδριον τοῦτο εἰκὸς ἦν ἀρετὰς
κεκτῆσθαι, ὅ γε τοσοῦτον παρὰ τῷ δήμῳ οὐ μόνον
ηὐδοκίμει ἀλλὰ καὶ διετέλει βεβαίαν διασῶζον τὴν
εὐδοκίμησιν, οἷα δὲ ἔμελλεν ἀγαθὰ ἀπεργάσεσθαι εἰ
ἐκεῖνοι ἠπίσταντο κατὰ τὸ προσῆκον τῆς ἀξίας θαυμά-
ζειν;

The oration which seems to have been delivered on
the occasion of the embassy by which the Olynthians
sought alliance with Athens, appears to have been designed
to animate the Athenians to a contest from which they
were disposed to shrink through fear of Philip's overwhelming power. The fears to which the orator addresses
himself were in themselves very reasonable : and the less
they were really felt by his hearers, the more advisable he
might think it to suggest them, not of course in order to
damp their spirit, but to rouse them to an effort worthy of
the greatness of the struggle. There were some, as he
had observed in his speech on the Rhodians, who were
used to represent Philip as a despicable antagonist : this
he knew would be a false and dangerous way of inspiring
the people with courage. He wished that they should
recognise Philip's power as truly formidable, but that they
should be convinced it had become so only through their
own remissness and unwise policy.

THIRLWALL.

Τῷ δὲ λόγῳ, ὃν εἰκὸς ῥηθῆναι τότε ὅτε Ὀλύνθιοι ἐπρεσβεύοντο δεόμενοι Ἀθηναίων συμμαχίας, ὅδε φαίνεται σκοπὸς εἶναι, εἴ πως τούτους παραθαρρύνοι βουλομένους ἀποκνεῖν τὸν ἀγῶνα, ἅτε τὴν ὑπερβάλλουσαν Φιλίππου δύναμιν ἐκπεπληγμένους. ὁ δὲ φόβος οὗ ὁ ῥήτωρ ἅπτεται αὐτὸς μὲν καθ' αὑτὸν οὐκ ἄλογος ἦν· ὅσῳ δὲ ἧττον πρὸς οὓς ἔλεγε τούτῳ ἦσαν τῷ ὄντι ἔνοχοι, τοσούτῳ μᾶλλον τάχ' ἂν ἴσως εἰ ὑποτιθείη αὐτὸν νομίζοι συμφέρειν, οὐχ ἵνα δῆλον ὅτι προθυμουμένους καταφοβοίη, ἀλλ' ὡς εἰς ἔργον τι τοσούτου ἀγῶνος ἄξιον παρακελευσόμενος. ἦσαν γὰρ οἵ, ὥσπερ καὶ αὐτὸς ἤδη εἶπεν ἐν τῷ περὶ τῆς Ῥοδίων ἐλευθερίας, τὸν Φίλιππον κατεμέμφοντο ὡς ἄρα φαῦλος εἴη προσπολεμεῖν· ὅτι δὲ λόγῳ οὔτ' ἀληθεῖ οὔτ' ἀκινδύνῳ χρώμενος ἀνδρείαν τοῖς πολίταις ἐμποιεῖν ἐπιχειρήσει εὖ ἐπιστάμενος, ἠξίου αὐτοὺς τὴν τοῦ Φιλίππου δύναμιν ὁμολογεῖν μὲν ὅτι φοβερὰ εἴη ἀναμφισβητήτως, καταμαθεῖν δὲ ὅτι τοσαύτη αὐξηθείη ῥᾳθυμούντων αὐτῶν καὶ ἀφρόνως πολιτευομένων.

But these reflections were not made, nor had we enough considered the example of Elizabeth, the last of our princes who had made any considerable figure abroad, and from whom we might have learned to act with vigour, but to engage with caution, and always to proportion our assistance according to our abilities, and the real necessities of our allies. The frontiers of France were now so fortified, her commerce and her naval force were so increased, her armies were grown so numerous, her troops were so disciplined, so inured to war, and so animated by a long course of successful campaigns, that they who looked on the situation of Europe could not fail to see how difficult the enterprise of reducing her power was become. Difficult as it was, we were obliged, on every account and by reasons of all kinds, to engage in it: but then we should have engaged with more forecast, and have conducted ourselves in the management of it, not with less alacrity and spirit, but with more order, more economy, and a better application of our efforts. But they who governed were glad to engage us at any rate: and we entered on this great scheme of action, as our nation is too apt to do, hurried on by the ruling passion of the day.

BOLINGBROKE.

Ἀλλ᾽ οὔτε γὰρ ταῦτα ἐνετεθυμήμεθα, οὔτε Ἐλίσσῃ
ἱκανῶς παραδείγματι ἐχρησάμεθα τῇ ὑστάτῃ δὴ τῶν γε
τῆς ἡμετέρας βασιλέων ἀξιόλογόν τι ἐν τῇ ἀλλοτρίᾳ
ἀποφηναμένη, ἐξὸν μέντοι παρ᾽ αὐτῆς μανθάνειν θαρ-
ραλέως μὲν δρᾶν, δεδιότας δὲ τὰς βοηθείας ἐπαγγέλ-
λεσθαι, καὶ ταύτας μέχρι τῆς τε ἡμετέρας αὐτῶν
δυνάμεως καὶ τῆς ὡς ὄντως τῶν συμμάχων χρείας ἀεὶ
ὁρίζεσθαι. ἐπὶ τοσοῦτον γὰρ ἤδη τῇ Γαλατίᾳ τετει-
χισμένων μὲν τῶν μεθορίων, ἐπηυξημένης δὲ τῆς τε
ἐμπορίας καὶ τοῦ ναυτικοῦ, ἔτι δὲ κεκτημένων αὐτῶν
τοσαῦτα μὲν τῶν στρατοπέδων τὰ πλήθη, τοσαύτην δὲ
τὴν τοῦ ὁπλιτικοῦ ἐμπειρίαν, ἀνδρῶν συγκεκροτημένων
τε τὰ τοῦ πολέμου καὶ διὰ τὸ πλεῖστα ἐν στρατείαις εὖ
φέρεσθαι ἐπαιρομένων, τούτων δὲ οὕτως ἐχόντων τίνα
ἂν λάθοι τὰ τῆς Εὐρώπης σκοπούμενον τὸ καταστρέ-
ψασθαι τὴν τοιαύτην δύναμιν ὡς χαλεπὴ εἴη καὶ ἡ
ἐπιχείρησις; οὐ μὴν ἀλλὰ καίπερ χαλεπὸν ὂν διὰ
πάντα τε καὶ ἀπὸ παντοίων αἰτιῶν πολλὴ ἀνάγκη
ἦν ἅπτεσθαι τούτου. καίτοι ἔδει πολλῷ πλείονα
ἔχοντας τὴν προμηθίαν, ἐν δὲ τῷ ἔργῳ οὐ μὰ Δί᾽ οὐχὶ
ἧττον προθύμως ἢ ἀπροφασίστως, ἀλλὰ καὶ εὐτακ-
τότερόν τε καὶ φειδομένους μᾶλλον τῶν χρημάτων, ἔτι
δὲ καὶ βέλτιον χρωμένους ταῖς ἐπιχειρήσεσιν. ἀλλ᾽ οἵ
τε γὰρ τότε ἐν τέλει ὄντες ἀσμένως ἡμῶν ἐφ᾽ ὁποιαοῦν
προφάσει ἐπηγγέλλοντο τὴν βοήθειαν, αὐτοί τε τὸ
μέγιστον τοῦτο ἔργον ἐνεστησάμεθα, ὅπερ καὶ φιλεῖ
ἡ πόλις ἥδε τῇ ἀεὶ κρατούσῃ ὀργῇ βιάζεσθαι.

Here then is the example, not of a virtue in principle, but of a virtue in performance, with all the indispensable benefits of that performance, being sustained on the soil of selfishness. Were a profound observer of human life to take account of all the honesties of mercantile intercourse, he would find that, in the general amount of them, they were mainly due to the operation of this cause; or that they were so prevalent in society, because each man was bound to their observance by the tie of his own personal interest—insomuch that, if this particular tie were broken, it would as surely derange or break up the world of trade, as the world of matter would become an inert or turbid chaos on the repeal or suspension of the law of gravitation. Confidence, the very soul of commercial enterprise, and without which the transactions of merchandise were impossible, is the goodly result, not of that native respect which each man has for another's rights, but of that native regard which each man has for his own special advantage. This forms another example of a great and general good wrought out for society—while each component member is intently set only on a certain and specific good for himself—a great interest which could not have been entrusted to human virtue, but which has been skilfully extracted from the working of selfishness. In so far as truth and justice prevail in the world, not by the operation of principle but of policy, in so far the goodness of man has no share in it : but so beneficent a result out of such unpromising materials speaks all the more emphatically both for the wisdom and the goodness of God.

CHALMERS.

Παραδεῖγμα τοίνυν τόδε ἔχομεν ἀρετῆς τινός, κατὰ προαίρεσιν μὲν ἐξ ἀρχῆς οὐκ οὔσης, ἐνεργείᾳ δὲ ἀποτελουμένης, ἡ αὐτή τε καὶ ὅσα ἀναγκαίως δεῖ συνέπεσθαι ἀγαθὰ τρέφεται ἀπὸ τῆς φιλαυτίας. εἰ γάρ τις τὰ ἀνθρώπινα κατ᾽ ἀκρίβειαν θεωρήσας σκέψαιτο ὅσα ἀψευδοῦσιν οἱ περὶ χρηματιστικήν, ὡς τὰ πολλὰ ἂν εὕροι εἰς τὴν αἰτίαν ταύτην παντὸς μᾶλλον δεῖν τὰ τοιαῦτα ἀναφέρεσθαι· καὶ ἐπὶ τοσοῦτον δὴ ἐν ἅπασιν ἐπιπολάζειν διότι τὴν τοιαύτην νόμισιν συνδεῖ ἑκάστῳ τὸ ἰδίᾳ συμφέρον, ἐπεὶ τοῦ συνδεσμοῦ τούτου λυθέντος οὐδὲν ἂν ἧττον συνταραχθείη ἢ ἀναιρεθείη ἡ ἐμπορικὴ σύστασις, ἢ πᾶσα ἡ γένεσις εἰς ἄκριτόν τι καὶ ταραχῶδες φύροιτο εἴ τις ἀνέλοι ἢ ἄκυρον θείη τὸν νόμον καθ᾽ ὃν πάντα κάτω φέρεται. τὴν γὰρ πίστιν, ὅπερ σῶμα τῆς χρηματιστικῆς, καὶ μὴ ὑπαρχούσης αὐτῆς οὐδὲ συμμένειν δύναται τὰ τῆς ἐμπορίας, τοῦτο τὸ κάλλιστον ἔκγονον ἀποτίκτει οὐχ ὅτι πέφυκεν ἕκαστός τις λόγον ἔχειν τῶν ἀλλοτρίων, ἀλλὰ καὶ τοῦ αὐτῷ ἰδίᾳ συμφέροντος ἐπιμελεῖσθαι. τόδε τοίνυν ἄλλο παράδειγμα φαίνεται τοῦ εἰς τὸ κοινὸν ἀπειργασμένου ἀγαθοῦ, καίπερ ἑκάστων τῶν μορίων τῷ οἰκείῳ καὶ ἰδίῳ συντόνως προσεχόντων· καὶ τοῦτο μεῖζον μέν τι ἢ κατὰ τὴν τῆς ἀνθρωπίνης ἀρετῆς ἐπιτροπείαν, ἐκ δὲ τῆς τῶν ἀνθρώπων φιλαυτίας ἐνεργούσης ἐπιστημόνως ἀποβαῖνον. ἐφ᾽ ὅσον μὲν οὖν ἐπιπολάζει παρὰ τοῖς ἀνθρώποις τό τε ἀψευδὲς καὶ τὸ δίκαιον, ἐνεργοῦντος τοῦ συμφέροντος ἀλλὰ μὴ τοῦ καλοῦ, μέχρι τοσούτου μὲν οὐδὲν μετέχει ἥ γε ἀνθρωπίνη ἀρετή· τὸ δὲ ἐκ τῶν ἀνεπιτηδείων καὶ τῶν τοιούτων αἰτιῶν τὰ τοιαῦτα ἀποβαίνειν, τοῦτο δὲ τοσούτῳ ἐπιφανέστερον τοῦ θείου ὡς σοφοῦ ἅμα καὶ φιλανθρώπου ὄντος κατηγορεῖ.

Since the soil will maintain many more than it can employ, what must be done, supposing the country to be full, with the remainder of the inhabitants? They who by the rules of partition (and some such must be established in every country) are entitled to the land, and they who by their labour upon the soil acquire a right in its produce, will not part with their property for nothing; or rather they will no longer raise from the soil what they can neither use themselves nor exchange for what they want. Or, lastly, if these were willing to distribute what they could spare of the provision which the ground yielded to others who had no share or concern in the property or cultivation of it, yet still the most enormous mischiefs would ensue from great numbers being unemployed. The idleness of one half of the community would overwhelm the whole with confusion and disorder. One only way presents itself of removing the difficulty which this question states, and which is simply this; that they whose work is not wanted nor can be employed in the raising of provision out of the ground, convert their hands and ingenuity to the fabrication of articles which may gratify and requite those who are so employed, or who by the division of lands in the country are entitled to the exclusive possession of certain parts of them. By this contrivance all things proceed well.

PALEY.

Ἐπειδὴ δὲ ἡ γῆ πολλῷ πλείονας τρέφειν ἱκανὴ ἢ
κατὰ τοὺς ἐργαζομένους αὐτήν, ἐὰν ἄρα πολυάνθρωπος
ᾖ, τί χρηστέον τῷ περιττεύοντι ἀριθμῷ; ὅσοι τε γὰρ
διὰ τοὺς νόμους τοὺς διανεμητικοὺς (τὸ δὲ τοιοῦτον
πανταχοῦ δεῖ καθεστηκέναι) δίκαιοι ἂν εἶεν κύριοι
ὑπάρχειν τῆς κτήσεως, οἷς τε ἄτε γεωργοῦσι προσγε-
γένηται δικαίως τὸ τῶν γε γιγνομένων μετέχειν, οὐ-
δέτεροι δῆλον ὅτι τῶν σφετέρων προῖκα προήσονται·
μᾶλλον δὲ οὐκέτι ἐθελήσουσιν ἀπὸ τῆς γῆς παρασκευάζειν ὧν μήτε σφίσι χρεία μηδεμία, ἀλλάττειν
τε ὧν δέονται ἀδύνατα. εἰ δὲ καὶ τούτοις βουλομένοις
εἴη τὸ περιττὸν τῆς τροφῆς τῆς ἐκ τῆς γῆς φυομένης
διαδοῦναι οἷς μέτεστι μηδὲν μήτε τῆς κτήσεως μήτε
τῆς γεωργίας, ὅμως ἂν ὑπερφυᾶ ὅσα κακὰ συμβαίη,
τοσούτων ἀργῶν τρεφομένων. τὸ γὰρ ἥμισυ τῶν ἐνοι-
κούντων μηδὲν ἐργαζόμενον τοὺς σύμπαντας ἀνάγκη
περιβαλεῖν ταραχῇ καὶ ἀνομίᾳ. τῆς δὲ ἀπορίας ταύτης ἣν ζητοῦμεν μία τις λύσις εὑρίσκεται· λέγω δὲ
τὴν τοιάνδε· εἰ ἐκεῖνοι, ὧν μηδεμία χρεία τῆς ἐργασίας
μηδὲ δυνατὸν χρῆσθαι αὐτοῖς εἰς τὰ γεωργικά, τρέποιεν
τήν τε ἐργασίαν καὶ τὴν ἀγχίνοιαν εἰς τὰ χειρουργήματα, ἅμα μὲν ὡς χάριν ἀποδώσοντες ἅμα δὲ εἰς
ἀπόλαυσιν τοῖς ἄλλοις τοῖς τε γεωργοῦσι καὶ τοῖς
τῶν κλήρων ἁπλῶς κυρίοις διὰ τὴν ἐν τῇ πόλει
ταύτῃ διανομὴν τῶν χωρίων. τῇ γὰρ τοιαύτῃ μηχανῇ
χρωμένοις πάντ' ἂν εὖ προχωροίη.

But the king of Scotland, though he would not formally retract his judgement of Perkin, wherein he had engaged himself so far; yet in his private opinion, upon often speech with the Englishmen, and divers other advertisements, began to suspect him for a counterfeit. Wherefore in a noble fashion he called him unto him, and recounted the benefits and favours that he had done him in making him his ally, and in provoking a mighty and opulent king by an offensive war in his quarrel, for the space of two years together; nay more, that he had refused an honourable peace, whereof he had a fair offer, if he would have delivered him; and that, to keep his promise with him, he had deeply offended both his nobles and people, whom he might not hold in any long discontent: and therefore required him to think of his own fortunes, and to choose out some fitter place for his exile: telling him withal, that he could not say but the English had forsaken him before the Scottish, for that, upon two several trials, none had declared themselves on his side; but nevertheless he would make good what he said to him at his first receiving, which was that he should not repent him for putting himself into his hands; for that he would not cast him off, but help him with shipping and means to transport him where he should desire.

BACON.

Ὁ δὲ Καληδόνιος καίπερ οὐ βουλόμενος ἃ περὶ
Περκίνου ἐγνωκὼς ἦν, ἐπὶ τοσοῦτόν γε ἤδη ὑπεσχημένος,
ταῦτα φανερὸς εἶναι διαρρήδην ἀνατιθέμενος, ἰδίᾳ μέντοι
ἄλλοθέν τε πολλαχόθεν τεκμαιρόμενος καὶ ἐξ ὧν πρὸς
Ἄγγλους διελέχθη, ἤδη ἐν ὑποψίᾳ εἶχε μὴ ἀλαζών τις
εἴη. διὸ καὶ πάνυ μεγαλοπρεπῶς μεταπεμψάμενος καὶ
διεξιὼν ὅσα τε καὶ ἡλίκα εὖ πεποιηκὼς εἴη, ἅμα μὲν
γράψας ξύμμαχον, ἅμα δὲ βασιλέα μέγαν καὶ εὐδαίμονα
ὑπὲρ αὐτοῦ ξυνεχῶς τρίτον ἔτος τουτὶ προσπολεμω-
σάμενος, ἔτι δὲ ὅτι καλῶς παρασχὸν αὐτῷ ἐπὶ μηδενὶ
αἰσχρῷ, ἐφ᾽ ᾧτε προδοῦναι αὐτόν, εἰρήνην ποιεῖσθαι,
οὔτε βούλοιτο, τοῖς τε εὐπατρίδαις ἅμα καὶ τῷ δήμῳ
ἵνα μηδὲν ψεύσαιτο ὧν ὑπέσχητο διαβεβλημένος εἴη,
πρὸς οὓς οὐχ οἷόν τε ἔτι πλείω χρόνον ἐπιφθόνως δια-
κεῖσθαι, οὕτω δὴ ἠξίου αὐτὸν τῶν ἑαυτοῦ ἐπιμελεῖσθαι
ζητοῦντα ὅποι καὶ ἄλλοσε ἐπιτηδειότερον φεύγων
διατελεῖ· ἅμα λέγων αὐτῷ ὅτι οὐ λόγος εἴη μὴ οὐ τοὺς
Ἄγγλους πρότερον ἢ σφεῖς προδοῦναι, δὶς γὰρ ἀποπει-
ρασαμένῳ οὐδὲ εἷς προσχωρήσειεν. οὐ μέντοι ἀλλὰ ἃ
πρότερον ὑποδεξάμενος ὑπόσχοιτο, ἦ μὴν μηδέποτε
μεταμελήσειν αὐτῷ παρὰ σφᾶς καταφυγόντι, ταῦτα καὶ
ποιήσειν· οὔτε γὰρ προήσεσθαι βοηθήσειν τε ναυσί τε
καὶ τοῖς ἄλλοις ὥστε ὅποι ἂν βούληται περαιωθῆναι.

When they were come before Exeter, they forbare to use any force at the first, but made continual shouts and outcries to terrify the inhabitants. They did likewise in divers places call and talk to them from under the walls, to join with them and be of their party; telling them that the king would make them another London, if they would be the first town that should acknowledge him. But they had not the wit to send to them, in any orderly fashion, agents or chosen men, to tempt them and to treat with them. The citizens on their part showed themselves stout and loyal subjects : neither was there so much as any tumult or division amongst them, but all prepared themselves for a valiant defence, and making good the town. For well they saw, that the rebels were of no such number or power, that they needed to fear them as yet ; and well they hoped, that before their numbers increased, the king's succours would come in. And, howsoever, they thought it the extremest of evils, to put themselves at the mercy of those hungry and disorderly people. Wherefore setting all things in good order within the town, they nevertheless let down with cords, from several parts of the walls privily, several messengers, that if one came to mischance, another might pass on, which should advertise the king of the state of the town and implore his aid. Perkin also doubted that succours would come ere long ; and therefore resolved to use his utmost force to assault the town. And for that purpose having mounted scaling-ladders in divers places upon the walls, made at the same instant an attempt to force one of the gates.

BACON.

Προσκαθεζόμενοι δὲ τὴν Ἐξωνίαν πρῶτον ἀπέσχοντο μὲν μὴ βιάζεσθαι κραυγῇ δὲ καὶ βοῇ ξυνεχῶς ἐχρῶντο, εἴ πως φοβήσειαν τοὺς ἔνδοθεν. προσκαλέσαντες δὲ καὶ ἄλλοι ἄλλοθεν ὑπὸ τοῦ τείχους διελέγοντο αὐτοῖς, προσχωρῆσαι κελεύοντες καὶ παρὰ σφίσι θέσθαι τὰ ὅπλα, ὡς Περκίνου ἀντὶ τοῦ δευτέρου ἀστέως προτιμῶντος ἐὰν πρῶτοι προσδέξωνται αὐτόν· οὐ μέντοι νουνεχόντως προσέπεμψαν ἄνδρας ἐπιλέκτους τινὰς πρέσβεις οἵτινες πειράσαντες τρόπῳ τινὶ ἐπιτηδείῳ πράξουσιν αὐτοῖς. οἱ δὲ αὐτόθεν ἀνδρείως ἅμα καὶ πιστῶς φρονοῦντες τὰ τοῦ βασιλέως διεφάνησαν· οὔτε γὰρ στάσεως οὐδὲ θορύβου οὐδ᾽ ὁτιοῦν ἦν, πάντες τε παρεσκευάσαντο ὡς προθύμως ἀμυνούμενοι καὶ βεβαίαν παρέξοντες τὴν πόλιν, ἐπιστάμενοι μὲν ὅτι οὔπω τοσοῦτον εἴη τῶν ἐπαναστάντων οὔτε πλῆθος οὔτε δύναμις ὥστε εἰκότως φοβηθῆναι αὐτούς, ἅμα δὲ ἐλπίζοντες πρὶν ἔτι μείζους αὐξηθῆναι παρέσεσθαι τὴν παρὰ τοῦ βασιλέως βοήθειαν. κακῶν δ᾽ οὖν ἔσχατον εἶναι ἐνόμισαν τῷ πεινῶντι καὶ ἀτάκτῳ καὶ τῷ τοιούτῳ ὄχλῳ παραδοῦναι αὐτούς. κατὰ τοῦτο πάντα ἐν τῇ πόλει καλῶς θέμενοι ἀγγέλους ὅμως τινὰς ἄλλους ἄλλοθεν τοῦ τείχους σπαρτίοις κρύφα καθίμων, καὶ ἔμελλεν ὁ μὲν παθεῖν τι ὁ δὲ φθάσας διασωθῆναι καὶ ἀγγείλας τῷ βασιλεῖ τὰ τῆς πόλεως ὡς ἔχοι οὕτω δεῖσθαι ὅπως βοηθήσει· τῷ δὲ Περκίνῳ ἐδόκει, ὃς καὶ αὐτὸς ἡγεῖτο τοὺς βοηθήσοντας ὅσον οὔπω παρέσεσθαι, πάσῃ ἰσχύι κατὰ τὸ δυνατὸν προσβολὴν ποιήσασθαι, καὶ ταύτῃ τῇ διανοίᾳ κλίμακας προσθεὶς πολλαχόσε τοῦ τείχους ἅμα κατὰ μίαν τῶν πυλῶν ἐπειρᾶτο βιάζεσθαι.

The Whigs impeached and attainted me. They went farther—at least in my way of thinking, that step was more cruel than all the others—by partial representation of facts, and pieces of facts put together as it best suited their purpose and published to the whole world, they did all that in them lay to expose me for a fool and to brand me for a knave. But then I had deserved this abundantly at their hands according to the notions of party justice. The Tories have not indeed impeached nor attainted me; but they have done and are still doing something very like to that which I took worse of the Whigs than the impeachment and attainder; and this after I have shown an inviolable attachment to the service and almost an implicit obedience to the will of the party—when I am actually an outlaw, deprived of my honours, stripped of my fortune, and cut off from my family and my country for their sakes.

BOLINGBROKE.

Εἰσαγγειλάντων δὲ τῶν πολλῶν ἠτιμώθην. ὃ δ' οὖν τῶν ἄλλων ἁπάντων, ἐμοί γε δοκεῖν, δεινότατον· ὑπερβολὴν γὰρ ποιούμενοι καὶ τὰ πεπραγμένα ἢ ἁπλῶς ἢ κατὰ μόρια οὐκ ἀπ' ἴσης ἀποφαινόμενοι, ἀλλὰ συντιθέντες ὡς μάλιστα σφίσι κατὰ νοῦν, πανταχῇ τῆς οἰκουμένης διήγγελλον, οὐδὲν ἐλλείποντες τὸ ἐπὶ σφᾶς εἶναι τὰ μὲν ὡς ἀμαθῆ με γέλωτα ποιεῖν τὰ δὲ ἐστιγμένον πανοῦργον ἀποκαλεῖν. οὐ μὴν ἀλλὰ πολλῶν ἔνεκα τούτων γε αὐτοῖς ἄξιος ἦν, καθάπερ δὴ δικαιοῦσι πρὸς ἀλλήλους οἱ ἀντιπολιτευόμενοι. οἱ δ' ὀλίγοι εἰ μὴ εἰσήγγειλάν με μηδ' ἠτίμωσαν, παραπλήσιον ὅμως τι ἔπραξάν τε καὶ πράττουσι τοῖς παρ' ἐκείνων ἐφ' οἷς οὐχ ἧττον ἠγανάκτουν τῆς εἰσαγγελίας καὶ τῆς ἀτιμίας· καὶ ταῦτα φανεροῦ ὄντος ἐμοῦ ἀμεταβόλως θεραπεύοντος τὰ συμφέροντα ταύτῃ τῇ προαιρέσει καὶ ὡς ἐπὶ τὸ πολὺ ἀπροφασίστως ἀκολουθοῦντος ταῖς βουλήσεσιν, ἔτι δὲ ὑπὲρ ταύτης αὐτῆς φυγάδος τῷ ὄντι γεγονότος καὶ τὴν ἐπιτιμίαν ἀφῃρημένου, καὶ ἀποβεβληκότος μὲν τὴν οὐσίαν ἐκπεπτωκότος δὲ τῶν τε οἰκείων καὶ τῆς πατρίδος.

What is there, then, ye will say to me, in this third ordinance, which thou so mislikest? I will answer you in a few words: I mislike the changing of the laws of our fathers, especially when these laws have respect to the worship of the gods. Many things, I know, are ordered wisely for one generation, which notwithstanding are by another generation no less wisely ordered otherwise. There is room in human affairs for change: there is room also for unchangeableness. And where shall we seek for that which is unchangeable, but in those great laws which are the very foundation of the commonwealth; most of all in those which, having to do with the immortal gods, should be also themselves immortal? Now it belongs to these laws that the office of consul, which is as it were the shadow of the majesty of Jove himself, should be held only by men of the houses of the patricians. Ye know how that none but the patricians may take any office of priesthood for the worship of the gods of Rome, nor interpret the will of the gods by augury. For the gods, being themselves many, have set also upon earth many races of men and many orders; and one race may not take to itself the law of another race, nor one order the law of another order. Each has its own law, which was given to it from the beginning; and if we change these, the whole world will be full of confusion. These laws are not of today, nor of yesterday: we know of no time when they have not been: may neither we nor our children ever see that time when they shall have ceased to be!

ARNOLD.

Τί δὲ καταμέμφει, τάχ᾽ ἂν εἴποι τις, τοῦ τρίτου τοῦδε ἐπιτάγματος; πρὸς τοῦτον ἀποκριναίμην ἂν ἐν βραχέσι. καταμέμφομαι γὰρ τὸ μεταβάλλεσθαι τοὺς νόμους τοὺς τῶν πατέρων, ἄλλους τε καὶ ὅσοι ἐπιμελοῦνται τῆς περὶ τὰ θεῖα νομίσεως. οἶδα μέντοι πολλὰ τῇ μὲν γενεᾷ σωφρόνως ἐπιταττόμενα, τῇ δὲ οὐδὲν ἧττον ἄλλως πως ἀποβαίνοντα· ἐπὶ γὰρ τῶν ἀνθρωπίνων ἐγχωρεῖ μὲν ἔστιν ὅτε ζητεῖν μεταβολάς, ἐγχωρεῖ δὲ καὶ ἔχεσθαι τοῦ ἀκινήτου. καὶ τίς ἂν ἄλλοθί που ἐπιζητοίη τὸ ἀκίνητον ἢ ἐν τοῖς νομίμοις τούτοις τοῖς μεγίστοις ἐφ᾽ οἷς ἵδρυται αὐτὴ ἡ πολιτεία, ὅσα πλεῖστα πρὸς τοὺς ἀθανάτους θεοὺς συντείνοντα προσήκει δήπου καὶ αὐτὰ ἀθάνατα εἶναι; ταῦτα δὲ πρὸς τί ἀποβλέπει; δῆλον ὅτι πρὸς τὸ τῆς ὑπατείας, ἣν ἅτε εἰκόνα οὖσαν τῆς αὐτοῦ τοῦ Διὸς ἐξουσίας μόναι αἱ τῶν εὐπατριδῶν οἰκίαι δίκαιαι ἂν εἶεν ἐπιτετράφθαι. ὅτι γὰρ οὐδενὶ ἄλλῳ ἢ τοῖς ἐκ τούτων ἔξεστι τῶν πρὸς τοὺς θεοὺς ἐπιμελεῖσθαι οὔτε ἱερωσύνης κληρουμένῳ οὔτε ἐξηγουμένῳ δι᾽ οἰωνῶν καὶ αὐτοὶ ἐπίστασθε. οἱ γὰρ θεοὶ πολλοὶ ὄντες καὶ αὐτοὶ πολλὰ κατέστησαν ἐπὶ τῆς γῆς καὶ τὰ φῦλα καὶ τὰ ἔθνη τῶν ἀνθρώπων, καὶ πῶς ἐνδέχεται ἄλλο ἄλλου τιμᾶς οἰκειοῦσθαι ἢ φῦλον φύλου ἢ καὶ ἔθνος ἔθνους; ἐπεὶ ἑκάστῳ ὁ οἰκεῖος νόμος ἐξ ἀρχῆς παραδέδοται, μεταβαλλομένων δὲ μεστὰ ἀπορίας πάντα ἂν εἴη. οὐδὲ γὰρ χθές τε καὶ πρώην ταῦτα κατέστη τὰ νόμιμα, μᾶλλον δὲ οὐδεὶς οἶδεν ἐξ ὅτου χρόνου ἐφάνη· μὴ τοίνυν τὸν χρόνον ἴδοιμεν μήτ᾽ αὐτοὶ μήτε οἱ ἐσόμενοι ἐν ᾧ ὑπάρχοντα παύσεται.

And as to the judgement of Cato the censor, he was well punished for his blasphemy against learning, in the same kind wherein he offended ; for when he was past threescore years old, he was taken with an extreme desire to go to school again, and to learn the Greek tongue, to the end to peruse the Greek authors ; which doth well demonstrate, that his former censure of the Grecian learning was rather an affected gravity, than according to the inward sense of his own opinion. And as for Virgil's verses, though it pleased him to brave the world in taking to the Romans the art of empire, and leaving to others the arts of subjects ; yet so much is manifest, that the Romans never ascended to that height of empire, till the time they had ascended to the height of other arts. For in the time of the two first Cæsars, which had the art of government in greatest perfection, there lived the best poet Virgilius Maro, the best historiographer Titus Livius, the best antiquary Marcus Varro, and the best or second orator Marcus Cicero, that to the memory of man are known. As for the accusation of Socrates, the time must be remembered when it was prosecuted ; which was under the thirty tyrants, the most base, bloody and envious persons that have governed ; which revolution of state was no sooner over, but Socrates, whom they had made a person criminal, was made a person heroical, and his memory accumulate with honours divine and human : and those discourses of his which were then termed corrupting of manners, were after acknowledged for sovereign medicines of the mind and manners, and so have been received ever since till this day.

BACON.

Ὅσα μὲν γὰρ Κάτων ὁ τιμητὴς ἐπικαλούμενος ἔκρινεν εἰς τὰ μαθήματα βλασφημῶν δίκην ἔδωκε κατὰ τὰ αὐτὰ ἃ καὶ ἡμαρτήκει. ἑξηκονταέτη γὰρ γεγονότα πόθος τις κατέλαβεν αὐτὸν ὑπερφυὴς ὅσος τοῦ πάλιν ἐξ ἀρχῆς φοιτῆσαι εἰς διδασκάλου ὡς τὸ ἑλληνίζειν μαθησόμενον καὶ ἔμπειρον γενησόμενον ὧν συνέγραψαν. ὃ καὶ τεκμηριοῖ ὅτι ἃ πρότερον ἐπετίμησε τῇ Ἑλλάδι προσποιήτως μᾶλλον ἐσεμνύνετο ἢ ἃ καὶ αὐτῷ ἐδόκει ἔλεγεν. εἰ δὲ καὶ ὁ Μάρων ἔπη ποιῶν πάνυ καταφρονητικῶς ἔχων πρὸς τοὺς ἄλλους τοῖς μὲν Ῥωμαίοις ᾤετο δεῖν τὴν ἀρχικὴν ἐπιστήμην περιθεῖναι τοῖς δὲ λοιποῖς τὰς τῶν ὑπηκόων, τοσοῦτον μέντοι φανερὸν ὅτι πορρωτάτω τῶν ἄλλων τεχνῶν προβεβηκότες ἐκεῖνοι οὕτως ἤδη καὶ τῆς ἀρχικῆς ἐφίκοντο. ἐπὶ γὰρ τοῖν πρώτοιν Καισάροιν, οἳ ἀκριβέστατα τὴν τοῦ ἄρχειν τέχνην ἠπίσταντο, οἱ ἀκρότατοι ὧν γε ἴσμεν ἀκοῇ καθ' ἑκάστην τὴν ἐπιστήμην ἐγένοντο τῶν μὲν ποιητῶν ὁ Μάρων, τῶν δὲ συγγραφέων Λίβιος, τῶν δὲ περὶ τὰ ἀρχαῖα πεπονημένων Βάρρων, τῶν δὲ ῥητόρων πολὺ δεύτερός γε Κικέρων. τὴν δὲ Σωκράτους κατηγορίαν οὐδ' ἐκεῖνο δεῖ λεληθέναι ἐφ' ὧντινων ἡ γραφὴ εἰσῆλθεν, ἐπὶ τῶν τριάκοντα, ἀνδρῶν εἴπερ καί τινες ἄλλοι ὠμοτάτων τε καὶ αἰσχίστων καὶ φθονερωτάτων. ἡ δὲ τοιαύτη κατάστασις οὐκ ἔφθη καταπαυθεῖσα, καὶ τῷ Σωκράτει, ὃν ἀλιτήριόν τινα ἀπεκάλεσαν, αὐτῷ μὲν ὡς ἥρωϊ τιμὴν εἴτε θείαν εἴτε ἀνθρωπίνην οὐδεμίαν ἥντιν' οὐ περιῆψαν, οἱ δὲ λόγοι αὐτοῦ πρότερον μὲν διαφθείρειν τοὺς νέους ἐδόκουν, ὕστερον δὲ ἐν φαρμάκων εἴδει ὡς μάλιστα σωτηρίων καὶ ὑγιεινῶν μέχρι τοῦ δεῦρο νομίζονται.

s. 15

According to our view of this celebrated society, it is not surprising that it should have presented such a variety of aspects, as to mislead those who fixed their attention on any one of them, and withdrew it from the rest. It was at once a philosophical school, a religious brotherhood, and a political association; and all these characters appear to have been inseparably united in the founder's mind. It must be considered as a proof of upright intentions in Pythagoras, which ought to rescue him from all suspicion of selfish motives, that he chose for his coadjutors persons whom he deemed capable of grasping the highest truths which he could communicate, and was not only willing to teach them all he knew, but regarded the utmost cultivation of their intellectual faculties as a necessary preparation for the work to which he destined them. His lessons were certainly not confined to particular branches of mathematical or physical science, but were clearly meant to throw the fullest light on the greatest questions which can occupy the human mind. Those who were to govern others were first to contemplate the world, and to comprehend the place which they filled in it. The Pythagorean philosophy may indeed appear singularly foreign to the business of a statesman: but we know that some of the greatest both in ancient and modern times have been nourished in such speculations, and the effects of the exercise are not to be measured by the importance of the scientific results.

THIRLWALL.

Τῆς δὲ πολυθρυλήτου ταύτης περὶ κοινωνίας εἴπερ ὀρθῶς ὑπειλήφαμεν οὐδὲν θαυμαστὸν εἰ παντοῖα αὐτῆς ἐφαίνετο τὰ εἴδη ἄλλῳ ἄλλη σκοπουμένῳ ὥστε παράγειν ἂν τὸν ἑνί γέ τῳ μέρει προσέχοντα ἀμελοῦντα δὲ τῶν λοιπῶν. τριῶν γὰρ ἅμα μία οὖσα εἴχετο, φιλοσοφίας, θεοσεβείας, πολιτικῆς, ἃ καὶ συνάπαντα ἐν τῇ τοῦ συστησαμένου διανοίᾳ ἀδιαχωρίστως δοκεῖ συζευχθῆναι. ὅτι δὲ τὰ δίκαια βουλόμενος συνεστήσατο ὁ Πυθαγόρας ὥστε μηδοτιοῦν δεῖ τοῦ φιλαύτου ὕποπτον εἶναι, τεκμήριον καὶ τόδε· τούς τε γὰρ συμπράξοντας προείλετο ὅσοι ἐπίδοξοι δοκοῖεν ἃ ἀκρότατα ἔχοι παραδιδόναι τούτων ἐφικέσθαι, καὶ οὐχ ὅτι ἐβούλετο ἃ εἰδείη αὐτὸς καὶ τούτους διδάσκειν, ἀλλὰ καὶ ὅτι μάλιστα τὰ τῆς διανοίας πεπαιδευμένους ᾤετο οὕτως ἀναγκαίως ἂν εἰς τὸ μέλλον ἔργον προπαρασκευασθῆναι. τὴν γοῦν διδαχὴν δῆλον ὅτι οὐχ ὡρίζετο μέχρι γεωμετρικῶν τινῶν ἢ φυσικῶν ἀφωρισμένων μορίων, τοὐναντίον δὲ ὅσα μέγιστα ἡ ἀνθρωπίνη μεταχειρίζεται διάνοια, ταῦτα τὰ ἐρευνήματα ὡς ἀκριβέστατα ἐβούλετο διασαφῆσαι. τοὺς γὰρ μέλλοντας ἄλλων ἄρχειν πρῶτον ἔδει τὰ τοῦ κόσμου θεωρῆσαι ὡς τὴν ἰδίαν ἕκαστον χώραν μαθησομένους. διὸ καὶ τὴν τοῦ Πυθαγόρου σοφίαν ἐνδέχεται μὲν τοῦ πολιτικοῦ διαφερόντως δὴ ἀλλοτρίαν δοκεῖν εἶναι, ἴσμεν δὲ τοὺς μάλιστα νῦν τε καὶ τότε ἀξιολόγους ἐν ταῖς τοιαύταις ζητήσεσι τρεφομένους· τὰ δ' οὖν συμβεβηκότα τοῖς μελετῶσι ταύτας οὐδαμῶς κρίνεσθαι δεῖ πρὸς τὸ εὖ ἢ μὴ τῶν κατὰ ἐπιστήμην ἀποτελουμένων.

You will observe that all I was charged with, and all by consequence that I am answerable for, was to solicit this court, and to dispose them to grant us the succours necessary to make the attempt, as soon as we should know certainly from England in what it was desired that these succours should consist, and whither they should be sent. Here I found a multitude of people at work, and every one doing what seemed good in his own eyes : no subordination, no order, no concert. Persons concerned in the management of these affairs upon former occasions have assured me, this is always the case. It might be so to some degree ; but I believe never so much as now. The Jacobites had wrought one another up to look upon the success of the present designs as infallible. Every meeting-house which the populace demolished, every little drunken riot which happened, served to confirm them in these sanguine expectations ; and there was hardly one amongst them who would lose the air of contributing by his intrigues to the restoration, which, he took it for granted, would be brought about, without him, in a very few weeks.

                                        BOLINGBROKE.

Ἐνθυμήθητε δὲ ὅτι τοσοῦτον ἐπιτετραμμένος ἦν,
ὥστε μηδ' ἑνὸς ἄλλου δεῖν ὑπεύθυνον εἶναι, εἰ δεόμενος οὕτω διαθείην τοὺς ἐκεῖ ἐν τέλει ὄντας ὅπως τὴν
ἐπὶ τὴν πεῖραν ἱκανὴν βοήθειαν ψηφιοῦνται ἐπειδὴ
τάχιστα παρὰ τῶν οἴκοθεν ἀπαγγελθείη ὁποίας δέοι
ταύτης καὶ ὅποι πεμφθησομένης. ἐνταῦθα δὲ πολλοὺς
εἶδον ἀθρόους μὲν διαπραττομένους, ἕκαστον δὲ ὅ τι
δοκοίη αὑτῷ· οὔτε γὰρ εὔτακτον οὐδέν, οὔτε κατὰ
κόσμον ἢ ὁμόνοιαν ἐγίγνετο. καὶ φασὶ μὲν δὴ οἱ περὶ
τὰ τοιαῦτα πεπονημένοι ὡς ἄρα ταῦτα ὡσαύτως ἀεὶ
γίγνεται· ἀληθῆ γε ἴσως μέχρι του λέγοντες, ἀλλ' οὐδεπώποτε πρότερον οἶμαι ὡς τότε. οἱ γὰρ Ἰακωβίζοντες
ἐπὶ τοσοῦτον δὴ ἀλλήλους ἤδη ἐπέρρωσαν ὡς μηδ'
εἴ τι γένοιτο τῆς γε παραυτίκα πείρας ἀποτευξόμενοι.
εἴτε γὰρ οἰκημάτιόν τι κατασκάψειε τὸ πλῆθος, εἴτε
ἄλλο ὁτιοῦν παροινηθείη, ἐπὶ τὸ μᾶλλον ἔτι εὐέλπιδας
γενέσθαι συνεβάλλετο· ὥστε οὐδεὶς ἦν ὡς ἔπος εἰπεῖν
ὅστις ἂν ἑκὼν ἑαυτὸν ἀποστεροίη τοῦ δοκεῖν εἰς τὴν
κάθοδον καὶ αὐτός τι συμπρᾶξαι, τὴν μέλλουσαν δὴ
καὶ ἄνευ αὐτοῦ οὐ διὰ πολλοῦ ἀποβήσεσθαι.

But were the other, or at least the democratic, states in as bad a condition as Athens? Here we are deserted by history; which has preserved little information on the subject of judicature. But though at Athens several accidental causes, partly arising from the national character, and partly from the political power of that city (for the importance of state-trials increases with the importance of the state) contributed to multiply this class of lawsuits; it by no means follows that the number was much smaller in most of the other Grecian cities. Popular tribunals are the sources of political revolutions, and what states abounded in them more than the Grecian? The man of influence, always an object of envy, was the most exposed to accusations, where it was so easy to find a ground of accusation; but the man of influence had also the greatest resources without the precincts of the court. Supported by his party, if conscious of possessing sufficient strength, he would have recourse to arms, and instead of suffering himself to be banished from the city, prefer to terminate the action by driving away his enemies. Were we more intimately acquainted with the history of the numberless political revolutions in Greece, how often would this same succession of events recur? But though we are not always able to establish them by historical evidence, they cannot on the whole be doubted; and they distinctly exhibit the close connection which existed between the ancient states and their judicial institutions.

HEEREN.

Σκεπτέον δ' ἐνταῦθα καὶ τὰς ἄλλας πόλεις ἤτοι τάς γε δημοκρατουμένας ἢ ἁπάσας εἰ κατὰ τὰ αὐτὰ κακῶς διέκειντο καὶ αἱ Ἀθῆναι· τὸ γὰρ χωρίον τοῦτο ἐκλιπὲς τοῖς συγγράψασιν ἤ τι ἢ οὐδὲν περὶ τῶν δικαστικῶν παραδιδοῦσιν. εἰ δὲ καὶ Ἀθήνησι πολλὰ καὶ ἀπὸ ταὐτομάτου τὰ μὲν διὰ τὸ ἦθος τὸ ἐπιχώριον τὰ δὲ τῆς πολιτικῆς δυνάμεως ἐμποιούσης (ἅμα γὰρ αὔξεται ἡ πόλις καὶ αἱ γραφαὶ αἱ δημόσιαι) εἰς τὸ πληθύειν τὰς τοιαύτας δίκας ἦν τὰ συμβαλλόμενα, οὐκ οὖν διὰ τοῦτό γε πολλῷ ἐλάττονες ἦσαν ἐν τῷ ἄλλῳ ὡς ἔπος εἰπεῖν Ἑλληνικῷ. τὰ γοῦν δικαστήρια δημοτικὰ ὄντα ὡς ἐπὶ τὸ πολὺ νεωτερίζει τὰς πόλεις, τὸ δὲ τοιοῦτον εἴπερ που καὶ ἄλλοθι καὶ ἐν τῇ Ἑλλάδι πλεῖστον καθειστήκει. ὁ γὰρ δυνατὸς ἀεὶ ἐπίφθονος ὢν καὶ εὐδιαβολώτατος ἦν τοσαύτης γε ὑπαρχούσης τῆς ἀφθονίας τῶν κατηγοριῶν· ὁ δὲ αὐτὸς οὐχ ἥκιστα παρασκευάσασθαι ἠδύνατο ἔξωθέν γε τοῦ δικαστηρίου. πεποιθὼς γὰρ τῷ ἑταιρικῷ εἴ ποτε συνειδείη ἑαυτῷ ἱκανῶς ἰσχύοντι, ἐπὶ τὰ ὅπλα ἂν ἐτρέπετο, ὡς προελόμενος πρὸ τοῦ αὐτὸς ἐκπεσεῖν τῆς πόλεως φυγαδεύσας τοὺς ἀντιστασιάζοντας οὕτω τελέσασθαι τὴν δίκην. εἰ δ' οὖν ἀκριβέστερον εἴχομεν τὰς ἐν Ἑλλάδι τῶν πολιτειῶν μεταβολὰς ἀναριθμήτους ὅσας γενομένας διεξιέναι πολλάκις ἂν εἰκὸς τὰ αὐτὰ ὡσαύτως ἀνακυκλεῖσθαι· εἰ δὲ καὶ ἐπιμαρτυρομένοις τοὺς συγγράψαντας ἀδύνατον ταῦτα ἀεὶ παντὶ ἑξῆς τεκμηρίῳ βεβαιώσασθαι οὐκ οὖν διὰ τοῦτό γε ὡς ἐπὶ τὸ πολὺ ἀμφισβητητέον· φανεροῖ δ' οὖν τὰς ἀρχαίας πόλεις ὡς ἐγγυτάτω εἴχοντο τῶν δικαστικῶν.

These reflections, and such as they suggest naturally to the mind, make it evident, that the future prosperity and safety of this country depend on the speedy diminution of our national debts. Nothing else can secure us effectually against contingent events that may be of fatal consequence to both. Recent experience has shown how unfit we are become in every respect, except the courage of our common seamen and soldiers, to engage in war. We shall not therefore, I suppose, provoke it easily, or soon. But war may be brought upon us, though we should not provoke it, nor go to the continent to seek it. Nay, we may be reduced to the melancholy dilemma of increasing our annual expense to assert our rights, to protect our trade, and to maintain our dignity ; or of sitting tamely down and sacrificing them all. I think, nay I hope, that we should not do the last : and yet we should have much greater difficulties to struggle with in our present situation, than we had in the former, great as they were, if we attempted to do what was then so shamefully neglected.

BOLINGBROKE.

Ταῦτα δὲ ἐνθυμουμένοις αὐτά τε καὶ ὅσα παρα-
πλήσιά τῳ ἂν εἰκότως ἐπίοι, φανερὸν ὅτι κεῖται τῇ
πόλει τῇδε ἐν τῷ συντέμνειν ὡς τάχιστα τὰ δημοσίᾳ
ὠφειλημένα ἡ ἐσομένη εὐδαιμονία τε καὶ σωτηρία. ἐπεὶ
τά γε ἀμφοτέραις μετ' ἀνηκέστου κινδύνου ἂν συμβαί-
νοντα τί ἂν ἄλλο ἱκανῶς ἐχέγγυον εἴη ὥστε προφυ-
λάξασθαι; πεπειραμένοις γὰρ ἀρτίως δεδήλωται ὅτι
παντάπασιν, εἰ μή τις τοῦ στρατιωτικοῦ τοῦ τε πεζοῦ
καὶ τοῦ ναυτικοῦ τὴν ἀρετὴν λογίσαιτο, ἄπειροι ἤδη
γεγενήμεθα ἐς τὸ αἴρεσθαι πόλεμον. σχολῇ τοίνυν ἂν
οἶμαι καὶ βραδέως προκαλεσαίμεθα αὐτόν· καίτοι τάχ'
ἂν ἐπιόντα ἀμυντέον εἴη, καὶ ταῦτα μήτε προκαλεσα-
μένοις μήτε ἐς τὴν ἀλλοτρίαν ἐπιδημήσασιν ὥστ'
ἐπιζητεῖν. ἀλλὰ μὴν ἐς τοσοῦτό γε ἀτυχίας καὶ ἀπορίας
τάχ' ἂν κατασταῖμεν ὥστε ἤτοι τὰ κατ' ἔτος ἀπαναλισκό-
μενα ἔτι μᾶλλον δαπανᾶν ὑπερμαχοῦντες μὲν τῶν δικαίων
βοηθοῦντες δὲ τῇ τε ἐμπορίᾳ καὶ αὐτῷ τῷ ἀξιώματι,
ἢ καταρρᾳθυμοῦντες ταῦτα πάντα καθάπαξ προΐεσθαι.
καὶ τοῦτο μὲν οἶμαι μᾶλλον δὲ ἐλπίζω οὐδ' ἂν εἴ τι
γένοιτο ἡμᾶς γ' ἂν ποιῆσαι· καίτοι πολὺ ἂν ἐλαφροτέ-
ροις δέοι τοῖς τότε, καίπερ οὐδ' ἐκείνοις ἐλαφρῶς ἔχουσιν,
ἀντιστῆναι ἢ τοῖς νῦν, εἰ τὰ τότε μὲν αἰσχρῶς ἠμελή-
σαμεν, τὰ δὲ νῦν ἐπιχειρήσαιμεν πράττειν.

There is according to Plato properly no knowledge, but only opinion concerning things sensible and perishing, not because they are naturally abstrusive and involved in darkness, but because their nature and existence is uncertain, ever fleeting and changing. Or rather because they do not, in strict truth, exist at all, being always generating or *in fieri*, that is in a perpetual flux, without anything stable or permanent in them to constitute an object of real science. The Pythagoreans and Platonics distinguish between that which is ever generated and that which exists. Sensible things and corporeal forms are perpetually producing and perishing, appearing and disappearing, never resting in one state, but always in motion and change, and therefore in effect not one being but a succession of beings : while τὸ ὄν is understood to be something of an abstract or spiritual nature, and the proper object of intellectual knowledge. Therefore, as there can be no knowledge of things flowing and instable, the opinion of Pythagoras, and Theaetetus, that sense was science, is absurd. As understanding perceiveth not, that is, doth not hear or see or feel, so sense knoweth not ; and although the mind may use both sense and fancy, as means whereby to arrive at knowledge, yet sense, or soul, so far forth as sensitive, knoweth nothing. For, as it is rightly observed, science consisteth not in the passive perceptions, but in the reasoning upon them.

BERKELEY.

Περὶ δὲ τὰ αἰσθητὰ καὶ φθαρτὰ κατὰ Πλάτωνα κυρίως δόξα μὲν ἂν εἴη, ἐπιστήμη δὲ οὔ. οὐχ ὡς φύσει ἀποκεκρυμμένου καὶ σκοτεινοῦ ὄντος ἑκάστου τούτων, ἀλλ' ὅτι πέφυκεν ἀβέβαια εἶναι, ἅτε ὑπορρέοντα ἀεὶ καὶ ἀλλοιούμενα· μᾶλλον δὲ ὅτι, ὡς ἀκριβεῖ λόγῳ εἰπεῖν, πάνυ οὐδὲ ἔστιν, ἀλλ' ἀεὶ γίγνεται ἐν ῥοῇ τινὶ συνεχεῖ ὄντα διὰ τὸ μηδὲν στάσιμον αὐτοῖς ἐνυπάρχειν καὶ πάγιον ὥστε καὶ ὡς ἀληθῶς ἐπιστητὰ εἶναι. οἵ τε γὰρ Πυθαγόρειοι καὶ οἱ ἀμφὶ Πλάτωνα διαιροῦνται τὸ ὂν καὶ τὸ ἀεὶ γιγνόμενον· ὡς ἄρα τὸ μὲν αἰσθητὸν καὶ σωματοειδὲς οὐδέποτε παύεται γεννώμενόν τε καὶ ἀπολλύμενον καὶ ὁτὲ μὲν φαινόμενον ὁτὲ δὲ ἀφανιζόμενον, οὐδὲ ἐν τῷ αὐτῷ μένει χρόνον οὐδένα, ἀλλ' ἀεὶ κινεῖται καὶ μεταβάλλει, ὥστε μηδὲ τὸ μᾶλλον δὲ τὰ δεῖν ὀνομασθῆναι· τὸ δέ γε ὂν ὡς χωριστόν τι αὐτὸ καθ' αὑτὸ καὶ ἀσώματον ὑποληπτέον, οὗ ἐφάπτεται ἡ ἐπιστήμη καὶ ἡ διάνοια. διὸ καὶ ἐπειδὴ τὰ ἐν ῥοῇ καὶ κινήσει οὐκ ἐπιστητά ἐστιν, ἀτόπως ᾤοντο Πυθαγόρας καὶ Θεαίτητος, αἴσθησιν ἐπιστήμην ἀποφαινόμενοι. ὡς γὰρ ἡ διάνοια οὐκ αἰσθάνεται, οὔτε γὰρ ὁρᾷ οὔτε ἀκούει οὔτε ἅπτεται, ὡσαύτως οὐδὲ ἡ αἴσθησις ἐπίσταται· τῇ δὲ αἰσθήσει καὶ φαντασίᾳ εἰ καὶ χρησάμενος ὁ νοῦς οὕτω διὰ τούτων τῆς ἐπιστήμης ἐφικνεῖται, ἀλλ' οὔτ' ἐκεῖναι οὔθ' ἡ ψυχὴ καθ' ὅσον αἰσθητικὴ οὐδὲν ἐπίσταται, ὀρθῶς εἰρημένον ὅτι ἐν μὲν τοῖς παθήμασι τοῖς διὰ τῶν αἰσθήσεων οὐκ ἔνι ἐπιστήμη, ἐν δὲ τῷ περὶ ἐκείνων συλλογισμῷ.

Is it possible, trow you, that king Richard should damn his soul, and foul his name with so abominable a murder, and yet not mend his case? Or do you think that men of blood, that were his instruments, did turn to pity in the midst of their execution? Whereas in cruel and savage beasts, and men also, the first draught of blood doth yet make them more fierce and enraged. Do you not know that the bloody executioners of tyrants do go to such errands with an halter around their neck; so that if they perform not, they are sure to die for it? And do you think that these men would hazard their own lives, for sparing another's? Admit they should have saved him; what should they have done with him? Turn him into London streets, that the watchmen, or any other passenger that should light upon him, should carry him before a justice, and so all come to light? Or should they have kept him by them secretly? That surely would have required a great deal of care, charge, and continual fears. But, my lords, I labour too much in a clear business. The king is so wise, and hath so good friends abroad, as that he knoweth duke Perkin from his cradle. And because he is a great prince, if you have any good poet here, he can help him with notes to write his life; and to parallel him with Lambert Simnel, now the king's falconer.

BACON.

Ἦ δοκεῖτε Ῥίχαρδον, κινδυνεύοντά τε τὴν ἐν Ἅιδου
τιμωρίαν καὶ τῷ αὐτοῦ ὀνόματι δόξαν τὴν αἰσχίστην
περιάψοντα, τὸν καταρατὸν τουτονὶ φόνον ἀπεργάσασθαι
ὥστε μηδὲν πλέον ἀποβῆναι ; δοκοῦσι γὰρ ὑμῖν ἄνδρες
μιαιφόνοι, οἷοι καὶ ὑπηρέτησαν αὐτῷ, μεταξὺ ἀποκτιν-
νύντες εἰς ἔλεον τραπέσθαι ; τὸ δὲ ἐπὶ τῶν ἀγρίων
θηρίων τε καὶ ἀνθρώπων τὸ ἅπαξ γεύσασθαι αἵματος
ἔτι σκληρότερα καὶ μανικώτερα ἀπειργάσατο ἀμφότερα.
ἴστε γὰρ δήπου ὅτι ὅσοι διὰ φόνου τὰ τοιαῦτα ὑπουρ-
γοῦσι τοῖς τυράννοις βρόχοις αὐχένα δεδεμένοι βαδί-
ζουσιν εἰς τὸ ἔργον, ὡς ἐὰν μὴ διαπράξωσι καὶ αὐτοὶ
ἀνταποθανούμενοι. καίτοι πῶς οἷόν τε τοὺς τοιούτους
τῆς ἀλλοτρίας ψυχῆς φειδομένους ὑπὲρ τῆς σφετέρας
κινδυνεῦσαι ; καὶ δὴ ἔσωσαν αὐτόν· τί μέντοι ἐχρή-
σαντο ; ἀλλὰ νὴ Δί᾽ εἰς ἀγυιὰς διέφρησαν, ὅπως δὴ οἱ
τοξόται ἢ καὶ τῶν παριόντων τις παρὰ τοὺς δικαστὰς
ἀπαγαγὼν οὕτω δὴ εἰς φανερὸν κατέστησε τὸ πρᾶγμα.
ἀλλὰ κρύβδην οἴκοι παρ᾽ ἑαυτοῖς ἔτρεφον· ἀλλὰ τοῦτό
γε πολλῆς ἂν ἔδει τῆς ἐπιμελείας καὶ οὐκ ἄνευ δαπάνης
καὶ φόβου συνεχοῦς ἂν ἐγένετο. ἀλλὰ γὰρ ἐν ὁμολο-
γουμένῳ τῷ πράγματι λίαν ταλαιπωρῶ. ὁ γὰρ βασιλεύς,
αὐτός τε σοφὸς ὢν καὶ πολλοῖς τῶν ἔξωθεν φίλοις
χρώμενος, τὸν Πέρκινον τουτονὶ οἷός ἐστιν ἤδη ἐκ
παιδὸς δίοιδεν. ἅτε δὲ γενναίου ὄντος τουτουί, εἴ τις
ἄρα ὑπάρχει τῶν ἐνθένδε ἀξιόλογος ποιητής, συγγρά-
ψειεν ἂν τὰ τουτῳὶ βεβιωμένα βοηθοῦντος ὑπομνήμασι
καὶ αὐτοῦ τοῦ βασιλέως, ὥστε ἐξισοῦσθαι τῷ Λαμβέρτῳ
τῷ Σιμνήλῳ ἐπικαλουμένῳ, ὃς καὶ νῦν τῶν ὀρτυγο-
τρόφων ἐστὶ τῶν βασιλείων.

Not that I can tax or condemn the morigeration or application of learned men to men in fortune. For the answer was good that Diogenes made to one that asked him in mockery, 'How it came to pass that philosophers were the followers of rich men, and not rich men of philosophers?' He answered soberly, and yet sharply, 'Because the one sort knew what they had need of, and the other did not.' And of the like nature was the answer which Aristippus made, when having a petition to Dionysius, and no ear given to him, he fell down at his feet; whereupon Dionysius staid, and gave him the hearing, and granted it; and afterward some person, tender on the behalf of philosophy, reproved Aristippus, 'that he would offer the profession of philosophy such an indignity, as, for a private suit, to fall at the feet of Dionysius.' But he answered, 'it was not his fault, but the fault of Dionysius, that he had his ears in his feet.' Neither was it accounted weakness, but discretion in him that would not dispute his best with Adrianus Cæsar; excusing himself 'that it was reason to yield to him that commanded thirty legions.' These and the like applications, and stooping to points of necessity and convenience, cannot be disallowed: for though they may have some outward baseness, yet in a judgement truly made, they are to be accounted submissions to the occasion and not to the person.

BACON.

Οὐ μὴν οὐδὲ τοῖς φιλοσόφοις τό γε ὑποπίπτειν τοῖς πλουσίοις καὶ προστάτας ἐγγράφεσθαι αὐτοὺς οὐδὲν οὔτ' ἔχω ἐπιτιμᾶν οὔτε κατηγορῶ. κομψὸν γὰρ τὸ Διογένους, ὃς τῷ σκωπτικῶς ποτε ἐρομένῳ διότι φιλόσοφοι ἀκολουθοῖεν τοῖς ἔχουσιν ἀλλ' οὐχὶ οὗτοι ἐκείνοις, σωφρόνως μὲν ὀξέως δὲ ἀποκρινόμενος, ὅτι οἱ μέν, ἔφη, ἴσασιν ὧν δέονται οἱ δὲ οὔ. παραπλήσιον δέ τι ἀπεκρίνατο καὶ Ἀρίστιππος· δεόμενος γάρ τι Διονυσίου οὐχ ὑπακούοντος παρὰ τοὺς πόδας αὐτῷ προσέπεσε· διὸ καὶ ὁ Διονύσιος παραμείνας καὶ προσσχὼν ἐχαρίσατο. ὕστερον δέ τις φιλοτιμούμενος ἐπὶ τῇ φιλοσοφίᾳ ἐπέπληξε τῷ Ἀριστίππῳ οἷα τὸ τοιοῦτον ἐπιτήδευμα ἀτιμάσειεν ἰδίας χρείας ἕνεκεν ἀνδρὶ τυράννῳ παρὰ τοὺς πόδας προσπεσών. ὁ δὲ οὐκ ἔφη αὐτὸς αἴτιος εἶναι ἀλλ' ἐκεῖνον τοῦ γε ἔχειν ἐν τοῖς ποσὶ τὰ ὦτα. οὐδέ γε ἐκεῖνος ἠλίθιος ἐδόκει εἶναι μᾶλλον ἢ φρόνιμος ὃς Ἀδριανῷ τῷ Καίσαρι ἀμφισβητῶν εἰρωνεύετο· ἀπελογεῖτο γὰρ ὅτι λόγον ἔχοι ὑποχωρεῖν τῷ γε τριάκοντα στρατοπέδων ἄρχοντι. ταῦτα δὴ καὶ τὰ τοιαῦτα θεραπεύειν ἔστιν ὅτε τῇ ἀνάγκῃ καὶ τῷ ὠφελίμῳ ὑπείκοντα ἐατέον. αἰσχρὰ γὰρ οὑτωσὶ μὲν σκοπεῖν τάχ' ἂν φανείη, τῷ μέντοι λόγῳ λαμβάνοντι τῷ καιρῷ δοκοῦσιν οἵ γε τοιοῦτοι ὑπείκοντες ἀλλ' οὐ τῷ ἀνθρώπῳ.

Again, since there can be no goodness desired which proceedeth not from God himself, as from the supreme cause of all things ; and every effect doth after a sort contain, at leastwise resemble the cause from which it proceedeth : all things in the world are said in some sort to seek the highest, and to covet more or less the participation of God himself.   Yet this doth nowhere so much appear as it doth in man, because there are so many kinds of perfections which man seeketh.   The first degree of goodness is that general perfection which all things do seek, in desiring the continuance of their being.   All things therefore coveting as much as may be to be like unto God in being ever, that which cannot hereunto attain personally, doth seek to continue itself another way, that is by offspring and propagation.   The next degree of goodness is that which each thing coveteth by affecting resemblance with God in the constancy and excellency of those operations which belong unto their kind.   The immutability of God they strive unto, by working either always or for the most part after one and the same manner : his absolute exactness they imitate, by tending unto that which is most exquisite in every particular.   Hence have risen a number of axioms in philosophy, showing how ' the works of nature do always aim at that which cannot be bettered.'

HOOKER.

Ἔτι δὲ ἐπεὶ οὐδενὸς ἀγαθοῦ ἐπορεγόμεθα, ὃ μὴ ἀπὸ
τοῦ θείου αὐτοῦ ἀποβαίνει· τοῦτο γὰρ κυριώτατον
πάντων αἴτιον· τὸ δὲ ἀποβαῖνον τούτῳ ὅθεν καὶ
ἀποβαίνει ἤτοι ὡμοίωταί γε ἢ τρόπον τινὰ περιέχει
αὐτό· ἅπαντα μὲν δηλονότι ἐπιζητεῖν πως λέγεται
τὸ ἀκρότατον, ἐφιέμενα τὰ μὲν πλέον τὰ δὲ ἔλαττον
τῆς τοῦ θείου αὐτοῦ μεθέξεως· ἐπὶ δὲ τοῦ ἀνθρώπου
τοῦτο εἴπερ καὶ ἐπ' ἄλλου του τοσούτῳ μάλιστα
ἐμφαίνεται, ὅσῳ ἂν καὶ πλεῖστα ᾖ τὰ τέλεια ἃ ὁ
τοιοῦτος ἐπιζητεῖ. τῆς δὲ ἀρετῆς πρῶτον μὲν τὸ ἁπλῶς
τέλειον πάντα ἐπιζητεῖ· ἐπορέγεται γὰρ τοῦ ἀεὶ ὄντα
διατελεῖν· ὥστε κατὰ δύναμιν ἐφιέμενα ὡμοιῶσθαι τῷ
θείῳ ἀεὶ ὄντι, τὸ μὴ αὐτὸ καθ' αὑτὸ τούτου τυχεῖν
δυνάμενον ἄλλως πως διατελεῖν ὂν ἐπιζητεῖ, λέγω δὲ
οἷον διὰ σπόρου καὶ τοῦ τοιοῦτον οἷον αὐτὸ καταλιπεῖν.
τῆς δὲ δευτέρας ἐπορεγόμενα ἐφίεται τῆς τοῦ θείου
ὁμοιώσεως τῷ ἀτρεμεῖς ἔχειν καὶ καλλίστας τὰς
ἐνεργείας κατὰ τὸ οἰκεῖον ἕκαστον εἶδος. τῆς δὲ
ἀμετακινήτου τούτου φύσεως ὂν μὲν τρόπον ἐπορέγεται,
ἕνα τινὰ καὶ τὸν αὐτὸν ἀεὶ ἢ ὡς ἐπὶ τὸ πολὺ ἐνεργεῖ·
τὴν δὲ αὐτάρκειαν τὴν τελειοτάτην μιμούμενα ὅ τι ἂν
ᾖ καθ' ἕκαστον εἶδος αἱρετώτατον εἰς τοῦτο ἀποβλέπει.
σημεῖον δὲ τὰ πολλάκις ὑπὸ σοφῶν ἀνδρῶν θρυλούμενα,
ὅτι τὰ φύσει ἀεὶ ἐπορέγεται τοῦ ἀνυπερβλήτου.

Those who believe a future state of rewards and punishments act very absurdly, if they form their opinions of a man's merit from his successes. But certainly, if I thought the whole circle of our being was concluded between our births and deaths, I should think a man's good fortune the measure and standard of his real merit, since Providence would have no opportunity of rewarding his virtue and perfections, but in the present life. A virtuous unbeliever, who lies under the pressure of misfortunes, has reason to cry out, as they say Brutus did a little before his death, O Virtue, I have worshipped thee as a substantial good, but I find thou art an empty name. But to return to our first point. Though prudence does undoubtedly in a great measure produce our good or ill fortune in the world, it is certain there are many unforeseen accidents and occurrences, which very often pervert the finest schemes that can be laid by human wisdom. Nay it very often happens that prudence, which has always in it a great mixture of caution, hinders a man from being so fortunate as he might possibly have been without it. A person who only aims at what is likely to succeed, and follows closely the dictates of human prudence, never meets with those great and unforeseen successes, which are often the effect of a sanguine temper, or a more happy rashness ; and this perhaps may be the reason that, according to the common observation, Fortune, like other females, delights rather in favouring the young than the old.

ADDISON.

Ὅστις τοῖς ἐκεῖσε ἀφικομένοις τοῖς μὲν ἀγαθὰ τοῖς
δὲ κακὰ ὑπάρχειν νομίζει ἀτοπώτατόν τι ποιεῖ εἰ κατὰ
τὰ ἀποβαίνοντα ἑκάστῳ καὶ περὶ τῆς ἀξίας αὐτοῦ
δοξάζει. εἰ μέντοι περιγεγράφθαι ἡγούμην ὅλον τὸν
βίον ἡμῶν ἐν τῷ μεταξὺ γενέσεως καὶ τελευτῆς, ᾠόμην
ἂν δηλονότι μέτρον εἶναι τῆς ἀληθοῦς ἀξίας καὶ κριτή-
ριον τὴν εὐπραγίαν ἑκάστου, ἄλλοθί που μὴ ἐξὸν εἰ μὴ
μόνον ἐνθάδε τῷ θείῳ μισθὸν ἀποδοῦναι τῆς τελείας
ἀρετῆς. εἰκότως τοίνυν ἂν ἀγανακτοίη ἅπερ φασὶ
Βροῦτον ὀλίγον πρὸ τοῦ θανάτου ὁ ἀγαθός, νομίζων
μὲν μηδὲν ταῦτα ταλαιπωρίαις δὲ πιεζόμενος, ὅτι

> ὦ τλῆμον ἀρετή, λόγος ἄρ᾽ ἦσθ᾽· ἐγὼ δέ σε
> ὡς ἔργον ἤσκουν.

ἀνίωμεν δὲ εἰς τὰ πρότερα. πολλὰ μὲν εἰς εὐτυχίαν
ἡμῶν ἔτι ζώντων ἡ φρόνησις συμβάλλεται· ἀναμφισ-
βήτητον δὲ κἀκεῖνο ὅτι συχνὰ ἐνδέχεται καὶ συμβαίνει
ὅσων οὐδὲν προορώμεθα, ἃ πλειστάκις τῶν τοῖς γε
σοφωτάτοις κάλλιστα δοξάντων φθαρτικὰ ἂν εἴη.
ἀλλὰ μὴν καὶ ἥ γε φρόνησις αὐτή, ἧς ἀεὶ πολὺ μετέχει
ἡ εὐλάβεια, πολλάκις ἐκώλυσέ τινα μὴ τοσοῦτον
εὐδαιμονῆσαι ὅσον ἐνεχώρει ἀπούσης αὐτῆς. ὁ γὰρ
μηδενὸς ἄλλου ἢ τῶν κατορθοῦσθαι ἐπιδόξων ἐφιέμενος
καὶ ὅσα ἐξηγεῖται ἡ φρόνησις ἡ ἀνθρωπίνη συνεχῶς
ἀκολουθῶν, τῶν μεγάλων οὐδέποτε τυγχάνει κατορθω-
μάτων, ἃ προὖπτα μὲν οὔ, πολλάκις δὲ τοῦ ἀποβαίνειν
αὐτὰ αἴτιός ἐστιν ὁ εὔελπις ἢ καὶ ὁ ἀπερισκέπτως μὲν
εὐτυχῶς δὲ κινδυνεύων. ὅπερ καὶ τάχ᾽ ἂν ἐπαληθεύοι
τὸ λεγόμενον, ὥσπερ τὸ ἄλλο θῆλυ γένος καὶ ἡ τύχη
φιλεῖ μᾶλλον χαρίζεσθαι τοῖς νέοις ἢ τοῖς γεραιτέροις.

We entered a small square: it had been a market-place: the roofs of the stalls were demolished, and the stones of several columns, not one of which was standing, thrown down to supply the cramps of iron and the lead that fastened them, served for the spectators, male and female, to mount upon. Five men were nailed on crosses; two others were nailed against a wall, from scarcity, as we were told, of wood. Can seven men have murdered their parents in the same year? cried I.

No, nor had any of the seven, replied the first who had spoken. But when heavy impositions were laid upon those who were backward in voluntary contributions, these men, among the richest in our city, protested by the gods, that they had no gold or silver left. They protested truly. And they die for this! inhuman, insatiable, inexorable wretch! Their books, added he, unmoved at my reproaches, were seized by public authority and examined. It was discovered that instead of employing their riches in external or internal commerce, or in agriculture, or in manufactories, instead of reserving it for the embellishment of the city, or the utility of the citizens, instead of lending it on interest to the industrious and the needy, they had lent it to foreign kings and tyrants, some of whom were waging wars against their neighbours by these very means, and others were enslaving their own country. For so heinous a crime the laws had appointed no specific punishment.

LANDOR.

Εἰσελθόντες δὲ εἰς χωρίον τι οὐ μέγα, ὅπου ἀγορὰ πρότερον ἦν—αἱ δὲ ὀροφαὶ τῶν σκηνῶν ἤδη κατεσκαμμέναι ἦσαν, τῶν τε στηλῶν, ὧν οὐδεμία ἔτι συνειστήκει, τούτων οἱ λίθοι καθῃρημένοι εἰς χρείαν μολυβδίνων ἢ σιδηρῶν συνδέσμων τοῖς θεωμένοις, ἀνδράσι τε ἅμα καὶ γυναιξί, βῆμα ὑπῆρχον—εἰσελθόντες δὲ ἑπτὰ ἄνδρας κατελάβομεν· ὧν οἱ μὲν πέντε ἀνεσταυρωμένοι ἦσαν, οἱ δὲ δύο προσήλωντο τῷ τοίχῳ, ἅτε σπανίζοντος ὡς ἔφασαν τοῦ ξύλου. τί δέ; ἦν δ' ἐγώ· ἑπτὰ γὰρ ἄνθρωποι τοὺς γονέας ἐν τῷ αὐτῷ ἐνιαυτῷ ἀπεκτονότες ἂν εἶεν; οὐδὲ γὰρ εἷς τῶν ἑπτά, ἦ δ' ὃς ὁ πρότερον διαλεχθείς, ἐπειδὴ δὲ μεγάλας ζημίας εἰσεπραττόμεθα τοὺς μὴ ἑκουσίως ἐπιδιδόντας, οὗτοι δὴ ἐν τοῖς πλουσιωτάτοις τῶν ἀστῶν διεμαρτύραντο τοὺς θεοὺς ἦ μὴν μήτε χρυσίου μήτε ἀργυρίου μηδὲν σφίσι περιεῖναι, ἀληθῆ γε διαμαρτυρόμενοι. εἶτα τούτων γε ἕνεκεν ἀποθνήσκουσιν, ὦ ἀναιδέστατε σύ, καὶ μάλιστ' ἀνθρώπων ἄπληστε καὶ ἀπαραίτητε; προσκαλεσάμενοι δὲ οἱ ἄρχοντες, ἦ δ' ὅς, ὀνειδίζοντός μου οὐδὲν ἐντρεπόμενος, εἰς ἐμφανῶν κατάστασιν, ἐξήταζον τὰ γραμματεῖα, φανεροὶ δ' ἐνταῦθα ἐγένοντο ἀντὶ μὲν τοῦ ἀναλῶσαι εἰς ἐμπορίαν τὰ χρήματα εἴτε ἔνδημον εἴθ' ὑπερορίαν, ἢ γεωργίαν ἢ καὶ χειρουργήματα, ἀντὶ δὲ τοῦ περιποιήσασθαι εἴτε εἰς κόσμον τοῦ ἄστεος εἴτε εἰς τὸ συμφέρον τοῖς πολίταις, ἀντὶ δὲ τοῦ τοκίσαι τοῖς φιλέργοις καὶ ἀπορωτέροις, ἀλλὰ καὶ δανείσαντες τοῖς ἀλλοφύλοις τυράννοις τε καὶ βασιλεῦσιν, ὧν οἱ μὲν ἀπ' αὐτῶν τούτων ἀδίκως τοῖς πλησιοχώροις ἐπολέμουν οἱ δὲ τὴν οἰκείαν κατεδουλοῦντο. τῇ δὲ ἀδικίᾳ ταύτῃ ἐν ὑπερβολῇ οὔσῃ οὐδεμία ἀφωρισμένη ζημία ἔκειτο.

And what signifies to me the esteem of others, if I cannot obtain my own ? I sometimes carry the mean idea I entertain of my own abilities even to contempt. What advantage have I derived from them ? Have I ever been able to obtain public employments, the offices of magistracy, or the applause and honours which I daily see bestowed on those base orators who betray the state ? Though my panegyric on Athens made those rhetoricians blush who had before treated the same subject, and discouraged others from again attempting it, I have always spoken of my successes with modesty, or rather with humility. My intentions are pure ; I have never either by writings or accusations done injury to any man ; yet I have enemies. What then ! must you not expect to pay the tribute of your merit by some disquietudes ? Your enemies are more to be pitied than yourself. An unwelcome voice perpetually reminds them that kings, generals, statesmen, historians, and authors in every branch of literature, are numbered among your disciples ; that whole colonies of learned and ingenious men from time to time issue from your school, who spread your doctrines far and wide ; that you govern Greece by your pupils ; and, to make use of your own expression, that you are the stone that whets the instrument. —True ; but it is not the stone that cuts.

                                        ANACHARSIS.

Τί δὲ μέλει μοι τοῦ ὑπ' ἄλλων ζηλοῦσθαι μηδέν γε ὑπ' ἐμαυτοῦ ζηλουμένῳ; τὴν γὰρ ἐμὴν φύσιν ἀεὶ καταμεμφόμενος ἔστιν ὅτε προάγομαι καὶ πάνυ καταφρονεῖν. τί γὰρ ἐνθένδε πώποτέ μοι γεγένηται ὄφελος; τίνα γὰρ ἀρχὴν ἦρξα, τίνα δὲ χειροτονίαν ἐχειροτονήθην, τίνος δὲ καὶ ἐπαίνου ἢ τίνων τιμῶν ἔτυχον οἵων τοὺς αἰσχροὺς τουτουσὶ ῥήτορας τοὺς τὴν πόλιν προπεπωκότας καθ' ἡμέραν ὁρῶ ἀξιουμένους; εἰ δὲ καὶ ἐν τῷ πανηγυρικῷ εὐλογήσας τὰς Ἀθήνας τοὺς μὲν περὶ τὰ αὐτὰ πρότερον πεπονημένους εἰς αἰσχύνην ἔτρεψα, τοὺς δὲ μηκέτι τοῦ λοιποῦ ἐπιχειρῆσαι κατέπαυσα, ὅμως δὲ περὶ τῶν κατωρθωμένων μοι μετρίως ἀεὶ μᾶλλον δὲ ταπεινῶς διαλέγομαι. ἔτι δὲ τὰ δίκαια ἀεὶ διανοούμενος καὶ οὐδένα πώποτε οὔτε γράφων οὔτε γραφόμενος βλάψας, ὅμως ἔστι πρὸς οὓς ἐπιφθόνως διάκειμαι. τί δαί; εἰκὸς γάρ πού σε ἀντὶ τῆς εὐδοκιμήσεως ὡσπερανεὶ ἀποφοράν τινα ἀποτῖσαι ὀλίγ' ἄττα ἀνιώμενον· οἱ γὰρ ἐχθροὶ ἐλεεῖσθαι ἀξιώτεροι ἢ αὐτός, οἷς γε φωνή τις ἀηδὴς ἀεὶ διατεθρύληται τοῖς ὠσίν, ὅσοι βασιλεῖς τε καὶ ἄνδρες πολιτικοί, συγγραφεῖς ἅμα καὶ περὶ παντοίας μαθήσεις πραγματευόμενοι τῆς σῆς συνουσίας ἀπολαύουσιν. ὅτι δὲ παρὰ σοῦ ἀποικίαι ὅλαι ἀνδρῶν σοφῶν τε καὶ εὐφυῶν ἑκάστοτε ἀποπεμπόμεναι ἑκασταχόσε τὰ σὰ μαθήματα ἐκφέρουσιν, ὥστε καὶ ἤδη διὰ τῶν μαθητῶν σὲ ἄρχειν τῆς Ἑλλάδος, καί, ὥσπερ φὴς καὶ αὐτός, εἶναι ἀκόνην τὴν θήγουσαν τὸν σίδηρον. ναί· ἀλλ' οὐκ αὐτή γε τέμνει ἡ ἀκόνη.

Instead of selfishness seducing a man, which it often does, from the observations of truth and honesty, it is vastly oftener on the side of these observations. Generally speaking, it is not more his interest that he should have men of integrity to deal with than that he himself should, in his own dealings, be strictly observant of this virtue. To be abandoned by the confidence of his fellows, he would find to be not more mortifying to his pride, than ruinous to his prosperity in the world. We are aware that many an occasional harvest is made from deceit and injustice ; but, in the vast majority of cases, men would cease to thrive when they ceased to be trusted. A man's actual truth is not more beneficial to others, than the reputation of it is gainful to himself. And therefore it is that, throughout the mercantile world, men are as sensitive of an aspersion on their name, as they would be of an encroachment on their property. The one, in fact, is tantamount to the other. It is thus that, under the constraints of selfishness alone, fidelity and justice may be in copious and current observation among men ; and while perhaps the principle of these virtues is exceedingly frail and uncertain in all hearts, human society may still subsist by the literal and outward observation of them.

CHALMERS.

Τὸ δὲ φίλαυτον οὐχ ὅπως παράγει τοὺς ἀνθρώπους, καίπερ καὶ τοῦτο ἔστιν ὅτε ποιοῦν, τοῦ μὴ τό τε ἀψευδεῖν καὶ τὸ ἀληθὲς νομίσαι, ἀλλὰ καὶ συχνῷ πλεονάκις πρὸς τῆς νομίσεως ταύτης ἂν εἴη. ὡς γὰρ ἐπὶ τὸ πολὺ οὐ μᾶλλόν τι συμφέρει τῷ ἀνθρώπῳ πιστοῖς χρῆσθαι τοῖς πρὸς αὐτὸν κοινωνοῦσιν, ἢ καὶ ἀκριβῶς αὐτὸν τοιουτότροπον γενέσθαι. τὸ γὰρ μηκέτι πιστεύεσθαι πρὸς τοὺς πλησίον καταμάθοι ἂν οὐ μόνον αὐτῷ λυπηρὸν εἶναι ἐφ' ἑαυτῷ ὡς εἰκὸς μέγα φρονοῦντι, ἢ καὶ βλαβερὸν προσκοινωνοῦντι πρὸς τοὺς ἄλλους. καίτοι σύνισμέν γε ἔστιν ὅτε πολλοῖς πολλὰ τῆς ἀδικίας καὶ φενακισμοῦ καρπωσαμένοις· πολλῷ μέντοι ἐπὶ πλειόνων ἅμα τις οὐκέτι ἐπιστεύθη καὶ ἐπαύσατο εὖ πράττων. τὸ γὰρ δίκαιον εἶναι οὐ τοῖς πέλας ὠφελιμώτερον ἢ τὸ δοκεῖν ἑαυτῷ λυσιτελέστερον. διὸ καὶ συμβαίνει τοῖς χρηματιζομένοις ὅτι ταὐτὸν πάσχουσι κακῶς ἀκούοντες καὶ εἴ τις ἐπινέμοι τι τῆς οὐσίας. ταὐτὸν γὰρ δῆλον ὅτι θάτερον τῷ ἑτέρῳ. ὅθεν καὶ κρατοῦντος καὶ μόνου τοῦ φιλαύτου, ἐνδέχεται παρὰ τοῖς ἀνθρώποις πλειστάκις νομίζεσθαι καὶ ἐπιπολάζειν τό τε πιστὸν καὶ τὸ δίκαιον, τῶν δὲ ἀρετῶν τούτων τὴν μὲν προαίρεσιν ὡς ἀστάθμητόν τι καὶ εὐμετάβολον εἴπερ τι καὶ ἄλλο ἐν τῇ διανοίᾳ καθιδρῦσθαι, τὴν μέντοι ἀνθρωπίνην κοινωνίαν συμμένειν οὑτωσὶ καὶ ἐπιπολῆς νομιζομένων αὐτῶν.

It is certain then that if ever such men as call themselves friends to the government, but are real enemies to the constitution, prevail, they will make it a capital point of their wicked policy to keep up a standing army. False appearances of reason for it will never be wanting as long as there are pretenders to the crown : though nothing can be more absurd than to employ in defence of liberty an instrument so often employed to destroy it : though nothing can be more absurd than to maintain that any government ought to make use of the same expedient to support itself as another government, on the ruins of which this government stands, was subverted for using : though nothing can be proved more manifestly by experience than these two propositions ; that Britain is enabled by her situation to support her government when the bulk of the people are for it, without employing any means inconsistent with her constitution : and that the bulk of the people are not only always for the government, when the government supports the constitution, but are even hard and slow to be detached from it, when the government attacks and undermines the constitution, and when they are by consequence justified, and even obliged in conscience to resist the government.

BOLINGBROKE.

Φανεροὶ δ' εἰσὶν οἱ τοιοῦτοι, οἱ λόγῳ μὲν εὖνοι τοῖς πολιτευομένοις τῷ δὲ ἔργῳ δύσνοι τοῖς καθεστῶσιν, ὅτι ἐὰν ἄρα ποτὲ ἰσχύσωσι, τοῦτο εἴπερ καί τι ἄλλο ὅτι μάλιστα πονηρεύσονται ὅπως στρατιά τις ὑπάρξει ἀίδιος. οὐδὲ γὰρ ἐνδεήσει προφάσεων καίπερ ψευδῶν οὐσῶν, ἕως ἂν ὦσιν οἱ ἀντιποιούμενοι τῆς βασιλείας· καίτοι τί ἂν εἴη ἀλογώτερον ἢ τοῦτο, τὸ πολλάκις διαλῦον τὴν ἐλευθερίαν, τοῦτο αὐτὸ τοὺς προπολε- μοῦντας ὑπὲρ ἐλευθερίας ἐπιτηδεύειν; ἀλογώτατον δὲ κἀκεῖνο ὅστις ἰσχυρίζεται ὡς ἄρα οἱ μὲν τῇ τοιαύτῃ πολιτείᾳ χρώμενοι κατεπαύθησαν, τοὺς δέ, οἳ καὶ ἐκείνων ἐκπεσόντων οὕτως ἤδη καὶ αὐτοὶ ἀντικα- θεστᾶσι, τούτους δὲ τῇ αὐτῇ προσήκει χρῆσθαι τῆς σφετέρας αὐτῶν σωτηρίας ἕνεκεν. ἔτι δὲ τί πεπειρα- μένοις σαφέστερον δεδήλωται ἢ ταῦτα; τοῦτο μὲν ὅτι ἡ Βρεταννία, ἅτε αὐτάρκη θέσιν κειμένη, ἱκανή ἐστι βοηθεῖν τοῖς πολιτευομένοις ἔχουσί γε τὸ πλῆθος σύμμαχον, καὶ ταῦτα μηδὲν ἀλλότριον τῶν καθεστώτων ἐργαζομένη· τοῦτο δὲ ὅτι τὸ πλῆθος αὐτὸ ἀεὶ πρὸς τῶν πολιτευομένων ἂν εἴη βοηθούντων γε τοῖς καθεστῶσιν, ἀλλὰ καὶ ἤτοι λάθρᾳ γε ἢ βίᾳ ἐπιβουλευόντων αὐτοῖς σχολῇ καὶ μόλις ἀφίστανται καίπερ ἐνταῦθά γε δίκαιον ὂν ἀλλ' οὐδ' ὅσιον μὴ οὐ πάσῃ μηχανῇ ἀντιστῆναι.

Euphranor. Tell me, Alciphron, are there not diseases of the soul, as well as of the body ?

Alciphron. Without doubt.

Euph. And are not those diseases vicious habits ?

Alc. They are.

Euph. And, as bodily distempers are cured by physic, those of the mind are cured by philosophy ; are they not ?

Alc. I acknowledge it.

Euph. It seems therefore that philosophy is a medicine for the soul of man.

Alc. It is.

Euph. How shall we be able to judge of medicines, or know which to prefer ? Is it not from the effects wrought by them ?

Alc. Doubtless.

Euph. Where an epidemical distemper rages, suppose a new physician should condemn the known established practice, and recommend another method of cure, would you not, in proportion as the bills of mortality increased, be tempted to suspect this new method, notwithstanding all the plausible discourse of its abettors ?

Alc. This serves only to amuse and lead us from the question.

Crito. It puts me in mind of my friend Lamprocles, who needed but one argument against infidels. I observed, said he, that as infidelity grew, there grew corruption of every kind, and new vices. This simple observation on matter of fact was sufficient to make him, notwithstanding the remonstrance of several ingenious men, imbue and season the minds of his children betimes with the principles of religion. The new theories, which our acute moderns have endeavoured to substitute in place of religion, have had their full course in the present age, and produced their effect on the minds and manners of men.

BERKELEY.

Εὐφ. Εἰπέ μοι, ὦ Ἀλκίφρον, ἄλλο τι ὥσπερ καὶ τοῦ σώματος καὶ τῆς ψυχῆς νόσοι ὑπάρχουσιν;

Ἀλκ. δηλονότι καὶ τῆς ψυχῆς.

Εὐφ. οὐκοῦν τὰς νόσους ταύτας καχεξίας λέγεις;

Ἀλκ. λέγω γάρ.

Εὐφ. καὶ τὰς καχεξίας τὰς μὲν σωματικὰς ὁ ἰατρὸς ἀπαλλάττει, τὰς δὲ ψυχικὰς ὁ φιλόσοφος· ἢ οὔ;

Ἀλκ. πάνυ μὲν οὖν.

Εὐφ. κινδυνεύει τοίνυν φάρμακον εἶναι τῇ ψυχῇ τῇ τοῦ ἀνθρώπου ἡ φιλοσοφία.

Ἀλκ. κινδυνεύει μέντοι.

Εὐφ. περὶ δὲ τῶν φαρμάκων ἔστιν ὁπόθεν τις ἂν ἄλλοθεν ἔχοι κρίνειν καὶ διειδέναι ὁποῖα αἱρετέα, ἢ ἀφ' οἵων ἂν ἀποτελῇ αὐτά;

Ἀλκ. οὐκ ἄλλοθεν.

Εὐφ. τί δ' εἰ καινοτομῶν τις ἰατρός, ἐπινεμομένης τῶν νόσων τινὸς τῶν ἐπιπολαζουσῶν, τῇ μὲν ἰατρεύσει τῇ εἰωθυίᾳ καὶ νενομισμένῃ ἐπιτιμήσειεν, ἄλλην δέ τινα προστάττοι, οὐκ ἂν καὶ σύ, ὅσῳ ἂν πλείονες αὐξηθῶσιν οἱ ἀπογιγνόμενοι, τὴν καινὴν ταύτην δίαιταν ἐν ὑποψίᾳ ποιεῖσθαι ἐπαρθείης, κἂν εἰ ὡς διὰ πιθανω- τάτων βοηθοίη τῷ προστάγματι;

Ἀλκ. ἀλλ' οὗτός γε ὁ λόγος χαριεντισμὸς ὢν οὐδὲν ἄλλο ἢ παράγει τοῦ προκειμένου.

Κρίτ. καίτοι ἐμέ γε ὑπομιμνήσκει Λαμπροκλέους τῶν ἑταίρων τινός· φησὶ γὰρ τούτῳ μόνῳ ἰσχυρίζεσθαι θεοὺς εἶναι, ὅτι, ὅσῳ ἂν μειζόνως οἱ μὴ εἶναι ἀρνούμενοι ἐπιδιδῶσι, τόσῳ ἐπιδίδωσι καὶ ἁμαρτήματα παντοῖα καὶ καίν' ἄττα εἴδη πονηριῶν. ἀρκεῖν ἄρα τοῦτ' αὐτὸ σκοπουμένῳ ἀπ' αὐτοῦ τοῦ πράγματος οὕτω ποιεῖν, καίπερ πολλῶν καὶ λόγου ἀξίων ἀντιλεγόντων, προ- παρασκευάζειν τὰς τῶν παίδων ψυχὰς ὡς πρωϊαίτατα ὥστε δέξασθαι ὥσπερ βαφὴν τὴν περὶ τὰ θεῖα νόμισιν. ἃ δ' οὖν σοφίζονται οἱ νῦν κομψοὶ ἀντὶ τῆς τοιαύτης νομίσεως τὰ νέα σπουδάζοντες ὅπως εἰσάξουσι, ταῦτα, οὐδενὸς ἐφ' ἡμῶν ὄντος ἐμποδίου, ἤδη οἷα εἰκὸς ἐγκατέ- λιπεν ἐν ταῖς τε διανοίαις καὶ τοῖς ἤθεσι τοῖς τῶν ἀνθρώπων.

We are not to forget that a play is, or ought to be, a very short composition : that if one passion or disposition is to be wrought with tolerable success, I believe it is as much as can in any reason be expected. If there be scenes of distress, and scenes of humour, they must either be in a double or single plot. If there be a double plot, there are in fact two. If they be in chequered scenes of serious and comic, you are obliged continually to break both the thread of the story and the continuity of the passion : if in the same scene, it is needless to observe how absurd the mixture must be and how little adapted to answer the genuine end of any passion. It is odd to observe the progress of bad taste : for this mixed passion being universally proscribed in the regions of tragedy, it has taken refuge and shelter in comedy, where it seems firmly established ; though no reason can be assigned why we may not laugh in the one as well as weep in the other. The true reason of this mixture is to be sought for in the manners which are prevalent amongst a people. It has become very fashionable to affect delicacy, tenderness of heart, and fine feeling, and to shun all imputation of rusticity. Much mirth is very foreign to this character : they have introduced therefore a sort of neutral writing.

BURKE.

Δεῖ δὲ μηδ' ἐκεῖνο λεληθέναι ὅτι ἐν βραχεῖ δὴ κεῖται τό γε ἀληθῶς δρᾶμα· ὥστε δοκεῖν μοι ἀγαπητὸν ἂν εἶναι, εἰ ἕν τι πάθος ἢ διάθεσιν μετρίως τις ἀπεργάζοιτο. εἰ δὲ ἐπὶ τῆς σκηνῆς τά τε σπουδαῖα καὶ τὰ γέλοια μέλλοι τις μιμήσεσθαι, ἤτοι ἁπλοῦς ἢ διπλοῦς ἂν εἴη ὁ μῦθος. εἰ δὲ ἄρα διπλοῦς δῆλον ὅτι διττώ ἐστον. εἰ μὲν οὖν τὰ ἐπὶ τῆς σκηνῆς τὰ μὲν γέλοια τὰ δὲ σπουδαῖα ἐναλλάξ πως εἰσέρχεται, τό τε συνεχὲς τοῦ μύθου καὶ τὸ ἐφεξῆς τοῦ πάθους δέοι ἂν διαλύειν. εἰ δὲ ἅμα φαίνεται, αὐτὸ δηλοῖ ὡς ἄτοπον τὸ τῆς συγκράσεως καὶ ὡς ἀνεπιτήδειον εἰς τοῦτο ὅποι δεῖ τελευτῆσαι τό γε γνήσιον πάθος. χαρίεν δὲ σκέψασθαι ἐφ' ὅσον προκεχώρηκεν ἡ ἀπειροκαλία· τὸ γὰρ μικτὸν πάθος πανταχόθεν ἐκπεσὸν τῆς τραγῳδίας καταπέφευγεν ἐν τῇ κωμῳδίᾳ, ἐν ᾗ δοκεῖ τελέως καθιδρῦσθαι, καίπερ ἀδύνατον ὂν διορίσασθαι διότι ἐν τῇ μὲν γελᾶν ἐν δὲ τῇ δακρύειν οὐκ ἔξεστιν. αἴτιον δὲ τῆς συγκράσεως τὸ ἀεὶ ἐπιχώριον ἦθος· νενόμισται γὰρ μεταποιεῖσθαι μὲν τοῦ τε χρηστοήθους καὶ τοῦ φιλανθρώπου καὶ τῆς εὐγνωμοσύνης, τῆς δ' ἀγροικίας μηδ' αἰτίαν ἔχειν ἀποφεύγειν· τῆς δὲ ἕξεως ταύτης πάνυ ἀλλότριον τὸ γέλοιον πολὺ ὄν· διὸ καὶ λέξιν τινὰ οὐδ' εἰς ἕτερον ῥέπουσαν κατέδειξαν.

Now if we are really under any obligations of duty at all to magistrates, honour and respect in our behaviour towards them must doubtless be their due. And they who refuse to pay them this small and easy regard, who 'despise dominion and speak evil of dignities,' should seriously ask themselves, what restrains them from any other instance whatever of undutifulness. And if it be principle, why not from this? Indeed free government supposes, that the conduct of affairs may be inquired into and spoken of with freedom. Yet surely this should be done with decency for the sake of liberty itself; for its honour and security. But be it done as it will, it is a very different thing from libelling and endeavouring to vilify the persons of such as are in authority. It will be hard to find an instance in which a serious man could calmly satisfy himself in doing this. It is in no case necessary, and in every case of very pernicious tendency. But the immorality of it increases in proportion to the integrity and superior rank of the persons thus treated. It is therefore in the highest degree immoral when it extends to the supreme authority of a prince from whom our liberties are in no imaginable danger, whatever they may be from ourselves; and whose mild and strictly legal government could not but make any virtuous people happy.

BUTLER.

Εἰ δὲ ὡς ἀληθῶς κατὰ τὸ δέον τι ὀφείλομεν τοῖς
ἄρχουσι κἂν ὁτιοῦν ᾖ, ἔν γέ τι δήπου ὀφείλομεν προσ-
ομιλοῦντες αὐτοῖς, λέγω δὲ οἷον τιμὴν καὶ θεραπείαν
ἀπονέμειν. ὅσοι δὲ ταῦτα φαῦλα καὶ εὐτελῆ ὄντα
ἀποστεροῦντες τῶν μὲν κυρίων καταφρονοῦσι περὶ
δὲ τῶν ἐν ἀξιώματι βλασφημοῦσι, δέοι ἂν ἀκριβῶς
ἐκεῖνό γε ἐξετάσαι ἄλλην τινὰ ὁποιανοῦν ἀθεραπευσίαν
ὅ τι ἐστὶ τὸ κωλῦον· εἰ γὰρ προαίρεσις, τί οὐ καὶ
ταύτην; οὐ μὴν ἀλλὰ τῆς τῶν ἐλευθέρων ἀρχῆς ὑπαρχούσης εἰκὸς καὶ ἐλευθέρως ἐξετάζοντας ἐλέγχειν τὰ
τῶν πολιτευομένων. καίτοι εἴπερ μέλλει κατὰ τὴν
ἀξίαν συμμένειν ἡ ἐλευθερία, ὑπὲρ αὐτῆς γε ταύτης δέοι
ἂν τοῦτο πρεπόντως ποιεῖν. ἕτερον δ᾽ οὖν τοῦτο καὶ τὸ
εἰς τοὺς ἐν τέλει βλασφημεῖν ὡς καταμεμψομένους τὴν
ἐξουσίαν· σχολῇ γὰρ ἂν εἷς ὁστισοῦν ὃς καὶ σπουδῇ
λογίζεται τοῦτό γε ποιῶν ἀγαπῴη. πότε γὰρ ἀναγκαῖον; πότε δὲ οὐ βλαβερώτατον; ἀλλὰ μὴν ὅσῳ
ἀμείνονες καὶ εὐγενέστεροι οἱ βλασφημούμενοι τοσούτῳ
καὶ πονηρότερον τὸ ἔθος. συμβαίνει ἄρα ὑπερβάλλειν
τῇ πονηρίᾳ, εἴ τις τῆς ἐξουσίας τῆς κυριωτάτης ἐπιλαμ-
βάνεται, ὅταν τὴν ἐλευθερίαν ὑφ᾽ ἡμῶν μὲν ἐνδέχηταί
τι παθεῖν, ὑπὸ δὲ τοῦ βασιλέως μηδ᾽ ὁτιοῦν ἐπίδοξος ᾖ·
ἐπεὶ ὁ μετρίως καὶ κατὰ νόμους ἄρχων τίνας οὐ κατ᾽
ἀρετὴν ἐνεργοῦντας εὐδαίμονας ἂν παρέχοι;

These men are ready, I know, to tell us that the influence
they plead for is necessary to strengthen the hands of those
who govern ; that corruption serves to oil the wheels of
government, and to render the administration more smooth
and easy ; and that it can never be of dangerous consequence under the present father of our country. Absurd
and wicked triflers—according to them our excellent constitution (as one of your correspondents has observed
exceedingly well) is no better than a jumble of incompatible
powers, which would separate and fall to pieces of themselves, unless restrained and upheld by such honourable
means as bribery and corruption.

BOLINGBROKE.

Οἱ δὲ τοιοῦτοι δῆλον ὅτι ῥᾳδίως θρυλοῦσιν ὡς
ἄρα ἀνάγκη ὑπάρχειν τὴν ἐξουσίαν ταύτην ὑπὲρ ἧς
ἀμφισβητοῦσιν, εἴπερ μέλλει ἰσχυρὰ εἶναι τὰ τῶν πολιτευομένων. ἡ γὰρ δωροδοκία, καθάπερ τὸ ἔλαιον τοῖς
τροχοῖς, οὕτω καὶ αὕτη συμφέρει τῇ πολιτείᾳ ὥστε
εὐτροχώτερον καὶ λειότερον προιέναι· ἐπικίνδυνος δὲ
οὐδέποτε μὴ γένηται ἐπὶ τούτου γε ὥσπερ πατρὸς ἐν
παισὶ βασιλεύοντος. ἄτοπά γε, οἶμαι, καὶ πονηρὰ
παραληροῦντες· κατὰ γὰρ δὴ τούτους ἡμῶν ἡ πολυ-
θρύλητος πολιτεία—καθάπερ καὶ πάνυ εὖ εἴρηκέ τις
τῶν σοι διαλεγομένων—οὐδὲν ἄλλο ἂν εἴη ἢ ἀσυνθέτων
ὄχλος τις δυνάμεων, αὐτῶν καθ᾽ αὑτὰς διαλυθεισῶν ἂν
καὶ συμπεσουσῶν εἰ μὴ δέοι καὶ συνέχοι τὸ δωρο-
δοκεῖν καὶ διαφθείρειν καὶ τὰ τοιαῦτα δὴ καλὰ ἐπιτηδεύματα.

TRANSLATIONS

INTO LATIN VERSE

A hundred torches, flashing bright,
Dispell'd at once the gloomy night
    That lour'd along the walls,
And show'd the King's astonish'd sight
    The inmates of the halls.
Nor wizard stern, nor goblin grim,
Nor giant huge of form and limb,
    Nor heathen knight was there ;
But the cressets, which odours flung aloft,
Show'd by their yellow light and soft
    A band of damsels fair.
Onward they came like summer wave
    That dances to the shore ;
A hundred voices welcome gave,
    And welcome o'er and o'er !
A hundred lovely hands assail
The bucklers of the monarch's mail,
And busy labour'd to unhasp
Rivet of steel and iron clasp.
One wrapt him in a mantle fair,
And one flung odours on his hair ;
His short curl'd ringlets one smooth'd down,
One wreath'd them with a myrtle crown.
A bride upon her wedding-day
Was tended ne'er by troop so gay.

SCOTT.

Centum coruscae lampades ignibus
caliginosam parietibus fugant
 repente noctem ; iam stupenti
  atria rex oculo incolentes

cernit ; sed illic non lemures nigri,
non se minaci Porphyrion statu,
 non fronte gens torva magorum,
  opposuit : vaga luce flava

non una odores taeda iacit supra et
pandit puellarum attonito manum ;
 fit obvia, haud aestiva saltans
  ipsa aliter lavit unda litus.

salvere regem plurima vox iubet,
linguae salutantum ingeminant sonos ;
 centena loricae catenas
  ecce petit studiosa virgo,

si forte solvat dextera fibulas,
hamos refigens sedula ferreos ;
 haec veste circumdat decora,
  malobathro rigat illa crines,

tortos capillos ordinat haec, caput
vult illa sertis cingere myrteis :
 tam festa vix umquam chorea
  visa novam est celebrare nuptam.

If thou beest he—but Oh how fallen ! how changed
From him !—who, in the happy realms of light,
Clothed with transcendent brightness didst outshine
Myriads though bright—if he whom mutual league,
United thoughts and counsels, equal hope
And hazard in the glorious enterprise,
Joined with me once, now misery hath joined
In equal ruin ; into what pit thou seest
From what highth fallen ; so much the stronger proved
He with his thunder : and till then who knew
The force of those dire arms ? Yet not for those,
Nor what the potent Victor in his rage
Can else inflict, do I repent, or change,
Though changed in outward lustre, that fixed mind,
And high disdain from sense of injured merit,
That with the Mightiest raised me to contend,
And to the fierce contention brought along
Innumerable force of Spirits armed,
That durst dislike his reign, and, me preferring,
His utmost power with adverse power opposed
In dubious battle on the plains of Heaven,
And shook his throne.

MILTON.

Fallor an ille idem es? sed quantum heu! lapsus ab illo,
mutatus quantum, dias per luminis oras
qui quondam eximio indutus fulgore phalanges
unus caelicolum innumeras anteire solebas!
es, quem iuncta datae nuper mihi foedera dextrae
spesque eadem eventus et consociata voluntas
et par consilium magnique pericula coepti
iunxerunt comitem? nunc nos commiscuit uno
strages exitio—quanta delapsus ab arce
in quantum sentis barathrum! tanto illius ira
fortior evasit rubraeque tonitrua dextrae:
experti quid dira queant iam novimus arma.
non tamen haec propter, nec si quid cogitat ultra
victrix ira manus, quicquam me paenitet ausi,
nec frontis quamquam externos mutatus honores
cetera item muto. superest mihi fastus et idem
ille animus, spretae superest iniuria laudis,
unde ego commotus bellum miscere Tonanti
ausus eram, mecumque una in certamina misi
milia caelicolum, qui tristia regna perosi
posthabuere meis, ausique opponere summis
viribus adversas vires soliumque movebant
et dubio campos foedabant Marte beatos.

In yonder grave a Druid lies,
　　Where slowly winds the stealing wave ;
The year's best sweets shall duteous rise
　　To deck its poet's sylvan grave.

In yon deep bed of whisp'ring reeds
　　His airy harp shall now be laid,
That he, whose heart in sorrow bleeds,
　　May love through life the soothing shade.

Then maids and youths shall linger here,
　　And, while its sounds at distance swell,
Shall sadly seem in Pity's ear
　　To hear the woodland pilgrim's knell.

Remembrance oft shall haunt the shore
　　When Thames in summer wreaths is drest,
And oft suspend the dashing oar
　　To bid his gentle spirit rest.

And oft as Ease and Health retire
　　To breezy lawn or forest deep,
The friend shall view yon whitening spire,
　　And 'mid the varied landscape weep.

But thou, who own'st that earthy bed,
　　Ah ! what will every dirge avail ?
Or tears which Love and Pity shed,
　　That mourn beneath the gliding sail ?

Yet lives there one, whose heedless eye
　　Shall scorn thy pale shrine glimm'ring near ?
With him, sweet bard, may Fancy die,
　　And Joy desert the blooming year.

COLLINS.

Caespite sub molli vatis sacra membra quiescunt,
    devia furtivo serpit ubi unda pede ;
anni primitiae dulcissima munera donant
    in vatis cineres officiosa sui.
inter harundineos ubi murmurat aura susurros
    Aeoliae iaceant fila reposta lyrae ;
scilicet assiduo cui saucia pectora luctu
    semper habet quo se mulceat umbra loci.
hanc puer hanc virgo dum saepe moratur ad oram
    det lyra longinquos quos bibat aure sonos ;
dum sonat illa procul, miserantia pectora fingent
    funereos vati concinuisse modos.
Mnemosyneque memor ripam persaepe reviset
    cum Tamesa aestivo flore coronat aquas,
et rapidos inhibens remos pia vota profundet :
    'molliter in tumulo molliter ossa cubent!'
sive valetudo nemorum descendere in umbras,
    sive quies gelidos visere suadet agros,
suspicit ut celsi candentia moenia templi
    per varias ruris flebit amicus opes.
at tibi, quem gelido caespes tegit ille sepulcro,
    quid tibi iam prodest nenia ? quidve dolor ?
quid lacrimae, quotiens laetae cumba explicat aurae
    carbasa, quas pietas quas tibi fundit amor ?
quis tamen est oculo qui dedignetur inani
    dum relegit tumuli pallida busta tui ?
huic pereat si quid placitum lusere Camenae,
    deneget huic laetas quas habet annus opes.

Adam, well may we labour still to dress
This garden, still to tend plant, herb, and flower,
Our pleasant task enjoined ; but, till more hands
Aid us, the work under our labour grows,
Luxurious by restraint : what we by day
Lop overgrown, or prune, or prop, or bind,
One night or two with wanton growth derides,
Tending to wild. Thou, therefore, now advise,
Or hear what to my mind first thoughts present.
Let us divide our labours—thou where choice
Leads thee, or where most needs, whether to wind
The woodbine round this arbour, or direct
The clasping ivy where to climb ; while I
In yonder spring of roses intermixed
With myrtle find what to redress till noon.
For, while so near each other thus all day
Our task we choose, what wonder if so near
Looks intervene and smiles, or objects new
Casual discourse draw on, which intermits
Our day's work, brought to little, though begun
Early, and the hour of supper comes unearned !

MILTON.

Dulce quidem hoc opus est, hos quod curare iubemur
semper agros, semper frutices et florea rura
excoluisse manu : sed nec tamen ulla labori
additur interea socium manus, omnia late
exsuperant magis et crescunt lasciva premendo.
quae cohibemus enim, quae falce resecta diurna
vimine fulcimus posito, nox altera totum
ridet opus nimioque docet silvescere ramo.
dic modo quid facias vel quae mihi prima recurrant
accipe : seiunctos hinc in diversa labores
suscipias moneo, qua te tua forte voluntas
quave operis ducat ratio, seu bracchia malis
nectere tu cytisi mollesque intexere frondes,
sive hederae monstrare viam lapsusque sequaces.
at nos interea, mista qua plurima myrto
insurgit rosa, quae dextrae medicamina poscant
pergimus in medios usque exornare calores ;
namque operi, totas iuxta dum tendimus horas,
quid mirum ? iocus obstat et arridentia furtim
lumina, et insoliti si quid miramur inanem
sermonem inducit : sic intermittitur omnem
cura diem, primaque labor quem accepimus hora
occidit omnis et immeritae stant vespere cenae.

Joy the halls of Troy surrounded,
　　Ere the lofty city fell ;
Golden hymns of gladness sounded
　　From the harp's exulting swell.
All the warriors' toils are over,
　　Arms no more the heroes bear ;
For Pelides, royal lover,
　　Weds with Priam's daughter fair.

Laurel wreaths their temples pressing,
　　Many a festive train with joy
Throng, to supplicate a blessing
　　From the deities of Troy.
Sounds of mirth and gladness only
　　Through the streets tumultuous flow,
Save where, in its sorrow lonely,
　　One sole bosom beats with woe.

Joyless, joys around unheeding,
　　Desolate, alone to rove,
Silently, Cassandra speeding
　　Sought Apollo's laurel grove.
To the wood's remote recesses
　　The prophetic maiden fled,
And, with wildly-flowing tresses,
　　Thus with angry grief she said.

　　　　　　　　　　From SCHILLER.

Aedes Iliacas prius
urbs est exitio quam data, gaudia
   cingunt ; et citharae sonant
laetanti populo plenius aureae.

   iam defuncta laboribus
bellantum arma gerit nulla manus ducum ;
   Pelides amat, et datur
regi uxor Priami filia nobilis.

   vincti tempora laurea
multi, festa cohors templa petentium,
   ' quod vertat bene ' supplices
exposcunt precibus numina Troica.

   auditur iocus undique et
ingenti strepitu per plateas lepor,
   unius licet aestuent
luctu corda gravi. laetitiae immemor

   quae circumvolat, ipsa egens
omnis laetitiae, sola petit nemus
   Cassandra et tacito gradu
ad laurus proprias tendit Apollinis.

   silvae non placido pede
virgo per latebras praescia devias,
   passis Thyias uti comis,
haec incensa iacit verba doloribus.

Ask not the cause why sullen Spring
     So long delays her flowers to bear;
Why warbling birds forget to sing,
     And winter storms invert the year:
Chloris is gone, and Fate provides
To make it Spring where she resides.

Chloris is gone, the cruel fair!
     She cast not back a pitying eye,
But left her lover in despair,
     To sigh, to languish, and to die.
Ah, how can those fair eyes endure
To give the wounds they will not cure?

Great God of Love, why hast thou made
     A face that can all hearts command,
That all religions can invade,
     And change the laws of every land?
Where thou had'st placed such power before,
Thou should'st have made her mercy more.

When Chloris to the temple comes,
     Adoring crowds before her fall;
She can restore the dead from tombs,
     And every life but mine recall.
I only am by Love designed
To be the victim for mankind.

                         DRYDEN.

Desine mirari cur dudum veris acerbi
  durities proprias ferre recuset opes.
cur volucres cessent oblitae carminis, aut cur
  sic anni cursum turbida mutet hiems.
nempe abiit Chloris, fatisque iubentibus unum
  ver quibus in terris ipsa moretur adest.
hinc abiit neque me miseranti Chloris ocello
  respexit puerum dura puella suum ;
sed desperato suspiria linquit amanti,
  sed languere diu, sed iubet illa mori.
cur oculi fax ista potest dare vulnera quis non
  ipsa simul medicam reddere callet opem ?
cur veneres formae finxisti, magne Cupido,
  pectora quae saeva sub dicione premat ?
quae valeat leges totum mutare per orbem,
  irrita quae passim reddere sacra queat ?
debuerat certe cor mollius esse puellae,
  muneribus tantis quam cumulare placet.
undique adorantum, quotiens se Chloris in aedem
  transtulit, ante pedes procubuere chori.
ex tumulo illa potest animas iam morte peremptas,
  unius ast animam non revocare meam.
discrepat heu ! mea sors aliis : nempe unus et ipse
  pro cunctis fiam victima fecit amor.

Come, sweet harp, resounding
Teian strains of yore,
With soft airs abounding,
Round the Lesbian shore :
Doric shell, awake thy soft themes no more.

Talk no more of maiden,
Fair with beauty's wiles,
Youth with blessings laden,
Whom new life beguiles—
Smiling as it flies, flying as it smiles.

Wisdom which ne'er wrongeth,
Born of God above,
Toils in birth and longeth
Your sweet chords to prove,
And hath bid me flee woes of earthly love.

What is strength or glory ?
Beauty, gold, or fame ?
What renown in story,
Or a kingly name,
To the thoughts of God—cares which bring no blame ?

One o'er steeds is bending,
One his bow hath strung,
One his gold is tending,
One by youth is sung,
For bright looks and locks o'er his shoulder hung.

Mine be the low portal,
Paths in silence trod,
Knowing not things mortal,
Knowing things of God,
Whilst still at my side Wisdom holds her rod.

O qui sonabas, barbite, Teïo
percussus olim pollice Lesbium
    ad litus, et circum solebas
        suaviloquos iterare cantus,

tandem modorum desine mollium;
ne iam dolosae, Dorica, virginis
    te forma, testudo, moretur,
        neve puer cumulatus omni

splendore vitae, quem nova credulum
nunc fallit aetas, praeterit at brevi
    lusura risu. iam novatum
        ede melos; Sophia en recenti

divi propago fallere nescia
partu laborat; iam properat fides
    temptare terrenique amoris
        nos vetuit celebrare luctus.

quid robur, aut quid gloria? quid valet
aurum aut puellae gratia? quid decus
    et nomen ornatum Camenis?
        stemmata quid titulique regum?

me cura summi detineat Dei
culpanda nulli. pars stupet aureis
    intenta gazis; hic feroci
        gaudet equo puer, ille tendit

arcum; est protervi quem iuvenum chori
laudant, natantesque ex umeris comas
    pulchrosque vultus; at modestum
        fas mihi sit subiisse limen,

virgaque flectat me Sophia, ut loca
tutus pererrem trita silentio,
    curaque mortali solutus
        nosse Dei monitus laborem.

In Ida vale (who knowes not Ida vale?)
When harmlesse Troy yet felt not Græcian spite,
An hundred shepheards wonn'd, and in the dale,
While their faire flockes the three-leaved pastures bite,
The shepheards boyes with hundred sportings light
   Gave winges unto the times too speedy hast:
   Ah, foolish lads! that strove with lavish wast
   So fast to spend the time that spends your time as fast.

Emong the rest, that all the rest excel'd,
A dainty boy there wonn'd, whose harmlesse yeares
Now in their freshest budding gently sweld;
His nimph-like face nere felt the nimble sheeres,
Youth's downy blossome through his cheeke appeares;
   His lovely limbes (but love he quite discarded)
   Were made for play (but he no play regarded)
   And fit love to reward and with love be rewarded.

His joy was not in musique's sweet delight,
(Though well his hand had learnt that cunning arte,)
Or dainty songs to daintier eares indite,
But through the plaines to chace the nimble hart
With well-tun'd hounds; or with his certaine dart
   The tusked boare or savage beare to wound;
   Meantime his heart with monsters doth abound.
   Ah, foole! to seeke so farre what neerer might be found.

His name (well knowne unto those woody shades,
Where unrewarded lovers oft complaine them,)
Anchises was: Anchises oft the glades
And mountains heard, Anchises had disdained them:
Not all their love one gentle looke had gain'd them.
   That rocky hills, with ecchoing noyse consenting,
   Anchises plain'd; but he no whit relenting,
   Harder than rocky hills, laught at their vaine lamenting.

SPENSER.

Valle sub Idaea—quisnam est qui nesciat Idam?—
ante Pelasgiacos quam sensit Troia furores,
pastores posuere casas; saltusque per imos,
gramina dum tondent pecudes herbamque trilicem,
sescentos agitat pubes pastoria ludos,
pernicemque diem levioribus instruit alis:
o nimium incautos! quis sit male prodiga cura
perdere vestram eadem perdentia tempora curam.
emicat aequales inter, cui conscia nondum
corda doli, primique tumet iam flosculus aevi
integer, ambiguo vultu propriorque puellae,
intonsasque genas tenera lanugine vestit.
quot veneres pandunt ludo sat idonea membra,
apta quidem ludo sed et invitantia amorem;
ast amor, ast illum ludus pellexit inertem.
olli non mira dulcedine corda Thalia
perculit—at docto novit bene pollice chordas
tangere—non mollem sua mollia fundere in aurem
carmina, sed mediis clamosa immittere campis
ora canum iuvat et dammas agitare fugaces,
seu certis aprum iaculis seu figere cervos.
ast intus puerum interea quam plurima vexant
monstra! quid imprudens prope quae sunt obvia quaeris
ista procul? silvis notum bene nomen opacis,
multus amans ubi despectum sibi plorat amorem,
Anchises cluet; Anchisen persaepe recessus,
immemorem Anchisen (cuius fastidia nondum
vicerat omnis amor) montes persaepe loquuntur:
ipsa repercussae rupis concordia saxa
Anchisen resonare: sed idem durior ipsis
rupibus irridet gemitus immotus inanes.

He ceas'd ; for many an eager hand
Had urg'd the barges from the strand.
Their number was a score and ten,
They bore thrice threescore chosen men.
With such small force did Bruce at last
The die for death or empire cast !

　Now on the darkening main afloat,
Ready and mann'd rocks every boat ;
Beneath their oars the ocean's might
Was dash'd to sparks of glimmering light.
Faint and more faint, as off they bore,
Their armour glanc'd against the shore,
And, mingled with the dashing tide,
Their murmuring voices distant died.—
' God speed them ! ' said the priest, as dark
On distant billows glides each bark ;
' O Heaven ! when swords for freedom shine,
And monarch's right, the cause is thine !
Edge doubly every patriot blow !
Beat down the banners of the foe !
And be it to the nations known,
That victory is from God alone ! '
As up the hill his path he drew,
He turn'd his blessings to renew,
Oft turn'd, till on the darken'd coast
All traces of their course were lost ;
Then slowly bent to Brodick tower,
To shelter for the evening hour.

　　　　　　　　　　　　　　SCOTT.

Desierat dux plura loqui ; nam solverat ora
  subductas alacris plurima dextra rates.
ter denas numerare datur ; datur ordine lectos
  vicenos novies imposuisse viros.
alea iactanda est haec ultima, sive potiri
  dat solio, sequitur pars quota, sive mori.
iam mare per nigrans vehitur iactantibus undis
  remigio puppis quaeque parata suo.
iam verrunt remi ; scintillis luminis ingens
  oceani dubiis vis agitata micat.
tandem iter emensis maius, quibus arsit harena
  ignibus, armorum fit minor ille nitor.
et rabies aestus sopit distantia vocum
  murmura, et amoti conticuere soni.
lapsa super fluctus visa est vanescere linter
  omnis, et antistes ' quod bene vertat' ait ;
' si quando populi aut regis ius vindicat ensis,
  caelicolae, vestra est causa ; favete piis.
vos facite ut mucro duplicem det civibus ictum,
  hostibus ut domitis irrita signa cadant.
caelicolis debetur enim victoria solis,
  sit notum populis hoc quoque posse deos.'
dixit, et adscendens acclivi tramite collem
  respicit et faustas vult iterare preces ;
saepe retro versus vestigia donec euntum
  iam caliganti litore tota latent.
inde senex lento turris petit ardua gressu ;
  hoc monet hospitio vesperis hora frui.

And fast beside there trickled softly downe
A gentle streame, whose murmuring wave did play
Emongst the pumy stones, and made a sowne,
To lull him soft asleepe that by it lay:
The wearie Traveiler, wandring that way,
Therein did often quench his thristy heat,
And then by it his wearie limbes display,
Whiles creeping slomber made him to forget
His former payne, and wypt away his toilsom sweat.

And on the other syde a pleasaunt grove
Was shott up high, full of the stately tree
That dedicated is t' Olympick Jove,
And to his sonne Alcides, whenas hee
In Nemus gayned goodly victoree:
Therein the mery birdes of every sorte
Chaunted alowd their chearefull harmonee,
And made emongst themselves a sweete consort,
And quickned the dull spright with musicall comfort.

SPENSER.

Nec procul hinc levi descendens tramite flumen
innocuum carpebat iter, cui lympha canoro
saxa movens ludo circum iucunda ferebat
murmura, securos animo inducentia somnos.
saepe vagans illuc tremulo pede fonte viator
fluminis infuso sitientia labra rigavit,
lassaque deponens viridanti in margine membra
oblitusque mali—tantum potuere soporis
gaudia—sudantem detersit corpore guttam.
at nemus ex alia parte est adsurgere ad auras
aetherias visum, procera ubi floruit arbos
plurima, Olympiaci Iovis Alcidaeque potentis
auspiciis nati felix, quo tempore victor
rettulit optatam Nemeae de fronde coronam.
omnigenae volucres illic comitante iocosa
harmonia vario contendunt gutture voces ;
dumque sua inter se captae dulcedine certant,
vivescunt pigri lyrico solamine sensus.

Come, peace of mind, delightful guest!
Return and make thy downy nest
    Once more in this sad heart.
Nor riches I nor power pursue,
Nor hold forbidden joys in view;
    We therefore need not part.

Where wilt thou dwell if not with me,
From avarice and ambition free,
    And pleasure's fatal wiles?
For whom alas! dost thou prepare
The sweets that I was wont to share,
    The banquet of thy smiles?

The great, the gay, shall they partake
The Heaven that thou alone canst make?
    And wilt thou quit the stream
That murmurs through the dewy mead,
The grove and the sequestered shed,
    To be a guest with them?

For thee I panted, thee I prized,
For thee I gladly sacrificed
    Whate'er I loved before;
And shall I see thee start away,
And, helpless, hopeless, hear thee say—
    'Farewell! we meet no more'?

COWPER.

O blanda cordis solliciti hospita,
pax alma, mollem in pectore saucio
   repone nidum. non honorum
     non nimii sitis urget auri,

nec me voluptas per vetitum et nefas
ducit sequentem. quid fugis, improba?
   quo tendis aspernata sedes,
     diva, meas, aliena luxu

cui mens et aegri pura cupidinis?
feliciori tradere cui placet
   quas ipse depasci solebam
     delicias epulasque risus?

ergo iuventas et procerum cohors
proterva carpet munera quae paras
   divina? mutabisne saltu et
     fontibus irriguaque valle

et tale seducta hospitium casa?
te semper aegro sector anhelitu,
   quodcumque delectabat olim
     pone tuos posuisse risus

libens amavi; me tamen invida
spe destitutum et praesidio fugis,
   et voce suprema salutas:
     'postmodo non erimus sodales'?

                                        As bees
In spring-time, when the Sun with Taurus rides,
Pour forth their populous youth about the hive
In clusters ; they among fresh dews and flowers
Fly to and fro, or on the smoothèd plank,
The suburb of their straw-built citadel,
New rubbed with balm, expatiate, and confer
Their state-affairs : so thick the aery crowd
Swarmed and were straitened; till, the signal given,
Behold a wonder ! They but now who seemed
In bigness to surpass Earth's giant sons,
Now less than smallest dwarfs, in narrow room
Throng numberless—like that pygmean race
Beyond the Indian mount ; or faery elves,
Whose midnight revels, by a forest-side
Or fountain, some belated peasant sees,
Or dreams he sees, while overhead the Moon
Sits arbitress, and nearer to the Earth
Wheels her pale course ; they, on their mirth and dance
Intent, with jocund music charm his ear ;
At once with joy and fear his heart rebounds.
                                        MILTON.

Ac veluti cum vere novo Phoebi accipit orbem
Taurus, apes iuvenum properorum examina fundunt,
immensasque trahunt nubes : at gramina circum
exsultant roresque novos, lignove dolato
balsama quod dulci tinxere recentia suco
arcis stramineae limen spatiantur, et urbis
concilio res expendunt : tanta aere turba
conglomerata volat, densis exercitus alis.
tum signo certo monstrum mirum adspice ! visi
nuper terrigenas corpus superare gigantas
nunc minimis similes nanis densantur in arto
inclusi spatio ; veluti genus id super Indos
Pygmaeum montes, dictataque numina silvae,
quorum intempestas saltus prope nocte choreas,
aut ubi fons oritur scatebris, remoratus agrestis
aut videt aut vidisse putat, dum caerula testes
intendens oculos luna imminet, et prope terram
pallentem flectit currum : sed gaudia curant
illa chorosque simul ; iucundis cantibus aures
oblectant ; micat ille metu gaudentia corda.

Emblem of England's ancient faith,
  Full proudly may thy branches wave,
Where loyalty lies low in death,
  And valour fills a timeless grave.

And thou, brave tenant of the tomb,
  Repine not if our clime deny,
Above thine honour'd sod to bloom,
  The flowrets of a milder sky.

These owe their birth to genial May;
  Beneath a fiercer sun they pine,
Before the winter storm decay—
  And can their worth be type of thine?

No! for, 'mid storms of Fate opposing,
  Still higher swell'd thy dauntless heart,
And, while Despair the scene was closing,
  Commenc'd thy brief but brilliant part.

'Twas then thou sought'st, on Albyn's hill,
  (When England's sons the strife resign'd,)
A rugged race, resisting still,
  And unsubdu'd though unrefin'd.

Thy death's hour heard no kindred wail,
  No holy knell thy requiem rung;
Thy mourners were the plaided Gael,
  Thy dirge the clamorous pibroch sung.

Scott.

Laeta super sanctam, priscae pietatis imago
  Anglorum, iacta bracchia, quercus, humum,
fortis ubi in tumulo virtus requiescit, et urnam
  intempestivam nacta sacrata fides.
nec te paeniteat, talis praeclare sepulcri
  hospes, inornati qui premit ossa loci,
dona quod ex sancto, nutrit quae mitior aer,
  temperies nasci caespite dura negat.
aura parit flores Maii genitalior illos ;
  sub caelo marcent fervidiore rosae.
ante rosae marcent hiemis quam decidit imber ;
  non instar pretii flos habet ille tui.
namque tibi impavidum fati generosius inter
  sensimus oppositas cor tumuisse minas :
occiderat sociis spes desperata salutis,
  cum brevis at splendens pars tua coepit agi.
tempore quo cessant fessi certaminis Angli,
  saxa Caledonii tu petis alta iugi :
aspera corda virum sed adhuc obsistere certa,
  gens si culta minus non minus illa ferox.
te neque cognati morientem nenia plangit,
  nec tuba maesta canit : ' molliter ossa cubent.'
sed tua virgati comitantur funera Celtae :
  bucina clamoso te iubet aere, ' vale.'

Εἰνοδία θύγατερ Δάματρος, ἀ τῶν
νυκτιπόλων ἐφόδων ἀνάσσεις,
καὶ μεθαμερίων ὅδωσον δυσθανάτων
κρατήρων πληρώματ᾽, ἐφ᾽ οἷσι πέμπει
πότνια πότνι᾽ ἐμὰ χθονίας
Γοργοῦς λαιμοτόμων ἀπὸ σταλαγμῶν
τῷ τῶν Ἐρεχθεϊδᾶν
δόμων ἐφαπτομένῳ·
μηδέ ποτ᾽ ἄλλος ἄλλων ἀπ᾽ οἴκων
πόλεως ἀνάσσοι
πλὴν τῶν εὐγενετᾶν Ἐρεχθειδᾶν.
εἰ δ᾽ ἀτελὴς θάνατος σπουδαί τε δεσποί-
νας, ὅ τε καιρὸς ἄπεισι τόλμας,
ᾇ τε νῦν φέρετ᾽ ἐλπίς, ἢ θηκτὸν ξίφος ἢ
λαιμῶν ἐξάψει. βρόχον ἀμφὶ δειρήν,
πάθεσι πάθεα δ᾽ ἐξανύτουσ᾽
εἰς ἄλλας βιότου κάτεισι μορφάς.
οὐ γὰρ δόμων γ᾽ ἑτέρους
ἄρχοντας ἀλλοδαποὺς
ζῶσά ποτ᾽ ὀμμάτων ἐν φαενναῖς
ἀνέχοιτ᾽ ἂν αὐγαῖς
ἁ τῶν εὐπατριδᾶν γεγῶσ᾽ οἴκων.

EURIPIDES.

Praeses viarum, quam peperit Ceres,
quae nocte caeca dirigis impetus,
   adsis, et incursus diurni
     diva potens, Hecate, secundos

pleno veneni da cyatho exitus;
quem nostra caeso e sanguine Gorgonis
   commiscet ausuro potiri
     Cecropidis solioque patrum

regina; genti nolumus extera
det iura quisquam barbarus a domo;
   sed sola Erechthidarum avitis
     progenies dominetur aulis.

sin forte letum senserit irritum
regina vanas insidias struens,
   si spes et opportuna deerit
     hora novum scelus incohanti,

ferri recludet pectora cuspide
nodosve collo nectet eburneo,
   et prisca finitura damnis
     damna vices alias inibit

vitae, superbum scilicet exsulem
exosa recto lumine sedibus
   spectare regnantem paternis,
     nobilium suboles avorum.

I'me no slave to such as you be ;
Neither shall that snowy brest,
Rowling eye, and lip of ruby,
Ever robb me of my rest :
    Goe, goe, display
    Thy beautie's ray
To some more-soone enamoured swaine ;
    Those common wiles
    Of sighs and smiles
Are all bestowed on me in vaine.

I have elsewhere vowed a dutie :
Turn away thy tempting eye :
Show me not a painted beautie :
These impostures I defie.
    My spirit lothes
    Where gawdie clothes
And fained othes may love obtaine :
    I love her so,
    Whose looke sweares No,
That all your labours will be vaine.

Can he prize the tainted posies
Which on every brest are worne,
That may plucke the virgin roses
From their never-touchèd thorne ?
    You labour may
    To lead astray
The heart that constant shall remaine :
    And I the while
    Will sit and smile
To see you spend your time in vaine.

WITHER.

Nec tibi nec tali potero succumbere flammae :
   nec nivei candor pectoris iste capit :
non mihi, qui iactant oculi nimis acriter orbes,
   non adimunt somnos aemula labra rosis.
i nunc, et citius si quem potes urere amantem,
   pande cupidineas pande, puella, faces.
quae passim risus, passim suspiria vendit,
   crede mihi, vanis me petit insidiis.
scilicet alterius iuravi in verba puellae ;
   sit vultus nimium lubricus iste procul.
este procul vos o ! pictae tectoria formae ;
   mens est fucatis inviolata dolis.
et nitidam vestem et falsae periuria linguae
   odimus ; est aliis inde petendus amor.
hanc ego depereo, quae denegat oscula recto
   lumine ; tuque operam perdis inepta tuam.
an placeant puero marcentia serta coronae
   unde caput quodvis se redimire queat,
virgineas ipsi cui sit data copia semper
   ex illibato carpere sente rosas ?
tu tamen in peius deflectere corda laboras,
   at superest constans intemerata fides ;
integer interea subridens fronte sedebo,
   tuque diem, illusa paelicis arte, teres.

And wilt thou weep when I am low?
   Sweet lady! speak those words again;
Yet, if they grieve thee, say not so—
   I would not give that bosom pain.

My heart is sad, my hopes are gone,
   My blood runs coldly through my breast;
And when I perish, thou alone
   Wilt sigh above my place of rest.

And yet, methinks, a gleam of peace
   Doth through my cloud of anguish shine:
And for a while my sorrows cease,
   To know thy heart hath felt for mine.

Oh lady! blessed be that tear—
   It falls for one who cannot weep;
Such precious drops are doubly dear
   To those whose eyes no tear may steep.

Sweet lady! once my heart was warm
   With every feeling soft as thine;
But beauty's self hath ceased to charm
   A wretch created to repine.

BYRON.

Ergo favillam, Lydia, fletibus
sparges? amatos dic iterum sonos;
   sin forte te vexant, recuso:
      molle nefas lacerare pectus.

mens aegra marcet, spes iacet irrita,
venisque sanguis labitur horridus;
   tu sola defuncti querelis
      flebilibus decorabis urnam.

at pacis almae nescio quod iubar
inter doloris nubila praenitet;
   et cura discedit parumper,
      te, mea lux, miserante nostri.

nam sancta cordi gutta cadit meo,
cui flere tandem lumina nesciunt;
   sortem quod eluxi malignam,
      bis pretio valet iste fletus.

qui corde fervet, Lydia, sub tuo
me fovit olim mollior impetus;
   plorare sed nato levamen
      ipsa negat Cytherea luctus.

The king was on his throne,
 The satraps throng'd the hall :
A thousand bright lamps shone
 O'er that high festival.
A thousand cups of gold,
 In Judah deem'd divine—
Jehovah's vessels hold
 The godless heathen's wine !

In that same hour and hall,
 The fingers of a hand
Came forth against the wall,
 And wrote as if on sand :
The fingers of a man,
 A solitary hand
Along the letters ran,
 And traced them like a wand.

The monarch saw, and shook,
 And bade no more rejoice :
All bloodless wax'd his look,
 And tremulous his voice.
' Let the men of lore appear,
 The wisest of the earth,
And expound the words of fear
 Which mar our royal mirth.'

Chaldea's seers are good,
 But here they have no skill ;
And the unknown letters stood,
 Untold and awful still.
And Babel's men of age
 Are wise and deep in lore ;
But now they were not sage,
 They saw—but knew no more.

A captive in the land,
 A stranger and a youth,
He heard the king's command,
 He saw that writing's truth.
The lamps around were bright,
 The prophecy in view ;
He read it on that night,—
 The morrow proved it true.

' Belshazzar's grave is made,
 His kingdom pass'd away,
He, in the balance weigh'd,
 Is light and worthless clay ;
The shroud his robe of state,
 His canopy the stone ;
The Mede is at his gate !
 The Persian on his throne !' BYRON.

Ipse sedet solio satrapis celebrantibus aulam :
mille die festo collucent lampades, auro
pocula mille nitent, Solymis sacrata Iehovae
credita; nunc vino rex imbuit impius illas
barbarico pateras. eadem tamen adspicit hora,
aula eadem, dextrae digitos in pariete celso
prodire in strata velut inscribentis harena,
humanos dextrae digitos. percurrere visa est
una notas manus, ut magicae vestigia virgae.
'laetitiae date finem,' hoc territus omine mandat ;
vultumque exsanguis tremula sic voce profatur:
'quicquid habet docti tellus, quem sancta magorum
educat ars, eia haec nobis edissere verba,
plena metu verba et regis turbantia luxus.'
educat ars Chaldaea magos, sed lingua perita
hic silet ; haec restant non nota, interprete nullo,
signa tremenda manus. se gens Babylonia doctis
iactat et ipsa viris, senibus sapientibus : ipsis
deest tamen hic doctrina ; ipsi obticuere videntes.
captus adest puer; is iussa audit regis et iras
exsul veridicas scriptorum intellegit unus.
lampades effulgent mille undique; praescia verba
clara patent oculis. pueri nox illa legentis,
crastina lux veram probat esse interpretis artem :
'iam tibi fit tumulus—iam tu diademate patrum,
Bele, cares. iam tu, suspensus lancibus aequis,
es leve vile lutum. quae vestit purpura, busto
coicitur; praebet saxum conopea. Medus
ad portas fremit ; en solio sedet advena Cyrus !'

And straight a stony shower
Of monstrous hail does downwards pour,
Such as ne'er winter yet brought forth,
From all her stormy magazines of the north.
It all the beasts and men abroad did slay,
O'er the defaced corpse, like monuments, lay;
The houses and strong-body'd trees it broke,
Nor asked aid from the thunder's stroke;
The thunder but for terror through it flew,
The hail alone the work could do.
The dismal lightnings all around,
Some flying through the air, some running on the ground,
Some swimming o'er the water's face,
Filled with bright horror every place;
One would have thought, their dreadful day to have seen,
The very hail, and rain itself, had kindled been.

COWLEY.

Nec iam moratus devolat aethere
saxosus imber grandinis horridae ;
   quem non procellosis sub Arcto
     carceribus peperit December.

foris trucidat saecla hominum et greges,
ceu signa corpus per mutilum iacet ;
   quin tecta nodosasque quercus
     non ope fulminea refringit.

perrupit oras aetherias, metus
vani minister, fulmineus fragor ;
   nam sola perfecisse munus
     noverat exitiale grando.

horrenda passim fulgura, nunc levi
cursu per auras excita, nunc humi
   illapsa, nunc summas per undas
     igniferum iaciunt pavorem.

quod si videres terribilem diem,
posses et ipsam credere grandinem,
   posses et exarsisse, mirum,
     igne novo pluvias et imbres.

Beside the ungathered rice he lay,
    His sickle in his hand ;
His breast was bare, his matted hair
    Was buried in the sand.
Again, in the mist and shadow of sleep,
    He saw his native land.

Wide through the landscape of his dreams
    The lordly Niger flowed ;
Beneath the palm-trees on the plain
    Once more a king he strode ;
And heard the tinkling caravans
    Descend the mountain-road.

He saw once more his dark-eyed queen
    Among her children stand ;
They clasped his neck, they kissed his cheeks,
    They held him by the hand :
A tear burst from the sleeper's lids,
    And fell upon the sand.

And then at furious speed he rode
    Along the Niger's bank ;
His bridle-reins were golden chains,
    And, with a martial clank,
At each leap he could feel his scabbard of steel
    Smiting his stallion's flank.

LONGFELLOW.

Sic temere intonsam propter recubabat oryzam :
    vix falcem servi dextra tenebat iners.
pectus erat nudus latum, incomptusque capillus
    subter harenosam semisepultus humum.
ecce inter tenebras caligantemque soporem
    visus erat patriam rursus adire domum.
visus et in somnis inter sua rura vaganti
    maximus ingentes volvere Nigris aquas ;
supra palmiferos ostendit campus honores ;
    per proprias iterum rex spatiatur opes ;
plaustra iterum crepitare novis tinnitibus audit,
    ut de clivoso tramite montis eunt.
coniugis ille nigros oculos perlustrat amatae,
    natorum in medio stantis, ut ante, choro.
bracchia circumdant collo, dant oscula labris,
    illa patris dextram parvula dextra tenet.
tum subito in guttas solvunt se lumina obortas ;
    sopiti lacrima subter harena madet.
inque vicem ad ripas insanis cursibus amnis
    ferrata indomitum calce lacessit equum.
aurea cornipedem constringunt frena minacem,
    ungula pulsat humum quadrupedante sono.
utque gradus glomerat, velut ipso in Marte, superbos,
    ilia vaginae pulsibus icta gemunt.

As after Numa's peaceful reign
The martial Ancus did the sceptre wield,
Furbished the rusty sword again,
Resumed the long-forgotten shield,
And led the Latins to the dusty field :
So James the drowsy genius wakes
Of Britain, long entranced in charms,
Restiff, and slumbering on its arms :
'Tis roused, and with a new-strung nerve the spear already
    shakes.
No neighing of the warrior steeds,
No drum or louder trumpet needs
T' inspire the coward, warm the cold ;
His voice, his sole appearance, makes them bold.
Gaul and Batavia dread th' impending blow ;
Too well the vigour of that arm they know ;
They lick the dust, and crouch beneath their fatal foe.
Long may they fear this awful prince,
And not provoke his lingering sword ;
Peace is their only sure defence,
Their best security his word.
In all the changes of his doubtful state,
His truth, like Heaven's, was kept inviolate ;
For him to promise is to make it fate.
His valour can triumph o'er land and main :
With broken oaths his fame he will not stain,
With conquest basely bought, and with inglorious gain.

                             DRYDEN.

Quieta sicut tempora post Numae
sceptro potitus belliger ensibus
    robiginem abstersit vetustam
        et clipeum repetivit Ancus,

campique in ipsum Martia pulverem
duxit Latinorum agmina; sic pigro
    nuper soporatae veterno et
        depositis recubantis armis

vinctaeque dudum carmine Thessalo
solvit Metellus membra Britanniae;
    en surgit intentisque nervis
        pila iterum renovata vibrat.

iam bellicosi non fremitus equi,
non rauca consors bucina classicis
    hortatur ignavos novosque
        suscitat in pavidis calores;

at vultus et vox sola animat ducis:
ictum imminentem Gallia contremit:
    experta iam robur lacerti
        mordet humum, validaque dextra

procumbit hostis strata Batavia.
diu expavescant principis impetus
    lentumque ne ferrum lacessant;
        non nisi pax columen fidesque

servata regis; per dubias vices
quae mansit ut vox numinis integra:
    quodcumque nam promisit, illud
        esse ratum voluere Parcae.

terraque victor continuo ac mari
nescit superbam turpi inhians lucro
    partisve per fraudem tropaeis
        perfidia maculare famam.

Look once more, ere we leave this specular mount,
Westward, much nearer by south-west; behold
Where on the Ægean shore a city stands,
Built nobly, pure the air, and light the soil—
Athens, the eye of Greece, mother of arts
And eloquence, native to famous wits
Or hospitable, in her sweet recess,
City or suburban, studious walks and shades.
See there the olive-grove of Academe,
Plato's retirement, where the Attic bird
Trills her thick-warbled notes the summer long;
There, flowery hill, Hymettus, with the sound
Of bees' industrious murmur, oft invites
To studious musing; there Ilissus rolls
His whispering stream. Within the walls then view
The schools of ancient sages—his who bred
Great Alexander to subdue the world,
Lyceum there; and painted Stoa next.
There shalt thou hear and learn the secret power
Of harmony, in tones and numbers hit
By voice or hand, and various-measured verse,
Æolian charms and Dorian lyric odes,
And his who gave them breath, but higher sung,
Blind Melesigenes, thence Homer called,
Whose poem Phœbus challenged for his own.

                                        MILTON.

Ante tamen quam de specula descenderis alta
rursum flecte oculos. zephyrum qua proximus urget
africus, Aegaeo patet urbs in litore, celsis
turribus aedificata ; ibi ridet purior aer,
fecundoque solum ditat putris ubere gleba ;
panditur ille oculus Graiae telluris, Athenae,
artibus eloquioque parens : illa ipsa virorum
sustulit ingenia alta aut blanda excepit amico
hospitio, spatia intra ipsam seu praebuit urbem,
sive suburbanis studium invitantibus umbris.
en oleas Academi atque otia grata Platoni,
Atthis ubi aestatem quam longa ex gutture pleno
vibrat avis modulos ; operosa immurmurat illic
dulce apis, et studium florens invitat Hymettus,
Ilissusque vagis clamosum illabitur undis :
dein intra muros sapientum introspice sedes :
illius ante alios quo sub monitore potentem
debellare orbem didicit stirps magna Philippi :
porticus hinc picta adsurgit coniuncta Lycaeo.
nec minus harmoniae vires audire latentes,
percussosque manu numeros seu voce perita
inde datur ; licet et vario pede discere versus,
Aeolios, seu quid lyrici dat tibia Dorum,
quique animam inflasti, tamen altius ipse canebas,
caece Melesigenes, an Homere libentius audis,
cui numeros ipse et vates invidit Apollo.

' A sister's faithful love, for you
   I'll ever cherish, knight.
For other love, O do not sue—
   Yours I can ne'er requite.
I would be calm when you are near,
   And calm when you depart.
I cannot understand this tear,
   Altho' it rends my heart.'

He hears her words; with grief opprest,
   His heart within doth bleed:
He clasps her to his panting breast,
   Then springs upon his steed:
He summons forth his vassals all,
   In trusty Switzerland.
They take the Cross t' obey his call,
   And seek the Holy Land.

And soon the hero's mighty deeds
   Resound throughout the land,
Into the thickest throngs he leads
   To victory his band;
And at the Toggenburgher's name
   The frightened Moslem start—
But when could glory cure, or fame,
   The pangs of love-sick heart?

From SCHILLER.

'Fida soror fratri foveo quem debet amorem
hunc tibi semper, eques.
sat tibi talis amor—ne plura poposceris—istum
quem petis haud refero.

fronte ego te placida video prope adesse, videbo
linquere te placida.
cur fundas lacrimam fallit me causa; sed aegrum
cor mihi dilacerat.'

audierat voces; quantus dolor opprimit intus
saucia corda viri!
pectus amore micat trepidisque amplectitur ulnis;
alite vectus equo

inde vocat cunctos Helvetia fida clientes
quos habet; illa cohors
audit, avens in verba Dei iurare, vocantem,
et loca sancta petit.

nec mora longa: viri per totam ingentia terram
undique gesta sonant.
et comitum in spissas fertur duce freta catervas
vincere certa manus.

Teutonici ducis ad nomen famamque paventum
gens Arabum trepidat:
luctibus at quando pereuntis amore mederi
gloria lausve valet?

The glories of our blood and state
  Are shadows, not substantial things;
There is no armour against fate;
  Death lays his icy hand on kings:
    Sceptre and crown
    Must tumble down,
And in the dust be equal made
With the poor crooked scythe and spade.

Some men with swords may reap the field
  And plant fresh laurels where they kill:
But their strong nerves at last must yield;
  They tame but one another still:
    Early or late
    They stoop to fate,
And must give up their murmuring breath
When they, pale captives, creep to death.

The garlands wither on your brow;
  Then boast no more your mighty deeds;
Upon Death's purple altar now
  See, where the victor-victim bleeds:
    All heads must come
    To the cold tomb;
Only the actions of the just
Smell sweet, and blossom in their dust.

SHIRLEY.

Ergo quid umbrarum instar inanium
prodest aviti gloria sanguinis?
    non arma vim fati coercent,
        at gelida Libitina dextra

reges et ipsos opprimit; infimo
sceptra et coronae pulvere corruunt
    et rursus aequantur recurvis
        falcibus aut humili ligoni.

est qui cruentos demetat ensibus
agros et inter funera conserat
    laurum: sed immanes lacerti
        deficiunt domitorque tandem

sensit domantem. serius ocius
cessere fato corpora pallida et
    cum murmure exspirant anhelo
        vitam, avidae data praeda morti.

en serta fronti marcida decidunt:
iactare noli gesta superbiens.
    iam victima extremum cruorem
        purpureae, modo victor, Orci

effundis arae; scilicet omnibus
pulsanda Ditis limina frigidi;
    at sola florescit piorum
        post cineres redoletque virtus.

Part on the plain, or in the air sublime,
Upon the wing or in swift race contend,
As at the Olympian games or Pythian fields;
Part curb their fiery steeds, or shun the goal
With rapid wheels, or fronted brigads form:
As when, to warn proud cities, war appears
Waged in the troubled sky, and armies rush
To battle in the clouds; before each van
Prick forth the aery knights, and couch their spears,
Till thickest legions close; with feats of arms
From either end of heaven the welkin burns.
Others, with vast Typhœan rage, more fell,
Rend up both rocks and hills, and ride the air
In whirlwind; Hell scarce holds the wild uproar:
As when Alcides, from Œchalia crowned
With conquest, felt the envenomed robe, and tore
Through pain up by the roots Thessalian pines,
And Lichas from the top of Œta threw
Into the Euboic sea. Others, more mild,
Retreated in a silent valley, sing
With notes angelical to many a harp
Their own heroic deeds, and hapless fall
By doom of battle, and complain that Fate
Free Virtue should enthrall to Force or Chance.

                                        MILTON.

Ast alii in campo aut sublime per aera vecti
alati certare aut cursu praepete, quales
Pythia quosve trahunt felicis Olympia palmae.
spumantes pars frenat equos, atque axe citato
evitat metas, obversasque instruit alas.
haud aliter trepido, populos monitura superbos,
bella geri visa in caelo ; concurrere nubes
per medias acies ; a prima fronte cohortum
prosiliunt equites protentis acriter hastis
aerii ; miscent densae mox proelia turmae ;
ardet uterque polus bellantum immanibus armis.
pars alia insanis agitata Typhoëos iris
convellit saxa ac montes, equitatque per auras
turbinibus ; strepitum ingentem vix continet Orcus.
qualis ubi Alcides, victor modo latus ab oris
Oechaliae, sensit tunicae fatale venenum,
Thessalicasque dolens pinus radicibus ipsis
eruit, Oetaeoque Lichan de vertice pontum
iecit in Euboicum.   ast alii, quis mitior aestus,
caelicolum numeris, secreta valle recepti,
multarum ad cantus fidium sua fortia facta
concelebrant lapsumque gravem discrimine Martis ;
virtutemque gemunt fatorum lege maligna
viribus indomitam aut caecae succumbere sorti.

Shall I tell you whom I love?
Hearken then awhile to me:
And if such a woman move
As I now shall versifie,
Be assured 'tis she or none
That I love and love alone.

Nature did her so much right
As she scorns the help of art,
In as many vertues dight
As ere yet imbraced a hart.
So much good so truely tride,
Some for less were deifide.

Wit she hath without desire
To make known how much she hath;
And her anger flames no higher
Than may fitly sweeten wrath.
Full of pitty as may be,
Though perhaps not so to me.

Such she is; and if you know
Such a one as I have sung;
Be she browne, or faire, or so,
That she be but somewhile young;
Be assured 'tis she or none
That I love and love alone.

BROWNE.

Dicamne quae me torreat ignibus?
paulisper audi; carmine feminam
   fingamus; hac uror, sed una
      crede mihi, modo vivat, uror,

natura quam tot dotibus instruit
ut spernat artis munera. quot meam
   ornant venustates puellam,
      quot numeris cumulata virtus,

spectata veris testibus! ordines
ipsos deorum laus minor attigit;
   quae novit at iactare passim
      eximios animi lepores

fastidit; ipsam qui decet, impetu
quae fervet irae; mollis amantium
   votis, sed heu! frustra vocanti
      dura, nimis mihi dura virgo.

nosti puellam carmine quam meo
finxi? sit albo corpore, sit nigro,
   dum flore paulisper iuventae
      rideat, haud alia calebo.

How sweet thy modest light to view,
  Fair star, to love and lovers dear!
While trembling on the falling dew,
  Like beauty shining through a tear;
Or, hanging o'er that mirror-stream,
  To mark that image trembling there;
Thou seem'st to smile with softer gleam,
  To see thy lovely face so fair.
Though, blazing o'er the arch of night,
  The moon thy timid beams outshine
As far as thine each starry light,
  Her rays can never vie with thine.
Thine are the soft enchanting hours
  When twilight lingers on the plain,
And whispers to the closing flowers
  That soon the sun will rise again.
Thine is the breeze that, murmuring bland
  As music, wafts the lover's sigh;
That bids the yielding heart expand
  In love's delicious ecstasy.
Fair star, though I be doomed to prove
  That rapture's tears are mixed with pain,
Ah! still I feel 'tis sweet to love,
  But sweeter to be loved again.

                                        LEYDEN.

Stella micans, quam suave iubar spectare modestum,
 cuius gaudet amans numine, gaudet amor,
rore tremis quotiens leviter depicta caduco
 lumina ceu flentis lucidiora micant :
seu iuvat in speculo magis impallescere lymphae,
 ut tremula in vitreis forma resurgit aquis,
mollior interea splendescere luce videris,
 scilicet es specie capta quod ipsa tua.
sidereos tua lux quantum supereminet ignes,
 luna potest radios exsuperare tuos ;
plenior illa licet nocturno effulgeat arcu,
 non eadem tibi quae gratia lucis erit.
cum remorantur adhuc iam sera crepuscula campo,
 conscia praesentis mollior hora tui est ;
nam super obductos spirantia sibila flores
 lumina Titanis mox reditura monent.
est tua, quae blando suspiria reddit amantum
 murmure, vocales aura imitata modos,
et tandem Veneris faciles in gaudia mentes
 edocuit furiis incaluisse novis.
stella pudens, quamquam medio de fonte leporum
 semper amaritiem surgere nosse meum est,
dulce tamen fateor si quem fax torret amoris,
 dulcius at si quem mutuus ardet amor.

Then straight commands that, at the warlike sound
Of trumpets loud and clarions, be upreared
His mighty standard.   That proud honour claimed
Azazel as his right, a Cherub tall :
Who forthwith from the glittering staff unfurled
The imperial ensign ; which, full high advanced,
Shone like a meteor streaming to the wind,
With gems and golden lustre rich emblazed,
Seraphic arms and trophies ; all the while
Sonorous metal blowing martial sounds :
At which the universal host up-sent
A shout that tore Hell's concave, and beyond
Frighted the reign of Chaos and old Night.
All in a moment through the gloom were seen
Ten thousand banners rise into the air,
With orient colours waving : with them rose
A forest huge of spears ; and thronging helms
Appeared, and serried shields in thick array
Of depth immeasurable.   Anon they move
In perfect phalanx to the Dorian mood
Of flutes and soft recorders, such as raised
To highth of noblest temper heroes old
Arming to battle.

                                            MILTON.

Continuo ad sonitum litui sonitumque tubarum
belligeros acuentum animos spectabile signum
attolli iubet aetherium ; quem laetus honorem
ipse suum, divus procero corpore praestans,
vindicat Azazel, fulgentique explicat hasta
continuo regale decus. volat illud in auras,
ut quondam in ventos multa cum luce moventur
obliquae per inane faces, altoque coruscat
aethere distinctum gemmis aurique nitore
signaque caelicolum referens et picta tropaea.
interea aerisonos accendunt cornua cantus
martia : tum vero audires uno ore frequentes
vociferare acies ; clangor cava Tartara rupit,
et tremuit Chaos, et priscae penetralia Noctis.
nec mora : per tenebras consurgere milia multa
signorum Eois agitata coloribus ; una
silva hastarum ingens, confertaque casside cassis
et clipeus clipeo, non enarrabilis ordo.
continuo iustas acies complere phalanges,
Dorica quas molli concentu ducit euntes
tibia ; qualem olim perhibent in limine Martis
accendisse animos et fortia facta virorum.

O thou who bad'st thy turtles bear
Swift from his grasp thy golden hair,
   And sought'st thy native skies;
When War, by vultures drawn from far,
To Britain bent his iron car,
   And bade the storms arise.

Tired of his rude tyrannic sway,
Our youths shall fix some festive day
   His sullen shrines to burn:
But thou who hear'st the turning spheres,
What sounds may charm thy partial ears,
   And gain thy blest return?

O Peace! thy injured robes upbind,
O, rise, and leave not one behind
   Of all thy beamy train;
The British Lion, Goddess sweet,
Lies stretched on earth to kiss thy feet,
   And own thy holier reign.

Let others court thy transient smile;
But come to grace thy western isle
   By warlike Honour led:
And while around her ports rejoice,
While all her sons adore thy choice,
   With him for ever wed.

                           COLLINS.

O quam nefando crinibus aureis
ex hoste raptis ala fidelium
   pernix columbarum revexit
     in superas, tua regna, sedes ;

quando remotis e regionibus
Mavors Britanna ad litora vultures
   currusque ferratos adegit
     terribiles glomerans procellas ;

ut feriato proruerit die
duri iuventus indocilis iugi
   delubra, Gradivique tristem
     igne sacro violarit aedem,

fastidiosam, quae bibis orbium
cantus vagantum, cui reseres sono
   aurem ? quis optatum reducat,
     Pax, reditum ? precor, huc resurgas

succincta laesos, inclita, vestium
nodos, chorea non sine lucida.
   en stratus advectae Britannus
     crura leo tua lambit ore

iam sanctioris conscius imperi.
captare risus fas aliis breves ;
   ast occidentales ad oras
     cuspide Honor positoque telo

te ducat ; una moenia portuum
festo salutantum omine personent,
   ut foedus aeternes in aevum
     digna viro sociata digno.

>   The mountain-ash,
> Decked with autumnal berries that outshine
> Spring's richest blossoms, yields a goodly show
> Among the leafy woods, and ye have seen
> By a brookside or solitary tarn
> How she her station doth adorn : the pool
> Glows at her feet, and all the gloomy rocks
> Are brightened round her. In his native vale
> Such, and so glorious, did this youth appear :
> A sight that kindled pleasure in all hearts
> By his ingenuous beauty, by the gleam
> Of his fair eyes, by his capacious brow,
> By all the graces with which Nature's hand
> Had lavishly arrayed him. As old bards
> Tell in their idle songs of wandering gods,
> Pan or Apollo, veiled in human form ;
> Yet, like the sweet-breathed violet of the shade,
> Discovered in their own despite to sense
> Of mortals (if such fables without blame
> May find chance-mention on this sacred ground),
> So, through a simple rustic garb's disguise,
> In him revealed a scholar's genius shone ;
> And so, not wholly hidden from men's sight,
> In him the spirit of a hero walked
> Our unpretending valley.

WORDSWORTH.

Qualis ubi autumni bacarum induta racemos
exsuperat veris gemmas atque ornus amictu
purpureo silvarum inter nitet ardua frondes :
propter aquam—vidistis enim—aut ad sola paludis
en quantum ipsa suam decorat pulcherrima sedem :
ardet sub pedibus lacus, atque immania circum
saxa renidescunt. talis convalle paterna
conspicitur iuvenis, species praeclara tueri,
laudandus vultu ingenuo, dulcedine qualis
pectora succendat mira spectantibus olli
torvum ardere oculum latamque patescere frontem,
prodiga quae Natura manu sua dona profudit.
carmine ceu vano veteres cecinere deorum
errores, ludentem hominis sub imagine Phoebum
Maenaliumve deum ; sed enim mortalibus ipsi,
sicut odor violam latitantem prodit in umbra,
inviti patuere oculis, si forte sacrata
talia mentiri in terra sine fraude licebit.
sic olli quamquam agresti sub tegmine operta
vivida vis sophiae non dissimulata refulsit.
haud aliter non ille latens in valle reducta
obtutus hominum manifestus prodiit heros.

Or will you deem them amply paid in health,
Labour's fair child, that languishes with wealth?
Go, then! and see them rising with the sun,
Through a long course of daily toil to run;
See them beneath the Dog-star's raging heat,
When the knees tremble and the temples beat;
Behold them, leaning on their scythes, look o'er
The labour past, and toils to come explore;
See them alternate suns and showers engage,
And hoard up aches and anguish for their age;
Through fens and marshy moors their steps pursue,
When their warm pores imbibe the evening dew.
There may you see the youth of slender frame
Contend with weakness, weariness, and shame;
Yet, urged along, and proudly loth to yield,
He strives to join his fellows of the field;
Till long-contending nature droops at last,
Declining health rejects his poor repast,
His cheerless spouse the coming danger sees,
And mutual murmurs urge the slow disease.
Yet grant them health, 'tis not for us to tell,
Though the head droops not, that the heart is well.
Or will you praise that homely, healthy fare,
Plenteous and plain, that happy peasants share?
Oh! trifle not with wants you cannot feel,
Nor mock the misery of a stinted meal;
Homely not wholesome, plain not plenteous, such
As you who praise would never deign to touch.

CRABBE.

At mala pensari dicis, cum nata laboris
  alma valetudo langueat inter opes.
adspice nunc una cum Phoebo surgere, ut orbem
  perpetuum, nacti pensa diurna, trahant ;
dum coquit arentes insana Canicula messes,
  quo saliant motu tempora, genua tremant.
ut baculo innixi reputent anteacta laborum,
  et quae venturo sint subeunda die.
adspice ut alternos soles patiantur et imbres,
  in senium ut morbos tristitiamque parent.
stagnaque limosae per vespertina paludis
  ut gelidos rores fervida vena bibat.
hic pueri videas macie luctantia membra,
  qui gemit invitus quem gemuisse pudet.
interea miserum mens cedere nescia torquet,
  nititur et sociis par tamen esse suis.
dum tandem natura malis, certamine lassa,
  fit minor et parcum respuit ore cibum.
prospicit infelix ventura pericula coniunx,
  et morbi accelerat mixta querela moras.
sit tamen ut valeant ; sed enim non dicere nostrum est,
  si bene sit capiti, corda vacare malo.
at plenam laudas mensam victusque salubres
  munera felicis simpliciora casae.
ne tibi inexperto moveat penuria risum,
  quaeque parum dirae sufficit esca fami.
mensa licet simplex neque plena neque esca salubris,
  laudatos pudeat te tetigisse cibos.

H.   My dearest love, since thou wilt go,
        And leave me here behind thee ;
     For love or pitie, let me know
        The place where I may find thee.

A.   In country meadowes, pearled with dew,
        And set about with lillies,
     There, filling maunds with cowslips, you
        May find your Amarillis.

H.   What have the meads to do with thee,
        Or with thy youthfull houres ?
     Live thou at court, where thou may'st be
        The queen of men, not flowers.

     Let country wenches make 'em fine
        With posies, since 'tis fitter
     For thee with richest jemmes to shine,
        And like the starres to glitter.

                                        HERRICK.

H.   Ergo, noster amor, fugis
    sic nos destituens ? dic quibus in locis
      te forte inveniam, precor
    per te si quid amor, si pietas valet.

A.   visas roscida liliis
    commendata suis rura ; ibi lutea
      praeda florum Amaryllida
    complentem calathos invenies tuam.

H.   tecum prata quid umida aut
    horis cum teneris ? tu potius fove
      aulam, verba homines ubi
    iurent in tua, non flos tibi serviat.

    istis rustica Phidyle
    sertis se decoret : gemmea tu nite—
      sic est verius—auream
    ut te sidereae non superent faces.

There is a place, deep, wondrous deep, below,
Which genuine Night and Horror does o'erflow ;
No bound controls th' unwearied space, but hell,
Endless as those dire pains that in it dwell.
Here no dear glimpse of the sun's lovely face
Strikes through the solid darkness of the place ;
No dawning morn does her kind reds display ;
One slight weak beam would here be thought the day :
No gentle stars with their fair gems of light
Offend the tyrannous and unquestion'd night.
Here Lucifer, the mighty captive, reigns ;
Proud 'midst his woes, and tyrant in his chains ;
Once general of a gilded host of sprites,
Like Hesper, leading forth the spangled nights ;
But down like lightning, which him struck, he came ;
And roar'd at his first plunge into the flame :
Myriads of spirits fell wounded round him there ;
With dropping lights thick shone the singed air ;
Since when, the dismal solace of their woe
Has only been weak mankind to undo ;
Themselves at first against themselves they excite
('Their dearest conquest and most proud delight),
And if those mines of secret treason fail,
With open force man's virtue they assail :
Unable to corrupt, seek to destroy,
And where their poisons miss, the sword employ.

COWLEY.

Qua comes ingenitae nocti scatet additus horror
est locus, immenso terrae mira antra recessu
subdita : nec spatiis ullus nisi Tartara limes,
Tartara Tartareo sedes aequata dolori.
his adeo numquam solidis offusa tenebris
exserit os roseum lampas Phoebea, nec umquam
se domus in facilem Aurora nascente ruborem
induit ; obscurae fuerit pro sole cavernae
nescio quod vel tenue iubar. neque enim astra coruscant
mitia ne liquidis lucem spirantia gemmis
imminuant noctis non exsuperabile regnum :
nimirum amissis devinctus honoribus aulae
Lucifer exili male praesidet, ut tamen ipsis
regem agat in vinclis luctusque superbiat inter.
scilicet in superis dux olim incesserat auris
agminis auricomi, qualis tu, Phosphore, noctis
praevius illuces : atqui Iovis ignibus ictus
ocior igne cadit, flammaque immersus et Orco
continuo ingemuit : nec milia caelicolarum
qui caesi caderent deerant : nempe ipse caducis
actutum facibus flammans incanduit aer.
ex quo non alia solantibus arte dolorem
praeda fuere hominum gens imbecillior : ipsis
comminus in se ipsos (nec carior ulla voluptas,
nulla umquam tanti laurus) certamina suadent.
sin minus occulta est grassari fraude, minaces
irrumpunt, si fors vi debellatus aperta
se dedat tecta qui non corrumpitur arte :
procuduntque feros enses pereunte veneno.

She came—she is gone—we have met—
   And meet perhaps never again.
The sun of that moment is set,
   And seems to have risen in vain.
Catharina has fled like a dream,
   (So vanishes pleasure, alas!)
But has left a regard and esteem
   That will not so suddenly pass.

The last evening ramble we made,
   Catharina, Maria and I,
Our progress was often delayed
   By the nightingale warbling nigh.
We paused under many a tree,
   And much was she charmed by a tone,
Less sweet to Maria and me,
   Who so lately had witnessed her own.

My numbers that day she had sung
   And gave them a grace so divine,
As only her musical tongue
   Could infuse into numbers of mine.
The longer I heard, I esteemed
   The work of my fancy the more,
And e'en to myself never seemed
   So tuneful a poet before.

COWPER

Visa semel rapta est. ergo convenimus, eheu!
  vix ubi nos iterum conveniamus erit.
me miserum! frustra sol ille videtur obortus,
  protinus hesperias sol rediturus aquas.
siccine nos Galatea levis velut umbra reliquit?
  sic fugiunt celeri gaudia nostra pede.
at desiderium memor, at manet ille superstes
  non subito gressu praeteriturus amor.
non cadit ex animo lux vespertina, Corinna
  qua fuit et nostrae pars Galatea viae.
proxima dum deflebat Ityn Philomela peremptum,
  ut placuit segnes substituisse pedes.
fronde sub arborea quotiens consedimus : illam
  illecebris quotiens detinuere modi.
me tamen hi sociamque minus potuere morari ;
  quale suum nuper fuderat ipsa melos.
ipsa meas paulo recitaverat ante Camenas ;
  divinis inerat gratia quanta sonis.
vox ea dulcis erat ; quales infundere norat
  carminibus veneres sola puella meis.
quo magis ausculto, magis auscultare placebat ;
  certe habuit nostrum quo caperemur opus.
carmina tum demum, fateor, numerosa sonabant,
  ipse mihi vates denique visus eram.

The steed is vanish'd from the stall ;
No serf is seen in Hassan's hall ;
The lonely spider's thin gray pall
Waves slowly widening o'er the wall ;
The bat builds in his haram bower,
And in the fortress of his power
The owl usurps the beacon-tower ;
The wild dog howls o'er the fountain's brim,
With baffled thirst and famine grim ;
For the stream has shrunk from its marble bed,
Where the weeds and the desolate dust are spread.
'Twas sweet of yore to see it play
And chase the sultriness of day,
As springing high the silver dew
In whirls fantastically flew,
And flung luxurious coolness round
The air, and verdure o'er the ground.
'Twas sweet, when cloudless stars were bright,
To view the wave of watery light,
And hear its melody by night.
And oft had Hassan's childhood play'd
Around the verge of that cascade ;
And oft upon his mother's breast
That sound had harmonized his rest ;
And oft had Hassan's youth along
Its bank been sooth'd by beauty's song ;
And softer seem'd each melting tone
Of music mingled with its own.

BYRON.

Non equus in stabulis, non alta servus in aula :
    iam fugit tacitam gratia prisca domum.
crescentes sensim suspendit aranea telas,
    solaque funerea moenia veste tegit.
immundae thalamis nidum posuere volucres,
    et vigil in summa noctua turre gemit.
aspera delusaque sibi rabieque fameque
    nunc ululat sicci fontis ad ora canis.
notos namque locos undae fugere loquaces,
    gramineque et foedo pulvere sordet humus.
atqui suave fuit ludentem cernere lympham
    effuso rapidum rore fugare iubar :
dum saliens variis errabat in orbibus unda
    tamquam incompositos duceret ipsa choros ;
grataque fundebat torrentes frigora in auras
    et viridi ornabat caespite semper humum.
suave erat undarum, sine nube micantibus astris,
    luce coruscantes cernere nocte vias.
suave audire sonos : nam mille puertia ludos
    luserat ad strepitum desilientis aquae.
saepe susurrantis resupini in pectore matris
    fontana fuerat consona voce quies.
saepe etiam Hassani fuerat se margine in illo
    virgineis vinci passa iuventa modis ;
suavia qua lympham verba interfusa sonabant
    nec nihil in magico carmine fontis erat.

Look back, old Janus, and survey
From Time's birth till this new-born day,
All the successful seasons bound
With laurel wreaths, and trophies crown'd:
Turn o'er the annals past, and where
Happy auspicious days appear,
Mark'd with the whiter stone that cast
On the dark brow of th' ages past
A dazzling lustre, let them shine
In this succeeding circle's twine,
Till it be round with glories spread:
Then with it crown our Charles his head;
That we th' ensuing year may call
One great continued festival.
Circle with peaceful olive boughs
And conquering bays his regal brows:
Let his strong virtues overcome,
And bring him bloodless trophies home:
Strew all the pavements where he treads
With loyal hearts or rebel heads;
But, Byfront, open thou no more
In his blest reign the temple door.

CAREW.

Saeclorum ab ortu fac, precor, ultimo
usque ad recentem, Iane vetus, diem
   horas coronatasque palmis
     respicias propriaque lauru;

fastosque volvas praeteritos, ubi
bene ominatus conspicitur dies,
   et siqua signasti notanda
     tempora candidiore creta,

caliginosam lumine quae replet
aevi prioris frontem, age, da iubar
   orbi secuturo novatum,
     necte meo diadema regi

splendore lucens (annus aget sequens
sic feriatos perpetuos dies);
   victrice mox lauru superbum
     cinge caput placitaeque paci

sertis olivae; regia Caesaris
virtus ut iras dissipet hostium
   constans, ut expertes cruoris
     in patriam referat triumphos,

ut fida corda aut colla rebellium
sternant pavimentum undique; sed fores,
   in posterum ut regnet beatus,
     parce, Bifrons, reserare templi.

To whom Satan, turning boldly, thus:—'Ye Powers
And Spirits of this nethermost Abyss,
Chaos and ancient Night, I come no spy
With purpose to explore or to disturb
The secrets of your realm, but, by constraint
Wandering this darksome desert, as my way
Lies through your spacious empire up to light,
Alone and without guide, half lost, I seek,
What readiest path leads where your gloomy bounds
Confine with Heaven; or, if some other place,
From your dominion won, the Ethereal King
Possesses lately, thither to arrive
I travel this profound. Direct my course:
Directed, no mean recompense it brings
To your behoof, if I that region lost,
All usurpation thence expelled, reduce
To her original darkness and your sway
(Which is my present journey), and once more
Erect the standard there of ancient Night.
Yours be the advantage all, mine the revenge!'

MILTON.

Quis Satanas audax obversus talia fatur:
'di, quibus est infra tutela voraginis imae,
vos, Chaos et Nox prisca, ego non huc arte dolosa
exploraturus venio aut turbare paratus
regni arcana nigri, verum deserta peragrans
et tenebras, quoniam vestrae dicionis iniqua
per spatia est iter ad lucem, non sponte, sed errans
fraude loci solus nullo duce, semita siqua est
prompta peto ad fines ubi vos contermina caelo
atra loca incolitis; vel si regione subacta
forte aliam aetherius nuper rex obtinet oram,
vestrum illuc properans studeo transire profundum:
este duces mihi vos; merces, si tramite certo
ire queo, non vilis erit, cum partibus istis
depulero amissis qui vos spoliavit, et umbras
reddidero antiquae caliginis—hoc iter illud
cogitat imperium ut sit vos penes, ipse vetustae
extollam rursus Noctis sublimia signa—
vestrum erit omne lucrum, mihi sat vindicta rependet.'

Lawrence, of virtuous father virtuous son,
    Now that the fields are dank, and ways are mire,
    Where shall we sometimes meet, and by the fire
    Help waste a sullen day, what may be won
From the hard season gaining ? Time will run
    On smoother, till Favonius reinspire
    The frozen earth, and clothe in fresh attire
    The lily and rose, that neither sowed nor spun.
What neat repast shall feast us, light and choice,
    Of Attic taste, with wine, whence we may rise
    To hear the lute well touched, or artful voice
Warble immortal notes and Tuscan air ?
    He who of those delights can judge, and spare
    To interpose them oft, is not unwise.

                        MILTON.

O sancta sancti progenies patris,
dum tesqua sordent, manat in hispidos
   dum nimbus agros, quos licebit
      ante focos reparare quondam

lusus, acerbum frangere quos diem?
quod dura cedant tempora, quid frui
   cessamus? en anni morantis
      hora volat leviore lapsu,

mox et favoni rura nivalia
flatus fovebit; liliaque et rosas
   ornabit expertes laborum
      veste nova reserata tellus.

quae cena simplex nos manet, Atticos
spirans lepores, non sine Massico?
   cum saepe sub noctem sonabit
      virgineo lyra tacta plectro,

seu vox Camenas callida fundere
cantusve Tuscos. desipit has miser
   qui novit at notis pepercit
      deliciis sapienter uti.

The castled crag of Drachenfels
Frowns o'er the wide and winding Rhine,
Whose breast of waters broadly swells
Between the banks which bear the vine,
And hills all rich with blossom'd trees,
And fields which promise corn and wine,
And scatter'd cities crowning these,
Whose far white walls along them shine,
Have strew'd a scene, which I should see
With double joy wert thou with me.

And peasant girls, with deep blue eyes,
And hands which offer early flowers,
Walk smiling o'er this paradise;
Above, the frequent feudal towers
Through green leaves lift their walls of gray;
And many a rock which steeply lowers,
And noble arch in proud decay,
Look o'er this vale of vintage-bowers;
But one thing want these banks of Rhine,—
Thy gentle hand to clasp in mine!

I send the lilies given to me;
Though long before thy hand they touch
I know that they must withered be,
But yet reject them not as such;
For I have cherished them as dear,
Because they yet may meet thine eye,
And guide thy soul to mine even here,
When thou behold'st them drooping nigh,
And know'st them gather'd by the Rhine,
And offered from my heart to thine!

BYRON.

Ecce super rupes veteris tutela draconis
  despiciens Rheni torva minatur aquas.
flexibus hic latis sinuatur et inter amictas
  vite sua ripas unda superba tumet.
plurimus hic ridet frondoso vertice collis,
  praebet ager Cereris spemque, Lyaee, tui.
urbe coronantur rara loca; turribus albis
  oblectant oculos moenia visa procul.
pulchra quidem regio; sed ter mihi pulchra videnti
  si posses nostrae tu comes esse viae.
nec non caeruleo quae ridet lumine virgo
  hos habitat, proles rustica, multa lares,
primitiasque adfert veris; super ardua fronde
  in viridi turris semisepulta latet.
praeceps adsurgit rupes; vallemque columna
  despicit exesa fronte, superba tamen.
deficit hoc unum—dat cetera gaudia Rhenus—
  dextra quod est dextrae non tua iuncta meae.
haec tibi quae mihi sunt dono data lilia mitto,
  heu nimium celeri deperitura vice:
ante, nec ignoro, dominae quam dextera tangit
  marcida, sed quamvis marcida dona cape.
ista, velim credas, mihi sunt pretiosa, quod olim
  forsan erunt oculis obvia serta tuis.
me forsan recoles, surget mea forsan imago,
  ut pueri absentis marcida dona vides.
tuque memor dices: ‘haec Rheni in margine carpta
  accipit a fido fida puella proco.’

Meanwhile the tepid caves, and fens, and shores,
Their brood as numerous hatch from the egg, that soon,
Bursting with kindly rupture, forth disclosed
Their callow young; but feathered soon and fledge
They summed their pens, and, soaring the air sublime,
With clang despised the ground, under a cloud
In prospect. There the eagle and the stork
On cliffs and cedar-tops their eyries build.
Part loosely wing the region; part, more wise,
In common, ranged in figure, wedge their way,
Intelligent of seasons, and set forth
Their aery caravan, high over seas
Flying, and over lands, with mutual wing
Easing their flight; so steers the prudent crane
Her annual voyage, borne on winds; the air
Floats as they pass, fanned with unnumbered plumes.

                                              MILTON.

Interea lacus et ripae tepidaeque paludes
quaeque suos generant aequali foedere partus.
continuo implumes rupto genitaliter ovo
exsiliunt pulli; nec longum tempus et alae
munera plumigeri capiunt, perque aera sursum
astra fuga sublime petunt, plausuque sonoro
spernit humum gens tota et scandere nubila temptat.
inde lares aquilae dulcesque ciconia nidos
rupibus excelsis cedrive in vertice nectunt.
pars vaga per sudum volitant: pars doctior una
agmen agunt, cuneoque viam communiter urgent,
horarum non immemores, celsoque volatu
per mare per terras, sociatis mutua pennis,
nubivagos fallunt cursus; labor omnibus aequus;
sollemnem quo more grues gens provida cursum
arte regunt; ventis expandunt carbasa, et aura
plumarum sonat innumeris agitata flabellis.

When the British warrior queen,
　Bleediug from the Roman rods,
Sought, with an indignant mien,
　Counsel of her country's gods;

Sage beneath the spreading oak
　Sat the Druid, hoary chief;
Every burning word he spoke
　Full of rage and full of grief:

'Princess, if our aged eyes
　Weep upon thy matchless wrongs,
'Tis because resentment ties
　All the terrors of our tongues.

Rome shall perish—write that word
　In the blood that she has spilt;
Perish, hopeless and abhorred,
　Deep in ruin as in guilt.

Rome, for empire far renowned,
　Tramples on a thousand states:
Soon her pride shall kiss the ground—
　Hark! the Gaul is at her gates!

Other Romans shall arise,
　Heedless of a soldier's name;
Sounds, not arms, shall win the prize,
　Harmony the path to fame.

Then the progeny that springs
　From the forests of our land,
Armed with thunder, clad with wings,
　Shall a wider world command.

Quando cruentis secta Quiritium
virgis minaci fronte Britanniae
   regina bellatrix deorum
      indigetum repetebat aras;

illic sedebat sub patulae comis
incanus aevo rex Druidum ilicis;
   exarsit in diram canentis
      fata dolor rabiesque vocem:

'o passa casus plus vice simplici,
regina, si te lumina flent senis,
   non verba desunt, at minantem
      ira potest cohibere linguam.

delenda Roma est—sit titulus memor
scriptus tepenti sanguine quo rubet—
   exspes et infamis suoque
      mersa pari scelere ac ruina.

nunc insolenti freta superbia
late illa gentes proterit, ast humum
   mox ipsa mordebit—minaci
      iam strepitu furit ante portas

(audisne?) Gallus; mox nova Martii
nascetur aetas nominis immemor,
   ensemque deponet perita
      voce petens citharaque palmam.

tum magna nostris saltibus edita
gens latiores imperio premet
   terras, inaudito volatu et
      fulmineo ruitura cursu.

Regions Caesar never knew
  Thy posterity shall sway;
Where his eagles never flew,
  None invincible as they.'

Such the bard's prophetic words,
  Pregnant with celestial fire,
Bending as he swept the chords
  Of his sweet but awful lyre.

She, with all a monarch's pride,
  Felt them in her bosom glow :
Rushed to battle, fought and died ;
  Dying hurled them at the foe.

' Ruffians ! pitiless as proud,
  Heaven awards the vengeance due ;
Empire is on us bestowed,
  Shame and ruin wait for you.'

COWPER.

tum longa tellus Caesaris inscia
tuos nepotes sentiet, ut plagis
 dent iura quo numquam per hostes
  explicuit sua signa victor.'

sic fata vates certa canit, novis
divi furoris percitus ignibus,
 chordis ut incumbens canorae
  fila lyrae metuenda pulsat.

ast ipsa, regum mater ovantium,
perculsa laeto ferbuit omine et
 tandem per obstantes catervas
  sic repetit moribunda fatum :

' nil non adortae poena superbiae
vos digna (divis sic placitum) manet ;
 sunt sceptra nobis, at paratus
  Romulidis pudor ac ruina.'

The swallows in their torpid state
　　Compose their useless wing,
And bees in hives as idly wait
　　The call of early spring.

The keenest frost that binds the stream,
　　The wildest wind that blows,
Are neither felt nor fear'd by them,
　　Secure of their repose.

But man, all feeling and awake,
　　The gloomy scene surveys ;
With present ill his heart must ache,
　　And pant for brighter days.

Old Winter, halting o'er the mead,
　　Bids me and Mary mourn ;
But lovely spring peeps o'er his head,
　　And whispers your return.

Then April, with her sister May,
　　Shall chase him from the bowers,
And weave fresh garlands every day,
　　To crown the smiling hours.

And if a tear, that speaks regret
　　Of happier times, appear,
A glimpse of joy, that we have met,
　　Shall shine and dry the tear.

COWPER.

Iam vacuas iterum pennas componit hirundo,
    torpet et in lentas desidiosa moras.
dumque lacessat apem veris vox alma renati
    delituit propriis segnis et ipsa favis.
sive premit rivi glacies acerrima cursus,
    flamina seu venti turgidiora furunt :
otia apis secura fovet, secura volucris :
    nil premit has boreae cura metusve noti.
nostra tamen semper quae gens vigil omnia sentit
    tristitiam foedi lustrat ubique loci.
et mala dilacerant praesentia pectus, et optat
    si radio surgat candidiore dies.
fronte senilis hiems serpens pede clauda per agros
    me iubet, at frustra, teque, Corinna, queri :
nam caput optatum supereminet inque susurris
    ver reditum socii iam prope adesse monet.
addere se facilis properat iam Maius Aprili,
    dum fugiat nostris saltibus exsul hiems :
inque dies cinctura comas ridentibus Horis
    nectere amant flores in nova serta novos.
quod si praeteritos quotiens desiderat annos
    ex oculis furtim debita gutta cadit,
at iubar e tenebris, quod nos convenimus olim,
    emicat et siccas deserit unda genas.

Thence to the famous Orators repair,
Those ancient whose resistless eloquence
Wielded at will that fierce democraty,
Shook the Arsenal and fulmined over Greece
To Macedon and Artaxerxes' throne.
To sage Philosophy next lend thine ear,
From heaven descended to the low-roofed house
Of Socrates—see there his tenement—
Whom, well inspired, the oracle pronounced
Wisest of men ; from whose mouth issued forth
Mellifluous streams, that watered all the schools
Of Academics old and new, with those
Surnamed Peripatetics, and the sect
Epicurean, and the Stoic severe.
These here revolve, or, as thou likest, at home,
Till time mature thee to a kingdom's weight ;
These rules will render thee a king complete
Within thyself, much more with empire joined.

MILTON.

Mox oratorum veterum admirabere celsa
ingenia, insanam quorum facundia plebem
impulit ut voluere : armamentaria tota
indomitas sensere minas, et sensit Achaia
et Macedo et Persa ipse horrenda tonitrua linguae.
inde tuam lenis sapientia mulceat aurem,
desuper in parvam caelo demissa tabernam
Socratis—ecce humiles cernas licet illius aedes—
percita non falso quem numine Pythia dixit
ante alios sapientem : ex quo fluxere loquenti
melliti latices, quorum omnes undique sectae
sive Academiae vetus et nova fonte rigantur,
seu quod Aristoteles Epicureique docebant,
Stoicus et norma vitae graviore severus.
hic mea sive domi malis praecepta revolvas,
donec onus regni tempus te praebeat aptum
ferre umeris ; quoniam privata sorte manentem
iussa valent haec te perfectum reddere regem,
quo magis, ipsa tibi modo sit coniuncta potestas.

The winds were laid, the air was still,
  The stars they shot alang the sky;
The fox was howling on the hill,
  And the distant echoing glens reply.
The stream adown its hazelly path
  Was rushing by the ruined wa's,
Hasting to join the sweeping Nith,
  Whase distant roaring swells an' fa's.
The cauld blue north was streaming forth
  Her lights wi' hissing eerie din;
Athort the lift they start an' shift,
  Like fortune's favours, tint as win.
By heedless chance I turned mine eyes,
  And by the moonbeam shook to see
A stern and stalwart ghaist arise,
  Attired as minstrels wont to be.
Had I a statue been o' stane,
  His daring look had daunted me;
And on his bonnet graved was plain
  The sacred posy—Libertie.
And frae his harp sic strains did flow,
  Might roused the slumbering dead to hear:
But oh! it was a tale of woe,
  As ever met a Briton's ear!
He sang wi' joy his former day,
  He weeping wailed his latter times.
But what he said it was nae play,
  I winna venture 't in my rhymes.

                                 BURNS.

Iam posuere aurae, et tacitum per inane vibrata
    sidera per geminos visa micare polos.
ardua iam collis vulpes ululatibus implet,
    silva repercussos dat procul icta sonos.
unda ruinosas lambit violentior arces
    dum terit insanam per coryleta viam ;
dum properat sese fluvio immiscere rapaci,
    qui strepit inque vices unda remota silet.
caerula trans caelum flammis radiaverat Arctos,
    spectra suos miscent, sibila turba, sonos.
illa vibrat variatque faces ceu munera fallax
    quae fors alterna datque rapitque manu.
forte pererrantem lunae sub luce salebras
    terrebant oculis obvia visa meis.
torvus et humano maior citharaque decorus
    nescio quis media visus adesse via.
non ego, si Pario starem de marmore cautes,
    non potui frontis non timuisse minas :
cernere erat sacra in medio manifesta galero
    nomina quis 'patriae' scriptus inesset 'amor.'
posse putes citharam Manes excire sepulcris
    quos liquidos digito reddidit icta modos.
triste tamen crepuere fides, neque nenia in aurem
    Angliacam sonuit tristior ulla prius.
quos dedit exsultim saecli de laude prioris,
    excipiunt laetos flebiliora modos ;
tempora culpanti mutata ; at seria fudit
    carmina versiculis vix tenuanda meis.

'Tis sung in ancient minstrelsy
　　That Phœbus wont to wear
The leaves of any pleasant tree
　　Around his golden hair,
Till Daphne, desperate with pursuit
　　Of his imperious love,
At her own prayer transformed, took root
　　A laurel in the grove.

Then did the Penitent adorn
　　His brow with laurel green :
And 'mid his bright locks never shorn
　　No meaner leaf was seen :
And poets sage in every age
　　About their temples wound
The bay ; and conquerors thank'd the Gods
　　With laurel chaplets bound.

WORDSWORTH.

Olim venustam sic temere arborem
Phoebo placebat sumere, ut aureos
   ornaret ex quavis capillos
      (sic veteres cecinere Musae);

Daphne impotentem exosa cupidinem
se donec exspes contulit in nemus,
   laurumque mutavit puella,
      ipsa suis precibus potita.

exinde facti paenituit deum, et
frontem virenti non nisi laurea
   cingit, neque intonsi nitebant
      fronde iterum leviore crines.

doctique lauru saecula in ultima
vates et ipsi tempora vinciunt;
   victorque dis nectens coronas
      haud alias sua vota solvit.

As those who pause on some delightful way,
Though bent on pleasant pilgrimage, we stood,
Looking upon the evening and the flood
Which lay between the city and the shore,
Paved with the image of the sky. The hoar
And aery Alps, toward the north, appeared,
Thro' mist, a heaven-sustaining bulwark, reared
Between the east and west; and half the sky
Was roofed with clouds of rich emblazonry,
Dark purple at the zenith, which still grew
Down the steep west into a wondrous hue
Brighter than burning gold, even to the rent
Where the swift sun yet paused in his descent.
                                    SHELLEY.

Qualis qui circum divortia amoena moratur,
quamquam iter acceptum peragrans, constamus uterque
solisque occasum pariter fluctusque iacentes
litoris atque urbis medios spectamus, ut infra
unda repercussa radiaret imagine caeli.
Alpes aerio candentes vertice ad arcton
visae inter nimbos utrisque ex partibus orbis
surgere suggestae moles fulcimina caelo.
tunc et dimidio picto subtemine nubes
aethere substiterunt laquearia, vertice summo
nigrantes atra ferrugine, cum tamen infra
convexa occidui rutilo immiscerier auro
ardentemque magis flammis mutare colorem
discussum caeli ad finem solemque morantem.

TRANSLATIONS

INTO LATIN PROSE

In his private conduct he was severe, morose, inexorable; banishing all the softer affections, as natural enemies to justice, and as suggesting false motives of acting, from favour, clemency, and compassion; in public affairs he was the same: had but one rule of policy, to adhere to what was right; without regard to times or circumstances, or even to a force that could control him; for instead of managing the power of the great, so as to mitigate the ill, or extract any good from it, he was urging it always to acts of violence by a perpetual defiance; so that with the best intentions in the world, he often did great harm to the republic. This was his general behaviour; yet, from some particular facts explained above, it appears that his strength of mind was not always impregnable, but had its weak places of pride, ambition, and party zeal; which, when managed and flattered to a certain point, would betray him sometimes into measures contrary to his ordinary rule of right and truth. The last act of his life was agreeable to his nature and philosophy; when he could no longer be what he had been; or when the ills of life overbalanced the good, which, by the principles of his sect, was a just cause for dying; he put an end to his life, with a spirit and resolution which would make one imagine that he was glad to have found an occasion of dying in his proper character. On the whole his life was rather admirable than amiable: fit to be praised, rather than imitated.

Domi et intus tristis durus implacabilis molliores animi adfectus relegabat, tamquam a iustitia suopte ingenio abhorrerent et falsa quaedam agendi principia gratiae clementiae misericordiae suggererent. idem erat et in re publica, qui non nisi hanc sibi regulam statuisset, quod rectum esset uti id amplecteretur, nulla neque rerum neque temporum ratione habita, ut ne vim quidem coercentium respiceret. quem enim optimatium auctoritatem ita tractare oportebat ut si quid inesset mali molliret, si quid boni eliceret, idem ad atrocissima quaeque continuis provocationibus lacessebat, ita ut optimo quidem utens animo saepe obesset rei publicae. ita se plerumque gerebat. constat tamen ex quibusdam rebus, quarum supra mentionem fecimus, non semper inexpugnabilem fuisse animi constantiam, sed aditus quosdam superbiae famae studio partium praebuisse; quem si quis adsentationibus aliquatenus tractare vellet, a solida recti et veri norma facile erat deducturus. quae novissima egit et ingenio et disciplinae satis congruebant : postquam enim is esse qui fuerat non iam poterat aut bona vitae malis compensabantur—quam isti quidem philosophi satis iustam moriendi causam esse voluerunt—mortem sibi conscivit, eo usus animo ea constantia ut occasionem sibi convenienter moriendi libentissime nactum esse credideris. quid multa? is erat quem admireris potius quam ames, quem laudandum potius quam exemplo proponendum dixeris.

Certainly the true end of visiting foreign parts is to look into their customs and policies, and observe in what particulars they excel or come short of our own; to unlearn some odd peculiarities in our manners, and wear off such awkward stiffnesses and affectations in our behaviour as may possibly have been contracted from constantly associating with one nation of men, by a more free, general, and mixed conversation.

Another end of travelling, which deserves to be considered, is the improving our taste of the best authors of antiquity, by seeing the places where they lived, and of which they wrote; to compare the natural face of the country with the descriptions they have given us, and observe how well the picture agrees with the original. This must certainly be a most charming exercise to the mind that is rightly turned for it; besides that it may in a good measure be made subservient to morality, if the person is capable of drawing just conclusions concerning the uncertainty of human things, from the ruinous alterations time and barbarity have brought upon so many palaces, cities, and whole countries, which make the most illustrious figures in history. And this hint may be not a little improved by examining every spot of ground that we find celebrated as the scene of some famous action, or retaining any footsteps of a Cato, Cicero, or Brutus, or some such great virtuous man. A nearer view of any such particular, though really little and trifling in itself, may serve the more powerfully to warm a generous mind to an emulation of their virtues, and a greater ardency of ambition to imitate their bright examples, if it comes duly tempered and prepared for the impression. But this I believe you'll hardly think those to be, who are so far from entering into the sense and spirit of the ancients, that they don't yet understand their language with any exactness.

STEELE.

Is profecto verus finis externas visentibus regiones proponitur, ut alienas consuetudines et instituta dignoscamus, quatenus nostris aut cedant aut antecellant, ut inurbanos nescio quos et nobis proprios mores dediscamus, ut si qua forte ex unius populi commercio rusticitas gestus paulo inconcinnior ac putidior se prodiderit, eam libero magis et promiscuo hominum usu exuamus. sequitur alius peregrinantium isque memoratu dignus finis, quod maior inde ex optimo quoque scriptorum veterum quasi gustus voluptatis percipitur, visitatis ipsis locis ubi quisque habitaverit de quo quisque conscripserit, quod ingenio regionum cum eorum narrationibus collato, quantum exemplaribus imagines congruant conveniantque, facultas datur diiudicandi. quae exercitatio ut non dubium est quin menti ad eam rem aptae et accommodatae iucundissima sit, ita potest eadem magno opere ad bonos mores conducere, si quis porro ex tot regiis domibus tot urbibus tot nationibus denique, quas clarissimas nobis monumenta prodiderint, iisdem iam vetustate temporis aut barbarorum incursu commutatis aut prostratis, de instabili humanarum rerum fortuna facultatem nactus est colligendi. iam vero eadem cogitatio adhuc in melius promoveri potest, si quis singulorum locorum faciem contemplabitur sive praeclarum aliquod facinus, sive Catonis Ciceronis Bruti ceterorum aeque bonorum et illustrium hominum vestigia repraesentantium. res sane ipsa per se tenuis et exilis ; quo autem quisque propius introspexerit, qui quidem liberali animo adfectus satis imbutus et praeparatus ad concipiendam rem accesserit, eo acrius ad aemulandas virtutes accendetur, eo ardentius exempla egregia sibi imitationi propositurus est. quamquam eos qui tantum abest ut veterum scriptorum cogitationes et sententias perceperint ut ne linguam quidem satis accurate intellegant, equidem vix credo tibi hoc in numero reponendos videri.

It may happen that a republic, in its infant state, may be supported by as few laws as a barbarous monarchy, and may entrust as unlimited an authority to its magistrates or judges. But, besides that the frequent elections by the people are a considerable check upon authority, it is impossible but in time the necessity of restraining the magistrates, in order to preserve liberty, must at last appear, and give rise to general laws and statutes. The Roman consuls, for some time, decided all causes, without being confined by any positive statutes, till the people, bearing this yoke with impatience, created the decemvirs, who promulgated the twelve tables ; a body of laws, which, though, perhaps, they were not equal in bulk to one English act of parliament, were almost the only written rules which regulated property and punishment, for some ages, in that famous republic. They were, however, sufficient, together with the forms of a free government, to secure the lives and properties of the citizens ; to exempt one man from the dominion of another ; and to protect every one against the violence or tyranny of his fellow-citizens. In such a situation the sciences may raise their heads and flourish ; but never can have being amidst such a scene of oppression and slavery as always results from barbarous monarchies, where the people alone are restrained by the authority of the magistrates, and the magistrates are not restrained by any law or statute.

HUME.

Potest sane fieri ut rem publicam cum maxime nascentem perinde ac barbarorum dominationem et perpaucae leges contineant, et in utraque iis quibus magistratus aut iudicia mandantur potestas aeque infinita deferatur. verum tamen, praeterquam quod comitiis populi mandandorum magistratuum crebro habitis magna ex parte praefiniri solet imperium, cuinam dubium est quin eos quibus mandantur coercendi ideoque leges et instituta quae in universum valeant componendi tandem aliquando necessitas oriatur? Romae quidem aliquamdiu penes consules erant rerum omnium iudicia, ipsos ne ulla quidem lege scripta coercitos; donec a populo quem iugi pertaesum erat decem viri creati XII tabulas promulgarunt, fasciculum sane legum ne uni quidem senatus consulto civitatis nostrae parem, quo tamen praeclara illa res publica unico et praediorum retinendi et poenarum sanciendi iure per aliquot saecula utebatur. quamquam id praestabant XII tabulae, si rei publicae simul liberae iura respexeris, ut et vitae et possessionibus civium consuleretur, ut neque alius alii serviret et a vi aut ab impotentia ceterorum uni cuique caveretur. quo in rerum statu posse caput erigere et florere constat doctrinas; neutiquam vero esse possunt tanto in servitio tot in iniuriis quibus obnoxiae solent esse barbarorum dominationes, in quibus populus eorum quibus mandantur magistratus imperio coercetur, ii ipsi aliqua lege aut instituto non coercentur.

Though the good fortune of Cortes interposed so season-
ably on this occasion, the detection of this conspiracy filled
his mind with most disquieting apprehensions, and
prompted him to execute a scheme which he had long
revolved. He perceived that the spirit of disaffection still
lurked among the troops; that though hitherto checked
by the uniform success of his schemes, or suppressed by the
hand of authority, various events might occur which would
encourage and call it forth. He observed that many of
his men, weary of the fatigue of service, longed to revisit
their settlements in Cuba; and that upon any appearance
of extraordinary danger, or any reverse of fortune, it would
be impossible to restrain them from returning thither. He
was sensible that his forces, already too feeble, could bear
no diminution, and that a very small defection of his
followers would oblige him to abandon the enterprise.
After ruminating often, and with much solicitude, upon
these particulars, he saw no hope of success but in cutting
off all possibility of retreat, and in reducing his men to the
necessity of adopting the same resolution with which he
himself was animated, either to conquer or to perish.
With this view he determined to destroy his fleet: and, as
he durst not venture to execute such a bold resolution
by his single authority, he laboured to bring his soldiers
to adopt his ideas with respect to the propriety of this
measure.

ROBERTSON.

Ita opportune solita Cortesi fortuna huic rei inter-
venerat. patefacta tamen coniuratio eo metu perturbatum
animum cruciabat, ut quod diu iam secum volutabat consilium maturandum esse sibi constitueret. discordiam et
immodestiam in suorum animis etiam tunc latere; quam
adhuc utique rerum gestarum continuo tenore coercitam
aut vi et auctoritate restinctam posse tamen diversis causis
stimulari et resurgere. porro multos onerum et militiae
pertaesos Cubanam coloniam respicere. nimio aliquo exorto
periculo, sive fortuna coeptis adversaretur, eo revertenti-
bus quonam consilio posse obsisti? neque id penes se
esse virium de quo deminui aliquid res pateretur: perpaucorum defectione omittendum esse consilium. his diu
et anxie secum meditatis rationibus, ita demum prospere
geri res videbatur si, omni via regressus interclusa, qua
ipse obstinatione animatus esset, suos aeque et ipsos mori
aut vincere necesse esset animis destinare. itaque urendam
classem statuit, periculosius consilium quam quod ipse sua
auctoritate exsequi auderet et cum exercitu toto commu-
nicandum, si forte eadem et ipsis probarentur.

Again, suppose that though the necessities of the human race continue the same as at present, yet the mind is so enlarged, and so replete with friendship and generosity, that every man has the utmost tenderness for every man, and feels no more concern for his own interest than for that of his fellows. It seems evident that the use of justice would in this case be suspended by such an extensive benevolence, nor would the divisions and barriers of property and obligation have ever been thought of. Why should I bind another by a deed or promise, to do me any good office, when I know that he is already prompted by the strongest inclination to seek my happiness, and would of himself perform the desired service; except the hurt he thereby receives be greater than the benefit accruing to me? in which case he knows that, from my innate friendship and humanity, I should be the first to oppose myself to his imprudent generosity. Why raise landmarks between my neighbour's field and mine when my heart has made no division between our interests, but shares all his joys and sorrows with the same force and vivacity as if originally my own? Every man, upon this supposition, being a second self to another would trust all his interests to the discretion of every man, without jealousy, without partition, without distinction. And the whole human race would form only one family, where all would be in common, and would be used freely without regard to property; but cautiously too, with as entire regard to the necessities of each individual as if our own interests were most intimately concerned.

HUME.

Fac autem necessitates hominum easdem quas hodie
permanere, animos tamen eo usque dilatari, ea amicitia
ea liberalitate diffluere, ut unus quisque in unum quemque
summa caritate adficiatur neque suum potius quam alienum
commodum respiciat. quae si ita se habeant, videtur
constare diffusa tam late benevolentia supersederi posse
usu iustitiae, ne excogitatis quidem neque limitibus agrorum neque officiorum terminis. quid enim alium ut mihi
bene faciat aut stipulatione aut promisso obstringam, quem
acerrimis iam sciam stimulis excitatum esse ut meis volun-
tatibus inserviat, ipsumque optatam operam praestiturum
nisi plus ipse damni quam ego emolumenti percepturus
sim. quo in genere compertum habeat me, quae mihi
insita est humanitas et amicitia, tam inconsulte benevolo
ultro obstiturum. quid ego meum vicinique agros terminis
definiam, in quem ita animatus sim ut ne ullo quidem
discrimine utriusque commoda distinguam, sed eius omnia
laeta et adversa pari cura et ardore mecum communicem,
ac si ad me ipsum in primis pertinerent? hoc posito,
cum unus quisque uni cuique tamquam alter idem sit, sua
ceterorum omnium arbitrio permittat commoda, nulla
invidia, nulla partitione, nullo discrimine, totumque genus
humanum in unum ita coalescat, ut omnia sint in medio
posita, libere utenda, neque ulla proprii cuiusque ratione
habita, caute tamen ut necessitatibus unius cuiusque consu-
latur perinde ac si nosmet ipsos res potissimum attingeret.

Andranadorus, whose wife's ambition would never let him rest, and who till then had covered his designs with smooth dissimulation, believing it a proper time for disclosing them, conspired with Themistus, Gelon's son-in-law, to seize the sovereignty. He communicated his views to a comedian named Ariston, from whom he kept nothing secret. That profession was not at all dishonourable among the Greeks, and was exercised by persons of no ignoble condition. Ariston, believing it his duty, as it really was, to sacrifice his friend to his country, discovered the conspiracy. Andranadorus and Themistus were immediately killed by order of the other magistrates as they entered the senate. The people rose and threatened to avenge their death, but were deterred from it by the sight of the dead bodies of the two conspirators, which were thrown out of the senate-house. They were then informed of their pernicious designs ; to which all the misfortunes of Sicily were ascribed, rather than to the wickedness of Hieronymus, who being only a youth had acted entirely by their counsels. They insinuated that his guardians and tutors had reigned in his name ; that they ought to have been cut off before Hieronymus, or at least with him ; that impunity had carried them on to commit new crimes, and induced them to aspire to the tyranny ; that not being able to succeed in their design by force they had employed dissimulation and perfidy ; that neither favours and honours had been capable of overcoming the wicked disposition of Andranadorus, nor the electing him one of the supreme magistrates amongst the deliverers of their country, him who was the declared enemy of liberty ; that as to the rest they had been inspired with their ambition of reigning by the princesses of the blood royal, whom they had married, the one Hiero's, the other Gelon's daughter.

ROLLIN.

Andranadorus, quem uxoria cupiditas numquam con-
quiescere pateretur, dissimulata hactenus sub blanda
specie consilia ratus iam adesse proferendi tempus, cum
Themisto Gelonis genero regni occupandi coniurationem
iniit. is Aristoni cuidam comoedo, quem nihil celare
insueverat, rem aperit. ea ars haudquaquam inhonesta
apud Graecos, ultroque a quibusdam haud tenuioribus
exercebatur. sed Aristo ratus offici esse, id quod erat,
amicum patriae posthabere coniurationem defert. itaque
Andranadorus et Themistus ceterorum iussu praetorum
curiam cum maxime introeuntes interfecti. primo plebs
minari se mortem ulturos : dein coniuratorum corpora
extra curiam ostentui proiecta deterrebant. tum certiores
facti de nefariis utriusque consiliis : quibus Siculorum mala
omnia referenda potius quam ad Hieronymi nequitiam : quem
vixdum pubescentem ex eorum arbitrio egisse. neque enim
dubium quin tutores ac magistri eius nomine regnassent :
proinde aut ante Hieronymum aut certe cum Hieronymo
interfici oportuisse : impunitate ad nova scelera provectos
esse, atque adeo tyrannidem ipsam adfectare : ubi vis parum
provenisset dissimulatione usos esse ac perfidia : neque
beneficio neque honoribus pravam Andranadori indolem
vinci potuisse : ne eo quidem quod inter liberatores patriae
libertatis ipse hostis manifestus cooptaretur. ceterum
regios eis animos regias coniuges fecisse · alteri Hieronis
alteri Gelonis nuptas filias.

The mere philosopher is a character which is commonly but little acceptable in the world, as being supposed to contribute nothing either to the advantage or pleasure of society, while he lives remote from communication with mankind, and is wrapped up in principles and notions equally remote from their comprehension. On the other hand the mere ignorant is still more despised; nor is anything deemed a surer sign of an illiberal genius, in an age and nation where the sciences flourish, than to be entirely destitute of all relish for those noble entertainments. The most perfect character is supposed to lie between these extremes; retaining an equal ability and taste for books, company, and business; preserving in conversation that discernment and delicacy which arise from polite letters, and in business that probity and accuracy which are the natural result of a just philosophy. In order to diffuse and cultivate so accomplished a character, nothing can be more useful than compositions of the easy style and manner, which draw not too much from life, require no deep application or retreat to be comprehended, and send back the student among mankind full of noble sentiments and wise precepts, applicable to every exigence of human life. By means of such compositions virtue becomes amiable, science agreeable, company instructive, and retirement entertaining.

HUME.

Ipse per se philosophus partes agit minus acceptas
ceteris hominibus, nimirum quod videtur nihil conferre
neque ad commodum neque ad voluptatem iis quibuscum
versatur, sed abhorrere omnino ab hominum commercio
totusque esse in sententiis et cognitionibus non minus ab
eorum captu abhorrentibus. contra ipse per se insipiens
vel magis adhuc contemptui est, neque ulla alia est ingeni
inficeti certior significatio quam et in saeculo et in civitate
doctrinis abundante nihil quicquam ex hisce lautissimis
epulis delibare. qui perfectus totis numeris et absolutus
est videtur inter duas personas quas deformavimus medium
locum obtinere, qui pari ingenio et studio ad libros ad
convictum hominum et societatem ad negotia accedit,
qui in colloquiis limatam iudici elegantiam ex litteris
humanioribus ortam praestat, idem in negotiis diligentiam
et probitatem quam accurata philosophia suopte ingenio
progenerat. quae persona tot dotibus exornata ut excoli
et propagari possit nihil magis solet conducere quam quae
facili stilo et oratione sunt conscripta; quae cum non ita
multum a cotidianis rebus avocent abducantque, neque ut
intellegantur nimiam assiduitatem et vacationem officiorum
postulent, et eum qui legit ab umbratili studio foras
regredientem cogitationibus iustis et sapientibus praeceptis
praeditum efficiunt ad qualescumque vitae necessitates
accommodatis. ex huius modi scriptis id usu venit, ut
amabilior fiat virtus, doctrinae iucundiores, ut a convictu
hominum plus utilitatis, ab otio voluptatis fructus maiores
percipiantur.

His success in this scheme for reducing the power of the nobility encouraged Ximines to attempt a diminution of their possessions, which were no less exorbitant. During the contests and disorders inseparable from the feudal government, the nobles, ever attentive to their own interests, and taking advantage of the weakness or distress of their monarchs, had seized some part of the royal demesnes, obtained grants of others, and, having gradually wrested almost the whole out of the hands of the prince, had annexed them to their own estates. The titles by which the most of the grandees held these lands were extremely defective ; it was from some successful usurpation, which the crown had been too feeble to dispute, that many derived their only claim to possession. An inquiry carried back to the origin of these encroachments, which were almost coeval with the feudal system, was impracticable ; as it would have stripped every nobleman in Spain of great part of his lands, and must have excited a general revolt. Such a step was too bold, even for the enterprising genius of Ximines. He confined himself to the reign of Ferdinand ; and, beginning with the pensions granted during that time, refused to make any farther payment, because all right to them expired with his life. He then called to account such as had acquired crown lands under the administration of that monarch, and at once resumed whatever he had alienated. The effects of these revocations extended to many persons of high rank ; for though Ferdinand was a prince of little generosity, yet he and Isabella having been raised to the throne of Castile by a powerful faction of the nobles, they were obliged to reward the zeal of their adherents with great liberality, and the royal demesnes were their only fund for that purpose.

ROBERTSON.

Feliciter uti diximus imminuta nimia optimatium
auctoritas eo Ximinem impulit ut possessiones aeque et
ipsas immodicas recidere conaretur. nam inter tumultus
contentionesque feodali quod vocant imperio proprias sui
semper tenacissimi nobiles, regumque angustiis aut imbecil-
litate usi, agrum regium partim vi raptum partim dono
concessum universum fere principi e manibus extorserant
suisque ipsi praediis continuaverant. sed plerisque parum
valida possidendi auctoritas, cum complures eo demum
iure niterentur, quod principem infirmiorem quam ut
obsisteret feliciter despoliassent. quarum tamen occupa-
tionum in initium ipsi ferme imperio aequalium non potuit
fieri inquisitio; cum enim nobilissimum quemque per
Hispanias magna agrorum parte nudatura esset, verendum
erat ne in universum conflaretur seditio. periculosius
consilium quam pro audaci ipsius Ximinis ingenio. itaque
intra Ferdinandi regnum stetit : orsusque a pecuniis annuis
eo rege donatis negavit se quicquam in posterum soluturum,
rege enim mortuo periisse etiam ius accipiendi. dein
ab iis repetebat, si quis eodem tempore agrum regium
usurpasset, quicquid idem alieni iuris fecisset statim revo-
cato. ceterum ea res ad plerosque optimatium pertinebat.
Ferdinandus enim ceteroqui parum liberalis, cum tamen
et ipse et Isabella coniunx valida nobilium factione freti
regno Castiliensi potiti essent, studia partium summa
augere munificentia cogebantur : neque aliud suppetebat
nisi ager regius.

Amongst too many other instances of the great corruption and degeneracy of the age wherein we live, the great and general want of sincerity in conversation is none of the least. The world is grown so full of dissimulation and compliment, that men's words are hardly any signification of their thoughts; and if any man measure his words by his heart, and speak as he thinks, and do not express more kindness to every man than men usually have for any man, he can hardly escape the censure of want of breeding. The old English plainness and sincerity, that generous integrity of nature, and honesty of disposition, which always argues true greatness of mind and is usually accompanied with undaunted courage and resolution, is in a great measure lost amongst us : there hath been a long endeavour to transform us into foreign manners and fashions, and to bring us to a servile imitation of none of the best of our neighbours in some of the worst of their qualities. The dialect of conversation is nowadays so swelled with vanity and compliment, and so surfeited (as I may say) of expressions of kindness and respect, that if a man that lived an age or two ago should return into the world again he would really want a dictionary to help him to understand his own language, and to know the true intrinsic value of the phrase in fashion, and would hardly at first believe at what a low rate the highest strains and expressions of kindness imaginable do commonly pass in current payment; and when he should come to understand it, it would be a great while before he could bring himself with a good countenance and a good conscience to converse with men upon equal terms, and in their own way.

TILLOTSON.

Quam pravi sint et in deterius corrupti mores huiusce saeculi, ut exempla alia praetermittam quam plurima, id haudquaquam minimum arbitror quod fere in universum colloquendi veritas desideratur. referti enim eo usque iam sumus dissimulatione ac blanditiis, ut vix et ne vix quidem index interpresque cogitationum sit oratio: quod si quis ex animi sententia verba proferat, si eadem sentiat eadem loquatur, neque in quemlibet plus benevolentiae quam qua in quemquam fere adficimur significet, vix fieri potest ut rusticitatis crimen defugiat. enimvero vetus illa atque aperta nostratium sinceritas, simplex et vere honesta naturae ingenuitas, quae ut animi sane magni indicium praebet, ita fortitudinem et constantiam fere secum solet adsciscere, magna iam ex parte interiit. diu iam in eo laboratur ut exterorum mores consuetudinesque inculcemus, ut a peregrinis neque iis optimis pessima quaedam exempla serviliter mutuemur. ita blanditiis et adsentationibus sermo cotidianus turget, ita benevolentiae et observantiae significationibus ut ita dicam saginatus est, ut si quis paucis abhinc saeculis mortuus reviviscat, ad intellegendam linguam suam interpretem desideraturus sit, ut quid valeant quae cum maxime iactentur vocabula pro comperto habeat, nec nisi invitus credat quam vili pretio verba summam caritatem prae se ferentia in cotidiano usu ac commercio aestimentur; quo perspecto ac cognito sero demum id commissurus sit ut salva fronte ac conscientia in coetu hominum pari iure et ex aequo versetur.

The protector, before he opened the campaign, published a manifesto, in which he exposed all the arguments for that measure. He said that nature seemed originally to have intended the island for one empire, and having cut it off from all communication with foreign states and guarded it by the ocean, she had pointed out to the inhabitants the road to happiness and security. That the education and customs of the people concurred with nature; and by giving them the same language and laws and manners, had invited them to a thorough union and coalition. That fortune had at length removed all obstacles, and had prepared an expedient by which they might become one people, without leaving any place for that jealousy either of honour or of interests, to which rival nations are naturally exposed. That the crown of Scotland had devolved on a female, that of England on a male; and happily the two sovereigns, as of a rank, were also of an age, the most suitable to each other. That the hostile dispositions which prevailed between the nations, and which arose from past injuries, would soon be extinguished after a long and secure peace had established confidence between them. That the memory of former miseries, which at present inflamed their mutual animosity, would then serve only to make them cherish with more passion a state of happiness and tranquillity so long unknown to their ancestors.

HUME.

Sed prius quam bellum iniretur, tutor regni positis propalam libellis quae in rem essent omnia confirmavit: naturam aiebat id videri voluisse ut penes unum esset insula. interdixisse enim ei exterorum commercio et mari Oceano saepsisse tamquam ad secure inter se beateque vivendum viam praemonstrasset; neque vero a voluntate naturae disciplinam aut mores utriusque populi abhorruisse: quibus utique eadem lingua, instituta, iura, quid aliud eos quam in artissimum concordiae vinculum ultro appellitatos? fortunam insuper quae impedimento essent omnia amovisse, dato aditu per quem ita in unum coalescerent, ut nullus iam invidiae gloriae aut utilitatum ergo, cui obnoxios fere semper aemulos, locus patefieret. nam Caledoniorum sceptro feminam, Anglorum masculam stirpem potiri, peropportune inter se sicut loco ita aetate pares et accommodatos. ita utriusque gentis inter se inimicitias, ex praeteritis ortas iniuriis, brevi exstinctum iri, postea quam pax firma et diutina mutuam fidem conciliasset. sane veterum infortuniorum memoria mutuas invicem accendi adhuc simultates; eandem mox praestituram ut felicitatem et otium diu a proavis desideratum vehementius foverent.

He illustrates this by the example of Tully's son Marcus. Cicero, in order to accomplish his son in that sort of learning which he designed him for, sent him to Athens, the most celebrated academy at that time in the world, and where a vast concourse, out of the most polite nations, could not but furnish a young gentleman with a multitude of great examples and accidents that might insensibly have instructed him in his designed studies. He placed him under the care of Cratippus, who was one of the greatest philosophers of the age, and, as if all the books which were at that time written had not been sufficient for his use, he composed others on purpose for him. Notwithstanding all this, history informs us that Marcus proved a mere blockhead, and that nature (who it seems was even with the son for her prodigality to the father) rendered him incapable of improving by all the rules of eloquence, the precepts of philosophy, his own endeavours and the most refined conversation in Athens. This author therefore proposes that there should be certain triers or examiners appointed by the state to inspect the genius of every particular boy, and to allot him the part that is most suitable to his natural talents.

Plato in one of his dialogues tells us that Socrates, who was the son of a midwife, used to say that as his mother, though she was very skilful in her profession, could not deliver a woman unless she was first with child, so neither could he himself raise knowledge out of a mind where nature had not planted it.

BUDGELL.

Quam rationem ut patefaciat et illustret, exemplum ponit M. Tullium M. filium, quem cum pater doctrinis quas ei proposuisset excoli vellet, Athenas misit. ea tunc altrix scientiarum praestantissima habebatur; cumque eo magnus coetus ex humanioribus populis conveniret, non potuit fieri quin multis et praeclaris exemplis uteretur liberali ingenio praeditus, alia porro ei contingerent destinatis studiis sensim imbutura. ibi Cratippum principem eius aetatis philosophum puer audiebat; et tamquam si omnes libri hactenus conscripti parum sufficerent, pater ipse de industria fili in usum alios composuit. traditur tamen a scriptoribus Marcum filium germanum stipitem evasisse: naturamque, quo largiora patri donavisset, eo minora, ut videretur, compensaturam filio, id fecisse ut neque ex eloquentiae normis, neque ex praeceptis philosophorum, neque ex sua industria, ne ex Atheniensium quidem politissimo commercio, omnino quicquam emolumenti adsequeretur. itaque scriptor libri existimatores quosdam rei publicae cuivis seligendos esse statuit qui, singulis singulorum puerorum ingeniis perpensis et quasi examinatis, suas cuique partes proprias accommodent. iam Plato in dialogo quodam tradit Socratem, matre obstetrice natum, solitum esse dicere neque illam, artis sane suae peritissimam, prius operam parturienti dare potuisse, nisi quae praegnas facta esset, neque se e cuiusquam animo in lucem protrahere scientiam quam non ipsa natura ingenerasset.

But after all, it must needs be owned that Pompey
had a very difficult part to act, and much less liberty of
executing what he himself approved than in all the other
wars in which he had been engaged. In his wars against
foreign enemies his power was absolute, and all his motions
depended on his own will; but in this, besides several
kings and princes of the East, who attended him in person,
he had with him in his camp almost all the chief magistrates and senators of Rome; men of equal dignity with
himself, who had commanded armies and obtained triumphs,
and expected a share in all his counsels, and that, in their
common danger, no step should be taken but by their
common advice: and, as they were under no engagement
to his cause but what was voluntary, so they were necessarily to be humoured, lest through disgust they should
desert it. Now these were all uneasy in their present
situation, and longed to be at home in the enjoyment
of their estates and honours; and having a confidence
of victory from the number of their troops and the reputation of their leader, were perpetually teasing Pompey to
the resolution of a battle; charging him with a design
to protract the war for the sake of perpetuating his
authority; and calling him another Agamemnon, who was
so proud of holding so many kings and generals under his
command; till, being unable to withstand their reproaches
any longer, he was driven, by a kind of shame and against
his judgement, to the experiment of a decisive action.

                                            MIDDLETON.

Neque tamen dubitandum est quin durissimae partes agendae essent Pompeio, multoque minor quam in ceteris bellis omnibus quae sibi probarentur gerendi potestas praeberetur. quae enim cum externis hostibus bella administrasset, penes ipsum summa imperi fuerat, suo ex arbitrio omnia peregerat. tunc autem, praeterquam quod plurimi et duces et reges Asiatici ipsi in castris merebant, aderant etiam plerique omnes populi Romani magistratus ac senatores, pares et ipsi dignitate, imperatores, triumphales, flagitantes uti consiliis omnibus interessent, neve in communi periculo nisi communi consensu quicquam coeptaretur : cum autem partibus eius non nisi suapte sponte addicti essent, mos gerendus erat ne ob invidiam transgrederentur. simul praesentium taedio honores agrosque domesticos respicere. itaque et copiarum vi et virtute ducis confisi perpetuo Pompeium lacessebant ut certa spe victoriae rem in discrimen daret ; belli moras imperi prorogandi ergo imputantes, alterumque Agamemnona tot ducibus sibi parentibus, tot regibus subnixum appellantes, donec postremo impar conviciis pudore quodam et invitus in aleam belli impelleretur.

I am equally sensible of your affliction, and of your
kindness, that made you think of me at such a moment;
would to God I could lessen the one, or requite the other
with that consolation which I have often received from you
when I most wanted it! but your grief is too just, and the
cause of it too fresh, to admit of any such endeavour.
What, indeed, is all human consolation? Can it efface
every little amiable word or action of an object we loved
from our memory? Can it convince us that all the hopes
we had entertained, the plans of future satisfaction we had
formed, were ill-grounded and vain, only because we have
lost them? The only comfort, I am afraid, that belongs
to our condition, is to reflect—when time has given us
leisure for reflection—that others have suffered worse;
or that we ourselves might have suffered the same misfortune at times and in circumstances that would probably
have aggravated our sorrow. You might have seen this
poor child arrived at an age to fulfil all your hopes, to
attach you more strongly to him by long habit, by esteem,
as well as natural affection, and that towards the decline
of your life, when we most stand in need of support, and
when he might chance to have been your only support;
and then by some unforeseen and deplorable accident, or
some painful lingering distemper you might have lost him.
Such has been the fate of many an unhappy father!
I know there is a sort of tenderness which infancy and
innocence alone produce; but I think you must own
the other to be a stronger and a more overwhelming
sorrow.

GRAY.

Luctum perinde tuum atque amicitiam qui me in istis temporibus nolueris praetermittere, scito me perspexisse. ac medius fidius utinam possem et illum minuere et huic solaci vicem rependere quod saepe numero ubi maxime opus erat mihi tu attulisti. causa tamen doloris recens et ipse dolor satis iustus prohibebant quo minus tale aliquid conari auderem. nam hominum quidem solacia quantuli sunt! eorumne quos amavimus iucundissimi cuiusque dicti factive vel tenuissimi id efficiunt ut memoria dilabatur? cuinam probare possunt, quas quisque spes foverit, quae consilia in posterum fructus sibi proposuerit, propterea quod amiserit, ideo fluxa esse et instabilia? equidem vereor ne ad humanam sortem illud unicum solacium pertineat, si cogitaverimus—ut vacemus cogitationi dies curabit—et peiora alios expertos esse, et pati eadem nosmet ipsos potuisse tum rebus tum temporibus intercedentibus quae dolorem fortasse incendissent. quid si puer iste parvulus ad adulescentiam provectus spei suae quantaecumque respondisset? si cum diuturna consuetudine tum existimatione quadam, nec solum ipsius naturae commendatione, devinctiorem te sibi habuisset, cum praesertim vergentibus iam annis tuis tibi subsidio potissimum opus esset, is si fors ferret tibi unico futurus esset subsidio? si qui improvisus et acerbus casus aut malignior et cunctantior morbi vis eum talem tibi eripuisset? atqui huius modi miseriae quot iam patribus acciderunt! equidem scio esse aliquid caritatis quo pueri infantis sola innocentia animum adficiat. idem credo eam quam posui miseriam posse vehementiorem in modum cor adfligere ne ipsum quidem te infitiaturum.

The reception which he met with at Worms was such as he might have reckoned a full reward of all his labours, if vanity and the love of applause had been the principles by which he was influenced. Greater crowds assembled to behold him than had appeared at the emperor's public entry; his apartments were daily filled with princes and personages of the highest rank, and he was treated with all the respect paid to those who possess the power of directing the understanding and sentiments of other men— an homage more sincere, as well as more flattering, than any which pre-eminence in birth or condition can command. At his appearance before the diet he behaved with great decency, and with equal firmness. He readily acknowledged an excess of vehemence and acrimony in his controversial writings, but refused to retract his opinions, unless he were convinced of their falsehood, or to consent to their being tried by any other rule than the word of God. When neither threats nor entreaties could prevail on him to depart from this resolution, some of the ecclesiastics proposed to imitate the example of the council of Constance, and by punishing the author of this pestilent heresy, who was now in their power, to deliver the Church at once from such an evil. But the members of the diet refusing to expose the German integrity to fresh reproach by a second violation of public faith, and Charles being no less unwilling to bring a stain upon the beginning of his administration by such an ignominious action, Luther was permitted to depart in safety.

ROBERTSON.

Honestissime ibi exceptus satis ampla nactus esse laborum omnium praemia videbatur, si ad gloriae normam et aviditatem laudis vitae officia direxisset. nam maior spectantium quam quae ipsum imperatorem publice introeuntem celebraverat obvia facta est frequentia. cotidie eum conveniebant coetus principum quique summi ordinis erant salutantium et plenissimo honore prosequentium, tamquam qui animos hominum atque intellegentiam quo vellet flectere ac dirigere calleret; quo obsequio nihil sincerius neque honorificentius praestare potest generis aut loci dignitas. ceterum productus in concilium parem modestiam prae se ferebat ac constantiam. sane in controversiis quae scripsisset acrius aequo et iracundius disputata esse; nolle tamen aut opiniones immutare nisi quis falsas esse evicisset, aut ad aliam normam quam scripturas sacras perpendendas eas tradere. quae pervicacia cum neque minis neque precibus flecteretur, sacerdotibus aliquot censentibus concilium Constantinum imitarentur, ut animadverso in auctorem pestilentis sectae tandem sibi in manus traditum tanto in posterum malo ecclesiam liberarent, haud visum est iis qui concilio interessent iterum violatam fidem publicam Germanico nomini imputare. Carolo quoque, qui initia principatus tanto flagitio et ipse nollet foedare, placuit pactam fidem Luthero servari oportere.

First of all, a man should always consider how much he has more than he wants. I am wonderfully pleased with the reply which Aristippus made to one who condoled him upon the loss of a farm: 'Why,' said he, 'I have three farms still, and you have but one; so that I ought rather to be afflicted for you than you for me.' On the contrary, foolish men are more apt to consider what they have lost than what they possess; and to fix their eyes upon those who are richer than themselves, rather than on those who are under greater difficulties. All the real pleasures and conveniences of life lie in a narrow compass; but it is the humour of mankind to be always looking forward, and straining after one who has got the start of them in wealth and honour. For this reason, as there are none can be properly called rich who have not more than they want, there are few rich men in any of the politer nations but among the middle sort of people, who keep their wishes within their fortunes, and have more wealth than they know how to enjoy. Persons of a higher rank live in a kind of splendid poverty, and are perpetually wanting, because, instead of acquiescing in the solid pleasures of life, they endeavour to outvy one another in shadows and appearances. Men of sense have at all times beheld with a great deal of mirth this silly game that is playing over their heads, and by contracting their desires enjoy all that secret satisfaction which others are always in quest of.

ADDISON.

Id in primis velim secum quisque reputet, quanto plura quam pro necessitatibus possideat. quo in genere mihi quidem valde placet illud Aristippi responsum, qui amico cuidam ob amissum fundum consolanti, 'tune me,' inquit, 'tribus etiam nunc praediis abundantem, qui ipse unicum tantum habeas? ut me tui potius quam te mei misereri oporteat.' contra insipientium est desiderata magis quam retenta recensere; et in ditiores malle quam qui maioribus rerum angustiis laborant oculos intendere. arto quidem spatio concluduntur vitae oblectationes commoditatesque verae; at humanum est semper prospicere, et cum iis qui se divitiis aut honoribus antecellant totis viribus contendere. qua de causa cum neminem recte divitem appellaveris nisi cui plura suppetant quam pro necessitatibus, constat in excultioribus populis perpaucos esse divites nisi inter eos qui mediocris ordinis intra fortunas cupiditates contineant et plura quam quibus uti possint possideant. nam editiore quidem loco orti, splendidam quasi paupertatem agentes, semper egent, quippe qui tantum abest ut oblectamentis vitae solidis contenti sint ut vana specie et inanibus rerum antecellere alter alteri nitantur. quod ineptissimum ordinum superiorum certamen semper fit ut sapientes magno opere derideant, suaque ipsi vota in artum contrahentes, quam ceteri voluptatem numquam non aucupantur, eam secum ipsi percipiant.

From this era (260 years from the foundation of Rome) we date the commencement of the popular constitution of the Roman republic, a change operated by the unwise policy of the patricians themselves, who by yielding to just complaints, and humanely redressing flagrant abuses, might have easily anticipated every ground of dissatisfaction. The first wish of the people was not power, but relief from tyranny and oppression; and, had this been readily granted them, if not by abolishing the debts, at least by repressing enormous usury, and putting an end to the inhuman right of corporal punishment and the bondage of debtors, the people would have cheerfully returned to order and submission, and the Roman constitution have long remained, what we have seen it was at the commencement of the consular government, aristocratical. But the plebeians now obtaining magistrates of their own order with those high powers, we shall see it become the object of the magistrates to increase their authority by continual demands and bold encroachments. The people, regarding them as the champions of their rights, are delighted to find themselves gradually approaching to a level with the higher order; and no longer bounding their desires to ease and security are soon equally influenced by ambition as their superiors.

TYTLER.

Ducentesimum sexagesimum annum urbs agebat, cum
populariter constitui coepta est respublica. initium penes
ipsos patres inconsulto agentes : qui si iusta querentibus
concessissent et flagitiis comiter subvenissent, facile omnes
invidiae causas erant praeventuri. neque enim a principio
potestatem adfectabat plebes, sed ut servitium atque iniurias dominantium exuerent : quae si patres facile condo-
nassent, si non concessis novis tabulis, at saltem faenebri
malo coercito, vetitoque in posterum ne quis ius immane
verberum trahendique addictos exerceret, et plebes libenter
in ordinem atque obsequium redacta esset, et civitas
Romana, id quod consulari potestate recens constituta
fuisse constat, penes optimates diu permansisset. sed
impetrati iam plebeiis sui ordinis magistratus iique plena
potestate ornati continuo id agebant (id quod brevi patebit)
ut assiduis efflagitationibus et aliena audacter invadendo
suam auctoritatem promoverent. quos ipsa plebs, tamquam
sui iuris propugnatores rata, superiori ordini libentissime
paulatim adaequatur : nec iam intra otium et securitatem
cupiditatibus contentis, pari et ipsi haud multo post ambi-
tione adficiuntur.

But as the Stoics exalted human nature too high, so the Epicureans depressed it too low; as those raised it to the heroic, these debased it to the brutal state; they held 'pleasure to be the chief good of man: death the extinction of his being'; and placed their happiness consequently in the secure enjoyment of a pleasurable life; esteeming virtue on no other account, than as it was a handmaid to pleasure, and helped to ensure the possession of it, by preserving health and conciliating friends. Their wise man, therefore, had no other duty but to provide for his own ease; to decline all struggles; to retire from public affairs; and to imitate the life of their gods, by passing his days in a calm, contemplative, undisturbed repose, in the midst of rural shades and pleasant gardens. This was the scheme that Atticus followed; he had all the talents that could qualify a man to be useful to society; great parts, learning, judgement, candour, benevolence, generosity; the same love of his country, and the same sentiments in politics with Cicero, whom he was always advising and urging to act, yet determined never to act himself; or never, at least, so far as to disturb his ease, or endanger his safety. For though he was so strictly united with Cicero, and valued him above all men, yet he managed an interest all the while with the opposite faction, and a friendship even with his mortal enemies, Clodius and Antony; that he might secure, against all events, the grand point which he had in view, the peace and tranquillity of his life. Thus two excellent men, by their mistaken notions of virtue, drawn from the principles of their philosophy, were made useless in a manner to their country, each in a different extreme of life; the one always acting and exposing himself to dangers, without the prospect of doing good; the other, without attempting to do any, resolving never to act at all.

MIDDLETON.

Sed ut Stoici de natura hominum altiora disputabant ad heroicum quendam ordinem extollentes, ita Epicurei in humilius detrudebant, ut qui pecudum naturae exaequarent. nam volebant summum bonum esse voluptatem, morte animum exstingui ; ita in voluptaria vita secure fruenda positam esse beatam ; virtutem non nisi eo aestimandam quod ancillula quaedam esset voluptati, ad eamque confirmandam servata bona valetudine conciliatisque amicis potissimum conduceret. itaque sapientis nihil aliud interesse quam ut suum ipse otium respiceret, contentiones omnes devitaret, a re publica recederet, deorumque vitam imitatus inter nemorum umbracula hortorumque amoenitates placidam et tranquillam in cognitione rerum aetatem degeret. quam rationem vitae sibi Atticus proposuerat. quo in homine erant illa omnia quae ad civilem vitam idonea videntur, ingenium doctrina iudicium ingenuitas benevolentia liberalitas ; idem amor patriae, eadem voluntas, quae et ipsi Ciceroni ; quem cum semper hortaretur atque adeo lacesseret ut aliquid ageret, ita tamen ipse sibi agendum statuebat ut et otio et saluti consuleret. cum enim esset Ciceroni coniunctissimus, cui ceteros omnes posthaberet, id tamen agebat ut diversis partibus gratiosus esset atque etiam inimicissimis Clodio et Antonio familiariter uteretur—ut, qualiscumque fortuna intercessisset, id unicum praestaret, quod semper sibi proposuisset, vitae otium et securitatem. ita duo optimi sane homines, uterque philosophiam suam secuti dum aberrant a via virtutis, inutiles propemodum patriae evadebant : cum alter semper aliquid ageret et periculis se obnoxium redderet nulla spe bene faciendi proposita, alter ne conaretur quidem, nedum quicquam ageret.

s.   25

Cortes, receiving his commission with the warmest expressions of respect and gratitude to the governor, immediately erected his standard before his own house, appeared in a military dress, and assumed all the ensigns of his new dignity. His utmost influence and activity were exerted in persuading many of his friends to engage in the service, and in urging forward the preparations for the voyage. All his own funds, together with what money he could raise by mortgaging his lands and Indians, were expended in purchasing military stores and provisions, or in supplying the wants of such of his officers as were unable to equip themselves in a manner suited to their rank. Inoffensive and even laudable as this conduct was, his disappointed competitors were malicious enough to give it a turn to his disadvantage. They represented him as aiming already with little disguise at establishing an independent authority over his troops, and endeavouring to secure their respect or love by his ostentatious and interested liberality. They reminded Velasquez of his former dissensions with the man in whom he now reposed so much confidence, and foretold that Cortes would be more apt to avail himself of the power which the governor was inconsiderately putting in his hands, to avenge past injuries, than to requite recent obligations.

ROBERTSON.

Cortesius, accepto munere plenissimamque observantiae gratique in praefectum animi significationem professus, statim pro domo vexillum erigere, paludatus palam incedere, omnia novi honoris insignia induere. dein summa qua potuit gratia nitebatur et industria si amicis pluribus profiterentur nomina suaderet quaeque ad iter necessaria forent maturarent. nam quod praesto erat pecuniae, quod auri praediis servitiisque pignori oppositis corradebat, in impedimentis commeatuque comparando sive subveniendo sociis, si quibus sui pro ordine instruendi facultates deessent, id omne insumpsit. quam rationem innocentem atque adeo laudabilem ii tamen qui posthabiti sunt eo invidiae exarserunt ut in deterius interpretarentur. moliri enim eum, neque id iam occulto, sui iuris imperium in milites usurpare, suorumque observantiam aut amorem speciosa ac parum simplici munificentia conciliare. cogitaret praefectus quantae sibi adversus hominem cui tanto opere confideret olim intercessissent simultates. an Cortesium imperio prorsus inconsulte in manus tradito ad recentia potius usurum beneficia rependenda quam ad pristinas ulciscendas iniurias?

We have before observed that there is generally in nature something more grand and august than what we meet with in the curiosities of art. When, therefore, we see this imitated in any measure, it gives us a nobler and more exalted kind of pleasure than what we receive from the nicer and more accurate productions of art. On this account our English gardens are not so entertaining to the fancy as those in France and Italy, where we see a large extent of ground covered over with an agreeable mixture of garden and forest, which represent everywhere an artificial rudeness, much more charming than that neatness and elegancy which we meet with in those of our own country. It might, indeed, be of ill consequence to the public, as well as unprofitable to private persons, to alienate so much ground from pasturage, and the plough, in many parts of a country that is so well peopled, and cultivated to a far greater advantage. But why may not a whole estate be thrown into a kind of garden by frequent plantations, that may turn as much to the profit as the pleasure of the owner? A marsh overgrown with willows, or a mountain shaded with oaks, are not only more beautiful, but more beneficial, than when they lie bare and unadorned. Fields of corn make a pleasant prospect, and if the walks were a little taken care of that lie between them, if the natural embroidery of the meadows were helped and improved by some small additions of art, and the several rows of hedges set off by trees and flowers, that the soil was capable of receiving, a man might make a pretty landscape of his own possessions.

ADDISON.

Id iam supra memoravimus, inesse in natura aliquid
amplius et excelsius quam quod ex artium subtilitatibus
exquisitioribus fere percipitur. quam amplitudinem quotiens aliquatenus adumbratam videmus, suboritur nescio
quae voluptas maior et sublimior, quae in artificiis lima-
tioribus sane et politioribus desiderari solet. qua de causa
nostratium horti haud perinde sensum alliciunt ac Gallorum
aut Italorum ; apud quos magnus agri ambitus obversatur
alterna hortorum ac nemorum varietate distinctus et quasi
rude quoddam artificium imitatus, cuius amoenitati in
concinna illa nostrorum elegantia vix quicquam simile
reppereris. potest sane fieri ut perinde bono publico de-
trimento sit ac privatorum incommodo tot pastiones tot
arationes a suis usibus abalienare, praesertim ut in regione
et frequentissima et longe melius exculta. quid autem
obstat quo minus ex universo praedio crebris consitionibus
quasi hortus fiat, qui domino usui pariter pariter voluptati
inserviat ? palus quidem salictis obsita aut mons quercetis
opacatus nonne plus et in speciem et in utilitatem valent,
quam si eadem nuda et inornata iaceant ? suavis ipse per
se segetum prospectus : quod si intervallis limitum non
nihil curae adhibeatur, si pratis suapte natura pictis aliquid
adiumenti ornamentique accedat, si variis saepium ordinibus
flores arboresque uti fert soli ingenium commendationem
quandam adiciant, potest utique ex suis quisque praediis
amoenae regionis speciem praestare.

But notwithstanding the fortunate dexterity with which he had eluded this danger, Cortes was so sensible of the precarious tenure by which he held his power, that he despatched deputies to Spain with a pompous account of the success of his arms, with further specimens of the productions of the country, and with rich presents to the emperor, as the earnest of future contributions from his new conquests; requesting in recompense for all his services the approbation of his proceedings, and that he might be entrusted with the government of those dominions which his conduct and the valour of his followers had added to the crown of Castile. The juncture in which his deputies reached the court was favourable. The internal commotions in Spain, which had disquieted the beginning of Charles' reign, were just appeased. The ministers had leisure to turn their attention towards foreign affairs. The account of Cortes' victories filled his countrymen with admiration. The extent and value of his conquests became the object of vast and interesting hopes. Whatever stain he might have contracted by the irregularity of the steps which he took in order to attain power was so fully effaced by the splendour and merit of the great actions which they had enabled him to perform, that every heart revolted at even the thought of inflicting any censure on a man whose services entitled him to the highest marks of distinction.

ROBERTSON.

Quod periculum callide ac feliciter eluctatus, gnarus
tamen quam lubrico iure staret auctoritas Cortesius, missis
in Hispanias legatis qui, auctis in magnificum proeliis,
nova rerum quas fert regio exempla adderent, simul dona
imperatori deferrent, spem ex recens debellatis populis
fructus redituri, postulavit ut pro rebus gestis sua omnia
principi probarentur, sibique provinciarum quas suo ductu
suorumque virtute regno Castiliensi adiecisset imperium
traderetur. ceterum adeundi regis opportunum tempus
nacti sunt legati, sedatis iam per Hispanias intestinis
tumultibus qui novum adhuc principem turbaverant.
itaque ii qui a consiliis erant externis iam rebus vacabant.
porro civium animos auditae victoriae, quas ex tantis
hostibus tamque locupletibus reportaverat, ea admiratione
adfecere ut ingentes exitus spe iam praesumerent. ita si
quid labis suscepisset adfectato per illicita imperio, splendore
rerum ac gloria inde profectarum eo usque obscurata est ut
nemo esset cui ne cogitatio quidem carpendi hominis
propter res gestas nullos non honores adsecuturi plane
abhorrens videretur.

If the Italians have a genius for music above the English, the English have a genius for other performances of a much higher nature, and capable of giving the mind a much nobler entertainment. Would one think it was possible (at a time when an author lived that was able to write the Phaedra and Hippolitus) for a people to be so stupidly fond of the Italian opera, as scarce to give a third day's hearing to that admirable tragedy? Music is certainly a very agreeable entertainment, but if it would take the entire possession of our ears, if it would make us incapable of hearing sense, if it would exclude arts that have a much greater tendency to the refinement of human nature; I must confess I would allow it no better quarter than Plato has done, who banishes it out of his Commonwealth.

At present our notions of music are so very uncertain, that we do not know what it is we like; only, in general, we are transported with anything that is not English; so it be of a foreign growth, let it be Italian, French, or High-Dutch, it is the same thing. In short, our English music is quite rooted out, and nothing yet planted in its stead.

ADDISON.

Si Britannis Itali ingenio praestant quod ad musicam attinet, nobis tamen ad alia quaedam et quidem longe altiora quaeque animo cibum multo praeclariorem suppeditare possint facultas non deficit. ecquis ergo crediderit, praesertim incolumi eo qui Phaedram et Hippolytum docere noverit, populum aliquem posse in Italorum mimis tam perdite amantem haerere, ut admirabilem illam tragoediam tertium recitatam tantum non omnino neglexerit? pulcherrimum sane oblectamentum est musica; quod si aures nostras totas sibi arrogare, si rationi parum dicto audientes nos efficere, si artes alias et ad naturam nostram in humanitatem molliendam multo magis idoneas penitus vult excludere, fateor equidem me nihilo lenius quam Platonem ipsum in eam animadversurum, qui e Re publica sua ablegavit. hodie autem tam varia tamque incerta de musica sentimus ut nesciamus quidnam sit quod nobismet ipsis placeat, ita tamen ut in omnibus fere, modo nostra ne sint, stupeamus; dum apud exteros orta sint, nihil moramur utrum Itala an Gallica an Germanica. nostra denique musica penitus exolevit, nec quicquam adhuc in locum eius coeptum est inolescere.

The partisans of the confederates reasoned very differently. It is evident, said they, that Mary either previously gave consent to the king's murder, or did afterwards approve of that horrid action. Her attachment to Bothwell, the power and honours which she has conferred upon him, the manner in which she suffered his trial to be carried on, and the indecent speed with which she married a man stained with so many crimes, raise strong suspicions of the former, and put the latter beyond all doubt. To have suffered the supreme power to continue in the hands of an ambitious man, capable of the most atrocious and desperate actions, would have been disgraceful to the nation, dishonourable to the queen, and dangerous to the prince. Recourse was therefore had to arms. The queen had been compelled to abandon a husband so unworthy of herself. But her affection toward him still continuing unabated; her indignation against the authors of this separation being visible, and often expressed in the strongest terms; they, by restoring her to her ancient authority, would have armed her with power to destroy themselves, have enabled her to recall Bothwell, and have afforded her an opportunity of pursuing schemes fatal to the nation with greater eagerness, and with more success. Nothing therefore remained, but by one bold action to deliver themselves and their country from all future fears. The expedient they had chosen was no less respectful to the royal blood, than necessary for the public safety. While one prince was set aside as incapable of governing, the crown was placed on his head who was the undoubted representative of their ancient kings.

ROBERTSON.

At qui a coniuratis stabant alia omnia disserebant.
satis liquere Mariam caedem regiam aut incohatam com-
probasse aut patrati certe sceleris auctorem fuisse. nam
quod Botuellium perdite amaret, quod honoribus et potestate eundem cumulasset, quod iudicium sua sponte fieri
passa esset, quod nuptias denique hominis tot sceleribus
inquinati cum festinatione ac flagitio iniisset, ut illud in
suspicionem cadere, ita hoc procul dubio coargui. num penes
hominem avidissimum ad atrocissima quaeque proclivem
summam esse rerum oportuisse? at illud populo inhonestum,
matri turpe, periculosum filio. ideo ad arma decursum.
reginam virum se indignissimum coactam deseruisse. neque
tamen amorem imminui; quin in auctores discidi etiam
tum manifestas simultates, ultroque in acerbissimas saepe
iras prorumpere. quod si pristinam redintegrassent auctoritatem, quid aliud quam sui pessumdandi copiam instru-
cturos fuisse, data simul potestate et Botuelli revocandi et
consilia genti perniciosa facilius ac felicius moliendi? nihil
igitur superesse nisi ut unum ausi facinus et se et patriam
omni in posterum metu liberarent. rationem se iniisse
perinde stirpi regiae honorificam ac paci publicae salutarem.
sane alteram posthabitam tamquam regnando imparem;
at alterum subrogatum regum sine controversia antiquorum
sanguinem.

If there be but one body of legislators, it is no better than a tyranny; if there are only two, there will want a casting voice, and one of them must at length be swallowed up by disputes and contentions that will necessarily arise between them. Four would have the same inconvenience as two, and a greater number would cause too much confusion. I could never read a passage in Polybius, and another in Cicero, to this purpose, without a secret pleasure in applying it to the English constitution, which it suits much better than the Roman. Both these great authors give the pre-eminence to a mixed government, consisting of three branches, the regal, the noble, and the popular. They had doubtless in their thoughts the constitution of the Roman commonwealth, in which the consul represented the king, the senate the nobles, and the tribunes the people. This division of the three powers in the Roman constitution was by no means so distinct and natural, as it is in the English form of government. Among several objections that might be made to it, I think the chief are those that affect the consular power, which had only the ornaments without the force of the regal authority. Their number had not a casting voice in it; for which reason, if one did not chance to be employed abroad, while the other sat at home, the public business was sometimes at a stand, while the consuls pulled two different ways in it. Besides, I do not find that the consuls had ever a negative voice in the passing of a law, or decree of senate; so that indeed they were rather the chief body of the nobility, or the first ministers of state, than a distinct branch of the sovereignty, in which none can be looked upon as a part, who are not a part of the legislature. Had the consuls been invested with the regal authority to as great a degree as our monarchs, there would never have been any occasions for a dictatorship, which had in it the power of all the three orders, and ended in the subversion of the whole constitution.

ADDISON.

Sive penes unum est ordinem legum ferendarum ratio, quidnam discrepat a tyrannide? sive duos, neque erit qui rem suffragio dirimat, et inter lites ac certamina necessaria postremo fiet ut alter alterum obruat. quattuor iisdem quibus duo laborant incommodis, et in pluribus nimium perturbatur. quo in genere duos locos, alterum Polybi, Ciceronis alterum, equidem numquam lectitare soleo, quin nescio qua adductus voluptate ad rem publicam Britannicam malim, cui utique multo plus conveniunt, quam ad Romam referre. hi enim duo scriptores praestantissimi civitati ex tribus ordinibus regio patricio populari consociatae primas deferunt. sane iis in mentem venerat rei publicae Romanae, in qua consul regiam, senatus optimatium, tribunus plebis popularem vicem defendebant. quamquam haec tripartita ordinum distributio haudquaquam illa in civitate perinde atque in nostra rationi congruens erat et consentanea. nam, ut alia praetermittam quae iure quispiam obiecerit, id haud minimum arbitror quod ad consulatum pertinet, penes quem insignia quidem erant regia, auctoritas non item. pares enim numero paria etiam ferebant suffragia: qua de causa nisi alter domi alter foras rem ageret, cessabant interdum negotia publica in diversa trahentibus consulibus. porro iis intercedendi ius fuisse aut iubendae legi aut senatus consulto me quidem hactenus fugit. itaque potius primi inter principes habendi sunt quam ipsa per se pars principatus, cuius neminem iure participem appellaveris, nisi idem ferendis legibus intersit. quod si ut iis qui nunc regnant, ita consulibus par ius potestatis regiae concessum esset, dictatura numquam desideraretur: quae una in se trium ordinum iura amplexa postremo rei publicae in perniciem convertit.

But while Lorenzo seemed to be sunk in luxury, and affected such an appearance of indolence and effeminacy that he would not wear a sword and trembled at the sight of blood, he concealed under that disguise a dark, designing, audacious spirit. Prompted either by the love of liberty, or allured by the hope of attaining the supreme power, he determined to assassinate Alexander, his benefactor and friend. Though he long revolved this design in his mind, his reserved and suspicious temper prevented him from communicating it to any person whatever, and continuing to live with Alexander in their usual familiarity, he one night, under pretence of having secured him an assignation with a lady of high rank whom he had often solicited, drew that unwary prince into a secret apartment of his house, and there stabbed him, while he lay carelessly on a couch expecting the arrival of the lady whose company he had been promised. But no sooner was the deed done than, standing astonished and struck with horror at its atrocity, he forgot in a moment all the motives which had induced him to commit it. Instead of rousing the people to recover their liberty by publishing the death of the tyrant, instead of taking any step towards opening his own way to the dignity now vacant, he locked the door of the apartment, and, like a man bereaved of reason and presence of mind, fled with the utmost precipitation out of the Florentine territories. It was late next morning before the fate of the unfortunate prince was known, as his attendants, accustomed to his irregularities, never entered his apartment early.

ROBERTSON.

Sed Laurentius quamquam uti visus est in luxum
solutior tantum somni et inertiae ostentabat ut neque
accingeretur gladio visumque sanguinem contremisceret,
suberat tamen obscurum atrox et ad audacissima proclive
ingenium. itaque liberandae patriae studio adductus, an
spe illectus summae rei potiendae, Alexandri et amici et
optime de se meriti interficiendi consilium init. quod
cum diu secum volutaret, quo minus tamen alii cuiquam
impertiret animus suspicax et abstrusus prohibuit; sed
familiariter ut solitum Alexandro utebatur, donec noctem
feminae illustris, quam diu ille temptaverat, pollicitus,
in secreta aedium imprudentem subductum ibique temere
in lecto accumbentem spe promissae mulieris gladio trans-
verberat. simul autem patratum scelus est, et attonitus
defixusque propter rei flagitium, quibus rationibus ad
caedem impulsus esset derepente oblitus est. non evul-
gata tyranni morte, si ad reciperandam libertatem plebem
posset exstimulare, non molitus aliquid unde vacuo iam
imperio ipse potiretur, sed obseratis cubiculi foribus, tamquam vecors neque iam praesenti usus animo, praeceps
ex agro Florentino in fugam se convertit. sero demum
postridie de caede principis innotuit, cum ministri gnari
libidinum non nisi post multum diem cubiculum intrare
insuevissent.

The first thing every one looks after, is to provide himself with necessaries. This point will engross our thoughts till it be satisfied. If this is taken care of to our hands, we look out for pleasures and amusements ; and among a great number of idle people there will be many whose pleasures will lie in reading and contemplation. These are the two great sources of knowledge, and as men grow wise they naturally love to communicate their discoveries ; and others seeing the happiness of such a learned life, and improving by their conversation, emulate, imitate, and surpass one another, till a nation is filled with races of wise and understanding persons. Ease and plenty are therefore the great cherishers of knowledge : and as most of the despotic governments of the world have neither of them, they are naturally overrun with ignorance and barbarity. In Europe, indeed, notwithstanding several of its princes are absolute, there are men famous for knowledge and learning ; but the reason is because the subjects are many of them rich and wealthy, the prince not thinking fit to exert himself in his full tyranny like the princes of the eastern nations, lest his subjects should be invited to new-mould their constitution, having so many prospects of liberty within their view. But in all despotic governments, though a particular prince may favour arts and letters, there is a natural degeneracy of mankind, as you may observe from Augustus' reign, how the Romans lost themselves by degrees till they fell to an equality with the most barbarous nations that surrounded them. Look upon Greece under its free states, and you would think its inhabitants lived in different climates, and under different heavens, from those at present; so different are the geniuses which are formed under Turkish slavery and Grecian liberty.

ADDISON.

Id in primis laboratur ut necessaria sibi quisque suppeditet. qua in re toti sumus donec satis factum sit animo. sin hoc praesto ad manus fuerit voluptates et oblectamenta expiscamur, et inter magnam otiosorum frequentiam par est esse multos qui in lectitando aliquid aut cogitando voluptatem ponant. ex his duobus quasi fontibus potissimum derivatur scientia : quo autem longius in sapientia processeris eo libentius quae ipse inveneris aliis quoque impertire volueris. ita alii vitae in doctrinis actae quid beati insit edocti, ipsique ceterorum societate in melius provecti, aemulantur inter se imitantur et exsuperant donec tota gens gravibus et sapientibus viris referta sit. itaque otio ac rerum abundantia potissimum alitur scientia ; quibus cum pleraeque tyrannides careant, natura comparatum est ut inscitia et barbarie obruantur. sane in Europa, quamquam penes multos principes sui iuris dominatio est, constat haud paucos esse qui scientia doctrinisque conspiciantur : ideo quod multi inter cives opibus et divitiis adfluunt, princeps autem artius imperium inhibere, sicut Asiatici, non audet, veritus ne civibus, tot exemplis libertatis propositis, fiat res novas moliendi provocatio. verum tamen in omnibus huius modi dominationibus, quamquam fieri potest ut unus et alter princeps artibus et humanioribus litteris faveat, suopte ingenio homines in peius corrumpuntur ; cuius rei documento sint Romani iam inde ab Augusto principe sensim prolapsi donec populis circum circa incultissimis adaequarentur. quod si Graeciam illam liberam respexeris, alio sub sole alio caelo hos et illos credas habitasse : tantas ingeniorum discrepantias praebet libertas Graecorum et Turcomannorum servitium.

He felt that it would be madness in him to imitate the example of Monmouth, to cross the sea with a few British adventurers, and to trust to a general rising of the population. It was necessary, and it was pronounced necessary by all those who invited him over, that he should carry an army with him. Yet who could answer for the effect which the appearance of an army might produce? The government was indeed justly odious. But would the English people, altogether unaccustomed to the interference of continental powers in English disputes, be inclined to look with favour on a deliverer who was surrounded by foreign soldiers? If any part of the royal forces resolutely withstood the invaders, would not that part soon have on its side the patriotic sympathy of millions? A defeat would be fatal to the undertaking. A bloody victory gained in the heart of the island by the mercenaries of the States General over the Coldstream Guards and the Buffs would be almost as great a calamity as a defeat. No severer wound could be inflicted on the national pride of one of the proudest of nations. The crown so won would never be worn in peace or security. Many, who had hitherto contemplated the power of France with dread and loathing, would say that if a foreign yoke must be borne, there was less ignominy in submitting to France than in submitting to Holland.

MACAULAY.

Volutabat secum amentiam si imitatus Valerium,
paucis Anglorum profugis comitibus, transgrederetur spe
nimirum universae popularium defectionis. immo secum
transducendum esse exercitum et sibi et omnibus qui
appellassent patere. quem tamen posse praestare quidnam
sequeretur huius modi speciem exercitus? sane aulam
invidia laborare neque id immerito. quid tamen nationem
ipsam, quibus plane inusitata species exterorum Anglicis
se discordiis inserentium? futurosne ea mente ut in libera-
torem inclinarent alienigenarum copiis stipatum? quid
si irrumpentibus aliqua regiorum pars ferociter obstitisset?
quot millium brevi eo accessuram concordiam fas patriae
reputantium? sive vincerentur, eam cladem toti incepto
esse exitiabilem; sive vincerent, et ipsa insulae penetralia
praetori et tertianorum strage implerent Batavorum mer-
cenarii milites, victoribus fere eandem instare perniciem
ac si vincerentur. quippe gentem si quam aliam superbis-
simam; et ea certe victoria securim infligi gentili superbiae
haud alias acerbiorem. nullam imperium ita adepto aut
pacem aut securitatem. multos quidem hactenus Gallorum
vim reformidare ac detestari; at eosdem clamaturos, si
cedendum foret exterorum imperio, minui saltem flagitium
Gallis potius quam Batavis cedentium.

Another consideration, that may check our presumption in putting such a construction upon a misfortune, is this, that it is impossible for us to know what are calamities, and what are blessings. How many accidents have passed for misfortunes, which have turned to the welfare and prosperity of the persons in whose lot they have fallen? How many disappointments have, in their consequences, saved a man from ruin? If we could look into the effects of everything, we might be allowed to pronounce boldly upon blessings and judgements; but for a man to give his opinion of what he sees but in part, and in its beginnings, is an unjustifiable piece of rashness and folly. The story of Biton and Clitobus, which was in great reputation among the heathens (for we see it quoted by all the ancient authors, both Greek and Latin, who have written upon the immortality of the soul), may teach us a caution in this matter. These two brothers, being the sons of a lady who was priestess to Juno, drew their mother's chariot to the temple at the time of a great solemnity, the persons being absent who by their office were to have drawn her chariot on that occasion. The mother was so transported with this instance of filial duty, that she petitioned her goddess to bestow upon them the greatest gift that could be given to men; upon which they were both cast into a deep sleep, and the next morning found dead in the temple. This was such an event, as would have been construed into a judgement, had it happened to the two brothers after an act of disobedience, and would doubtless have been represented as such by any ancient historian who had given us an account of it.

ADDISON.

Iam vero alia ratio haud scio an prohibitura sit quo
minus infortunia arrogantius interpretemur, quod quaenam
bona sint, quaenam mala, nemo potest praesentire. quot
enim casus in infortuniis positi iidem iis quibus acciderint
in salutem atque emolumentum conduxere! porro quot
frustra et praeter spem habita is exitus consecutus est
unde calamitas averteretur! iam si liceret rerum omnium
eventus introspicere fidenter sane praemia divina et sup-
plicia auderemus dignoscere. qui contra id quod incohatum
et non nisi ex aliqua parte viderit diiudicare velit, nullam
habet excusationem huius modi temeritas et stultitia. quo
in genere ut caute progrediamur docent quae de Bitone
et Cleobi traduntur : notissima est veteribus fabula ; nemo
enim est qui de immortalite animi aut Graece aut Latine
conscripserit a quo non praedicetur. ferunt eos iuvenes
matris, sacerdotis Iunoniae, currum stato quodam sacrificio
ad fanum duxisse, cum forte abessent ii quorum id esset
ministerium. itaque matrem hac filiorum pietate perculsam
a dea precatam esse, ut illis praemium daret quod maximum
homini posset dari : post somno oppressos mane inventos
esse in templo mortuos. quisnam huius modi eventum non
interpretaretur tamquam poenam infensi numinis, si impie
rem gerentibus accidisset fratribus ? id certe haud dubium
est, quin nemo auctorum veterum de hac re scribentium
aliter iudicaturus fuerit.

By authorizing the right of appeal from the courts of the baron to those of the king, and subjecting the decisions of the former to the review of the latter, a new step, not less considerable than those which I have already mentioned, was taken towards establishing the regular, consistent, and vigorous administration of justice. Among all the encroachments of the feudal nobles on the prerogative of their monarchs, their usurping the administration of justice with supreme authority, both in civil and criminal causes, within the precincts of their own estates, was the most singular. In other nations subjects have contended with their sovereigns, and have endeavoured to extend their own power and privileges; but in the history of their struggles and pretensions we discover nothing similar to this right which the feudal barons claimed and obtained. It must have been something peculiar in their genius and manners that suggested this idea, and prompted them to insist on such a claim. Among the rude people who conquered the various provinces of the Roman empire, and established new kingdoms there, the passion of resentment, too impetuous to bear control, was permitted to remain almost unrestrained by the authority of laws. The person offended, as has been observed, retained the right not only of prosecuting, but of punishing his adversary. To him it belonged to inflict such vengeance as satiated his rage, or to accept of such satisfaction as appeased it. But while fierce barbarians continued to be the sole judges in their own cause, their enmities were implacable and immortal; they set no bounds either to the degree of their vengeance, or to the duration of their resentment.

ROBERTSON.

Concesso iam iure appellandi regis, ut quae decressent optimates eadem ille recognosceret, nova quaedam neque minor iis quarum mentionem fecimus via munita est ut aequius constantius et stabilius iudicia redderentur. nam inter ea quae adversus auctoritatem regiam feodales quos vocant proceres invaserant, id potissimum admirabile est, quod iuris dictionem nulli obnoxiam distrahendarum controversiarum et puniendorum maleficiorum causa sua quisque intra praedia occupaverant. sane in aliis populis adversus reges a civibus certatum est, suam potentiam sua iura in maius promoventibus ; sed eius modi certaminum et postulationum historia nihil huic simile suppeditat quod et flagitarunt et flagitatum consecuti sunt feodales proceres. itaque non potest fieri quin proprium quiddam ipsorum morum et ingeni et hanc spem iis iniecerit et ut enixe flagitarent adduxerit. nam inter gentes incultas quae debellatas imperi Romani provincias in nova regna distribuerunt vindictae studium effrenatum et cohibentium intolerans nulla fere legum coercitione teneri se patiebatur. penes laesum erat, id quod supra iam diximus, ius non solum reum postulandi sed in peractum etiam animadvertendi, sive poena adficeret quae iram satiaret seu satisfactione quadam mallet mitigari. cum tamen barbari et feri homines petitores essent iidem et iudices, inimicitias inexorabiles et immortales fovebant, nullo vindictae modo, nullo spatio diuturnitate irarum circumscripta.

It is hard to personate and act a part long; for where truth is not at the bottom, nature will always be endeavouring to return, and will peep out and betray herself one time or other. Therefore if any man think it convenient to seem good, let him be so indeed, and then his goodness will appear to everybody's satisfaction; so that upon all accounts sincerity is true wisdom. Particularly as to the affairs of this world, integrity hath many advantages over all the fine and artificial ways of dissimulation and deceit; it is much the plainer and easier, much the safer and more secure way of dealing in the world; it has less of trouble and difficulty, of entanglement and perplexity, of danger and hazard in it; it is the shortest and nearest way to our end, carrying us thither in a straight line, and will hold out and last longest. The arts of deceit and cunning do continually grow weaker and less effectual and serviceable to them that use them; whereas integrity gains strength by use, and the more and longer any man practiseth it, the greater service it does him, by confirming his reputation, and encouraging those with whom he hath to do to repose the greatest trust and confidence in him, which is an unspeakable advantage in the business and affairs of life.

STEELE.

Difficile est profecto diu partes agere et quasi alienam personam induere: nisi enim subest veritas, 'recurret usque natura,' et tandem aliquando sese in lucem prodat proferatque necesse est. qua de causa si quis sibi convenire statuerit uti probus videatur, esto probus: ita nimirum probitatem suam omnibus probaturus. itaque sicut ceteris in rebus haec vera est sapientia, ita in commerciis hominum cotidianis accuratiora fraudis simulationisque artificia longe exsuperat sinceritas: quae quo simplicior et facilior sit, eo tutiorem et munitiorem agendi rationem praestet; quae multo minus molestiarum et onerum, multo minus obscuritatis et erroris, aut periculi aleaeque in se contineat; quae brevissimam ad propositum finem viam praemonstret recta eo ducentem eandemque diutissime permansuram. enimvero doli artis et malitiae quo plus exercentur, eo minus validi sunt, eo minus commodi et utilitatis efficiunt; contra virtuti novae quaedam vires exercendo accedunt, et ut quisque in ea diutissime versatur, ita uberrimos inde fructus percipit; comprobatur enim bona existimatio, ii autem quibuscum res agenda est eo adducuntur ut summam tibi fidem habeant, id quod vix dici potest quanto in negotiis et rerum usu emolumento sit.

Immediately after the conclusion of the peace the French forces left Scotland, as much to their own satisfaction as to that of the nation. The Scots soon found that the calling to their assistance a people more powerful than themselves was a dangerous experiment. They beheld, with the utmost impatience, those who had come over to protect the kingdom taking upon them to command in it; and on many occasions they repented the rash invitation which they had given. The peculiar genius of the French nation heightened this disgust, and prepared the Scots to throw off the yoke before they had well begun to feel it. The French were in that age what they are in the present, one of the most polished nations in Europe. But it is to be observed, in all their expeditions into foreign countries, whether towards the south or north, that their manners have been remarkably incompatible with the manners of every other people. Barbarians are tenacious of their own customs, because they want knowledge and taste to discover the reasonableness and propriety of customs which differ from them. Nations, which hold the first rank in politeness, are frequently no less tenacious out of pride. The Greeks were so in the ancient world; and the French are the same in the modern. Full of themselves, flattered by the imitation of their neighbours, and accustomed to consider their own modes as the standard of elegance; they scorn to disguise, or to lay aside, the distinguishing manners of their own nation, or to make any allowance for what may differ from them among others. For this reason, the behaviour of their armies has on every occasion been insupportable to strangers, and has always exposed them to hatred, and often to destruction.

ROBERTSON.

Simul pax firmata et decessum est a Gallis Caledonia volentibus perinde ipsis ac popularibus. nam Caledoniis brevi cognitum est quanto suo cum periculo populi se potentioris societatem appellassent. id plane intolerandum, qui ad tutandum regnum advecti essent, eosdem iam imperium ipsum adfectare: esse quod paeniteat tam temere adsciti auxili. auxit invidiam Gallis proprium ingenium, ut Caledonii iugum vixdum experti exuere paratos sese ostentarent. Galli enim sicut hodie ita id quoque aetatis inter excultissimos Europaeorum populos conspiciebantur. illud tamen libet animadvertere, quocumque in externas gentes itinera fecerint, sive in meridiem seu septemtrionem versus, mores huius populi mirum quantum a ceteris omnibus abhorruisse. nam ut barbari suas consuetudines artissime amplectuntur, ut quibus neque peritia neque elegantia sufficiat ad dignoscendum quam apta ac naturae congruentia sint aliena instituta, ita quibus in humanitate primae deferuntur idem efficiunt prae superbia. cuius rei documento sint apud veteres Graeci, hodie Galli. toti enim in se conversi, aliorum sui imitatione deleniti, suaque instituta quasi normam quandam elegantiae soliti proponere, proprios ipsorum mores dissimulare vel exuere, aut si quid in aliis a suis institutis discrepet aliquid ignoscere prorsus dedignantur. qua de causa ita sese ubique exercitus gesserunt, ut externis populis haudquaquam tolerandi numquam non odio, saepe exitio obnoxii evaserint.

Nor need we fear that men, by losing their ferocity, will lose their martial spirit, or become less undaunted and vigorous in defence of their country or their liberty. The arts have no such effect in enervating either the mind or the body. On the contrary, industry, their inseparable attendant, adds new force to both. And if anger, which is said to be the whetstone of courage, loses somewhat of its asperity by politeness and refinement; a sense of honour, which is a stronger, more constant, and more governable principle, acquires fresh vigour by that elevation of genius which arises from knowledge and a good education. Add to this, that courage can neither have any duration, nor be of any use, when not accompanied with discipline and martial skill, which are seldom found among a barbarous people. The ancients remarked that Datames was the only barbarian that ever knew the art of war. And Pyrrhus, seeing the Romans marshal their army with some art and skill, said with surprise, 'These barbarians have nothing barbarous in their discipline!' It is observable that, as the old Romans, by applying themselves solely to war, were almost the only uncivilized people that ever possessed military discipline, so the modern Italians are the only civilized people, among Europeans, that ever wanted courage and a martial spirit.

HUME.

Neque vero est cur vereamur ne exuta feritate bellicum itidem homines animum exuant, neve in propugnando pro salute patriae aut libertatis minus impavidi constantesque evadant. neque enim ullam vim tantam habent artes egregiae ut aut corpus aut animum effeminent. quod contra, industria, quae artissime eas subsequitur, utrique novas vires solet adicere. quod si iracundiae, quam quasi cotem esse fortitudinis volunt, per humanitatem cultumque aliquid asperitatis deteritur, at appetitui famae, quod cum fortius ac constantius tum idem docilius est agendi principium, novus quidam vigor adcrescit, auctis nimirum per disciplinas et liberalem institutionem ingeniis. huc accedit ut neque durare neque prodesse quicquam possit virtus, quae non disciplina quadam ac scientia militari commendetur. id autem barbaris in civitatibus perraro invenimus. veteres quidem aiebant Datamen solum inter barbaros rei militaris peritum exstitisse. Pyrrhus quoque, cum Romanos arte quadam et scientia videret aciem instruere, fertur mirabundus exclamasse; 'at istis quidem barbaris nihil sane barbari in disciplina inest.' libet porro illud animadvertere, sicut antiquos Romanos, qui rei bellicae toti incumberent, solos fere inter incultas nationes disciplinam militarem attigisse; ita ex populis qui quidem hodie in Europa exstent humanissimis, nullis virtutem et bellicosum ingenium defuisse nisi Italis.

Meanwhile Charles, satisfied with the easy and almost bloodless victory which he had gained, and advancing slowly with the precaution necessary in an enemy's country, did not yet know the whole extent of his good fortune. But at last a messenger despatched by the slaves acquainted him with the success of their noble effort for the recovery of their liberty; and at the same time deputies arrived from the town, in order to present him with the keys of their gates, and to implore his protection from military violence. While he was deliberating concerning the proper measures for this purpose, the soldiers, fearing that they should be deprived of the booty which they had expected, rushed suddenly and without orders into the town, and began to kill and plunder without distinction. It was then too late to restrain their cruelty, their avarice or licentiousness. All the outrages of which soldiers are capable in the fury of a storm, all the excesses of which men can be guilty when their passions are heightened by the contempt and hatred which difference in manners and religion inspires, were committed. Above thirty thousand of the innocent inhabitants perished on that unhappy day, and ten thousand were carried away as slaves. Muley Hassan took possession of a throne surrounded with carnage, abhorred by his subjects, on whom he had brought such calamities, and pitied even by those whose rashness had been the occasion of them. The emperor lamented the fatal accident which had stained the lustre of his victory; and amidst such a scene of horror there was but one spectacle that afforded him any satisfaction. Ten thousand Christian slaves, among whom were several persons of distinction, met him as he entered the town, and falling on their knees thanked and blessed him as their deliverer.

Robertson.

Interea Carolus laetus victoria facile et propemodum citra sanguinem parta, cauteque ut in hostili agro et pedetemptim itineri insistens, nondum tamen compertum habuit quam prospere secum fortuna egisset. missus demum a servitiis nuntius certiorem facit egregium reciperandae libertatis ausum bene sibi evenisse: simul adsunt legati ab oppido qui traditis portarum clavibus militarem vim deprecarentur. cuius rei dum rationes animo volutabat, veritus miles ne spem praedae irritam haberent subito et iniussu in urbem irruere, rapere, trucidare. promiscua inde strages, nec iam licentiam saevitiam aut rapinas facile quis coercuerit. quod enim immanitatis in ardore ipso expugnationum possunt milites, quaecumque flagitia genus humanum audet quorum animos diversorum morum sacrorumve contemptus atque odium exstimulet, nihil infaustus ille dies praetermisit, insontium capitum occisis triginta millibus, decem in servitutem abductis. Hassanius regno inter medias caedes potitus est, popularibus quibus tot mala intulerat invisus, ne iis quidem penes quos temeritatis causa erat nisi miserabilis. foedatam fatali rabie victoriae famam miseratus imperator, quamquam tot flebilia offundebantur, uno demum spectaculo requievit. servi ad decem milia Christiani nominis, pars haud ignobili loco orta, ingredienti obvii facti et ad genua provoluti grates egerunt tamquam liberatori et fausta omnia precati sunt.

I am perfectly sensible of the very flattering distinction I have received in your thinking me worthy of so noble a present as that of your History of America. I have however suffered my gratitude to lie under some suspicion, by delaying my acknowledgement of so great a favour. But my delay was only to render my obligation to you more complete, and my thanks, if possible, more merited. The close of the session brought a great deal of very troublesome, though not important, business on me at once. I could not go through your work at one breath at that time, though I have done it since. I am now enabled to thank you not only for the honour you have done me, but for the great satisfaction and the infinite variety and compass of instruction I have received from your incomparable work. Everything has been done which was so naturally to be expected from the author of the History of Scotland and of the age of Charles the Fifth. I believe few books have done more than this towards clearing up dark points, correcting errors, and removing prejudices. You have too the rare secret of rekindling an interest on subjects that had so often been treated, and in which everything that could feed a vital flame appeared to have been consumed. I am sure I read many parts of your History with that fresh concern and anxiety which attend those who are not previously apprized of the event. You have besides thrown quite a new light on the present state of the Spanish provinces, and furnished us with materials and hints for a rational theory of what may be expected from them in future.

BURKE.

Quanto me honore cumulaveris dignum ratus ad quem rerum Americanarum historia tua, munus amplissimum, mitteretur, scito me penitus perspexisse. quamquam id commisi ut non nihil immemorem me fuisse suspiceris, qui benefici tanti sero demum gratias agam. id tamen habeto me non nisi ideo commoratum esse, ut et tu melius de me meritus esses, et ego gratias si id fieri potest debitas magis persolverem. nam cum rerum prolatio iam appropin- quaret permagna non illius quidem gravissimi sed moles- tissimi tamen negoti moles simul iniecta est. itaque non licebat quasi uno spiritu librum tuum haurire, id quod postea fecimus. iam vacat mihi tibi gratias agere, qui non solum tanto honore a te adfectus sim sed ex infinito paene ambitu ac varietate ista egregii operis amplissimos oblecta- tionis fructus perceperim. quod enim par erat eum qui Caledonias res et Caroli Quinti aequaliumque gesta con- scripsisti, satis respondisti exspectationi tuae. equidem credo, sive obscura enucleanda erant, sive errores demo- vendi, sive opiniones praeiudicatae exstirpandae, perpaucos libros plus isto opere profecisse. illud quoque tibi quod fere nemini permirum accidit, quod rebus iam decantatis, in quibus omnia quae vitalem ut ita dicam flammam alerent prorsus iam absumpta videbantur, novam facem attulisti. mihi quidem velim scias perlegenti historiam tuam aliquot locos ea cura ac studio animum retinuisse quibus ceteri eventu nondum perspecto fere adficiuntur. porro uti iam se habent Hispanorum coloniae, hanc rem nova quadam luce illustrasti, et unde coniectura satis probabili quinam in posterum exitus futurus sit augurari liceat et materiem et argumenta praebuisti.

In far different plight and with far other feelings than they had entered the pass of Caudium, did the Roman army issue out from it again upon the plain of Campania. Defeated and disarmed, they knew not what reception they might meet with from their Campanian allies : it was possible that Capua might shut her gates against them and go over to the victorious enemy. But the Campanians behaved faithfully and generously : they sent supplies of arms, of clothing, and of provisions to meet the Romans even before they arrived at Capua : they sent new cloaks, and the lictors and fasces of their own magistrates, to enable the consuls to resume their fitting state ; and when the army approached their city the senate and people went out to meet them, and welcomed them both individually and publicly with the greatest kindness. No attentions, however, could soothe the wounded pride of the Romans : they could not bear to raise their eyes from the ground, nor to speak to any one : full of shame they continued their march to Rome : when they came near to it all those soldiers who had a home in the country dispersed and escaped to their several houses singly and silently : whilst those who lived in Rome lingered without the walls till the sun was set, and stole to their homes under cover of the darkness. The consuls were obliged to enter the city publicly and in the light of day, but they looked upon themselves as no longer worthy to be the chief magistrates of Rome, and they shut themselves up at home in privacy.

ARNOLD.

Longe aliter adfecti et animo et corpore qui nuper
Furculas Caudinas intraverant in Campanum agrum evase-
runt. devictos et dearmatos quanam fide se recepturi
essent Campani socii anquirebant : posse et oppidanos
occlusis portis ultro in victoris partes transire. sed Cam-
panis nec fides nec benignitas defuit : arma vestimenta
commeatus exercitui nondum appropinquanti mittunt :
consulibus nova paludamenta, suorum magistratuum fasces
prout dignitas postulabat suppeditant : et venientibus
Capuam cunctus senatus populusque obviam egressi iustis
omnibus hospitalibus privatisque et publicis funguntur
officiis. nulla tamen comitate Romanorum ignominia et
indignitas leniri : neque oculos attollere, nec quemquam
alloqui : pudor omnium implere animos ad urbem profici-
scentium : ubi iam propius moenia adventum est, quibus ruri
praedia erant suam quisque in domum singuli ac silentes
dilabebantur : qui in urbe habitabant diu extra morati
sero demum post obortas tenebras intra tecta sese abdide-
runt. consules autem quibus palam intranda erat urbs et
interdiu rati se haudquaquam dignos qui primi populi
Romani magistratus haberentur domi se tamquam privati
clauserunt.

Plutarch tells us that Caius Gracchus, the Roman, was frequently hurried by his passion into so loud and tumultuous a way of speaking, and so strained his voice as not to be able to proceed. To remedy this excess, he had an ingenious servant, by name Licinius, always attending him with a pitch-pipe or instrument to regulate the voice; who, whenever he heard his master begin to be high, immediately touched a soft note; at which, it is said, Caius would presently abate and grow calm.

Upon recollecting this story, I have frequently wondered that this useful instrument should have been so long discontinued; especially since we find that this good office of Licinius has preserved his memory for many hundred years, which, methinks, should have encouraged some one to have revived it, if not for the public good, yet for his own credit. It may be objected, that our loud talkers are so fond of their own noise, that they would not take it well to be checked by their servants: but granting this to be true, surely any of their hearers have a very good title to play a soft note in their own defence. To be short, no Licinius appearing and the noise increasing, I was resolved to give this late long vacation to the good of my country; and I have at length, by the assistance of an ingenious artist (who works to the Royal Society), almost completed my design, and shall be ready in a short time to furnish the public with what number of these instruments they please, either to lodge at coffee-houses, or carry for their own private use. In the mean time I shall pay that respect to several gentlemen, who I know will be in danger of offending against this instrument, to give them notice of it by private letters, in which I shall only write, Get a Licinius.

STEELE.

Auctor est Plutarchus C. Gracchum saepe numero con-
tionantem ardore et ira in tantum impetum et vehementiam
prorupisse, ut ea dicendi contentio vocem obtunderet. cui
nimio studio ut mederetur, Licinium quendam, phonascum
haud imperitum, solitum esse adstare qui vocem modera-
retur, et quotiens excitatior esset pronuntiatio domini, subito
remissius fistula caneret; inde illum statim vim minuere et
requiescere. huius narrationis recordatus, soleo admirari tam
utile organum diu iam factum esse cum cessaverit, cum praesertim Licinio hoc ministerium praestiterit ut in tot saecula
nominis memoria supersit; quae res, opinor, stimularet
quempiam si non in utilitatem publicam saltem ut suae
famae consuleret, huius modi tibiam ad repraesentandam.
at enim iis qui loquendi contentione utuntur clamor suus
ita placet, ut aegro animo ferant parere servis cohibentibus.
verum id esto : at utique auditoribus causa satis iusta est,
cur ipsi suum in commodum remissius aliquid canant tibia.
ut brevi rem absolvam, cum neque iam Licinius exstet et
clamor augeatur, recens prolatis rebus bono publico mihi
inserviendum statui, et, ingenio usus artificis qui operas
dat philosophorum societati, opus propositum cum paene
exegerim, brevi curabo ut popularibus quot velint tibias
huius modi suppeditem, quas aut in tonstrinis deponant aut
suum quisque in usum circumportent. interim quibusdam,
qui scio periculum esse ne hanc in tibiam peccent, dabo
singulis singulas epistolas, hoc unum scripturus, 'fac emas
Licinium.'

There is no person in that age about whom historians have been more divided, or whose character has been drawn with such opposite colours. Personal intrepidity, military skill, sagacity and vigour in the administration of civil affairs, are virtues which even his enemies allow him to have possessed in an eminent degree. His moral qualities are more dubious, and ought neither to be praised nor censured without great reserve and many distinctions. In a fierce age he was capable of using victory with humanity, and of treating the vanquished with moderation. A patron of learning, which among martial nobles was either unknown or despised. Zealous for religion to a degree which distinguished him, even at a time when professions of that kind were not uncommon. His confidence in his friends was extreme, and inferior only to his liberality towards them, which knew no bounds. A disinterested passion for the liberty of his country prompted him to oppose the pernicious system which the princes of Lorrain had obliged the queen-mother to pursue. On Mary's return into Scotland, he served her with a zeal and affection to which he sacrificed the friendship of those who were most attached to his person. But, on the other hand, his ambition was immoderate; and events happened that opened to him vast projects, which allured his enterprising genius, and led him to actions inconsistent with the duty of a subject. His treatment of the queen, to whose bounty he was so much indebted, was unbrotherly and ungrateful. The dependence on Elizabeth under which he brought Scotland was disgraceful to the nation. He deceived and betrayed Norfolk with a baseness unworthy of a man of honour.

ROBERTSON.

Nemo aequalium exstitit de quo magis discrepet inter scriptores tam in diversum vitam eius depingentes. virtute bellica, rei militaris peritia, rei publicae administrandae vigore ac consilio, his artibus magno opere eum conspici ne ipsi quidem inimici infitiantur. de moribus res magis in dubio est, quos neque laudari neque reprehendi nisi caute et cum delectu aliquo oportuerit. in atrocitate temporum potuit victoria clementer uti et victis parcere. litterarum quoque fautor, quae inter nobiles belli avidos aut ignotae erant aut contemptui habitae, idem religionum studiosus ut supra aequales plerosque et ipsos idem studium prae se ferentes enitesceret. accedebat magna amicorum fiducia, maior tamen munificentia quae erat infinita. neque dubium est quin fatalibus consiliis in quae Lorranenses reginae matrem impulere incorrupto libertatis patriae amore adductus se opposuerit ; nec minus constat Mariae in Caledoniam reversae eo studio et caritate inservisse cui amicitiam sui amantissimorum posthabuerit. contra cupiditas gloriae erat immodica quaeque intercesserunt negotia ingenti spe proposita eo usque avidum ingenium allexerunt ut plus quam civilia agitaret. nam in reginam et sororem et optime de se meritam contra quam fratrem et beneficiorum memorem decet sese gerebat. utque Caledonia Elissae dedita civile erat dedecus, ita deceptus proditusque Norfolciensis comes turpem ipsius nomini infamiam intulit.

The next and higher use of history is to improve the understanding and strengthen the judgement, and thereby fit us for entering upon life with advantage. ' By contemplating' (as Lord Bolingbroke well observes) 'the vast variety of particular characters and events, by examining the strange combination of causes—different, remote, and seemingly opposite—that often concur in producing one effect, a man of parts may improve the study of history to its proper and principal use : he may sharpen the penetration, fix the attention of his mind, and strengthen his judgement : he may acquire the faculty and the habit of discerning quicker and looking further, and of exerting that flexibility and steadiness which are necessary to be joined in the conduct of all affairs that depend on the concurrence or opposition of other men.' Judgement as well as other powers must improve by exercise. Now history presents us with the same objects which we meet with in the business of life. They must consequently excite the same kind of reflections and give the same exercise to our thoughts, and thus produce the same turn of mind. History therefore may be called anticipated experience. By this means we begin our acquaintance with mankind sooner, and bring into the world and the business of it such a cast of thought and temper of mind as is acquired by passing through it, which will make us to appear to more advantage in it, and not such novices upon our introduction to it as we should otherwise be.

PRIESTLEY.

Iam vero sequitur altior legendorum historicorum utilitas, quod et intellegentiam promovent et iudicium corrobo-
rant ideoque uti melius instructi vitae munia ingrediamur
efficiunt. praeclare enim Cato noster : si quis incredibiles
rerum hominumque varietates contemplatus fuerit, si cau-
sarum discrepantium inter se diversarum utque visae sunt
repugnantium, in eundem tamen finem saepe numero coeun-
tium admirabiles nexus introspexerit, potest is, modo ingenio haud absurdus sit, in proprios ac primarios usus
historiae studium conferre : potest ingeni vim acuere,
intentionem animi augere, iudicium confirmare : potest
facilitatem consuetudinemque tum maturius diiudicandi
tum longius prospiciendi adipisci : accedit ut multiplicem
eandemque constantem agendi rationem praestare possit,
quae omni in negotio ex alieno adsensu sive repugnantia
apto necesse est consocietur. enimvero sicut aliae animi
facultates ita iudicium exercitando augetur. historia
autem eadem praebet quae in vitae usu cotidiano versantur.
itaque easdem cogitationes utrumque excitat, eandem
exercitationem animi, eandem informationem utrumque
efficit. qua de causa historiam quasi anteceptam quandam
experientiam haud iniuria appellaveris. ita enim maturius
cum hominibus versamur, iis cogitationibus ea animi infor-
matione ornati in curriculum vitae progredimur, quam
decurso demum spatio ceteri adipiscuntur : ut melius
instructi prodeamus ceteroqui tirones atque hospites ingres-
suri.

There is a sort of delight, which is alternately mixed with terror and sorrow, in the contemplation of death. The soul has its curiosity more than ordinarily awakened, when it turns its thoughts upon the conduct of such who have behaved themselves with an equal, a resigned, a cheerful, a generous or heroic temper in that extremity. We are affected with these respective manners of behaviour, as we secretly believe the part of the dying person imitable by ourselves, or such as we imagine ourselves more particularly capable of. Men of exalted minds march before us like princes, and are, to the ordinary race of mankind, rather subjects for their admiration than example. However, there are no ideas strike more forcibly upon our imaginations, than those which are raised from reflections upon the exits of great and excellent men. Innocent men who have suffered as criminals, though they were benefactors to human society, seem to be persons of the highest distinction, among the vastly greater number of human race, the dead. When the iniquity of the times brought Socrates to his execution, how great and wonderful is it to behold him, unsupported by anything but the testimony of his own conscience and conjectures of hereafter, receive the poison with an air of mirth and good humour, and as if going on an agreeable journey bespeak some deity to make it fortunate.

STEELE.

In contemplanda morte nescio quid voluptatis subesse solet quae alterno metu ac dolore compleatur. nimirum nescio qua praeter solitum cura commovetur mens quotiens obversantur ii qui in novissimis aequum constantem hilarem fortem et ut ita dicam divinum animum praestiterunt. ita singuli singulorum moribus adficimur prout moribundi hominis partes eas esse credimus quae nobismet ipsis imitabiles sint et ad nostrum ingenium potissimum accommodatae. nam praeclara quidem ingenia praeter oculos tamquam principes incedunt, quos longe maxima pars hominum admiretur potius quam exemplo sibi proponat. quamquam nullis aliis imaginibus vehementius pulsatur animus quam quae suboriri solent praeclarorum hominum et optimorum exitus contemplantibus. qui enim insontes tamquam rei habiti sunt iidemque optime de genere humano meriti inter plures —ita enim volunt esse mortuos—prae ceteris conspiciuntur. fingamus animo Socratem propter atrocitatem temporum summo supplicio adfectum, nulla alia re fretum nisi bene actae vitae conscientia et de postera quantum posset coniectura adsequi. quantum admirationis commovetur spectantibus cicutam comiter et alacriter accipere, et tamquam iter quoddam iucundum ingressurum a deo aliquo uti fortunet contendere.

The contrast between Charles' conduct and that of the
Pope at this juncture was so obvious, that it struck even
the most careless observers ; nor was the comparison which
they made to the advantage of Paul.   The former, a con-
queror, born to reign, long accustomed to the splendour
which accompanies supreme power, and to those busy and
interesting scenes in which an active ambition had engaged
him, quitted the world at a period of life not far advanced,
that he might close the evening of his days in tranquillity,
and secure some interval for sober thought and serious
recollection.   The latter, a priest, who had passed the early
part of his life in the shade of the schools, and in the
study of the speculative sciences, who was seemingly so
detached from the world, that he had shut himself up for
many years in the solitude of a cloister, and who was not
raised to the papal throne until he had reached the extremity of old age, discovered at once all the impetuosity
of youthful ambition, and formed extensive schemes, in
order to accomplish which he scrupled not to scatter the
seeds of discord, and to kindle the flames of war, in every
corner of Europe.   But Paul, regardless of the opinion or
censures of mankind, held on his own course with his
wonted arrogance and violence.   These, although they
seemed already to have exceeded all bounds, rose to a still
greater height upon the arrival of the Duke of Guise in
Italy.

                                                    ROBERTSON.

Inter Carolum id temporis et pontificem tanta erat
morum discrepantia ut vel maxime incuriosos adverteret, et
Paullo erat deterior comparatio. alterum enim triumpha-
lem, regiis incunabulis, summae fortunae splendori diu
adsuefactum devinctumque negotiis quae aviditatem famae
paulo acriorem illexissent, potuisse eundem non ita multum
provecta aetate e rebus publicis recedere ut occidentem
vitam tranquille finiret, et ad sobrie secum serioque medi-
tandum aliquid oti seponeret. alterum, sacerdotem, adole-
scentia in umbratili studio ac rerum cognitione peracta,
adeo, ut videretur, semotum ab hominum commercio ut
multos annos intra solitudinem sese abderet, et vergente
demum aetate pontificatu ornatus esset, subito tamen
impetu iuvenili et cupiditate exarsisse vastosque conatus
molitum esse, quos ut patraret non dubitasse semina dis-
cordiae bellique incendia per Europam spargere. ceterum
Paullus, validus spernendis vituperantium rumoribus, solita
superbia et vehementia cursum tenuit, quae ut adhuc
videbantur terminos exiisse ita in altius elatae sunt duce
Guisiano iam in Italiam advecto.

Clive was in a painfully anxious situation. He could
place no confidence in the sincerity or in the courage of his
confederate; and, whatever confidence he might place in
his own military talents, and in the valour and discipline
of his troops, it was no light thing to engage an army
twenty times as numerous as his own. Before him lay a
river over which it was easy to advance, but over which,
if things went ill, not one of his little band would ever
return. On this occasion, for the first and for the last time,
his dauntless spirit, during a few hours, shrank from the
fearful responsibility of making a decision. He called a
council of war. The majority pronounced against fighting;
and Clive declared his concurrence with the majority.
Long afterwards, he said that he had never called but one
council of war, and that, if he had taken the advice of that
council, the British army would never have been masters
of Bengal. But scarcely had the meeting broken up when
he was himself again. He retired alone under the shade
of some trees, and passed near an hour there in thought.
He came back determined to put everything to the hazard,
and gave orders that all should be in readiness for passing
the river on the morrow.

                                        MACAULAY.

Ea cura et sollicitudo ducem angebat. socii nec fidei
nec virtuti posse se quicquam confidere; posse sibi ad
militarem rem natura comparato, posse suorum ferociae et
armorum disciplinae; at grave onus confligere cum copiis
ita disparibus ut hinc unus illinc viginti proeliantium
numerarentur. sane transgressum obiecti amnis facilem;
sin res improspere evenisset, ne uni quidem perpaucorum
militum fore regressum. quid si rem in discrimen commit-
teret? quam rationem redditurum? eo metu animus
numquam alias pavidus neque tum nisi in breve tempus ab
incepto reformidavit. ita legatis in consilium adhibitis
pluribus moram pugnae suadentibus tum et ipse adsensus
est. una demum hac consultatione rei bellicae se usum
esse, his suasoribus si paruisset numquam Anglos India
potituros fuisse, ipse aliquanto post testabatur. sed statim
contio dilapsa est, et compos iam animi dux in solitudinem
silvae se recepit, ibi quid agendum esset horam fere cogita-
turus. revertenti summam rerum in aleam dari, quaeque
opus forent ad amnem die postero transeundum omnia
parata esse placuit.

Self-satisfaction, at least in some degree, is an advantage which equally attends the fool and the wise man ; but it is the only one, nor is there any other circumstance in the conduct of life where they are on an equal footing. Business, books, conversation ; for all of these a fool is totally incapacitated, and except condemned by his station to the coarsest drudgery remains a useless burden upon the earth. Accordingly it is found that men are extremely jealous of their character in this particular ; and many instances are seen of profligacy and treachery, the most avowed and unreserved, none of bearing patiently the imputation of ignorance and stupidity. Dicaearchus, the Macedonian general, who, as Polybius tells us, openly erected one altar to impiety, another to injustice, in order to bid defiance to mankind : even he, I am well assured, would have started at the epithet fool, and have meditated revenge for so injurious an appellation. Except the affection of parents—the strongest and most indissoluble bond in nature—no connexion has strength sufficient to support the disgust arising from this character. Love itself, which can subsist under treachery, ingratitude, malice, and infidelity, is immediately extinguished by it, when perceived and acknowledged ; nor are deformity and old age more fatal to the dominion of that passion. So dreadful are the ideas of an utter incapacity for any purpose or undertaking, and of continued error and misconduct in life.

HUME.

Stulto et sapienti, ceteroqui plane inter se dissimilibus, id quadam saltem tenus commune est commodum ut uterque sibi placeat; neque enim ulla in re alia pari iure vivitur. quid dicam libros? quid colloquia? quid negotia? quibus omnibus plane ineptus est insipiens; quem nisi ad sordidissima ministeria sors sua detruserit non nisi 'onus minus utile terris' maneat necesse est. quocirca hoc in genere tenacissimos existimationis suae constat esse homines; ut multos videas qui flagitia ac perfidias apertissime prae se ferant, qui stultitiae crimen aequo animo patiatur neminem. velut Dicaearchus dux ille Macedonum, quem auctor est Polybius duas aras alteram iniustitiae impietati alteram posuisse, tamquam communi omnium sensui in offensionem cadere non dubitaverit, ne is quidem, uti mihi persuadeo, si quis stultum appellasset, non calcitrasset poenasque statim probri a male dicentibus sumpsisset. nam remota parentium caritate, qua haud scio an nullum firmius vinculum natura homini ingeneraverit, nullam vim tantam habet necessitudo alia quae hac in re non fastidiat. quin ipse amor, quem neque dolus malus, neque immemor beneficiorum animus, neque malevolentia, ne laesa quidem coniugia solent exstinguere, hoc uno vitio cognito perspectoque statim opprimitur; ut ne turpitudo quidem formae aut senectus ipsa ad hanc animi adfectionem evellendam maiorem vim habeat. tantum ab iis reformidat animus, in quibus nullus omnino labor nulla industria, qui nec sibi nec alteri ut dicitur sed in perpetuo errore ac tenebris versantur.

Peter Alexiwitz of Russia, when he came to years of manhood, though he found himself emperor of a vast and numerous people, master of an endless territory, absolute commander of the lives and fortunes of his subjects, in the midst of this unbounded power and greatness turned his thoughts upon himself and people with sorrow. Sordid ignorance and a brute manner of life this generous prince beheld and contemned from the light of his own genius. His judgement suggested this to him, and his courage prompted him to amend it. In order to this he did not send to the nation from whence the rest of the world has borrowed its politeness, but himself left his diadem to learn the true way to glory and honour, and application to useful arts, wherein to employ the laborious, the simple, the honest part of his people. Mechanic employments and operations were very justly the first objects of his favour and observation. With this glorious intention he travelled into foreign nations in an obscure manner, above receiving little honours where he sojourned, but prying into what was of more consequence, their arts of peace and of war. By this means has this great prince laid the foundation of a great and lasting fame, by personal labour, personal knowledge, personal valour. It would be injury to any of antiquity to name them with him. Who, but himself, ever left a throne to learn to sit in it with more grace? Who ever thought himself mean in absolute power, till he had learned to use it?

STEELE.

Petrus Alexandri filius Sarmatarum rex, cum in suam iam tutelam venisset, videretque sibi permissam regionem nationum et latissime patentium et hominibus abundantium, penes se in capita fortunasque civium esse sui iuris arbitrium, ita infinitis opibus et dignitate fruebatur ut se suosque non sine dolore respiceret ; erat enim vir singularis sollers ingenio et si quid barbarae inscitiae et immanitatis dominaretur aptus ad discernendum despiciendumque, aeque callidus iudicio ac gnavus remediorum. cum huc incumberet, ad eam nationem unde ceteris humanitas sua derivata est noluit legatos mittere, sed ipse ultro exuta dignitate viam gloriae ac famae appetivit adfectato artium utilium studio quibus si quid popularium esset frugi simplex et industrium adsuefaceret. fabrum artificia, id quod aequum erat, potissimum animum et curam advertebant. itaque haec praeclara meditatus, externas regiones tamquam privatus visitare, ubi commoraretur validus spernendo honorum inania, sed, unde maior utilitas ostendebatur, belli pacisque artes rimari. his rationibus celeberrimus sibi princeps gloriae solidae et permansurae fundamenta iecit suo labore usus sua experientia sua fortitudine. itaque neminem ita cum Petro veterum contenderis ut ei non deterior sit comparatio. quis enim est alius qui principali loco se abdicaverit ut meliore cum dignitate implere disceret ? quis alius, cui infinita contigerat potestas, doctus demum sapienter uti, se contemnere dedidicit ?

It will seem strange to some that Cicero, when he had certain information of Catiline's treason, instead of seizing him in the city, not only suffered but urged his escape, and forced him as it were to begin the war. But there was good reason for what he did, as he frequently intimates in his speeches ; he had many enemies among the nobility, and Catiline many secret friends ; and though he was perfectly informed of the whole progress and extent of the plot, yet the proofs being not ready to be laid before the public, Catiline's dissimulation still prevailed, and persuaded great numbers of his innocence ; so that if he had imprisoned and punished him at this time, as he deserved, the whole faction were prepared to raise a general clamour against him, by representing his administration as a tyranny, and the plot as a forgery contrived to support it ; whereas by driving Catiline into rebellion, he made all men see the reality of their danger ; while from an exact account of his troops, he knew them to be so unequal to those of the republic, that there was no doubt of his being destroyed, if he could be pushed to the necessity of declaring himself, before his other projects were ripe for execution. He knew also, that if Catiline was once driven out of the city, and separated from his accomplices, who were a lazy, drunken, thoughtless crew, they would ruin themselves by their own rashness, and be easily drawn into any trap which he should lay for them : the event showed that he judged right ; and by what happened afterwards both to Catiline and to himself, it appeared, that, as far as human caution could reach, he acted with the utmost prudence in regard as well to his own, as to the public safety.

MIDDLETON.

Erunt sane qui demirentur Ciceronem, cuius de coniuratione certior factus esset, Catilinae non solum non in urbe vincula iniecisse, verum etiam in fugam se recipere sivisse atque adeo hortatum esse, tamquam ad inferenda ultro arma exstimulasset. sed agendi satis iustas fuisse causas testis et ipse multis in orationibus : esse enim inter optimates sibi complures invidos, multos Catilinae clam favere. sane exploratum sibi quanta iam facta esset quamque in latum spargeretur coniuratio ; at nondum ita maturatis testimoniis ut vulgarentur, illum etiam tum dissimulare, suamque multis innocentiam probasse. itaque si statim comprehensum supplicio merito adfecisset, totum coniuratorum corpus clamoribus se insectaturos, regnum consulatus appellantes ipsamque coniurationem in subsidium sui commenticiam. si contra ad inferenda arma eum adegisset, fore ut periculi magnitudo omnibus innotesceret. simul satis comperto quot armatos quamque contemnendos prae rei publicae copiis eduxisset, ei fore exitium si ad necessitatem belli aperte gerendi maturatis nondum consiliis coegisset. gnarum quoque, Catilina urbe semel eiecto nudatoque consciis, desides illos ebriosos improvidos greges ipsos se temeritate sua pessumdaturos, et in insidiis quascumque opposuisset facile posse intercludi. quod iudicium rei exitus comprobavit. nam ex iis quae et ipsi et Catilinae brevi evenerunt, satis constat caute eum ac sapienter, quoad homini datur, et suae et rei publicae saluti consuluisse.

For these reasons, even if it could be believed that the
court was sincere, a dissenter might reasonably have determined to cast in his lot with the church.   But what
guarantee was there for the sincerity of the court ?   All men
knew what the conduct of James had been up to that very
time.   It was not impossible, indeed, that a persecutor
might be convinced by argument and by experience of the
advantages of toleration.   But James did not pretend to
have been recently convinced.   On the contrary, he omitted
no opportunity of protesting that he had, during many
years, been, on principle, adverse to all intolerance.   Yet,
within a few months, he had persecuted men, women, young
girls, to the death for their religion.   Had he been acting
against light and against the convictions of his conscience
then ?   Or was he uttering a deliberate falsehood now ?
From this dilemma there was no escape ; and either of the
two suppositions was fatal to the king's character for
honesty.   It was notorious also that he had been com-
pletely subjugated by the Jesuits.   Whatever praises those
fathers might justly claim, flattery itself could not ascribe
to them either wide liberality or strict veracity.

MACAULAY.

His cogitationibus, etiam si probari posset fides regia,
par erat dissentientem a religione patriae suam alteri sectae
causam consociare. at fidem regiam quemnam praestiturum? patere omnibus quae ad illum ipsum diem rex
egisset. sane posse homini immisericordi quantum inesset
boni clementiae argumentatione aut usu persuaderi. at
regem ne fingere quidem recens sibi id persuasum. praeter-
misisse ultro nihil occasionis quo minus testaretur multos
iam annos suopte ingenio qualicumque intolerantiae obsti-
tisse. eundem intra paucos menses in viros, in mulieres,
in puellas, religionis ergo usque ad mortem saeviisse.
illudne contra veritatis lumen, contra quae sibi ipsi probarentur fecisse, an hoc de industria mentiri? hoc aut illud
pro certo esse, neque ullum perfugium; aut hoc aut illo
gladio fidem et probitatem regiam confici. porro iis qui se
societatem Iesu appellitarent esse eum obnoxium cui non
liquere? at quantumcumque laudis iis sacerdotibus iure
deberetur, satis liberale ingenium aut veritatis constantiam
ne adulatores quidem ipsos imputaturos.

After his departure, everything tended fast to the wildest anarchy. Faction and discontent had often risen so high among the old settlers, that they could hardly be kept within bounds. The spirit of the new comers was too ungovernable to bear any restraint. Several among them of better rank were such dissipated hopeless young men, as their friends were glad to send out in quest of whatever fortune might betide them in a foreign land. Of the lower order, many were so profligate or desperate that their country was happy to throw them out as nuisances in society. Such persons were little capable of the general subordination, the strict economy, and persevering industry, which their situation required. The Indians observing their misconduct, and that every precaution for sustenance or safety was neglected, not only withheld the supplies of provisions which they were accustomed to furnish, but harassed them with continual hostilities. All their subsistence was derived from the stores which they had brought from England; these were soon consumed; then the domestic animals sent out to breed in the country were devoured; and by this inconsiderate waste they were reduced to such extremity of famine, as not only to eat the most nauseous and unwholesome roots and berries, but to feed on the bodies of the Indians whom they slew, and even on those of their companions who sunk under the oppression of such complicated distress. In less than six months, of five hundred persons whom Smith left in Virginia, only sixty remained; and these so feeble and dejected that they could not have survived for ten days, if succour had not arrived from a quarter whence they did not expect it.

ROBERTSON.

Simul decessum est colonia et omnia in effrenatam licentiam retro ruere. nam et antiquis colonis pravitas et discordia saepe eo usque flagraverat ut sisti non posset ; et qui proxime adscripti sunt iis animus impotentior et coercentium impatiens ? quorum qui loco meliore nati sunt, perditos plerosque adulescentes et nulla spe boni propinqui qualemcumque fortunam in alieno experturos haud inviti relegaverant. vulgus autem improbissimum genus et flagitiosissimum libenter patria tamquam communem hominum pestem evomuerat. hi parum idonei videbantur qui pro necessitate loci aut apte parerent imperio aut parsimoniae consulerent aut graviter et strenue agerent. quos cum Indi male rem gerere neque salutis neque cibariorum rationem iam habere animadverterent, non modo solitos commeatus intercipere sed continuis proeliis lacessere. utensilia suppetebant nulla praeter quae secum ex Anglia apportaverant. quibus brevi absumptis carne bestiarum mansuetarum quae procreandi fetus causa domo emissae erant vescebantur ; donec inconsulte prodigi eo famis redacti sunt, ut non solum bacae et radices teterrimae et maximae pestiferae, sed Indorum quoque caesorum cadavera et ipsorum comitum quos tam multiplex calamitas confecerat victum necessarium praeberent. intra sex menses ex quingentis hominibus, is enim numerus ante legati discessum Virginiensium fuerat, vix sexaginta supererant, fessi et fracti animo neque in diem decimum vitam sustentaturi, ni ex inopinato subventum esset laborantibus.

INDEX OF FIRST LINES

TRANSLATIONS INTO GREEK VERSE

TRANSLATIONS INTO GREEK PROSE

TRANSLATIONS INTO LATIN VERSE

TRANSLATIONS INTO LATIN PROSE

For EU product safety concerns, contact us at Calle de José Abascal, 56–1°,
28003 Madrid, Spain or eugpsr@cambridge.org.

www.ingramcontent.com/pod-product-compliance
Ingram Content Group UK Ltd.
Pitfield, Milton Keynes, MK11 3LW, UK
UKHW012329130625
459647UK00009B/158